D1246806

Introduction to

CLASSICAL ARABIC LITERATURE

Introduction to
CLASSICAL ARABIC LITERATURE

With Selections from Representative Works
in English Translation

ILSE LICHTENSTADTER

SCHOCKEN BOOKS · NEW YORK

Learning Resource Center
Lincoln Trail College
Robinson, Illinois

First published by SCHOCKEN BOOKS 1976

Published by arrangement with Twayne Publishers, Inc.

Library of Congress Cataloging in Publication Data

Lichtenstadter, Ilse, 1907-
Introduction to classical Arabic literature.

Bibliography: p. 125
Includes indexes.
1. Arabic literature—History and criticism. 2. Civilization, Islamic. 3. Arabic literature—Translations into English. 4. English literature—Translations from Arabic. I. Title.

PJ7528.L5 1976 892'.7'09 76-9147

Manufactured in the United States of America

In Memoriam

JOSEF HOROVITZ

GIORGIO LEVI DELLA VIDA

R. A. NICHOLSON

SIR HAMILTON GIBB

GUSTAVE E. VON GRUNEBAUM

Contents

PART II: SELECTIONS FROM ARABIC LITERATURE

Preface

The close political and economic interdependence between East and West of recent times demands a deeper mutual understanding of each other's thought patterns and culture. In particular, the Western-educated person must become better acquainted with the intellectual stimuli, the artistic creativity, and the emotions that moved the Arab/Muslim mind since the appearance of Islam. In the Middle Ages the two worlds had many contacts, not always friendly (*vide* the Crusades) but always mutually fertilizing. Medieval Muslim philosophy, especially, was deeply inspired by ancient Greek thought; in turn, medieval Western philosophy was stimulated by the Muslim philosophers to whose preservation of much of the Greek heritage the West was greatly indebted.

In modern times, as a result of historical factors, the Eastern people had lived in contact with Europeans and had learned a good deal from and about Western civilization (though they have not always interpreted it correctly and have frequently adopted its outer forms without fully understanding its inner motivations). The West, on the whole, did not become deeply acquainted with Eastern culture and its expression in its life-style as well as its literature. Only recently have Western students begun to be sent by their universities to the Near and Middle East, as an integral part of their education; in the past, only individual students or scholars ventured to live in the countries whose languages, literatures, and arts they were studying, though admittedly some of the "civil servants" of colonial powers, while usually keeping socially aloof from the native inhabitants, used their experience to make important contributions to scholarship.

If the scholarly world did not feel the necessity of intimate contact (even such a great Orientalist as Theodor Noeldeke never in his long life set foot on Oriental soil), the general public in the West had even less knowledge of the intellectual achievements of the Arab/Muslim world. "Near Eastern Art"—which meant mainly ancient Egyptian, and, to a lesser degree, Assyrian-Babylonian art—was touched upon in high school and college courses; the Koran was mentioned in passing as one of the Holy Scriptures, and "the preservation of the

Classical heritage" was credited to the Arabs; but that was about all the average Western student would learn. It is still quite common to meet otherwise well-read people who know nothing about Arabic literature, apart from the *Arabian Nights* and the *Quatrains* of 'Umar Khayyâm, which are Persian, not Arabic poetry, and are known only through the mirror of their translator, Edward Fitzgerald.

This book was written to help fill the gap. It aims at giving the nonspecialist an inkling of the richness of Arab/Muslim literature and the depth of religious and philosophic thought it contains. It also intends to show the refinement of scholarship, the breadth of interest, and the exactness of method applied. Beyond that, the book also points to the many-sided problems of a religious, theological, or philosophical nature dealt with by the Muslim thinkers and shows the critical and analytical appraisal to which they subjected the creations of their intellectual leaders.

This essay is therefore concerned mainly with a representation of the ideas expressed in the literary works, the problems their authors were trying to solve, and the solutions they offered. It also presents the difference between the viewpoints of the Western Orientalist and those of the Muslim; some of these concern religious tenets which the Muslim considers outside the range of critical analysis because of their roots in Revelation.

The second part of this study contains excerpts from representative Arabic writings, chosen to show the variety of Arabic literature, while all-inclusiveness was not intended. The examples were selected partly for the interest they hold for the reader and partly to acquaint him with important facets of Muslim literary works. However, they were also chosen as being representative of their respective type, while at the same time being informative in contents. For example, the lengthy excerpts from the *Biography of the Prophet* (no. 8) present a sequence of decisive events in his development. The chapter from the *Travels of Ibn Jubayr* (no. 25) describes the rites of the Pilgrimage to Mecca as experienced by a medieval Muslim traveler who participated in them as a Believer. The excerpts from ar-Râzî (no. 13) were included as an example of the combination of scientific observation and philosophic speculation, while the passage from al-Ghazâlî (no. 12) conveys an intimate picture of the man and his philosophy. Thus, these excerpts serve a double purpose: to be examples of Arab writings and to introduce the reader to some salient features of medieval Muslim life, many of which are still alive today. The principle that guided this writer in the selection was not merely didactic, to teach the reader something about Muslim thought, but humanistic, to make "the Arab" or "the Muslim" come alive through his literary works and to induce the reader to further study (and enjoyment) of the vast body of this literature.

The Bibliography is intended to help in this endeavor. It is selective, as a guide for the nonspecialist to further reading; while most titles mentioned in it deal with broad aspects, many are included to lead those who desire to penetrate more deeply to more detailed studies. For the same reason, some anthologies with translations of specific subjects are included. Only a few Arabic texts are listed, since the book is addressed primarily to the nonspecialist; the Arabist and Islamist would be familiar with the literature in his field.

This essay may provoke comparison with two highly acclaimed works by two leading Orientalists, R. A. Nicholson's *A Literary History of the Arabs* and H. A. R. Gibb's *Arabic Literature*. It differs from both in intention and form. Nicholson's work combines the account of historical events with his presentation of the literary works created in each epoch; he also aims at comprehensiveness and discusses the works of a great number of authors at length. His book presents Arabic literature within the framework of the history of Islam. It is delightful reading; besides the scholarly competence of its author, it shows his artistic sensivity and his feeling for beauty of language and imagery.Though much additional material has come to light in the nearly seventy years since it was first published, it will not easily be surpassed either as a reference book or as a literary achievement.

Sir Hamilton Gibb's book is small in size, but not in scope. He had the gift—both in his writings and his lectures—of expressing complicated thought in precise, comparatively short statements. In this writer's judgment, this is not a book for the beginner, but presupposes a certain familiarity with Arab writers and their thought.

The present study emphasizes the emerging ideas and problems posed by the developing Muslim culture as discussed in the works of its protagonists. It also stresses the different approach to them by the Western Arabist and Orientalist who is not bound to accept many of the premises on which the Muslim concepts and solutions rest. This emphasis on the ideas and methods of the ancient authors made it unnecessary to aim at complete enumeration of authors and works; only the discussion of their representative exponents was required in the framework and the purpose of the present work.

The author's indebtedness to many scholars is obvious. The specialist will easily recognize the source for many of the facts and interpretations incorporated in this book; a good many of the latter are the author's own, and she accepts full responsibility for them. The notes are kept to a minimum; the Bibliography will suffice as a guide for anyone who wishes to know more about a specific subject or to verify certain statements.

The dedication acknowledges the author's indebtedness and deep gratitude to a group of Orientalists whom she was privileged to meet during her scholarly career: Josef Horovitz, her teacher as a young beginner in the field of Islamic studies; Giorgio Levi Della Vida, who became her mentor and friend after the former's death; R. A. Nicholson and Sir Hamilton Gibb, who aided her at a critical stage in her career. And, to her deepest regret, the name of G. E. von Grunebaum, with whom friendship linked her for more than thirty years, must sadly be added to this list of scholars and friends who are no longer with us.

ILSE LICHTENSTADTER

Harvard University

Acknowledgments

The author wishes to thank the following for permission to reprint excerpts from books and articles published by them:
George Allen & Unwin, Ltd., London: for selections from W. Montgomery Watt, *The Faith and Practice of al-Ghazâlî,* 1967;
Jonathan Cape, Ltd., London: for selections from *The Travels of Ibn Jubayr,* edited and translated by R. J. C. Broadhurst, 1952;
Cambridge University Press, Cambridge: for selections from R. A. Nicholson, *A Literary History of the Arabs,* 1907, 1930, and R. A. Nicholson, *Studies in Islamic Poetry,* 1921, reprinted 1969;
Islamic Culture, Hyderabad, India: for selections from volumes IV, no. 1: Josef Horovitz, "ʿAdî ibn Zayd, the Poet of al-Hîra"; IV, nos. 2 & 3: Josef Horovitz "ʿUyûn al-Akhbâr"; IX, nos. 1 & 3: D. S. Margoliouth, "The Table-Talk of a Mesopotamian Judge"; vol. IX, no. 1: D. S. Margoliouth, "The Devil's Delusions."
Islamic Research Institute, Islamabad, Pakistan: for selections from M. S. H. Maʿṣûmî, *Imâm Râzî's ʿIlm al-Akhlâq,* (1969);
Oxford University Press, Oxford: for selections from *The Life of Muhammad,* translated and with Introduction and Notes by A. Guillaume, Oxford University Press, Karachi, 1968;
Routledge & Kegan Paul, Ltd., London: for selections from Ibn Baṭṭûṭa, *The Travels in Asia and Africa 1325–1354,* translated by H. A. R. Gibb, 1929;
The University of Chicago Press, Chicago, Ill.: for selections from Gustave E. von Gruenebaum, *A Tenth-Century Document of Arabic Literary Theory and Criticism,* 1950.
The author also gratefully acknowledges the contributions of three young Orientalists, her former students at Harvard, who kindly gave her some original translations for inclusion in this book. They are Dr. Herbert Mason, now Professor at Boston University, Dr. John Damis, now Assistant Professor at Portland State University, and Dr. Wheeler McKintosh Thackston, Jr., now Assistant Professor at Harvard.
The unsigned translations are her own.

Transliteration Table

ء = ' (omitted at beginning of word)

ب = b	ص = ṣ	ه = h
ت = t	ض = ḍ	و = w
ث = th	ط = ṭ	ى = y
ج = j	ظ = ẓ	ة = t, h
ح = ḥ	ع = '	
خ = kh	غ = gh	
د = d	ف = f	ـَا = â (ā, á)
ذ = dh	ق = q	ـُو = û (ū, ú)
ر = r	ك = k	ـِى = î (ī, í)
ز = z	ل = l	ـَوْ = aw
س = s	م = m	ـَىْ = ay (ey)
ش = sh	ن = n	

PART I

Introduction

CHAPTER 1

The Environment of the Jâhilîyah

I *The Arabian Peninsula and Its Language*

The task of writing an introduction to Arabic literature is not an easy one. The author of a book on the literature of any other people—be it Russian, English, German, French, or Italian—can go right into the heart of the matter. At the most, he may have to deal briefly with the times and the events and problems dominating the lifetime and environment of the authors. He need not, however, begin with a definition of the term "literature" itself or of its various branches; nor need he examine the term "Russian" or "German," "French" or "Italian" for his readers to know its application in the context of his book.

This is not so when one undertakes to write a book on Arabic literature. Not only is the history of the Arabs unfamiliar to most readers, except perhaps in rather broad and general terms, but what is referred to, rather sweepingly, as "Arabic literature" is a complex and vast body of writing that encompasses many centuries and a variety of branches and subjects. Furthermore, ethnically, many of the most famed authors of works included in this term were not even Arabs.

It is, therefore, indispensable to start with an answer to the question: What is meant by the term "Arabic literature"? It has to be used in its broadest sense, embracing not only belles-lettres—the narrowest definition of the word given in the dictionaries—but also historical, religious, philosophic, and scientific works of all kinds. It does not describe only the literature of the Arabs as a people or of the inhabitants of the Arabian Peninsula where it originated. For, following a religious awakening, inspired by one man among them, the Arabs streamed forth beyond the confines of their homeland; they took their language and the new religion with them, stimulating, if not creating, the literature that became the *Arab* literature. From that time it developed in diverse environments through and among peoples that differed in ethnic origins and cultural backgrounds, the unifying factors being the use of the Arabic language and the fundament and "firm link" of Islam.[1]

Thus, the first definition for the term "Arabic literature" is partly negative. It is not the literature of a people, but of a culture. This literature spread from the barren land of Arabia where it originated and whose language it perpetuated and even sanctified eastward to Central Asia and the frontiers of China and westward into North Africa and Europe, to Sicily and the Iberian Peninsula, where some of its outstanding representatives were born and some of the finest of its poetry and philosophy developed. Thus, in the Middle Ages, the period of its highest achievement, the greatest representatives of Arab literature were not Arabs. Many of the authors using the Arabic language as their medium of expression were not even Muslims: in the Middle Ages Jews as well as Christians who lived in the environment of Muslim culture used Arabic as the medium of expression of their poetry and of their philosophic and religious thought.

Yet the use of the term "Arabic literature" is justified not only because the works were written in Arabic but also because the earliest extant works originated in the Arabian homeland and were indigenous to the Arabian Peninsula. These works received further stimulation—and their decisive direction—through the religion of Islam, which was born there and revealed in the Arabic language to an Arab prophet to be brought to the Arabs in their own "intelligible language."[2]

This leads to the second definition of the term "Arabic literature." A large proportion, if not the largest part, of the works to be thus characterized deals with religious subjects. It includes the Koran, the Holy Book of Islam, commentaries on it, biographies of leading ancient scholars, and a vast body of "Traditions" of the Prophet as well as canon law. It applies to historical writings born out of an interest in the events before the advent of Islam, the era called *al-Jâhilîyah,* "Time of Ignorance" (ignorance of the true religion and of the One God), and carried on as research into the life of the Prophet and the history of Islam in Arabia and its spread through conquest over much of the then-known civilized world. The term also includes scientific works, such as studies on geography, medicine, mathematics, and astronomy; it may be applied, too, to Muslim philosophy. Besides all these works, attractive for the scholar rather than the layman, a vast amount of belles-lettres, called *adab*, was created. Collections of poetry, together with learned commentaries on its meaning and biographical notes on the poets, were composed to preserve this ancient heritage. Philological commentaries, dictionaries, and works on grammar round out the variety of subjects included in the term.

The cradle of Arabic literature was the Arabian Peninsula, still one of the least explored regions of the world. Only very recently have parts of it become accessible to the outside, in particular the non-Muslim, world. Most of it remains largely unmapped and nearly inaccessible. It is still a major enterprise to venture into the interior from the inhabited regions along its periphery and its few cities; Central Arabia consists largely of deserts and steppes where, to this day, Bedouins roam as they did in the centuries before the country appeared on the historical scene. Indeed, it is the poetry of the nomadic tribes that represents to us, as it did to the classical Arab scholars, the earliest product of the Arab mind.

For from time immemorial, the Arab excelled in poetry which he cultivated long before Islam gave the impetus for collecting and studying it, not only for its own sake, but for the understanding of God's Word, the Holy Koran. To this day the Arabs take particular delight in reciting and listening to poetry. But its beginning is still shrouded in mystery. The oldest extant examples of Arabic poetry date only from the middle of the sixth century A.D., but show already a very involved, and at that stereotyped, form with definite and obligatory motifs and topics. Its origin and its earliest forms cannot yet be established or even examined for want of surviving examples.

The history of ancient Arabia can be divided into two distinctive epochs. The great divide is the appearance, in the early seventh century A.D., of the Prophet Muhammad who with his religious message of Islam ushered the Arabs onto the stage of history. The Muslims—and the ancient Arab writers themselves—recognize the importance of this event as the watershed in the history of their people; by terming the ages before Muhammad's appearance the Time of Ignorance, they attest to the different character of the epoch that began with the Prophet. The age before him was to them (as it still appears to many modern Western writers) not only one of lawlessness, with a society only loosely organized in tribes and with no established leader, a time in which tribe was pitted against tribe, the hand of all against all. Worst of all, it seemed to lack religious belief. Thus, in one word the generations after Muhammad characterized the era before his appearance as Messenger of God as, at the same time, crude and unpolished, and irreligious: the word *al-Jâhilîyah* implied godlessness as well as barbarism. Yet, the Arab still looks back to this age with a certain nostalgia, a certain pride.

Even though we should not accept this characterization in full, the use of the term *Jâhilîyah* for the period preceding the advent of the Prophet is convenient. However, we have to examine the extent to which the implication of barbarism—the lack of culture or civilization—is justified. True, no great monuments of past ages have been found in that part of the Peninsula that constitutes modern Saʿûdî Arabia. However, archeological exploration by excavation, the only way to uncover the remnants of ancient cultures, has hitherto been impossible. Not only is the region most important for elucidating the thoughts and the life-pattern of pre-Islamic Arabia—in particular Mecca itself—sacred ground (and the holy cities of Mecca and Medînah themselves and their *ḥaram*, "sacred banlieue," accessible to this day to none but a Muslim), the Wahhâbîs, the dominant politico-religious group in Arabia, are still very far from understanding the very necessity of carrying on such research.

From about the eighth century B.C. to the fifth or sixth century A.D., several highly organized states existed in South Arabia with kings or priest-kings at their head, with a flourishing agriculture, dependent on irrigation (which presupposes for its functioning a strong organized government). Only in this southernmost region, however, the Arabia Felix of the Ancients in Yemen and Ḥaḍramaut, has some limited exploration taken place. As a result, South Arabian history, religion, and social organization in the millennium before Christ has been studied on the basis of inscriptions on statues and temples and on bronze, stone, alabaster, and marble objects. The religious ideas, the system of government, and the social classes have been studied from this documentation, and the history, the feuds and alliances, the high points, and the decay of society have been established by modern scholars.

No such evidence exists for North Arabia. The earliest documents yet found are graffiti, engraved or scratched on rocks in South Arabian languages by members of the South Arabian caravans that plied the trade between the Indian Ocean and the Red Sea (via South Arabia), and the so-called Thamudean or proto-Arabic inscriptions by Aramaic-speaking Arab merchants from the north which date from the fifth century B.C. to the fifth century A.D. These are "literary" documents, that is, they are written statements, in contrast to sculpture and architecture or pottery—but they cannot be considered "literature." They are mostly short lines with few words, mainly of a religious character, a supplication or other devotional expression, a prayer to a deity for protection, or a name or two (just as modern tourists scribble their names on the walls of monuments or ruins to commemorate their visit). Only a very few of these documents—such as an often-quoted inscription of an Arab leader by the name of Imraʾ al-Qais, dated 328 A.D.—help to elucidate the early history of the Peninsula or deal with a historical personality or event.

Furthermore, these inscriptions are written in languages and scripts that differ from those employed in Arabic literature, which for us, and since the advent of Islam, are Arabic par excellence. Arabic is a member of the Western branch of the Semitic family of languages. Its Eastern branch, written in cuneiform characters, is familiar through the famous monuments from Assyria and Babylonia, exhibited in museums throughout the world; but the "Accadian" languages fell into disuse a millennium before the rise of Islam without leaving any trace. Arabic, both in its southern and northern form, belongs, with Ethiopic and Abyssinian, to the Southwest Semitic group of the Semitic languages. The best-known member of this West-Semitic branch is Hebrew, the language of the Old Testament and rabbinical literature, and surviving in the modern Hebrew spoken in Israel. The languages used in the inscriptions and graffiti of North Arabia are either South Arabic (Southwest Semitic) or some branch of Canaanite (Northwest Semitic, to which Hebrew and Aramaic also belong) in the so-called Nabataean inscriptions found there. Other West-Semitic languages, such as that of the Râs Shamra texts, written in cuneiform characters, and the South Arabian languages of the above-mentioned monuments, written in a script of their own, which is akin to the Abyssinian script, have died out leaving hardly a trace, while Syriac and its close relative Aramaic (the language spoken in Jesus' time over wide areas of the Near East) have survived in our time as church languages and are still spoken in three enclaves near Mosul in Iraq, Lake Urmia in Iran, and Lake Van in Armenia. South Arabic has survived as a spoken dialect only in some out-of-the-way places, remote from the stream of history, such as Soqotra, an island in the Indian Ocean, fronting on the southeast coast of Arabia.

In modern parlance, the term "Arabic language" refers to the language—known to us from about the fifth century A.D. in central and northern Arabia—which was used as the medium of expression for the works of poets, historians, theologians, philosophers, and other scholars from then on into the present time. Above all, it is the language in which Allâh revealed His Word, the Koran (*Qur'ân*), in a style which Muslim religious sentiment feels to be inimitable and unsurpassable —a sure proof of its divine origin. To this day Arabic is the language spoken and written by any Muslim who wants to reach through his work the whole Muslim world, not just his own native, non-Arab group. For, by being the language of Scripture and prayer, it has become—like Latin in the Christian church or Hebrew for the Jews throughout the time of the Diaspora—the theological lingua franca of Islam.

Modern literary Arabic, the so-called *naḥwî*, is almost identical with this classical tongue. To be sure, to fill the need to express modern thought as well as modern technology and science, new terms had to be created; its classical, sometimes cumbersome structure has also become somewhat modified. But, except for coping with an enlarged vocabulary, anyone familiar with classical Arabic will not find it difficult to understand the modern literary language. Not so the spoken vernacular. "Colloquial" Arabic, the so-called *'âmmî*, differs considerably from region to region, and from the classical and *naḥwî* language, in pronunciation and structure as well as in expression.

It is largely due to the feeling of awe for the language in which Allâh revealed His Word to the Prophet Muhammad that the creations of the Arab genius before his appearance have survived. According to the Koran, God revealed His Book to the Prophet in the language of his own people so that they, too, would possess a Scripture to guide them on the Right Path; for the earlier Revelations to the "People of the Book"—the Torah, the Evangelion, and the nameless Book of the "*Ṣâbi'ûn*"—had been revealed in languages not intelligible to them. Yet, the Arabic of the Koranic sermon was not that commonly spoken by the Arabs of that time. Not only did the Holy Book contain unfamiliar ideas, but these were expressed in phrases and terms not current in everyday speech. Nonetheless, the Koran had to be understood and, above all, to be recited in exactly the way in which it had been revealed. Thus, already at an early moment in Islamic development, the task arose to preserve the correct version, to establish the precise forms in which the Word of God had been revealed, and to comment on its explicit and implicit meaning.

Due to the peculiar structure which Arabic shares with all Semitic languages, this was not an easy task. For the most part, Semitic words possess three "radicals," that is, consonants which embody their intrinsic connotation. By internal changes—which do not, however, affect these consonants or alter their sequence—by doubling the second radical, by adding prefixes, infixes, or suffixes, by changing the vowels with which the consonants are pronounced (which may be long or short), the meaning of the word within the context is determined and modified. Every possible modification of a root is achieved in this manner: noun or adjective or verb; active or passive, causative, reflexive, or intensive meanings are expressed only in this way. This structure is complicated and leads to possible misunderstandings, a danger that is heightened by the fact that in written Arabic, as in all Semitic languages, the short vowels are not generally indicated. Only the consonants, both radicals and those that indicate modifications, are written down. Thus, the correct reading of a text depends on the understanding of its contents. At a very early time, therefore, the need was felt to establish the authentic reading of the holy Book.

A traditional story relates that Ziyâd ibn Abîhi, half-brother of the caliph Muʿâwiyah and his governor in Baṣra, was sitting one day with a group of Arabs when some newly converted Muslims of non-Arab stock were passing by, speaking faulty Arabic. Ziyâd commented on their errors and urged Abu'l-Aswad al-Du'alî (died 69 A.H./688 A.D.), who is considered by tradition to have been the first grammarian and the inventor of the system of Arabic grammar, to write a book on the correct use of the Arabic language. Al-Du'alî was disinclined to do that. However, when at some later time he heard God's Word mispronounced and distorted by faulty reading of the holy text, he felt compelled to compose a book to instruct the *ʿAjam*, the non-Arab Muslims, in the holy language. Thus was born the science of *naḥw*, "grammar."

But understanding Scripture required more than simply grammar. In searching for its meaning—of words and phrases as well as of ideas—scholars who lived long after the Prophet's time became interested in the life of those early generations of the Time of Ignorance—their outstanding personalities, their exploits, and their way of life. The endeavor to interpret words or phrases led the scholars to the literary treasures they had inherited from their forefathers, the poets and storytellers of pre-Islamic times who in their poetry and in their *gestes*, the so-called *aiyâm al-ʿarab* tales, had preserved the memory of the heroic deeds of past generations.

But these poems and tales of wars (*aiyâm al-ʿarab*, "battle days of the Arabs") had been transmitted from generation to generation solely by word of mouth, though writing, if not the commonplace necessity it is today, nor even the achievement of 15 or 20 percent of literates (as in underdeveloped countries of modern times) was not unknown in pre-Islamic Arabia. The above-mentioned graffiti were engraved by travelers, members of merchant caravans who were not craftsmen or professional scribes, as indicated by the mistakes they made in spelling and grammar. That there were professional scribes is confirmed by ancient Arabic poetry where writing is referred to many times as an admired art known to a small number of men who are identified as Yemenites or Jews. In poetry, too, the tattooing on the hands of the beloved, and the traces of an old encampment left in the desert sand which awake in the poet the bittersweet memory of a lost love, are compared to the writing in a book or to the lines written on parchment by a scribe.

However, in the Jâhilîyah this art was not used for the purpose of preserving poetic creations, though some of the poets were venerated, and their art often thought to have been inspired by their "familiar spirit." In pre-Islamic times, there were men called *râwî* whose task it was to memorize poetry and to recite it at the festivals and fairs held periodically in various parts of Arabia, and who were, in fact, themselves poets of renown. Yet a poet would not recite his own odes but would entrust their public recitation to his *râwî*; frequently he, in turn, would act as the latter's *râwî*. The ability of these men to store in their memory thousands of verses is amazing, especially since many of them acted as *râwî* to more than one poet, besides creating their own poetry. Indeed, it is for this reason that a small minority of modern scholars, one of them an admired and revered Arab scholar and littérateur, have doubted the genuineness of pre-Islamic poetry in its entirety, asserting that most of the poetry of the Jâhilîyah was the creation of later poets who attributed their own work to famed pre-Islamic bards and attached their name to their own imitations. This assertion has been repudiated not only by the Arabs, whose pride in this great national heritage of theirs was hurt, but also by the critical Western Orientalists who, despite their professional skepticism, did not see any reason to condemn the Arab pre-Islamic creations *in toto*. One need do no more than examine individual poems on the basis of inner criteria to uphold or discredit the validity of their claim to genuineness.

Poetry as well as the prose works of pre-Islamic times had to be gathered, written down, and annotated by the scholars of Islamic times before they could use them for their main purpose, namely, the interpretation of, and commentation on, the Koran. Thus, posterity owes even the survival of the creations of the Time of Ignorance to the religious zeal of pious Muslims.

Philological interest was not the only impulse that led Islamic scholars to collect pre-Islamic poetry and prose. They were keenly interested in the environment in which Muhammad grew up and developed into the Holy Prophet. The phrase "The *dîwân* [the historical records] of the Arabs is their poetry" was coined to express this motivation for undertaking the search for, and the preservation of, the old tales and poems. Later generations considered the ancient odes and the tales of the pre-Islamic "Days" to be the records of their nation's ancient history—of the relationships between its tribes and of the reasons for their alliances and feuds; they saw in them the chronicles of their heroes' exploits as well as of their scoundrels' misdeeds. Modern scholarship is not entirely convinced of the historical authenticity of the events described in Arabic poetry, even less of that of the explanatory stories found in the commentaries to the poems and the etiological tales explaining the proverbs and other literary products; yet, that they were composed in the Jâhilîyah and that their authors lived in that period cannot be doubted. Further, they truthfully—if possibly in a somewhat romanticizing and idealizing manner—reflect the state of Arabian culture, the social structure and pattern of thought in pre-Islamic times. Only in one respect must a reservation be entered: the surviving examples of pre-Islamic literature do not present a true reflection of religious attitudes in the pre-Muhammedan age, as will be discussed later.

II *The Arab Tribes, Their Social Organization, Their Religion*

Poetry as well as the prose works that originated in the pre-Islamic era serve to keep the memory of the Jâhilîyah fresh. That heritage which Muslim scholarship preserved is concerned almost exclusively with Bedouin tribes and their life; love, loyalty, bravery, war, and rivalry, but also treachery, brutality, and cowardice, are its subjects, both in prose and in verse. The protagonists of that age were Bedouins who lived in the deserts of Arabia roaming within large areas which were respected and acknowledged by other tribes as their traditional, hereditary domain. If they were disputed, war followed. In the waterless desert, the Bedouin depended on the camel for transportation and possibly more so for sustenance, particularly for its milk; on festive or other traditional occasions, or when an animal succumbed to the rigors of desert life, he ate its meat. Camel hides were used to make water skins and its wool was used to weave tents. We hardly ever hear of other domestic animals, such as sheep or goats, which their cousins, the nomadic Biblical Patriarchs, possessed, as do modern Bedouins of the Syrian desert and North Africa. But in pre-Islamic poetry we hear nothing of these utilitarian animals. Only the dog, detested but needed in the hunt, the aristocratic horse, and the doughty camel, the companion of the warrior and the stouthearted desert leader, were worthy of mention and praise.

The camel features prominently in Arabic poetry, for a considerable part of the *qaṣîdah,* "ode," customarily was devoted to the poet's travel through the desert on the back of his camel; he praises its stamina and characteristics in detail. The horse, too, a much more costly possession not within the reach of the ordinary Bedouin, was the subject of many tales, collected in works devoted especially to outstanding stallions and mares. But, in the characteristic Arab style, their story leads to that of their owner, his tribe and his time. The Bedouin wealth in camels must have been considerable, for we hear that a ransom of up to one thousand camels was paid for a captive king, that paid for a leading sheikh to have been several hundred, for a commoner one hundred camels, less for a captive woman. We also hear of leaders who commanded a thousand horse, though their number appears to have been small (one of our authorities lists some fifty such *jarrârûn*).[3]

Life as it is described in these prose and poetic epics was worth living—indeed possible—only within the closely knit tribal group. Only as a member of the tribe could the Bedouin Arab be assured of protection and help in his feuds and raids for the sake of revenge or booty. For Arabia, and in particular nomadic Arabia, lacked a solid, inflexible "political" organization. Leadership rested in the most admired and honored, since strongest, member of the tribe, the man who could guide because of superior wisdom and insight. He was at the same time dispenser of advice and charity, speaking with authority for the tribal community. In fact, the Arabic words for "leader" and "leadership" often denote the ability to speak, to give orders, and to think clearly, such as *amîr, zaʿîm*. But there was no set manner of selecting or electing the leader, nor was there any claim to inherited succession to that office. Indeed, leadership could hardly be characterized as an "office" in the modern sense; it could be assumed, as need arose, or on the spur of the moment, by anyone who felt the ability to cope with an exigency or emergency and who commanded, at the same time, the respect of the tribe. The temporary leader could retain his position only by continuously proving himself worthy of it: only success bred success.

However, it would be incorrect to describe the tribal organization as nearing anarchy, as has been done too often. The survival of the tribe as well as that of its individuals depended on discipline, cooperation, and submission of individual interests to that of the tribal community. The need for cooperation extended beyond the individual tribes, and alliances were concluded that either served temporary exigencies or developed into permanent associations. A tribe in need of help and support would seek the protection of another, more powerful one; men who found themselves in straitened or dangerous circumstances would seek shelter with a renowned warrior of their own or another tribe. For the tribe or the men who granted this *jiwâr*, "protection," it implied an acknowledgment of their superiority; their reputation grew with the number of their *jîrân*, the men under their *jiwâr*. This relationship between tribes might lead to a permanent alliance, with a new group name by which it was henceforth known, or it might cease with the passing of the emergency that necessitated it.

Thus, organization, not chaos, prevailed in the pre-Islamic Bedouin society. The individual knew where he belonged; he had the irrevocable right to a place in his tribe; as long as he did not commit a crime or violate its mores or rules and thus become an outlaw, he could count on its help and support. Women, too, were part of the tribal unit, and in the comparatively rare cases of exogamic marriage, they retained the right to return to the fold in case of divorce or the death of their husbands. However, in the time just prior to Islam, their sons remained with their father and were reared as members of his tribe.

Arabic sources reflect the diverse elements of which the pre-Islamic population of the Peninsula was composed. They preserve, in a stylized and systematized form, the memory of their origin. On the basis of probably very ancient tradition, the Arabs evolved an intricate system of kinship and genealogical relationship. Though oversystematized, it helped them—as it helps us—to distinguish between personalities and their relationship to each other, to remember historical events and keep track of participants in them; in short, it was their way of recording history. Thus, from time immemorial, the Arabs retained the memory that they were divided into two main groups—those tribes that originated in South Arabia and those from the North. They regarded as the original inhabitants of their land a number of almost or entirely legendary people that had perished without leaving any trace. We meet these alleged original, pure-blooded Arabs, *ʿarab ʿariba*, in the Koran where the vanishing of the ʿÂd and the Thamûd (see above p. 6) from the face of the earth is pointed out as a deterrent for the unrepentant sinners of the Prophet's own time. According to this assumption, they had taught the Arabic language to non-Arab settlers in South Arabia, descendants of Qaḥṭân (identified with the Biblical Yaqẓân); these became Arabicized *ʿarab mutaʿarriba* and formed the historical South Arabian tribes. Another group, also not of pure Arab blood, called *ʿarab mustaʿriba,* was formed by tribes that had settled in North and Central Arabia. To them belonged, among others, the Banû Quraysh, the most famous member of which was Muḥammad ibn ʿAbd Allâh who became the Prophet of Allâh. This construction, though of course merely a historical fiction, nonetheless shows that the Arabs were conscious that their group was not homogeneous but composed of many varied components.

Tracing their genealogy back to their eponym Ismâʿîl, the Biblical Ishmael, son of Abraham's concubine Hagar, the North Arabians consider themselves descendants of ʿAdnân. The consciousness of this division into ʿAdnân and Qaḥṭân groups was kept alive throughout the centuries, though many of the South Arabian tribes migrated into Central and North Arabia and played a role in pre-Islamic times as well as in the history of Islam. Thus, the Banû Kinda, one of whose princes was the famous pre-Islamic poet Imraʾ al-Qais, as well as the Banû Aus and the Banû Khazraj, the "Helpers" of the Prophet (who probably played the most decisive part in the success of his mission) were the descendants of South Arabians who had settled in North Arabia and in Yathrib—which later became *Medînat al-Nabî*, "the Prophet's City," then *al-Medînah*, "The City" par excellence. This division, and the rivalry and animosity, not to call it hostility, between them was still very much in evidence in early Islamic times; in the newly founded military settlements within the regions conquered by the Muslim armies, for example in Kûfah, it slowed down the undisturbed development of the new Muslim community. Indeed, one might even wonder whether the disharmony prevailing among modern Arabs in the various parts of the Arab world has not at least one of its roots in this ancient animosity between the different Arab groups.[4]

In spite of their alleged common ancestry, tribal feuds were common. Blood revenge was one frequent reason for outbreaks of hostilities. For every blood-guilt, whatever the motive for its being committed, imposed upon any member of the tribe the duty of revenging it; he was, in turn, legitimate prey for an avenger. Thus, wars between whole tribes or individual members were constant, and only willingness to offer and accept a ransom instead of paying with blood prevented them from continuing indefinitely. They are the subject of the *aiyâm* tales. Indeed, the famous "Dâḥis War,"[5] the protracted feud between the ʿAbs and Dhubyân tribes, arose from a trivial incident, but the strife and mutual blood revenge is said to have lasted for forty years. Much of the surviving poetry has praise for the heroes or scorn for the enemy as its main topic.

Tribal organization still prevailed also in the few settled habitations in the Arabian Peninsula. These developed from the presence of water in an oasis or grew up around a sanctuary, which in turn often owed its existence to the presence of a well, as was the case in Mecca, the most renowned of all. However, to call these settlements "cities," and contrast "urban" with Bedouin life, conveys a misleading impression in view of the modern associations these words evoke. Arabic poetry and prose sources do not justify the characterization of these settlements as "urban centers" and their inhabitants as "merchants" with their interests concentrated on trade. Their inhabitants kept in close contact with the neighboring Bedouin tribes—often relatives, "cousins" of theirs—and deep into Islamic times the custom of raising children in the desert, practiced before Islam, remained alive, especially among the aristocracy. The Prophet himself, though only a poor orphaned member of a leading tribe, is said to have been reared by a Bedouin woman. If we can take the emotions expressed in the poetry of "urban" poets at their face value and not regard them simply as obligatory motifs of a stylized genre of poetry, they were as close to the desert way of life as the Bedouin himself. But that is a debatable, and much debated, point.

Moreover, some of these places were inhabited only for short periods, at the time of the fairs to which "all Arabia" came during the holy months in which a *Pax Arabica* reigned. ʿUkâẓ—often mentioned in prose and poetry and, next to Mecca, with its Kaʿbah, the most important site for pre-Islamic gatherings—came to life only in this period. But even in the permanent settlements, such as Ṭâʾif, Yathrib, Khaybar, and Mecca, the tribal organization prevailed. Even in Mecca, the tribes had their defined quarters within the town, as we know from the biography of the Prophet as well as from the works on its history. In Yathrib, this arrangement was carried to such an extreme that the oasis with its rich palm groves was nothing but a concentration of clan-homesteads with independent water supplies and storage facilities and fortified against attacks from fellow Yathribians. Indeed, in the decades before Islam, Yathrib was in the throes of feuds between the dominant tribal groups residing in it, a state of affairs that eventually led them to call upon Muhammad, as an independent impartial man from the outside with no ties to any faction in Yathrib, to act as an umpire and to restore peace within the strife-torn oasis. The impact of this step was farther reaching than any of the participants in this decision could have foreseen.

The importance of these settlements lay in their role as places for rest and replenishment of food and water for the caravans that passed through them on their way from South Arabia to Egypt and the Fertile Crescent and beyond. North Arabia itself had very little to contribute by way of merchandise to this trade; dates from the oases, riding and pack camels which the Bedouins bred and their wool and skins were about all the products that Central Arabia had to offer to the neighboring countries. Its inhabitants could not contribute incense or sandalwood and spices, such as the caravans brought from Yemen and Ḥaḍramaut and from faraway India. In our old sources we find descriptions of the "trade" in some of the pre-Islamic fairs, the names of their patrons and the tribes that frequented them, the merchandise traded in them, and the manner of bidding for it and of concluding the bargain.[6] Much of the trade was by barter. However, it seems that the renowned merchants of Mecca acted as middlemen in their city and the other depot posts of the caravan route; Mecca's much-vaunted two caravans of Muhammad's time, one in the summer, one in winter (Sûrah 106), do not bespeak really intense mercantile activity; they are at best, remnants of formerly more frequent caravans.

The religious attitudes and ideas prevailing in pre-Islamic Arabia require detailed discussion. Most scholars find only scant evidence of religious practices and emotions in our sources and aver that the pre-Islamic Arab in the centuries immediately before Islam had no religious feeling except a vague fear of the unknown and a rather primitive kind of "animism." Julius Wellhausen, in his volume on *Reste arabischen Heidenthums*, collected quite an impressive quantity of allusions to, and outright descriptions of, pagan rites, "superstitions," and beliefs, including the rites pertaining to the cults of the Kaʿbah and other sanctuaries. The sheer mass of material he assembled should have convinced the author himself, but must convince his readers, that the assertion of Arab irreligiosity has no basis. This lack of comprehension of a religiosity differing from the accustomed Western kind is due to the inability of men like Wellhausen to accept as religion anything but monotheism, partly because they were steeped in the Christian concept of religion, partly because of the thought prevailing in his time that "primitive" religion or "idolatry" was no religion, "primitive" culture no culture at all. In modern times, a better understanding of cultures that differ from our own has developed—due to the efforts of cultural anthropologists and the research into "patterns of cultures" other than that in which we live—so that we are able now to approach the religion of the Arabs in the Jâhilîyah with less bias and new insight. Our deep cultural roots in the "Judeo-Christian traditions," strengthened by the antipolytheistic attitude of Islam itself and those that confessed it, helped to support and perpetuate this contempt for the Jâhilîyah form of Arabian religiosity.

The silence of Arabic poetry on religious beliefs and the lack of expressions of religious emotions in it and in other forms of pre-Islamic literature were taken as proof that the Arab did not possess religiosity and was living for the here and now without meditating upon such religious questions as life after death or the existence and essence of a divine being or beings. But that lack was due to the censorship of the Islamic scholars who, generations later, purged all expressions of pre-Islamic beliefs from their literary written records and substituted the name of Allâh for those of pre-Islamic deities. (We know, too, that people changed their names which invoked pre-Islamic gods into such that called on Allâh.)

The dearth of evidence does not prove lack of religious feelings. If that assertion were true, how could we account for the existence of sanctuaries such as the Kaʿbah in Mecca and others near it which possessed such great religious power that Muhammad had to incorporate them into his new, so strongly monotheistic faith? For even his reinterpretation of the Kaʿbah in the Koran as a holy house founded by Ibrâhîm (Abraham) and its rites as memorials to him does not hide their source in pre-Islamic cults and their original pagan connotations. To minimize the pre-Islamic rites at the Kaʿbah, in Mîna, at ʿArafât, and elsewhere, as meaningless forms with no real religious awe behind them reveals a failure to grasp the meanings of ritual acts. These rites are expressions of man's dedication to his god; touching his sanctuary (as, for instance, touching the Black Stone at the Kaʿbah) meant sharing in its strength and partaking of its divine power. The circumambulation of the Kaʿbah, the running between Ṣafa and Marwah, as exercised before Islam, have their roots in rites performed in remote antiquity. At the *Sed* Festival, the ancient Egyptian god-king dedicated to the gods of Egypt the Field—which represented the land of Egypt—by crossing its length and breadth, on a fourfold course according to the points of the compass in a dancelike walk; he is also represented in a relief as performing a dancelike run between the two *Sed* pillars.[7]

Moreover, not to recognize the deep-seated religiosity of the pre-Islamic rituals is to fail to understand human needs and the working of human minds. In the harsh environment of the desert, exposed to hardships of climate and geography, constantly endangered by the hostility of man and nature, the Bedouin must often have felt small and in need of divine assistance. Furthermore—and this is no mean consideration—he lived in a region in which, since the dawn of civilization, religion and religions had risen. We moderns no longer worship the sun, the moon, and the stars; we do not worship any god of the mountains, though we, too, are still awed by their majesty. We do not understand the ancient symbols anymore; and that is the reason why men like Wellhausen give the name of "animism" or "pantheism" to the religion of men who regard the natural phenomena as manifestations of the gods and take, what we may possibly express in poetry or by symbols, for the divine, the deity, itself. The Prophet of Islam grew up in this environment, and however much the brands of Judaism and Christianity, or "*Ḥanîf*dom" in Arabia, may have influenced his thought in later periods, it was the Near East with its innate religiosity, its millennia-old symbols and images, that nurtured in him the deep religious ideas of his early meditations and sermons.

This religiosity is reflected in the Koran itself. In his earliest sermons, Muhammad constantly invokes the stars, the mountains, the ship, the city, and the fish—ancient symbols in Near Eastern religious belief for death and resurrection; he fills these ancient religious ideas with a new, deeper spiritual meaning than they had in antiquity. But their basic value, the memory of their antiquity, is ever present in his early sermons. From the earliest recorded times on, Near Eastern man speculated about the miracles which his immediate environment made so drastically evident to him. The seasonal revival of nature after its "death" in the heat of summer, recurring year after year, gave him hope for, even confident expectation of, a revival after death. The Egyptian myths of the death of the god and his resurrection, as for example, in the Osiris-Horus myths, the Canaanite legends of the death and return to life of Baʿal, the tragic mystery of the god-king's death and restoration closely connected in these myths with the perennial death and revival of nature, are echoed in the Koran. Muhammad proves his unshakable belief in the omnipotence of the One and Only God by this unalterable sequence of dying and revival in nature; even more was it for him undeniable proof of the certainty of man's resurrection after death.

Paradise and Hell, featured so prominently in the Koranic idea of life after death, are also rooted in the most ancient Near Eastern mythology. The Egyptian Abode of the Dead, the dreaded Netherworld, and the Field of the Blessed find their counterpart in the Koran—not always in obvious terms, as in the threats of The Fire (= Hell), but often in symbols that need interpretation in order to be understood. Very little expression of this idea was allowed to remain in the literary heritage that has come to us from the Jâhilîyah. Muslim censorship erased from old prose and poetry almost any reference to pre-Islamic deities; if it was allowed to remain, it was interpreted in Koranic terms; for example, every *Bayt Allâh,* "House of God," was taken to mean the House of God in Mecca, and every *Kaʿbah* mentioned was held to be the sacred Kaʿbah in Mecca. However, some surviving literary sources show that more than one *bayt Allâh,* more than one *kaʿbah* existed in pre-Islamic Arabia.

There is even evidence that the pagan Arab did ponder death and resurrection in the traditional ancient manner, a fact hitherto denied by Western Orientalists, because no explicit expression of this belief can be found in our texts. However, the Arabs must have had at least one symbol for this idea; its preservation in a few pre-Islamic poems (by

Zuhayr 19, v.15; ʿAbîd b. al-ʿAbraṣ, 8, vv. 5f.; Nâbighah, 5, vv. 44ff.; al-Aʿshà, 4, vv. 36ff.; 5, vv. 56ff.; 13, vv. 55ff.; 13, vv. 58ff.) is due to the fact that this particular symbol—the ship—is sanctified by its occurrence in Sacred Scripture. The comparison of death to a frightening experience symbolized by a passage in a boat through a stormy sea and of the resurrection as the abatement of the storm and the saving of the sailors in the ship was known in various myths and legends from Ancient Egypt to Christianity and was always interpreted as such. It is twice found in beautiful passages in the Koran (Sûrah 10, v.23 and 29, v. 65), and only lack of understanding of mythological thought and its expression in symbolic forms could result in interpreting it as a reminiscence of an actual crossing of the Red Sea by Muhammad.[8]

CHAPTER 2

The Literature of the Jâhilîyah

I *Pre-Islamic Poetry*

By far the most widely known and most often discussed genre of pre-Islamic literature is its poetry. Once the West became aware of its existence, it began to attract the attention of some of Europe's finest minds; it found translators and imitators and it inspired literary works and learned discussions. In Goethe's *West-Őstlicher Diwan,* the spirit of "Arab" poetry has found one of its highest literary expressions in Western garb, for the *Diwan* is not a translation of Arabic originals, as are, for example Rückert's translations, or the later ones by Sir Charles Lyall, or in our own time those of Arberry, but a recreation of, and an empathy with, the sentiments expressed in the originals. Goethe did not distinguish between Arabic and Persian poetry; but that does not detract from the validity of this assertion, for Hammer-Purgstall's *Geschichte der schönen Redekünste Persiens,* which gave Goethe the inspiration to cast his own personal emotions into this Oriental form, as he did in the *Ushk Nameh,* "Book of Love," of the *Diwan,* discusses Arabic, Persian, and Turkish poetry indiscriminately.

As it has come to us, Arabic poetry presents itself as a highly developed art, stylized in form as well as in contents. Already the earliest recorded poems, dating from the early decades of the sixth century A.D., manifest refinement of expression, polished metrics, and, above all, a uniformity of motifs that can only be explained if these poems are regarded as the end-result of a long period of development. Even the so-called *Rajaz* poems, the earliest pre-Islamic poetry, and at the same time formally the simplest type in existence, show the stereotyped motifs and style that are characteristic of Arabic poetry as a whole. Granted, the strict regulations of later Arab scholars as to what topics may or may not be treated in poetry, and their debates about the comparative merits of various poets and their creations must be considered as—rather sterile—judgments on the basis of the poetic heritage that had come down to them; yet, by the period in which the Arabic poetry that has been preserved was composed, a strict pattern with traditional topics expressed in set forms and images and cast into formal meters had already evolved.

This statement must, however, be modified to a certain degree. The material on which we base our judgments is limited both in character and in origin. Therefore, the uniformity that we observe may be due to limitations in the scholarly interest of its collectors; they looked for, and preserved, poetic and prose works that enhanced their insight into the environment from which their Prophet arose and which increased their knowledge of the origins of their faith. Thus the *dîwâns* of individual poets and the anthologies brought together by post-Muhammad scholars are devoted to the creations of members of certain tribes that represent—possibly only in their ideology—the "mainstream of Arab life" in the Jâhilîyah. For we possess, at least in the *dîwân* of the Hudhaylite poets, poetry of a different character, that of mountain people, with a harsher code of behavior, a cruder, more aggressive way of life. The motifs and even the dialect used in their poetry differ from those usually found in Arabic poems. Unfortunately, this is the only such *dîwân* of a different strain to have survived, though we may safely assume that there were others.

However, the Arab poet of the sixth century—considered the classical and golden age of pre-Islamic Arabic poetry—was limited in his creativity to certain topics and was forced to use them in a prescribed sequence. Among these he was free to emphasize one topic and play down another. But even within this limited freedom of selection he had to follow strict "esthetic" rules; only a limited number of motifs were considered worthy of treatment in poetry. Thus, Arabic poetry of the period immediately preceding Islam appears to the Western student on the surface as a rather stereotyped art form, restrained in imagery, almost entirely devoid of individual expression of emotion, fettered by the restrictions imposed on the artist by tradition and by the limitations of accepted and required motifs.

However, emphasizing this fact does not do justice to the ancient Arab poet and his art. In ancient times, Near Eastern poetry was not the expression of personal, individual, but of communal, religious, emotions; it performed a function within ancient society and its religious rites. The ancient temples resounded to the hymns in praise of the deities spoken by the priests; these survive, according to some scholars, as a remote echo in such parts of the Arabic *qaṣîdah* as the *nasîb*, "love poem".[1] Nor was Semitic poetry originally an art-for-art's-sake affair; it formed part of divine worship, and in the Ṣûfî poetry of later times it became again the vehicle for religious devotion. The very term *shâʿir* for "poet" in Arabic still conveys this religious connection, for it reminds us that in ancient times the *shâʿir* was a man endowed with deep intuition, guided by a higher power outside himself. Even in comparatively late times the Arabs still believed that the poet had a *jinn,* "familiar spirit," to inspire him and to enable him to speak for his community through his poetry.

Thus, poetry had a function in pre-Islamic Arabian life different from what is attributed to it in the West. It was not the expression of personal emotions; the poet did not, indeed *could* not, flourish in isolation. He was part of the tribe's life. In fact, he was often its spokesman and a person of influence whose word was counted, whose advice was heeded, and whose scorn could hurt equally a member of his own tribe or an enemy. The victor in a poetic match enhanced his tribe's reputation, and the poet stood before the battle line to taunt the foe, to be answered by the poet representing the enemy in a poem that took up the meter and rhyme of this provocation. That poetry was a potent weapon was still acknowledged in comparatively late times; a father ordered his son to lie down lest the "arrows" of the hostile poet's verse hit and hurt him;[2] the wounds inflicted through poetic curse and by the *hijà,* "taunt," of the Arab poet (as in the Biblical story of Balak's demand to curse the Children of Israel which God turned into blessing in Bileam's mouth) were felt as real ones by those who were hit.

The immense richness of the Arabic language as such which enables the poet to cast the common topic into an almost infinite variety of expression must also be taken into account in assessing the artistry of Arab poetry. Besides the mediocre poetaster who was able, because of its rigid contents, structure, and form, to compose verse that was acceptable but of no particular merit, even in the eyes of his compatriots, there were others who possessed the genius required to cast the commonplace topic into exquisite original poetry, filling it with their personal emotional experience though keeping within the prescribed pattern and the traditional motifs and forms. However, only those who are able to read and understand the original can savor the peculiar beauty and flavor of Arab poetry. Translations from the Arabic, in a higher degree than from any other language, cannot re-create the specific style and subtlety of the Arabic tongue nor adequately convey the flavor of its poetic imagination.

The form in which ancient Arabic poetry has come to us is called by the Arabs the *qaṣîdah.* In its most complete form, it consisted of several parts which had to deal with certain topics, each subject to the strict rules of imagery, expressions, and motifs of its own species. Even the sequence of these parts was predetermined. According to tradition, the *qaṣîdah* acquired its name from the fact that its climax was an "approach" to a prince, a sheikh, or some other influential and mighty person with a demand for a favor, be it to help the petitioner in his struggle against a foe or simply to reward the poet with a gift for the flattery addressed to his patron in his poem. This interpretation sounds, however, like an attempt to explain an expression the original and real meaning of which had long been forgotten.

A *qaṣîdah* begins with the so-called *nasîb,* an "amatory prelude" (as it is usually called), to the ode. This is invariably devoted to the memory of a lost love, never concerned with a love affair that is still alive. This is followed by a detailed description of the camel that carries the poet away from the place of his sad reminiscences in an arduous ride through the desert, which is the topic of the next part of the *qaṣîdah.* The goal of this ride is the main topic of the poem. In it, the poet may express his hostility toward an attacker; he may deride him and revile his character and that of his ancestors and his tribe. He may extol his own qualities, his generosity toward those in need, his heroic exploits in war. He may also sing the praise of the sheikh or prince whose favors he hopes to gain or whose help he needs to win. This part of the poem, called *fakhr,* "praise," or *iftikhâr,* "self-glorification," presents a very fine picture of the ideal Arab hero. Virile, enduring, a valiant fighter, he is the protector of the weak and the defender of the honor of his tribe and its women. No foe is able to withstand him; he will always be true to his given word. Chivalry and generosity, loyalty and courage, as well as wisdom, prudence, and inventiveness, and when needed also *ḥilm,* that is, wise restraint and knowledge of the limits to which he may go, are his characteristics. The enemy is charged with exactly the opposite of these qualities: treachery, cowardice, "eating of the poor," mistreatment of women are the accusations hurled at him. The former noble character traits are also the qualities extolled in the *marthiyah,* the dirge mourning a fallen hero, composed by women only. The most beautiful examples of these dirges are those devoted to the Hudhaylite hero Ṣakhr by his sister al-Khansâ',[3] the only pre-Islamic poetess whose poems have survived in a *dîwân* "collection."

In fact, the *fakhr,* the final, climactic part of the Arab ode, is also the most valuable for us because of its quasi-historical contents. For tribal rivalries, the struggle for supremacy among the groups, personal ambitions, and frustrations are a major theme in this, the principal part of the *qaṣîdah.* The compact style, the direct and outspoken condemnation of the foe, the vivacious language, and the hard-hitting, unflattering comparisons must have had a deep impact on the contemporary Arab listener familiar with the events and circumstances.

It is less easy for the modern scholar, be he Westerner or Arab, to elucidate the kernel of historical truth from them; even the early Islamic commentators on these poems had a hard time trying to do so. In spite of the attempts by both ancient and modern scholars, the many discrepancies between the poetical versions and the reports transmitted by Arab historians, the mixup in personalities involved (often due to the similarity of their names), and the fact that almost all knowledge was based on oral transmission prevent attaining historically reliable results. In modern native editions, the commentaries utilize mainly the ancient sources without attempting to separate traditional interpretation from historical fact.

Within each of the main parts of the odes, various topics are available for the poet's use, each with a limited variety of motifs from which the poet may either choose one or the other or use them all. The theme of the *nasîb,* mournful reminiscences of a love episode in bygone days, can be expressed poetically in three ways. The most often used, and the best known—possibly because Imra' al-Qais, the most famous of pre-Islamic poets and the most often quoted in both East and West, used it in his famous *Muʿallaqah*—is that of the aging lover stopping on his ride through the desert at a spot where traces of a ditch and of tent pegs, dry camel dung, and ashes from the cooking pit reveal an old camp site. He recognizes it as the place where he enjoyed long ago the company of a maid from a friendly tribe that had pitched its tents in the same camping ground. These traces awaken in him the old love for her; he remembers her beauty and describes it minutely: her hair, her eyes, her teeth, the way she walked, and her coquetry. Tears well up in his eyes, and he weeps as copiously as the rainfall in a thunderstorm or a sudden cloudburst, which results in covering the desert with a luxuriant verdure. But, looking at his camel, he regains his composure, shakes off his sadness, and continues his travel on his trusty camel whose endurance and beauty he then describes.

The second opening topic of the *nasîb,* and with it of the *qaṣîdah,* shows the poet watching the departure of the tribes after the happy spring season—the season of love—on their separate ways. With the neighborly tribe his beloved, too, is departing. The poet describes the scene vividly, the appearance of the laden camels with the towering litters of the women resembling ships.

The third theme of the *nasîb,* though not the most frequently used, is of great poetic impact. The poet, now old and white-haired, seems to see his beloved of many years ago coming at night to his resting place, phantomlike in all her youthful beauty. He marvels that such a frail woman could walk such a long distance. But the vision disappears, and he is left with the memory of her beauty and the sad realization of his old age and the passing of time. Like the first theme, both the second and the third may lead to a description of the beloved's beauty and the verdure of the desert in spring.

The fixed sequence of themes, together with their comparative limitation to certain permissible topics to the exclusion of any that had not become part of the poetic repertoire would seem to have resulted in a monotonous, stereotyped kind of poetry. That this is not the case—at least not in the Arabic original—is due to two factors. The first reason, as already mentioned, is the richness of the Arabic language, a veritable "ocean" (*qâmûs,* a word of Greek origin used for a famous classical lexicon which then became the generic term for any dictionary). But it is due far more to a characteristic feature of that poetry, its habit of using innumerable metonymic characterizations instead of a plain noun. Thus, a woman is described as "large-eyed" (*ḥûr al-ʿayn*) which literally means "[a gazelle] with the black of the pupil sharply distinct from the white [of her eye]"; the word then acquired the meaning of "beautiful woman" in general. Or descriptive epithets of the sword or the lance, a camel or a horse, or a characterization of an outstanding fighter are commonly used for "sword," "lance," "camel," "horse," "hero," and so on.[4]

Thus, the most striking characteristic of Arabic poetry is its conformance to strict rules of composition, of themes and motifs, of sequences, and, last but not least, of meters and rhymes. One may justly wonder whether, under these circumstances and with these restrictions, the Jâhilîyah produced any poet of individuality, or indeed, genius. Such a question, however, cannot properly be asked, given the character of the psychological environment in which pre-Islamic poetry flourished. For Bedouin society did not promote individuality; the personality traits it valued were exactly those developed within the tribe and those that furthered its well-being. Individual valor and bravery, courage and leadership grew within, and for, the societal tribal needs. Indeed, such men as Taʿabbaṭa Sharrà or ash-Shanfarà, famous heroes and individualists, were outlaws who had to live outside the tribal community, since they would not submit to its rules and to the limitations of their freedom. But even in the poetry of these men who dared to be different because their life was passed outside the accepted norm, the influence of the regular style makes itself felt. Where the conventional poet would speak of fellow tribesmen, ash-Shanfarà boasts of his fellowship with panther, hyena, and wolf, not with human companions. In the *fakhr,* he flaunts his exploits as is the custom, but he praises qualities not usually considered praiseworthy; his hair is unkempt and no oil has touched it; his belly is lean from constant and voluntarily prolonged lack of food. He boasts of his loneliness and lawlessness and compares his wild and dangerous life to that of his companions, the wild beasts.[5]

The Arab does not know lyrical poetry in the Western sense. There is no outpouring of individual emotions, or, one should rather say that, wherever these *are* present (as for instance in the poems of Imra' al-Qais), they were forced into the obligatory forms of expression. But, in spite of this, even the Western reader can feel the strong personal involvement underlying the stereotyped forms into which it was cast. Imraʾ al-Qais, the much maligned lover of many women—to this writer the greatest of Jâhilîyah poets—pours his outrage over the treacherous murder of his royal father into verses which, though strictly within the formal boundaries requested by convention, show his personal grief and at the same time the depth of his poetic gift. Al-Aʿshà, too, though not as spontaneous and personal in his style, had the gift of poetic expression, though keeping within the strict limits tradition imposed on poetry.

However, our Western standards of what makes "good" poetry do not suffice to appreciate the artistry of the Jâhilîyah poetry. The native judgments of the respective merits use criteria that differ widely from ours, and even from those of modern Arab critics.

In later generations, scholars began to develop theories evaluating the respective ranks of pre-Islamic poets. Establishing the traditional *qaṣîdah* as the norm, its topics and the manner of their treatment, the rules governing its metrics, and the limitations imposed on motifs as the standard by which to judge a poet and his creations, they began to pit poet against poet, *qaṣîdah* against *qaṣîdah,* and even verse against verse. Thus, a poet would be praised for the refinement of his camel description, another became famous for his *nasîb,* yet another for his handling of the *fakhr*; a poet might even be praised or faulted for a single verse, or his way of expressing an idea might be considered superior to the manner in which a rival had expressed a similar idea.

One important aspect of Arab poetry must not remain unmentioned since it contributes in a considerable measure to its poetic appeal, even to its emotional effect. This is especially, possibly only, effective when one listens to its being recited; in fact, Arabic poetry originally was meant to be heard, not read. To produce this effect, the Arab had at his disposal a variety of meters; each verse consisted of a number of feet with its rhythmic sequence of long, accented, and short, unaccented, syllables. At the end of each verse appears a rhyme which is contained in the last syllable only; it is produced by the vowel-consonant-vowel sequence of the last syllable of each verse which remains identical throughout the whole length of the *qaṣîdah*. The effect of this combination of meter and repeated rhyme-syllable is striking and fascinates the Arab attuned to the sound of his language; his intuitive understanding of the metonymies and his delight in the elegant style arouse him to enthusiasm and passion. It was thus in classical times, when poetry was *the* art of the Arabs, and it still affects him in this way today.

II *Pre-Islamic Prose Literature*

Poetry is not the only literary heritage from pre-Islamic times that has survived. An extensive amount of prose works exists, sufficient to supplement and clarify our knowledge of life in the Arabian Peninsula before the advent of Islam. However, prose, too, was not committed to writing until the interest of post-Muhammad scholars in the Jâhilîyah was aroused. Then they began to collect the stories hitherto only transmitted orally and to write them down, much in the same way and out of the same scholarly impulse that inspired the Brothers Grimm in the nineteenth century to collect the German folk- and fairy-tales in order to preserve them from oblivion. The Muslim scholars were motivated by an additional, somewhat different intention, that of fighting the arrogance of pure-blooded Arabs through their own recollections. Though partly they were engaged in an honest endeavor to preserve the memory of ancient events and customs, this added incentive may have appeared to them even more cogent.

In the wake of Muhammad's appearance in the Arabian Peninsula, the social order of the Arabs was bound to change. True, the Bedouins that remained in Arabia proper changed little, if at all; but the migration of masses of Arabs, in consequence of the Conquest, into the Fertile Crescent and beyond, their inevitable contact with the inhabitants of the conquered regions (some, though by far not all of which, were Arabs), and the moral duty of acknowledging the vanquished as brethren in Islam demanded a gradual reorientation of their social outlook as well as an adjustment in their order of values. Muhammad himself had set this process in motion through his passionate call for the brotherhood of all men under Islam. However, Arab arrogance—as the non-Arab saw it—heightened by their pride in having been chosen by Allâh as the people to whom He sent His Messenger, with the "last and definite" Revelation in the Arabic tongue, caused them to relegate the non-Arab convert to Islam to second-class status. But the *ʿAjam,* the "Barbarian," non-Arab, was aware of a cultural heritage of his own far superior to that of the Arab Bedouin: Did they not themselves constantly boast of their harsh, rough, uncivilized life in the desert? Thus the *ʿAjam* used the stories told by the Bedouins themselves to cut their detractors down to size and to defame them with their avowed barbaric customs. Where was their pride in ancestry? How often must they not have been unsure of their own origin and family in view of the constant raids on women and their abduction as captives left to the not-so-tender mercies of their captors.[6]

Thus, we owe the survival of the *akhbâr al-ʿArab,* the "tales of the pre-Islamic Arabs," and their *aiyâm,* "days of warfare," not wholly to admiration but, on the contrary, to the desire of the non-Arab convert to disparage them. These *ʿajam* scholars were the mouthpiece of an anti-Arab, pro-Iranian movement, designed to bolster the pride of the non-Arab Muslim. It derived its justification—and also its name of *Shuʿûbîyah*—from Revelation itself. Whether or not the famous verses of the Koran "The Believers are but brothers, so make peace between your two brothers and fear God, haply ye may obtain mercy . . . . O ye folk, verily we have created you of male and female, and made you races (*shuʿûb*) and tribes that ye may know each other. Verily the most honorable of you in the sight of God is the most pious of you; verily, God is knowing, aware" (Koran, Sûrah 49, vv. 10,13) are genuine or, as has been asserted, a tendentious interpolation by non-Arab converts to Islam, they doubtless reflect Muhammad's own conviction. These converts had to be integrated into Arab society, so to speak become "naturalized," since, at least during the first century and a quarter of Islam—to the end of the Umaiyad dynasty (123 A.H./740 A.D.)—Arab custom and outlook still prevailed. The ancient way of affiliation of a non-Arab with an Arab tribe—usually by manumitting a slave and incorporating him as *mawlà,* "client," of his former master into the tribal community—offered a traditional way of receiving an alien into the Islamic community, in which, especially in the first century of the *Hijrah* ('Hegira', Emigration), tribal organization still persisted.

These *mawâlî* became a powerful influence not only on the

social and political organization of the Muslim state but also on its literature and scholarship. They adopted Arabic as their working language in which they achieved mastery, together with Arabic names and surnames, usually derived from their native towns (the so-called *nisbah*); soon they began to outshine and even outnumber native Arabs in all the main branches of Muslim scholarship. They became prominent in the field of historiography (e.g., al-Ṭabarî, al-Balâdhurî, Yaʿqûbî, and others) and were leaders in religious Tradition, Canon law, and Koran interpretation; the outstanding philosophers and scientists writing in the Arabic language were of non-Arab origin. In the field of philosophy, for instance, only one prominent man, al-Kindî, was an Arab, as his name proclaims (his tribe, the Banû Kinda, could also boast of counting Imra' al-Qais among their prominent members). But for a long time, the ancient pride of the Arab in his *ʿarabîyah,* his Arabhood, expressed in hundreds of verses in pre-Islamic times, in the *fakhr,* still prevailed. This high self-esteem was enhanced by pride in having been chosen by Allâh as the people from among whom He called His Prophet. Thus, the Arabs became boastful and overbearing and provoked the anger of the non-Arab converts.

To defend themselves against Arab haughtiness, the *mawâlî* began to taunt them, using their own hereditary records from poetry and other traditional lore as arguments against them. This was the motivation which produced the anthologies of Arab prose and the *dîwâns* of pre-Islamic poetry with their commentaries and philological and historical explanations. Yet, like the Faustian "Kraft, die stets das Böse will und stets das Gute schafft" (Goethe), we owe to these non-Arab scholars and compilers the preservation of most, if not all, of the ancient (pre-Islamic) poetry and prose literature. Names like Abû ʿUbaydah (died 207 or 210 A.H./ca. 825 A.D.), Ibn Qutaybah (died 276 A.H./889 A.D.), al-Aṣmaʿî (died 213 A.H./830 A.D.), al-Madâʾinî (died 225 A.H./840 A.D.) are constantly quoted as the authorities on which the tales or the collections rely, and even the later compilations, such as Abu'l-Faraj al-Iṣfahânî's *Kitâb al-Aghânî* (died 366 A.H./976 A.D.), are founded on the material preserved by these early *mawâlî* predecessors.

In contrast to poetry where the individual poets were known and most poems could be accredited to their creator, the *aiyâm* and *akhbâr* stories are told anonymously. True, the scholar who had been the first to collect them and write them down henceforth became the authority cited to guarantee their authenticity. But these stories preserve the deeds of the pre-Islamic Arabs as they had been told and retold through the generations by anonymous storytellers. Gradually a typical style developed which combined straightforward recording of events as they happened with fanciful elaboration and real or imagined detail. In fact, a specific "*aiyâm* style" evolved.[7]

Typically, the story would deal with the relation between tribes or tribal groups, probing the reasons for their alliance or their enmity. All that was known or presumed about their affairs would be included in the narration and described in detail. As was the case in poetry, the story was told in a rather schematized manner: the outbreak of hostilities, the preparations made by the attacker, the fearful anticipation of the intended victims who often had received secret warnings of the impending raid through an informer, most often a woman captive in the enemy's camp. They would post watchmen on the heights overlooking the approaches to their camp who would—often in the nick of time—raise the hue and cry to warn of the approaching raiders. Camels and women would be abducted (the latter mainly for the sake of camels to be paid as ransom to the abductor); the men of the attacked tribe would pursue the enemy, and skirmishes and individual duels would ensue. With the scene thus set, the narrative would often disintegrate into detailed description of individual episodes in the pursuit, of combat between various heroes, and the fight and death of well-known leaders; the revenge taken for them or the blood-feuds resulting would be told in detail. The capture of a famous man or woman and their experience while in captivity might be the topic of another part of the story. Many episodes glorify well-known personalities, a sheikh, a poet, a king, or a woman who later became famous as the mother of heroes. Often these tales take on a romantic character, and the beginnings of future romances, such as that of the hero ʿAntar—still told by popular storytellers—are already found in the *aiyâm al-ʿArab* tales of the Jâhilîyah.

A prominent characteristic of the *aiyâm* style is the habit of interrupting the narrative with the recital of poems said to have been composed in connection with the "day," the subject of the tale, or referring to one of its celebrated episodes. Though they are almost invariably introduced as if they were an integral part of the *aiyâm* tale in which they appear, it is often almost impossible to connect the prose version with that of the poem. The stereotyped composition of Arabic poetry, discussed previously, prevents distinctive expression; the generalized style of praise, approval, exultation over victory, or disdain, taunting, provocation, and despair over defeat does not conjure up a precise image of either situation or personality. Thus, if we had only the poetry, it would be impossible to reconstruct the events by means of the allusions contained in the verses, or even to attribute a poem to a specific *yawm,* "day," and derive a coherent full report of the battle from it. The poem quoted may not even originally have been connected with the "day" to which it was ascribed, let alone with any of its episodes. However, if regarded not as a historical source but as a literary device, this interspersing of poetry into the prose recital of the *aiyâm* tale is very effective. It perpetuates a traditional artistic device already found in the Old Testament; it has, in fact, survived throughout the centuries and is the art form of popular storytellers from the *Alf Laylah wa-Laylah,* "Arabian Nights," to the modern *Sîrat ʿAntar* recital in the village coffee shop or the bazaars of the native city quarters. It also figures prominently in the classic *Biography of the Prophet.*

In fact, the question may be raised how far the *aiyâm* tales are history, how far literature. The answer must probably be: a little of both. If it were not for these tales, we would have hardly any evidence of the structure of pre-Islamic Arab society, of its tribal organization, or of the relationship, be it friendly or hostile, between the various groups. The utter lack of any other contemporary sources, such as inscriptions, papyri, or monuments, so common and so valuable elsewhere in the Near East (not to speak of classical antiquity), makes it imperative to use these stories for whatever historical truth they may preserve. That they do provide some basis for the elucidation of the "prehistory" of Islam has been brilliantly shown by such scholars as Noeldeke, Rothstein, and Bräunlich.[8] The original impulse was to record the tribal events as they happened; since the story was spread by word of mouth, it was inevitable that in the telling the heroes' exploits were exalted, the enemy's defeat deemed more decisive, the number of killed and wounded exaggerated, and, altogether, a small skirmish or a minor raid raised to undeserved importance. In addition, the Arab inclination—partly through the influence of poetry—toward type-casting caused a certain stylization of the report which resulted in the characteristic manner of the *aiyâm* tale. However, it played an important role in the development of later Muslim historiography:[9] it not only prepared the soil for creating an interest in recording events but also influenced the style of Muslim historians who retained certain of the characteristic features of the *aiyâm* style and even developed them further into what might be called "Islamic legends."

We do not find, at least in the literary sources at our disposal, any independent books or collections of *aiyâm* tales; they were preserved as part of other literary works. They are found in the commentaries to the great collections and anthologies of Arabic poetry as explanations and amplification of the allusions contained therein, such as the *Ḥamâsah,* "Poems of Bravery," the *Mufaḍḍaliyât,* the *dîwâns* of the poets, the *Naqâ'iḍ* of Jarîr and al-Farazdaq, in the "biographies" of the poets collected in the *Kitâb al-Aghânî,* "Book of Songs" or in the encyclopedic opus of Ibn al-Athîr, called *al-ʿIqd al-Farîd,* "The Unique Necklace". All these works offer a wealth of material wholly or partly based on *aiyâm* stories.[10]

Folkloristic elements abound in these tales and even more so in the related etiological commentaries to the *Amthâl al-ʿArab,* the "Proverbs of the Arabs," dating from approximately the same epoch. Many of these are of types found all over the world, many even surviving into modern times. Among them is the motif of the girl who had to be secretly saved from being buried alive at birth—as was the custom amongst pre-Islamic Arabs—and then became the wife of a famous hero for whom only an exceptional girl would be a worthy mate.[11] The motifs of divination, for example, through food, by casting arrows, through birds' flight, of *langage figuré*—communication by means of symbols or *double entendre*—of omina, are employed to enliven the tale. Thus, the *aiyâm al-ʿarab,* with the related *amthâl* literature, are a repository for the folklore of pre-Islamic Arabia; much of it can also give clues to its religious ideas, which have not yet been sufficiently explored, let alone utilized for the elucidation of pre-Islamic paganism.

The *aiyâm al-ʿarab* stories thus fulfilled an important function; they preserved the continuity between the pre-Islamic art of storytelling (if not, in fact, interest in the history of their people) and the interest of later generations in the historical development of Islam. They also generated the partly emotional-religious, partly objective-scholarly research into the life of its creator and its protagonists which led to the imposing annalistic and analytical works of the Muslim historians.

A word may be added about the *amthâl* themselves which gave rise to the explanatory story. They do not themselves deserve the classification of "literature" (except after they became the basis for the stories attached to them); yet they are indicative of the incisive and hard-hitting way in which an Arab would size up a situation in a short, often witty and ironical, comment, or characterize, very often adversely, a man's action or lack of it. Later scholars collected these exclamations or remarks,[12] uttered most often spontaneously and on the spur of the moment; frequently biting, sarcastic, and caustic, they exhibit, through the turn of a phrase or by a satirical comparison or image the sharp and quick tongue of the Arab. Interspersed in tales, as a comment on an act or event witnessed, the phrase "became a proverb," *ḍuriba mathalan.* Again the predilection for systematization led later scholars, such as al-Maydânî (died 518 A.H./1124 A.D.), not only to collect the *amthâl* themselves but also to add in a commentary the explanatory tale attached to it which ostensibly related the occasion at which the proverbial saying had been coined. Many of these tales are identical with the *aiyâm* stories; many others were invented solely for the purpose of furnishing an explanation to an old proverb that had become unintelligible.

CHAPTER 3

The Era of the Prophet

I *The Birth of Islam and the Koran*

During the last decades of the sixth century A.D. a child was born in the city of Mecca who was destined to have a profound influence not only on the history and ideas of the Arabian Peninsula but far beyond its confines. The exact date of Muhammad's birth is not known. Muslim tradition synchronizes it with the famous "Year of the Elephant" (*ʿÂm al-Fîl*), the year when the attempt of the South Arabian king Abraha to reach Persia by way of Central Arabia failed before Mecca through the decimation of his army by smallpox. That event is assumed to have happened circa 570 A.D.; it impressed the Arabs so deeply that it became, in the words of their chroniclers, "the beginning of an era." Because of Mecca's almost miraculous salvation, Islamic legend connected it with the equally momentous birth of the future Messenger of God. In fact, however, modern Western scholars contend that Abraha's campaign happened earlier than the date assumed by ancient Muslim tradition; they conjecture that the Prophet may have been born as late as ca. 580 A.D.

Mecca itself developed, as settlements in arid Arabia had to, at a spot where a well provided the necessary, though somewhat brackish, water for settlers. From time immemorial it was the site of a sanctuary, a cubic edifice erected near that well called Kaʿbah, "cube." In fact, the whole area around Mecca (or Becca, as it was called in ancient times as attested to in the Koran [Sûrah 3, v. 90]) was sacred, including, true to type, besides the Kaʿbah and its holy well, a holy mountain (ʿArafât), sacred pillars (Ṣafa and Marwah), and cairns. There were other sanctuaries and *kaʿbahs* in Arabia, but Mecca, strategically situated at the crossing of trade routes between the Indian Ocean and the Mediterranean, became a depot and a station for rest and replenishment of provisions for the caravans that plied these routes. It thus grew more prominent and prosperous than similar Arabian sanctuaries and way stations less fortunately located.

To the later Muslim legend and the historians of Islam, in particular the biographers of Muhammad himself, Mecca appeared as the holy of holies, destined from time immemorial to become the cradle of the

Prophet and thus of Islam. In their estimation, it competed with Jerusalem for the honor of being the "Navel of the Earth,"[1] the birthplace of Creation and the center of religious worship long before Muhammad's appearance. It was thus, to the Muslim, the logical, most appropriate place to be chosen by Allâh for the revelation of the Koran, the Scripture of the Arabs, revealed in their language and thus "intelligible" to them. This, to the Prophet himself, was the most telling proof for the truth of his revelations and for the validity of his claim that he was the transmitter of an ancient message that had its origin with God. It had been revealed before to other peoples in their tongue, alien and unintelligible to the Arabs, who were thus deprived of divine guidance (*hudà*). Muhammad felt called by Allâh to provide them with it in an "Arabic, clear Scripture" (Sûrah 12, v.2).

Even when discussed in the context of a work on the literature of the Arabs, the Koran must be analyzed as both a work of—*sit venia verbo*—art *and* as a religious document.[2] In fact, the two aspects overlap and complement each other in this stirring, strangely moving testimony to a searching mind. To the Muslim, the Koran is not an ordinary book, not even the work of an extraordinary and exalted man. It is the Word of God, revealed by His grace to a humble Arab to whom the very language of the message he was impelled to bring to his people appeared to be a miracle. There can be no doubt that Muhammad was convinced of the divine origin of the *âyât*, the verses of the Koran, that came from his mouth; in answer to the doubters he exclaimed: "Verily, it is a revelation from the Lord of the Worlds" (Sûrah 26, v.196); the Koran could not have been devised by anyone but Allâh (Sûrah 10, v.38). Though the revelations came to Muhammad in the rhymed prose style (*saj*ʿ) of the ancient soothsayers, he protested against being considered one of them; the words he uttered were God's words, the message, the one of the *Umm al-Kitâb,* the prototype of all revealed Books kept near God's throne.

Muhammad felt that he was sent to the Arabs to call them away from their paganism and their idolatry to the recognition and worship of the sole, One and Almighty God, the Lord of the Universe, the Creator, the Judge of the Day of Judgment at the end of time. It is in His power to create and re-create, to punish evil and reward good, to guide man on the straight path or allow him to stray from it. In passionate cadences he envisions the awesome events of Judgment Day which are announced by the shattering of the sky, the falling of the stars, the splitting of the moon, the darkening of the sun, when the trumpet sounds and the tombs open to spew out their dead. Then, accompanied by the two angels who carry in their hands the book in which the good and evil acts of all men are recorded, the soul is called before the Lord to account for its deeds and to be rewarded with bliss in Paradise or condemned to eternal hellfire. These awesome events of the Last Hour, the Day of Judgment, and the Sûrahs in which they are described, form the earliest stratum of the Koranic revelations.

From the beginning the Muslims themselves were aware of distinct phases in Muhammad's prophetic activity. The Prophet's life passed through distinct stages. First was the preprophetic period, in which Muhammad lived the life of a member of the Meccan community, distinguished only, perhaps, by a more contemplative mind which seems to have led him to lonely religious meditation. There followed the period of transformation into a visionary who received and answered the divine call to become the Warner of his people and their guide to righteousness and knowledge of the One and Only God. The third stage, reached not in his native environment but only after his emigration into an alien group and acceptance of its leadership, shows him as the creator and organizer of a new community, of a kind that had not hitherto existed in Arabia. The first period in Muhammad's life finds only faint echo in the Holy Book (Sûrah 93, v. 6: "Did he not find thee an orphan?") but is amply speculated upon in detailed later Islamic legend (see below Part II). The second and third stages, however, are so clearly reflected in the Koran that the Muslims at an early time distinguished between those revelations that were "sent down" in Mecca and those that were revealed in Medînah (Yathrib) after his migration (*Hijrah*, Hegira) to that city. Thus every Sûrah in the authoritative canon of the Koran carries a notation as to its place of origin: *makkîyah* or *madanîyah*, "a Meccan, a Medinian, sûrah."

Modern Western scholarship has gone a step further. Without sacrificing the reverence due to a book sacred to hundreds of millions of Believers, the great Orientalist Theodor Noeldeke (1836–1930) recognized, on the basis of internal criteria, four different stages in Muhammad's prophetic development. Contents as well as style, different motifs, cast into differing forms of expression, represent different aspects and moods in the revelations he received. This recognition does not imply that there is a "break" in his attitudes, "prophet" in Mecca, "lawgiver," "politician" in Medînah. Nothing can be further from the truth. In spite of the changes in style, an identity of ideas, a consciousness of his task as a prophet, a realization of his divine mission runs as a continuum through the whole Koran, from Muhammad's first vision to the last *âyah* revealed.[3] It is as evident in the dominant theme of his early sermon—the immutable sequence of birth, death, and resurrection—as it is in the "Legends of Divine Punishment" and in the laws and ethical principles laid down in Medînah.

The sûrahs attributed to each of the periods—three in Mecca and the Prophet's work in Medînah—show in contents as well as in expression the different emotions stirring in Muhammad's mind in each phase. The earliest sûrahs—short, passionate outbursts filled with the visions of the impending Hour of Doom—show the Prophet himself overwhelmed by the realization of having been chosen as the bearer of God's Message.[4] He wrestled with the difficult task of communicating his own inner experience to an unbelieving, even hostile, crowd; he invoked the stars, the dawn, the sky as witnesses that he truly had received a divine call, that he did not speak out of his own volition or of vain imaginations. The "Messenger" whom he had seen was real, and so was his message which he, Muhammad, relays. The greater the opposition he met with became, the more urgently he insisted on the truth of his mission. In the late first stage of his prophetic development, he began to point to the "Warners" Allâh had sent to peoples in ancient times: to the ʿÂd and Thamûd, and Iram, "She of the Pillars," of Arabian antiquity, all still remembered in Arabian poetry and legend, but of whom no trace existed in Muhammad's own time. "Biblical" names appear in this period—Firʿawn, "Pharaoh," "He of the Tent Pegs," and the "Man of the Fish," *Ṣâḥib al-Ḥût*, mentioned as examples of men of ancient times to whom divine events happened (not yet recorded in detail in that early period). Only gradually, and increasingly in the second Meccan period do these "Warners" emerge with greater clarity and become endowed with more and more details, until eventually, in the third Meccan period, there emerges a long line of Prophets and "Warners" of old times who had been sent by God to their people but whose warning words were disregarded. In the Medinian sûrahs knowledge of these "prophets" and their fate is taken for granted and only brief, though frequent, allusions to them occur.

These "Legends of Divine Punishment" (as Josef Horovitz called them) form the most important part of Muhammad's sermon in the later Meccan phase. The Prophet had to fight for recognition and acknowledgment of the veracity of his prophetic mission. His Meccan contemporaries did not accept his leadership; they resented his taking them to task for their way of life, for their adherence to ancient beliefs and customs, and for their unwillingness to believe in the truth of his message. Then Muhammad pointed to the fate of the ancient people and to the example of the cities of yore that disobeyed God's messengers—to the disappearance of the people and the utter destruction of the cities of the past. The same fate threatened the unrepenting, unbelieving Meccans. Only from that period on, and continuing in Medînah throughout the following years, do the Biblical stories, as well as those using New Testament personalities, resemble to a fairly high degree the Old Testament and Christian parallels, though they are never fully identical with them.

It may be allowed in a discussion of the Koran as literature to dwell for a moment on the problems these legends of divine punishment present.[5] Any reader of the Koran is struck by the fact that the stories dealing with Biblical personalitites—both Old and New Testament ones—do not tally with their "parallels" in the Torah or the Gospels. Western scholars used to accuse Muhammad with distorting the Biblical stories; they charged him with ignorance of the Old Testament versions as the Jews of his own time and environment had done. Neither his contemporaries nor his latter-day critics, nor, for that matter, the Muslim Believers themselves, understood the reasons for the lack of conformity between the Koranic and the Biblical or Gospel versions of events. Even if we accept the customary argument that the Koranic account is garbled and that it does not conform to the Biblical original, the discrepancies should be explained only as the result of Muhammad's use of the Biblical story and the manner in which he told it. He saw himself reflected in the earlier warners and prophets and emphasized those aspects in their story that resembled his own situation. Like them, he was exhorting his people by divine command, only to find himself rejected and his preaching disregarded. He identified himself with them and saw in the fate that befell those earlier unrepenting sinners an example of what would happen to Mecca if it rejected his warnings.

There is, however, a deeper reason for the Prophet's seeming "ignorance." In the early times of his mission, he was not telling "Biblical" stories; he was dipping deep into the reservoir of ancient Near Eastern myth from which those Biblical stories themselves had originally arisen. Thus, these variants represent several parallel streams of myth and legend that had developed in Near Eastern religious tradition and had emerged independently from this ancient well of Near Eastern mythology, gradually becoming "history." They were identical in their underlying symbolic meaning but not in the way they were remembered and told in the various cultural and religious environments. The earliest stratum of their appearance in the Koran represents the ancient myth remembered only as such; and only gradually, with the growing polemics and arguments, the "historical" details, as they are told, for example, in the Old Testament, were added, trait by trait.

The figure of Firʿawn is possibly the best example of this process. He is first mentioned in Sûrah 85, vv. 17f.: "Has there come to you the story of the hosts/of Firʿawn and Thamûd?" Nothing more is said of him here. Firʿawn, ʿÂd and Thamûd, and Iram, "She of the Pillars," are joined in the chronologically second Sûrah in which Firʿawn occurs (Sûrah 89). Here, he is given an epithet that contains a key to deciphering the mystery. He is called Firʿawn, "He of the Tent Pegs" (*Dhu-l-awtâd,* 89, v.9; thus also 38, v.11). The two sûrahs, 85 and 89, belong to the oldest Meccan group. In Sûrah 73, vv. 15f., Firʿawn is for the first time said to have opposed a messenger whose name, however, is still unknown: "Verily, We sent to you a messenger as a witness against you [*ʿalaikum*], as We sent a messenger to Firʿawn/ But Firʿawn rebelled against the messenger and We seized him with a rough seizure." Josef Horovitz considers this passage the first occurence of Muhammad's use of "history" in his argument with the Meccans.[6] But it is not—or not yet—history; it is still myth. Only gradually does the historical Pharaoh emerge. In Sûrahs 51,v.38 and 79, vv.15–26 (from late Mecca I), Firʿawn is mentioned for the first time together with Mûsà, Moses. While the former passage still rather perfunctorily refers to the warning example found "in Mûsà whom We sent to Firʿawn with an explicit [*mubîn*, "clear"] authority [*sulṭân*]," the latter adds slightly more, though still vague, detail: "Has there come to thee the story of Mûsà/ his Lord called to him in the hallowed valley of Ṭuwâ/ go unto Pharaoh, verily he is outrageous/ and say 'hast thou a wish to purify thyself/ and that I may guide thee to thy Lord and thou mayest fear'/ So he showed him the greatest signs/ but he called him a liar and rebelled/ Then he retreated hastily and gathered/ and said 'I am your Lord most High'/ but God seized him with the punishment of the future life and the former/ Verily in that is a lesson to him who fears." Only in Sûrah 20 (late Mecca II; cf. also Sûrahs 7, vv. 101–73 and 10, vv. 76–92 from Mecca III) is the full story of Mûsà and Firʿawn told in almost perfect accordance with the Biblical version of the Exodus from Egypt and the various episodes leading to it.

It is thus obvious that the early Koranic verses reflect not Pharaoh, the king of Egypt, but Pharaoh as the god of Egyptian mythology. Muhammad knew of the Egyptian god-king Pharaoh who, as sky-god, was thought to span the firmament and to be fastened to the earth on its outermost ends—as the Arabs' tents were fastened to the *awtâd,* the tent pegs. And Iram, mentioned only once in the Koran, together with Firʿawn in Sûrah 89, is not an earthly city the ruins of which may be (or, as has been asserted, have been) found somewhere in Arabia: it is a symbol for the world after death, for Paradise. This interpretation is in full accord with the Koranic ideas which, in the earliest sermons, are dominated by the themes of the immutable sequence of birth, death, and resurrection as proven by the seasonal "death" of nature and its eternal rebirth. As the author has tried to prove elsewhere,[7] these sûrahs reflect the idea that filled Muhammad's mind in this early phase of his prophetic development, the ever recurring cycle of creation, death, and rebirth. *Iram Dhât al-ʿImâd* is one of the symbols for the world after death, and Firʿawn, as in the Egyptian myth, its sovereign. These are not the only figures reminiscent of the ancient Near Eastern mythological concepts found in the Koran: *Ṣâḥib al-Ḥût* or *Dhu-n-Nûn*, "The Man of the Fish"—only later identified with Yûnus, the Biblical Jonah—is another striking figure, symbol, too, for death and resurrection, to have undergone the same evolution from myth to historical figure in the Koran as did Firʿawn. Another telling example for this mythological thinking of the Prophet is the fascinating *Sûrat al-Kahf,* "Sûrah of the Cave," (Sûrah 18) with its abundance of ancient Near Eastern symbols contained in the legends of the *Aṣḥâb al-Kahf,* "The Seven Sleepers," and the tale of *Dhu-l-Qarnayn,* "The Two-Horned One," and/or Mûsà searching for the *majmaʿ al-baḥrayn,* "the confluence of the two seas." Only after his audience—in particular the Jews of his environment—associated Muhammad's sermons with the familiar Biblical persons (who are themselves but the end-product of the same evolution, without having left in the Old Testament easily recognizable traces of the consecutive steps comparable to those in the Koran), only then did Muhammad gradually substitute the "historical" Firʿawn and the "historical" Yûnus for the mythological ones.

In this context a problem that has haunted Western scholarship for a long time may appropriately be discussed. It concerns the *dîwân* of the poet Umaiyah ibn Abî-ṣ-Ṣalt, a contemporary of the Prophet's, which contains numerous poems dealing with "Biblical" stories. Some of these can be proved to be based on the Koran, for internal reasons, as for example, literal quotations from the Koranic versions. These were interpolated into original poems by Umaiyah or are forgeries by later post-Muhammadan poets who attributed their creations to Umaiyah. But most of the poetry collected in this *dîwân* can be considered genuine and to have been composed contemporarily with or slightly before the Prophet's activity. In the minds of Western scholars this raised the question of the mutual relationship between the Prophet's Koran and

Umaiyah's poetry and their relative priority: Whose version was the original and who was the imitator? (For the Muslim, there could be no such doubt, since the Koran for him is not a creation of Muhammad's, but the Word of God.) However, no direct contact between the two men—creative minds both—has been proven on the evidence of the existing sources, nor is there any indication that either knew of the other. If the ideas developed in the preceding discussion are accepted, this so-called Umaiyah Problem ceases to be a problem, and even the discrepancies that exist between their way of tellling the same basic story become irrelevant (as does the question whether they used "different sources"). Both took their inspiration from the same source, the reservoir of Near Eastern mythological thought.

The Koran is a perfect mirror of the Prophet's spiritual growth. Even the style of the revelations reflects this evolution. The question of the chronology of individual revelations, a problem that already confronted the early Muslims, can be answered—though not for every individual verse or group of verses—by a detailed examination of their contents and their style. The latter is an outstanding means for attributing certain sûrahs or parts thereof to a specific period of Muhammad's activity. Each of its phases is characterized in the Koran by specific stylistic peculiarities, establishing them as hymns, prayers, admonitions, polemics, and, in the Medinian period, as legislation. Oaths abound in the earliest sûrahs, where Muhammad calls on the phenomena of nature, the sun, the stars, the mountains, the sky, the clouds, and the winds, as witnesses to the truth of his words, in the first Meccan period; he swears by "The Book," in the second Meccan phase; these oaths disappear in late Meccan times and in Medînah. Certain phrases and expressions indicate, almost like formulas, the beginning of distinct themes, for example, a narrative or a sermonlike passage, for which they are typical; others introduce a hymnic, still others a polemical or didactic, sequence. Even the appellations used for "God" are not the same throughout the Koran. *Rabb*, "Lord," and *Allâh* are the only ones that occur in the first Meccan period, in the second the term *ar-Raḥmân*, "The Merciful," predominates but almost disappears in the following, third Meccan, period, and is not used at all in the Medinian revelations.

The style of the Medinian sûrahs differs so strikingly from the Meccan revelations that analysts of the Prophet's message have postulated a deep-seated break in his religious development. He is said to have changed from prophet to politician, from religious visionary to lawgiver and organizer. It is true that the new needs of the developing Muslim community, based on a concept inherently different from the traditional Arab tribal system, forced the Prophet, as its founder and leader, to make decisions and to issue laws by which its life was to be regulated. But he never lost sight of the deeply felt religious fundament on which the conduct of his community had to rest. He retained the unshakable conviction that every utterance of his, every social or legal decision he made, originated in divine inspiration and thus was Allâh's, not his. The *Hijrah* inaugurated new secular tasks and problems for the Prophet but did not end his preoccupation with the eternal values. Rather, these became intermingled; the Prophet's newly founded community of Islam, the *Ummah*, became the secular organ through which the sacred demands were to be fulfilled.

The most important task the Prophet faced in the Medinian period was to mold the various heterogeneous elements into a unified Islamic community. The Koran—the only authentic contemporary document (except for the so-called Statute of Medînah, about which more later)—reflects the problem as well as its attempted solution. Already in Mecca Muhammad had begun to substitute for the divisive tribal makeup of Arabian society one that was founded on the allegiance to Islam and that disregarded membership in a particular tribe. The need to create an Islamic, in contrast to the traditional tribal, loyalty became even more evident in Medînah where the original inhabitants of Yathrib (its ancient name) were confronted with an influx of *Muhâjirûn*, "Emigrants," from Mecca; gradually a fairly large number of other tribes, too, accepted Islam, that is, acknowledged Muhammad's leadership.

To consolidate these heterogeneous elements he used the Biblical Patriarch Ibrâhîm (Abraham) whom they all recognized as their ancestor through his son Ismâʿîl (Ishmael). In Meccan times, Ibrâhîm had remained for Muhammad one of those men who worshiped God and were obedient to His Word, he was the "first Believer," *Ḥanîf*, and the "Friend of God," *Khalîl Allâh*; in Medînah, he acquired an added and weighty function. He was credited with having built the original Kaʿbah in Mecca, on the spot where God had saved his son Ismâʿîl from dying of thirst by miraculously creating the Zemzem well. To this day a well found in the precincts of the Kaʿbah is held sacred by being identified with that holy well. This Koranic legend served a twofold purpose. It stressed the common ancestry of the diverse tribal groups in the Muslim community, and it made possible the integration into Islam of the Kaʿbah cult in Mecca by attributing to it a monotheistic origin and emphasizing this fact. Its obvious pagan features could then be explained as aberration from the Straight Path by unbelieving sinners, and Muhammad's acceptance could be conceived as its restoration to its pristine monotheism.

Whether introduced by conscious intention or by unconscious attachment to his native city, the emphasis on the alleged common ancestor of all Arabs and his role in the establishment of the Kaʿbah served Muhammad well. It gave his new religion a supratribal, unifying Arab character, and it provided it with a focus in Arabia. In fact, the *qiblah*, "direction in prayer," hitherto toward Jerusalem, was replaced by that toward Mecca. The Koran reflects this development by reinterpreting, in its Medinian sections, the various stations of the ancient Meccan rites in terms of their connection with Ibrâhîm's and Ismâʿîl's actions, or events in their lives.

In Medînah, Muhammad had also to cope with the everyday demands of community life, and therefore the Koranic revelations of that period acquired a character not found in the Meccan sûrahs. Social and legal problems needed authoritative decisions by the Prophet who, as before, spoke in the name of Allâh and by His inspiration. Thus, pronouncements (both commands and prohibitions) on sacred and profane issues were revealed, all imbued with unalterable sanctity by being included in Holy Writ, for example, on inheritance, usury, marriage and divorce, the rites of the Pilgrimage, on crime and punishment, the Fast of Ramadhân, prayer, slavery, and so on. Such matters changed the mood of the revelations; thus, though the *sajʿ*, "rhymed prose," form was retained, a more discursive, interpretative style predominates in the sûrahs of the Medinian period. But in spite of this change, Muhammad remained convinced that he was the mouthpiece of Allâh, Who was the one Who decided and decreed. Nor have the Muslims yet given up the firm belief that every word contained in the Koran is Holy Writ, *Kalâm Allâh*, "the Word of God"; and, being that, the Koran is held to be inimitable.

In the course of a few centuries, as will be discussed more fully in a later chapter, a variety of dogmatic positions on the essential tenets of Islam emerged, all of which claimed to be based on Holy Writ; even the most esoteric among them pointed to the Koran as their fundament. Thus, it was inevitable that from early times on the true meaning of the Koranic revelations had to be established.

Though the Prophet claimed that Allâh had revealed to him "clear, unequivocal verses" (Sûrah 24, v.1), many of them, already often less than lucid for Muhammad's immediate audiences, lacked clarity for later generations. In addition, unlike the Torah which Jewish orthodoxy believes to have been given to Moses on Mount Sinai as one integral revelation, the Koran was acknowledged to have been sent down piecemeal. This fact remained undisputed together with the knowledge that the full Koran text had been compiled by the early caliphs "from the hearts of the people" or from widely dispersed manuscripts in the possession of individual Muslims or their families. The fourth caliph, ʿUthmân, declared one such compilation in the possession of Ḥafṣah, the daughter of ʿUmar ibn al-Khaṭṭâb, to be the authorized, canonical Koran; he ordered all other versions and heirloom manuscripts remaining in private hands to be destroyed.

The Muslims accepted the fact that this compilation did not follow the chronological sequence of the revelations but that it combined into sûrahs passages sent down at various times and dealing with different themes. For some of them the occasions, and in consequence the time and place, of their revelation was known. But the majority of the *âyât*, and particularly those of the early Meccan periods, were not connected with any specific events but spoke of religious ideas or contained ethical exhortations and theological doctrines often hidden in intricate images or in parables and legends. Therefore, the need for examination of these problems and for interpretation of sûrahs or *âyât* through penetrating analysis of the meaning intended by the Prophet became evident at an early time.

Consequently, those close to the Prophet and his Companions began to write down all they knew about the circumstances surrounding the sûrahs and their revelation. Examples of this endeavor are preserved in the works of the early historians such as the *Sîrah*, "Biography," of the Prophet by Ibn Isḥâq (see below). Gradually, these reminiscences developed into systematic commentaries, but only a few of the earliest works of this kind have survived. However, in the great *Tafsîr*, "Commentary," of al-Ṭabarî (d. 309 A.H./922 A.D.), much of the early material has been incorporated. This work, filling thirty volumes in the first printed edition (Cairo, 1321 A.H.) presents a *sûrah*-by-*sûrah*, *âyah*-by-*âyah* exegesis, paraphrasing difficult passages and discussing philological and grammatical problems of the text. The author also quotes comments of other authorities and discusses religious and theological issues of his own times connected with the passage under consideration.

Two other later commentaries, the *Kashshâf ʿan Ḥaqâʾiq al-Tanzîl*, "Unveiler of the Essence of Revelation," by Abuʾl-Qâsim Maḥmûd ibn ʿUmar al-Zamakhsharî (died 538 A.H./1143 A.D.), and that of ʿAbdallâh ibn ʿUmar al-Bayḍâwî (died either 685 A.H./1286 A.D. or 692 A.H./1292 A.D. or 710 A.H./1310 A.D.) gained great authority in the Muslim world. The former stresses grammatical and philological exegesis (as might be expected from one of the greatest Arab philologists and grammarians), but he also devotes much of his work to theological and philosophical problems which, as will be shown later on in this essay, were based on Koranic equivocal pronouncements. Al-Bayḍâwî's *Anwâr al-Tanzîl wa-Asrâr al-Taʾwîl*, "The Lights of Revelation and the Secrets of Commentation," is largely dependent on al-Zamakhsharî's work; his commentary abounds in grammatical and philological discussions and also offers variant readings of the Koran text. It is still greatly admired by the Muslims for the mass of information it contains, but it has been criticized by Western scholars as not always reliable.

Among the *tafâsîr* works of later generations the highest rank, in the eyes of the Muslims, is accorded to the so-called *Tafsîr al-Jalâlayn*, "Commentary of the Two [men called] Jalâl al-Dîn." These are Jalâl al-Dîn Muḥammad ibn Aḥmad al-Maḥallî (died 864 A.H./ 1459 A.D.) and his well-known disciple, the polyhistor Jalâl al-Dîn as-Suyûṭî. The latter (died 911 A.H./1505 A.D.) wrote a huge commentary on the Koran called *Tarjumân al-Qurʾân fiʾl-Tafsîr al-Musnad,* "Interpretation of the Koran with a Commentary [supported by] Isnâd," which in its title indicates the author's intention to restore the traditional exegesis based on the ancient authorities, in contrast to the widespread esoteric interpretations. This work seems to have been lost; but there exists an excerpt of it, called *al-Durr al-Manthûr fiʾl-Tafsîr al-Maʾthûr*, "Scattered Pearls concerning traditional Koran Interpretation," which comprises (in a Cairo edition of 1314 A.H.) six volumes. In the so-called *Tafsîr al-Jalâlayn* the commentary on Sûrahs 2 to 17 is by al-Suyûṭî, that on Sûrahs 18 to 114 by al-Maḥallî.

The commentaries of two modern Muslim scholars might be mentioned because of their exceptional approach and the fame they have acquired both in the Muslim world and among modern Orientalists. The first, and somewhat earlier one, is by the famous Egyptian scholar Muhammad ʿAbduh (1849–1905). As judge in Egypt and rector of the famous Azhar theological university in Cairo, he was a leader of the emerging new generation who attempted to reconcile reformatory endeavors, based on the new insights in science and the needs of modern society, with traditional beliefs. His Koran commentary remained unfinished but was edited and completed by his disciple

Rashîd Riḍâ.[8] The second modern scholar was the Indian leader Mawlana Abu'l-Kalam Azad (1888–1958) who also undertook a modern exegesis of the Koran which likewise remained a torso. His influence, however, was more apparent as a political leader in the Indian fight for Independence than in the religious sphere. He sided with Gandhi and Nehru and opposed the particularism and separation movement of Muhammad Iqbal and Jinnah; after Partition, he gained great influence in India, holding high office in its government. His influence as a Koranic scholar on modern Muslim reform movements is far overshadowed by that of Sheikh Muhammad ʿAbduh.

II *Muhammad in History and Legend*

At the Prophet's death, the only authentic surviving record of his ideas, intentions, and achievements was the Koran. Besides being the receptacle of his religious thought, it echoes his struggles, the arguments of his adversaries and his answers to them, even the difficulties he encountered within his own community. None of this was expressed plainly, in the manner of historical records: it was embedded in his utterances as the transmitter of divine revelation. The historical events that gave birth to them can be elucidated only by inference from the context and from the rather scanty reliable historical reports on his life and activity. During his lifetime and at his death, the ancient custom of oral tradition was still prevalent, and no systematic written records were kept. Only the Koranic revelations were committed to writing, in a rather haphazard manner, as they were pronounced, on bits of parchment or bones and on potsherds, or preserved "in the hearts of men." The contemporary non-Arab world took hardly any notice of this man whose new faith, and those who professed it, would only a century later dominate the whole tier of the Near and Middle East from the tip of Northwest Africa to the Indus and Oxus rivers.

However, one other genuine contemporary record of the highest value has somehow been preserved, though not the original document itself. Its text has found its way into the later historical works on Islam, in its fullest form in the earliest extant biography of the Prophet, the so-called *Sîrat an-Nabî'*, "Course of the Prophet's Life." In this work, which will be dealt with more fully below, a copy of this document—now usually referred to as the "Statute of Medînah"— has been inserted, with no word of explanation added.[9] (It is preceded in the *Sîrah* by a chapter on the events leading to the *Hijrah* and followed by a list of the *mu'akhât*, "brotherhoods," between Muhammad's adherents of different tribal kinships, and between *Muhâjirûn*, "Emigrants," from Mecca and *Anṣâr*, "Helpers," of Medînah.) It is simply introduced as a *kitâb*, "written agreement," that was drawn up between Muhammad and the various groups in Yathrib to establish their privileges and mutual obligations. Each tribe and clan of the original inhabitants of that town is listed individually in their relationship to Muhammad, who emerges from this document as the leader of the community established by the terms of this *kitâb* under the protection and in the name of Allâh. Most interestingly, the three large Jewish tribes of Yathrib, the Banû Naḍîr, the Banû Qurayẓah and the Banû Qaynuqâʿ, with their numerous subtribes and clients, are included in that pact and thus integrated into the *Ummat al-Islâm*, "Community of Islam," that it constituted; at the same time, their right to remain adherents of their own faith was explicitly guaranteed.

Several internal factors establish the authenticity of this document beyond any doubt for even the most critical historian. Throughout, Muhammad is called either simply by his name or *Rasûl Allâh*, "Allâh's Messenger"; he is not yet the Prophet par excellence, as he became later in his life and as he would doubtless have been called by a later forger. His authority is strictly limited to Yathrib (its ancient name being used throughout the Statute) and its inhabitants; the contract regulates only their internal relations. Their dealings—in particular their feuds—with groups outside the city were not subject to its provisions or to the Prophet's control; it extended exclusively to the contracting parties and obliged only these to obey its terms in their mutual dealings to the exclusion of all outsiders. Foremost among the latter were the Meccans. These limitations, and above all the fact that the Jews of Yathrib were included in the *ummah*, not only rule out the possibility of forgery but also postulate a very early date for the conclusion of this concordat. It must have been entered into in the first year of the *Hijrah* and before the battle of Badr in the year 2 A.H.

The *Sîrat an-Nabî*ʾ of Muḥammad ibn Isḥâq (died 150 or 151 A.H./767 or 768 A.D.), apart from being the earliest surviving full biography of the Prophet and, by virtue of this, the earliest existing history of Islam, contains another extremely valuable type of authoritative record. As in the pre-Islamic *aiyâm al-ʿarab* literature, the stylistic influence of which is still traceable in the *Sîrah*, poetry is inserted that allegedly was created in connection with events of the Prophet's life.[10] Later critics accused Ibn Isḥâq of accepting late forgeries as genuine contemporary poems for insertion into his work. This skepticism was, to a large extent, justified and must be shared by the modern scholar. Yet, in contrast to the poetic insertions in the *aiyâm al-ʿarab* tales, those within the *Sîrah* have a certain amount of historical value, though, like their older counterparts, they contain little, if any, precise information. For the ancient author has included not only poetry glorifying the Prophet and his Companions (in Medinian times of rather poor poetic value and mainly composed by the "court poet" Ḥassân ibn Thâbit) but also poems by his adversaries attacking him and his adherents. Of particular interest are the *marâthî*, "dirges," composed in honor of those who fell in battle on either side. Many of those bewailing the fallen men of Quraysh are ascribed to Hind bint ʿUqbah ibn Rabîʿah who was so violent in her hatred of the Prophet that she is said, in the same work,[11] to have mutilated the corpses of Muslim men, together with a few other women of Quraysh. She also allegedly tried to swallow the liver of Ḥamzah, the Prophet's uncle who fell at Uḥud, to avenge her father's death by Ḥamzah's hand in the battle of Badr. She was later one of the very few people whom the Prophet, after the Conquest of Mecca, ordered to be executed; she was, however, reprieved when she converted to Islam. There can be no doubt that the verses attributed to her were genuine and contemporary with the events; for no one in later times would have dared to compose poetry attacking the Prophet and the honored martyrs of Islam and extolling their early enemies.

These *marâthî* and poetical attacks, in the ancient *hijâʾ* style, show the depth of antagonism against Muhammad and the upheaval caused by his new concept of Islamic brotherhood in disregard of tribal allegiance. They are also a counter-argument against those modern scholars who assert that the Prophet's message struck a familiar note in the minds of the Meccans (meaning that he was preaching some kind of religion based on Judeo-Christian concepts with which the Meccans were said to be familiar). It is amazing that these strong expressions of hostility survived partisan censorship and were allowed to remain embedded in the *Sîrah* in spite of the great veneration in which it is held to this day.

Their very inclusion by the original author, Ibn Isḥâq, and their escape from the editorial criticism of his editor, Ibn Hishâm (died 218 A.H./ 833 A.D.), whose somewhat abridged version is, on the whole, the one we possess, is indeed astonishing, for the work contains traces of the evolving Muhammad legend and veneration. Historically, the circumstances of Muhammad's birth and early years are utterly unknown and were probably indistinguishable from those of any other child in his environment. Yet, Ibn Isḥâq tells us of miraculous signs and events connected with his birth and childhood. According to this legend, his father—historically a nondescript figure—showed signs of being destined to bring forth a prophet; his mother Âminah was surrounded during her pregnancy by a glow through which she could see the spires of Boṣra in faraway Syria. The puny fatherless baby (he was born after his father's death), refused by every other Bedouin wet nurse, turned out to be a blessing for Ḥalîmah and her family, the woman who had taken him with her lest she return to her tribe without a foster child. While he was with her, angels appeared, opened his breast, and "cleansed" his heart. He was born circumcised, a sign of his purity and of being one chosen by Allâh. As a youth, he is said to have participated in the rebuilding of the Kaʿbah. When the Quraysh were unable to replace the Black Stone, the future Prophet approached and restored it effortlessly to its proper position. Trees bowed to him, and the monk Baḥîrah recognized in him the signs of prophethood. The only circumstance of his youth for which there is valid and reliable proof is his having been poor and an orphan, for the Prophet himself attested to this fact in the Koran (Sûrah 93, v. 6).

But the unrecorded years of his infancy and his preprophetic life are not the only ones about which legends were spread that are found as early as in Ibn Isḥâq's *Sîrah*. Those years, too, in which he had attracted the attention of his contemporaries were said to have been full of miraculous events that could only have happened by virtue of his being chosen by Allâh. For instance, it is said that once when he was about to partake of food offered to him by his Jewish adversaries, the Prophet miraculously received a warning from the roasted sheep itself that it had been poisoned (this legend, by the way, is an early example of the developing anti-Jewish polemics). Thus, we find in the *Sîrah* the initial stages for the development of the prophetic legend which grew considerably in later Islamic literature.

Related to this elevation of the Prophet into a somewhat higher-than-ordinary rank of human experience was the desire to know fully what manner of man he was. This led to a search for information about minute details of his personal life and habits, his behavior, appearance, choice of food, mode of dress, long before the Prophet's *Sunnah*, "Way of Life," became (as we shall see later) the fundamental religious sanction for the Muslim way of life.

Parallel with the development of the Prophet's legendary personality grew the search for historical data about his time, his Companions, and the events in which they took a part. It is reported that the Prophet's contemporaries left written records (*ṣaḥîfah*, pl. *ṣaḥâʾif*);[12] but no manuscripts of the earliest scholars—of the Prophet's own and the following generations, that of the *Aṣḥâb* or *Ṣaḥâbah*, "Companions," that is, the early Muslims, and the *Tâbiʿûn*, their descendants—have survived. Yet, due to the technique of Muslim historiographers of faithfully quoting their sources, we have knowledge of works written by scholars that were born as early as the second decade after the *Hijrah*. In the gatherings of Medinian high society—that is, precisely the surviving early Muslims and their sons—the fateful events of early Islam and the role of individual men and women in them formed a favorite topic of conversation. Much of this was written down at that time and was passed on as treasured family records from father to son.[13] It was also transmitted orally in circles of students and disciples and found its way eventually into the works of later historians. This reliance on old authorities and the custom of quoting them also accounts for the fact that the reports contained in different later works are identical, with only slight variants, and are mostly based on the same ancient authorities; an example is Muḥammad ibn Muslim b. Shihâb al-Zuhrî (died 125 A.H./742 A.D.), whose own work has not been preserved but who is the principal authority for the account of such scholars as Ibn Isḥâq, Ibn Saʿd, and other early authors.

The battles fought by the Prophet and his followers and the expeditions and raids sent out by Muhammad against the neighboring tribes were the subject of the *maghâzî* works, recording the "Raids of the Prophet." This branch of literature originally was concerned only with the battles fought by the Prophet and his Companions; it also included the so-called *sarâyah*, that is, his expeditions into Arabia for the purpose of "converting the Arab tribes to Islam," or rather, to extend his political power beyond Medînah. Gradually the scope of inquiry was extended to include not only the Prophet's own era and the role of his Companions in the spiritual and political growth of Islam within Arabia but also the events that led to, and accompanied, its triumphant spread beyond its frontiers. Of necessity, this inaugurated an intense search for the most exact knowledge not only of the events themselves but also of the participants in them, the story of their life, and, in particular, the time and manner of their conversion to Islam and their relations with the Prophet. All this served as records from which the later historians developed their annals. The original *ṣaḥâʾif* have only survived through the often extensive quotations from them in later works, with the names of the reporter given as the guarantor for the authenticity of the report.

On account of the proximity to the generation of the Prophet and his Companions, these records must be accorded a fairly large amount of credence (though always to be submitted to critical evaluation) as reports of eyewitnesses, or, at the very least, as reports of earlier happenings whose echoes were still current in the reporter's lifetime. Partisan interpretation and even distortion came only later; yet, when based on a contemporary protagonist of the view expressed in them, these versions, too, reflect actual trends and thus carry considerable weight in evaluating their authenticity.

The best known and most often quoted among the *maghâzî* works is that of al-Wâqidî[14] (died 207 A.H./ 822 A.D.) though it is by no means the earliest of which we have knowledge. Though we possess it only in excerpts, it was one of the foremost sources for the *Kitâb al-Ṭabaqât al-Kabîr*[15], "The Great Book of Classes" (implying, of authorities) by Ibn Saʿd (died 230 A.H./845 A.D.), who was known as *Kâtib al-Wâqidî*, "al-Wâqidî's Secretary." But his master himself made extensive use of the notes and memoirs of his predecessors. In this manner, works of historians of later generations still reflect the vivid recollections of those who had witnessed the events and spoken of them to their sons and grandsons. To be exact, only part of Ibn Saʿd's work deals with the Prophet himself and the events of his own time and life. In the edition prepared by a group of scholars under the direction of Eduard Sachau of Berlin, only volumes one to three contain the so-called *Sîrah* and *maghâzî*; the remaining five volumes deal with the biographies and activities of the Companions and the succeeding generations (*ṭabaqât*) of authorities, including women, on whom not only the authenticity of historiography was based, but on whose testimony also rested the validity of the religious traditions and canon law (*sunnah* and *fiqh*).

In fact, the gradual rise of the *maghâzî* literature and the early history of Islam and the Prophet are an instructive example of the development and the technique of Islamic historiography. Reference to the source from which the information, called *khabar* or *ḥadîth*, "tale, report," was derived and the enumeration of the chain of transmitters through which it eventually reached the author of the historical work became fundamental requirements for proving the accuracy and authenticity of the recorded facts.

III *Muslim Historiography*[16]

From these beginnings developed one of the most important branches of Arabic literature. Once Islam had attained spiritual as well as political power, the historian's interest in its origins and the ways in which it had reached that eminence intensified. Partisan factions that arose among the conquering Muslims and the conquered peoples with axes to grind searched for justification of their claims to preeminence in the records of the past and used the traditions of their forefathers to support their demands. This interest in the origins and growth of the new religion and its political protagonists was in line with the old pre-Islamic tradition; only the central figures had changed. In the *aiyâm* literature the events and the personalities that shaped the destiny of the tribes formed the topic; with the widening scope of their experience, the focus shifted from Arabia to the Fertile Crescent and beyond. "World history" began to be felt as relevant; not only the contemporary, but also the ancient world needed to be known, events of the distant past were found to have a bearing on those of the Prophet's time and of the conquests and the creation and consolidation of the Muslim empire that followed. The history of neighboring empires and their rulers, such as Iran, too, entered into that survey, if only to demonstrate their weakness and to glorify the achievements of the conquerors.

Therefore, chronicles began almost invariably with the Creation of the world and the histories of the peoples of antiquity; those that had survived and those that had perished were included within their purview—not unexpectedly, for the Koran itself stressed their importance as warning examples for mankind, as they had been for the Unbelievers among the Quraysh. In fact, Muhammad himself had this awareness of historical continuity; his insistence on being a link in the great line of successive leaders, "prophets" as he called them, shows this clearly. His self-evaluation as the *Khâtam al-Nabî'în* "Seal of Prophets" (Sûrah 33, v. 40), has been interpreted by his followers as a claim to being the last prophet ever to appear in the world. However, as it seems to this writer, the Prophet expressed by this term only his conviction that he affirmed, through his revelation, the veracity of earlier "messages" brought by his prophetic predecessors; he joined their ranks, carrying on their work and projecting it into the future by confirming, as the seal does for a document, the eternal truth it conveys. This interpretation, it has to be admitted, is unacceptable to orthodox Muslims, though the Aḥmadîyah sect, a modern movement in Islam, favors a similar interpretation.

The Muslim historian accepted the importance of the history of the Ancients for their own generations as valid; it was to serve as an example for the Muslims, to give moral support to their actions and aspirations, and to justify their conquests as well as their institutions. The Ancients served as a kind of prelude to the Muslim experience. Therefore, the accounts start with the obvious beginning of everything, the Creation of the world. Legend, popular tales, and folklore as well as oral and written tradition formed the basis for these introductory chapters to the historical works. Much of this also figured in another literary genre, that of the *Qiṣaṣ al-Anbiyâ'*, "Tales of the Prophets," but was incorporated into the annals to make up for the lack of authentic historical records. Many of the *qiṣaṣ* stories are told on the authority of converts to Islam from Judaism or on that of the descendants of Jews. The most renowned of these was Kaʿb al-Aḥbâr who, when queried about Biblical personalities, and in particular about predictions in the *Tawrât*, "Torah," of the Prophet's coming, would have an alleged quotation from the Bible ready, though often he had to invent it, or, even more frequently, had recourse to tales from Jewish homiletics, the so-called Midrash.

Two types of historiography are characteristic: the annalistic, chronologically arranged works, and the "genealogical" ones which systematically record the part of leading families in the historical development throughout the period without regard to the exact chronological sequence. This latter method, exemplified best in al-Balâdhurî's (died 279 A.H./ 892 A.D.) *Kitâb Ansâb al-Ashrâf*, "Book of the Genealogy of the Aristocrats," has the advantage of showing the continuity or change of attitudes within a specific group to specific problems or conflicts, for example, the development of the Shîʿî movement leading to the debacle at Kerbelâ, but it interrupts this continuity by synchronizing the report with the events in successive reigns and circumstances contemporary with them.

The outstanding example of the former, the annalistic, arrangement is the *Ta'rîkh*, "Annals," of al-Ṭabarî (died 390 A.H./922 A.D.). Starting in the accustomed manner with the "prehistory" of Islam (the events in the ancient world from Creation to the Prophet's Mission, and with an account of the pre-Islamic Iranian empire), the author continues with a detailed report on the Prophet, his life, the circumstances of Allâh's Call, Muhammad's sermons, ministry, and activities to his death. While narrating the pre-*Hijrah* period, al-Ṭabarî conformed to the customary style of the *Sîrah* and, in fact, relied largely on Ibn Isḥâq's work or on the same original sources; but, beginning with the *Hijrah* to Medînah, he chose the annalistic, year-by-year narrative characteristic henceforth of his entire work. Every event is chronicled in the year it happened, or, if the exact date was doubtful, the arguments for its inclusion among those of a particular year were discussed, with confirming or contradictory evidence and its supporting authorities duly registered. Ṭabarî included any or all differing accounts of which he had knowledge, with the authorities for the variants carefully noted. Thus, not only the mainstream of tradition but also differences of opinion and various strains of historical reportage were preserved. The method he used was to give the chain of authorities on which the account following it rested, then to transcribe the report itself exactly as it had been transmitted through these authorities, followed, if necessary, by other accounts with their supporting transmitters and their variants. He did not attempt any reconciliation of contradictions or conflicts either in dates or in substance, but considered his task fully accomplished when he had recorded all the information available about persons, actions, battles, victories or defeats, riots, or any other happening.

Thus, clearly, al-Ṭabarî was not a historian in the modern sense of one who tries to elucidate the inner motivations, the sequence of causes and effects, the role of circumstance, or the influence of environment on events of the past or of his own time. He was a chronicler, a collector of "source material" who considered nothing too small to be preserved, of too little value to be entered into the record. In reading his work, however, we do not get the feeling that he had no judgment, that he was merely an "archivist," but that he held back his own judgment in order not to prejudge his sources. Indeed, by registering impartially all available evidence, al-Ṭabarî showed his awareness that even the smallest detail—particularly in controversial issues—might become a factor in bringing out the truth. He himself, however, abstained from any prejudgment; it is as if he were saying to his readers: "I have collected for you all the evidence—now you be the judge as to how it really came to pass."

The annalistic approach, though lacking somewhat in critical coordination, objective evaluation, and, above all, integrated representation, has its great value, exactly through its analytic documentation, for any scholar, ancient or modern, who intended to know the facts and details rather than to get an overall picture of trends, tensions, and partisanships. This advantage becomes quite clear in a comparison between Ṭabarî's work and the much later one called *al-Kâmil fi-l-Taʾrîkh,* "The Complete Book of Chronicles", of Ibn al-Athîr (died 630 A.H./ 1232 A.D.), which, being a synthesis, lacks this discrimination. Ibn al-Athîr used his predecessor's *Annals* and other earlier works the way a modern historian might use ancient documents to provide him with the raw material for his history. Ṭabarî did not attempt to harmonize the different versions nor did he discard or neglect information he had because it appeared to him faulty, biased, or otherwise untrue (often he did not even express any preference for one or the other version); in contrast, Ibn al-Athîr used his earlier sources eclectically, synchronizing contradictory dates, following one report and continuing with another without regard to ensuing conflicts and discrepancies in either chronology or historical data.[17] The resulting work is, in consequence, far more sophisticated in representing Islamic development, but factually far less reliable. Ibn al-Athîr's *Kâmil* was known to Western Orientalists and available in a Western edition before Ṭabarî's *Ta'rîkh,* and the discrepancies and inherent contradictions troubled the modern historians. Only when the *Annals* had been published did it become evident that Ibn al-Athîr, using indeed Ṭabarî's work extensively, was writing selectively and interpretatively, integrating disparate reports and thereby destroying the historical factuality of his work.

The second type of historiography is best represented by the voluminous work of-Balâdhurî (died 279 A.H./892 A.D.) called *Ansâb al-Ashrâf,* "Genealogies of the Aristocrats." This work, only slightly smaller than Ṭabarî's *Annals* and of equal importance, has not yet been published fully. Luckily, however, large and important parts of it have been made available in the excellent edition by scholars of the Hebrew University (who are continuing in this endeavor) with full annotations and an introduction which analyses the contents and structure of the whole work.[18] Another highly important section, dealing with the reign of Muʿâwîyah I, has been translated into Italian by G. Levi Della Vida and Olga Pinto, though the original text itself has not yet been published. Again the fact that both Ṭabarî and Balâdhurî had to use the same basic sources accounts for the sameness of large parts of their respective narratives. However, the essential difference between these two great historians is that al-Balâdhurî, writing somewhat earlier than al-Ṭabarî, still retains the ancient attitude which focused its interest on the aristocratic families. He therefore followed their various members through several generations and organized his work on the basis of their collective or individual participation in decisive events in the history of Islam. This "genealogical" arrangement often interrupted the sequence of representation; often an event would be reported within the history of the protagonist's family instead of its chronological place. Thus, for example, the death of the Prophet's grandson Ḥusayn in the battle of Kerbelâ is not discussed in full as one of the events of the reign of the caliph Yazîd ibn Muʿâwîyah, of the Umaiyad branch of the Quraysh, during which it occurred, but is recorded among the memorabilia of the family of his grandfather Abû Ṭâlib of the Banû Hâshim of Quraysh.

The genealogical structure of Balâdhurî's *Ansâb al-Ashrâf* begins with the history of Noah, the ancestor of all mankind after the Flood, then continues with his descendants to the forefathers of the Quraysh, Ibrâhîm and Ismâ'îl. The Banû Hâshim are the next group in this system, and the various Hâshimite families and their prominent members are treated in full, namely Muhammad, followed by Abû Ṭâlib and his son 'Alî and his family. A substantial part of the work (450 folios of the manuscript) is devoted to the Banû Umaiyah and the Umaiyad caliphs, whereas only a comparatively small section of the work (70 folios) is devoted to the history of the 'Abbâsides.

This kind of historiography underlines, though possibly not intentionally, an important factor in the historical development of the early Muslim empire. From the very beginning, the Muslim community was not a monolithic bloc, but was torn by strife and rivalry that led to intrigues, open battles, assassinations, and even to attacks on the holy city of Mecca itself. While Ṭabarî records all of these events and attitudes faithfully in their chronological place, without showing any open preference for one party or the other, Balâdhurî's arrangement stresses the participation of the various families and factions in them with perfect clarity, thus showing a certain bias for or against them.

By using the genealogical arrangement, Balâdhurî is carrying on the traditional way of recording history in Arabian society. Whether or not the ancient organization on tribal lines must be considered a fiction, an invention of later times as a means to establish an orderly system for a seemingly disorganized society, most, if not all, classical records accept it as a fact and are based on it. Thus, we find, at an early time, scholars that specialized in the field of "genealogy," the *nassâb*, whose fame was largely based on their outstanding competence in it. But "genealogy" meant far more than merely a knowledge of the tribes and their members, their relations and ramifications, and their ancestral roaming grounds; it included a full knowledge of their strife, the outstanding events in tribal history, their leading personalities, and their rivalries. This lore is embedded for the most part in the commentaries to the *dîwâns* of the Arab poets and anthologies of Arabic poetry, added by their compilators as an elucidation of the numerous allusions to ancient events and their protagonists; though not intended primarily to be "historiography," these notes, too, contribute greatly to the sum total of historical writing proper and of comments on poetic allusions, often based on the same authorities.

On the whole, the most ancient historians record the course of Islamic history factually, without taking a partisan stand for or against leading personalities and without bias in recounting decisive events. There is, however, one weighty exception. From the very beginning of its post-Muhammad development, the Muslim community was split into two camps, the Sunnîs and the Shîʿîs, a schism that continued into modern times. As most manifestations in the history of Islam, this division has both religious and political roots as well as effects. Its political origins and consequences are fairly easy to trace.

Strange as it may seem in so forceful a leader and so skillful an organizer, Muhammad never designated anyone in his entourage as his successor in the leadership of his *ummah*, various claims to the contrary notwithstanding. Thus, at the very moment of his death, the latent rivalries between the various factions that comprised the *ummah*—Meccan Emigrants (*Muhâjirûn*), Medinian Helpers (*Anṣâr*), and family and tribal groups within these larger parties—came to the fore, each claiming for themselves the right to succession. But for the forceful intervention of ʿUmar ibn al-Khaṭṭâb, one of the earliest adherents of the Prophet's, the Muslim community would have split right then and there.[19] Yet, in spite of their rallying under the "caliphate" (representation or succession) of the *al-Khulafâʾ al-Râshidûn*, the so-called Orthodox caliphs, this rivalry smoldered on and led to open warfare, murder, and usurpation of the office of *Khalîfah*, "the successor to the Prophet's office." The question of legitimacy in the succession as seen from this point of view was a political one; but that does not exhaust the problem.

Among the contenders was a group that asserted that divine right to the succession (as against secular political consideration) was inherent in the closest relative of the Prophet's and his family, namely ʿAlî ibn Abî Ṭâlib, who was not only Muhammad's cousin, but had married Fâṭimah, the Prophet's daughter by his marriage to his first, and during her lifetime only, wife, Khadîjah. This marriage brought forth two sons, Ḥasan and Ḥusayn. In the eyes of those who were convinced of ʿAlî's divine right to the leadership of the Muslim community, he and his family had been wrongfully deprived of it. To support this point of view, their representatives, the *Shîʿat ʿAlî*, "Party of ʿAlî" (hence commonly called Shîʿites), held that the Prophet himself had designated his cousin and son-in-law ʿAlî as his successor, if not in an explicit statement, yet in many hints and allusions. To bolster this claim, they asserted that the Prophet had elevated ʿAlî to the same relationship toward himself as that which had existed between Mûsà and Hârûn (Moses and Aaron), that the Prophet had assigned him the highest rank over the rest of his Companions and had entrusted him with secrets that he did not reveal to any other man. Some of ʿAlî's partisans went so far as to elevate ʿAlî into a godlike being, though these *ʿAlî-Ilâhîs*, as they were called, were considered "exaggerators" (*ghulât*), and their doctrine was rejected.

In the course of time, Shîʿism became a subdivision of Islam with a theology and religious philosophy and a literature of its own. This ideological division found an echo in all branches of Arabic (or Islamic) literature. Thus the historians of early as well as of later Islam show their Sunnî or Shîʿî coloration; others show their bias in more subtle allusions. Even post-Muhammed poetry was not unaffected by it; Shîʿite poets, such as al-Kumayt (died 126 A.H./743 A.D.) in his *Hâshimîyât* wrote poems in praise of the ʿAlide family and their cause.

Since the authenticity of the historic records—most, if not all, of which were, in the last analysis, based on oral tradition—had to be judged by the trustworthiness of their transmitters, a type of historical science developed which, in its scope and methods, seems to be unique. Its aim was to investigate the reliability of each authority individually. For this purpose it was necessary to search for and gather as much information as possible about their life, their studies, their movement from one center of learning to another, their teachers or other informants. This led to compilations of biographical data and their assembly in works which one might characterize as precursors of the modern biographical encyclopedias of the "Dictionary of National Biography" or the "Who's Who" type. The difference is that instead of the concise factualness of the modern works which include usually only the barest data, the Arab classical biographical dictionaries (as they are often called nowadays) aim at the greatest possible completeness. They resemble their modern counterparts in the inclusion of date and place, if known, of birth and death, names of parents and children, their studies and writings, their main fields of interest, and those on which their greatest fame rests. But these ancient works expand into frequently extensive reports on their activities, their travels to distant parts, their teachers and contemporaries, and their mutual relations. Comments on their environment or the historical events of their times as well as anecdotes showing their character and their standing in the circle of their friends or competitors and students often enliven the reports. The reader thus gains a knowledge not only of the scholar's own personality but also of his whole ambiance, his time, his family and friends, even the reputation he enjoyed in his time.

For the Muslim scholar of old, the fullness of these biographical records was an indispensable means for evaluating the trustworthiness and reliability of the authority on which he would have to depend for his material; for the modern user, they furnish an invaluable source of factual data together with a rich fund of social, economic, and political information. The surviving biographical works represent two types, the first mainly concerned with the historians, especially those of the earliest times of Islam and on the Prophet, the second arising from the special needs of the evolving science of *Ḥadîth*, "Tradition," and *Sunnah*, "the Prophet's Way of Life", though these two types often overlap. The *Book of Classes* by Ibn Saʿd has already been mentioned and its place in early Muslim historiography established. But it is also an outstanding example of the general biographical dictionary type, for it serves as well to elucidate the scholarly rank of those men on whom the soundness of Ḥadîth and, through it, the whole edifice of Islamic custom, tradition, law, and dogma rests.

The wider the scope of Muslim scholarship expanded, the greater became the need for secure information about its creators and their standing within the community of scholars. In consequence, compilation of biographical works continued to be considered a valuable and essential auxiliary science. The authors were guided by varying objectives which determined the selections; predominant among these was the desire to collect, evaluate, and sift the religious and theological authorities on which the religious dogmatics, *Fiqh* and *Sunnah* were based. But special interests, too, were served: works were devoted specifically to the scholars of one or the other of the Sunnî *madhâhib*, "schools," or to those who formed a circle around a renowned scholar. The representatives of the so-called "Greek" (*yûnânî*) sciences, that is, philosophy, mathematics, astronomy, and medicine, needed special investigation, which the works of Ibn Al-Qifṭî (died 646 A.H./1248 A.D.) and Ibn Abî Uṣaybiyah (606–69 A.H./1203–70 A.D.) provided. Ibn al-Athîr's (556–630 A.H./1160–1232 A.D.) *Usd al-Ghâba fî ʿIlm al-Ṣaḥâbah*, "The Lions of the Thicket on the Knowledge of the Companions," or Yâqût's (573–627 A.H./ 1177–1229 A.D.) *Irshâd al-Arîb ilà maʿrifat al-Adîb*, a large biographical compendium, Ibn Khallikân's (608–81 A.H./1211–82 A.D.), *Wafayât al-Aʿyân wa-Anbâʾ al-Zamân*, "Obituaries of Eminent Men and Knowledge of Contemporaries," or the later representative of this literary branch, the Spanish scholar Ibn Ḥajar al-Asqalânî (774–853 A.H./1372–1449 A.D.) are outstanding examples of this scholarly activity. It continued for many centuries, and these collections of biographies form one of the richest sources for our knowledge of the intellectual history of medieval Islam. Mention may here be made of the so-called *Fihrist*, "Index, Catalogue," of Ibn al-Nadîm (died 385 A.H./995 A.D.), a work intended to be a bookseller's and book collector's catalogue which has preserved for us a plethora of titles of works that have perished besides many more that have survived.

IV *Later Historiography*

During the first few centuries of the *Hijrah*, the birth of Islam, the environment from which it arose, the religious practices and tendencies it fostered and their representatives, remained the principal topic of historical research and historiography. An outgrowth of this emphasis were works that turned the spotlight on the two holy cities of Islam, Mecca and Medînah, which resulted in various monographs, such as that by al-Azraqî (died after 244 A.H./858–59 A.D.), al-Samhûdî (died 911 A.H./1505 A.D.), and others. But with the growing expansion of the Muslim Empire and the increasing consolidation of its components, the attention of the historians of later times turned away from contemplating its beginnings and from investigating the motivation for its founding and its religious premises. No longer were the lives, minds, and purposes of its earliest leaders and the shapers of its ideology the most important, almost the only, subject of their compilations. They began to turn their attention to the events that affected the individual cities and provinces and, last but not least, to chronicle the history and the fate of rising and ever more independent dynasties.

Thus, we find special works on Baghdâd (*Ta'rîkh Baghdâd* by al-Khatîb al-Baghdâdî, died 567 A.H. /1171 A.D.), Damascus (*Ta'rîkh al-Kabîr* by Ibn Asâkir, died 573 A.H./1177 A.D.), Mosul, Aleppo, Jerusalem, and so on, concentrating on local events and on the men, political personalities as well as scholars, who lived and worked in that particular locality. Some of these works were quite voluminous: for instance, Ibn Asâkir's *Ta'rîkh* filled eighty volumes. Special works dealt with the governors and the events during the time they held office, for example, the Egyptian author Muhammad ibn Yûsûf al-Kindî's (died in Fusṭâṭ in 350 A.H./ 961 A.D.) opus on the governors, and another one on the judges, of Egypt.

That region was the subject of a number of monographs. Cairo, with its vigorous, though unorthodox, Shî'î, Fâṭimide dynasty, with the Aiyubides, culminating in Ṣalâḥ ud-Dîn's (Saladdin, 533–89 A.H./1138–93 A.D.) victory over the Crusaders, and the peculiar, but powerful Mamlûk rulers (whose line, incidentally, was founded by a woman, Shajar al-Durr [died 648 A.H./1250 A.D.]) held special interest both politically and culturally. The age-old rivalry between the Nile and the Euphrates/ Tigris valleys—going back to antiquity and again visible in the competition between Syria/Iraq on the one hand and Egypt on the other in the second half of our twentieth century (and, incidentally, being fought out in the same area, the Jordan valley)—made the happenings in the Maghrib, especially in Egypt under the Fâṭimides and their successors, intensely noteworthy. Thus, it is not astonishing that Egypt, and its capital Cairo, with its mosques and the Azhar, its libraries and hospitals, became the subject of monographs and large works, of which the great history by Abu'l-Maḥâsin Ibn Taghribîrdî (died 874 A.H./ 1469 A.D.) *al-Nujûm al-Zâhira fî Mulûk Miṣr wa'l-Qâhira,* "The Brilliant Stars regarding the Kings of Egypt and Cairo," a record of the history of Egypt from the Arab Conquest to the year 1453 A.D., is the outstanding example. Taqî-al-Dîn Aḥmad al-Maqrîzî (766–846 A.H./ 1364–1442 A.D.) wrote his *al-Mawâ'iẓ wa'l-I'tibâr fî Dhikr al-Khiṭaṭ wa'-l-Âthâr*, ". . . an Account of the New Settlements and the Remains," a topography of Egypt and its monuments and history, and Jalâl al-Dîn al-Suyûṭî, born in Assiut in Upper Egypt (849–911 A.H./1445–1505 A.D.), composed his *Ḥusn al-Muḥâḍara fî Akhbâr Miṣr wa'l-Qâhira*, "A Beautiful Presentation of the History of Egypt and Cairo." Ibn Iyâs (died 930 A.H./1524 A.D.) chronicled Egypt's history in his *Badâ'i' al-Zuhûr fî Waqâ'i' al-Duhûr*, "Marvelous Flowers on the Events of the Times", up to the year 928 A.H./1522 A.D., that is, to within two years before his death. His journal is available in a French translation by Gaston Wiet.

In the East, too, the growing independence from the central government gave the events and the personalities of the rulers in that part of the realm increased importance. Bukhâra, Iṣfahân, Herât, and other cities, Ṭabaristân and other Eastern regions, became the subjects of special historical works, many of them, however, written in Persian. Spain, too, produced historians of its own who chronicled the events in the Iberian Peninsula.

A unique example of these regional chronicles is the history of the Berbers in Northwest Africa written by Ibn Khaldûn as part of his great work called *Kitâb al-'Ibar wa-Dîwân al-mubtada' wa'l-khabar fî aiyâm al-'Arab wa'l-'Ajam wa'l-Barbar wa-man 'aṣarahum min dhawî-l-Sulṭân al-Akbar*, "Book of Examples and Record of Origins and Events concerning the Days of the Arabs, Persians and Berbers and their Contemporaries who held great power." One of the most outstanding historians of medieval times, Ibn Khaldûn can claim high place in the ranks of creative minds of all times. In modern terms, he would be labeled a sociologist or political scientist. He himself would probably claim to be a historian, a theologian, or a jurist and administrator, all of which he, indeed, was at one time or another. All these professions brought forth the ideas on which his fame, at least in modern times, was founded.

ʿAbd al-Raḥmân Ibn Khaldûn was born in Tunis in 1332, the scion of a family that traced its origin to the South Arabian Kinda tribe, but had long been domiciled in Spain. The unsettled conditions there had forced his great-great-grandfather to emigrate to Northwest Africa. The political atmosphere in its various regions was far from tranquil; in consequence, Ibn Khaldûn paid allegiance for a time to one ruler, to shift it with the changing situation to another and then yet another; in consequence, he spent his life in many parts of the Maghrib, from Fez in Morocco to various cities in Tunisia, to Egypt, with two intervening periods in Granada, Spain. In all of his residences he was active politically and connected with the intellectual and political aristocracy. He died in 1406 in Cairo, where he had spent almost a quarter of a century (1382–1406 A.D.) holding prestigious positions at court and in academic circles, including a professorship and that of chief Mâlikî Qâḍî.

In the course of his frequent peregrinations he had spent some time with Maghribî Arab tribes. Trying to free himself from serving a not too friendly overlord, Abû Ḥammû of Tlemcen, he used a mission on behalf of that ruler to some of these tribes to seek asylum with them. He remained under their protection for a period of three years, during which time he began to write his world history and finished its introduction, which he called *al-Muqaddimah*, "The Introduction," in 1377. One of the results of this stay is the already mentioned account of the history of the Maghribî Arab and non-Arab (Berber) tribes which, being the only existing account of the Berbers written by a contemporary on the basis of firsthand observation and direct reportage, is of extreme value for the historian and forms one of the two unique aspects of Ibn Khaldûn's *Kitâb al-ʿIbar*.[21] The other is its *Muqaddimah*.

To quote from Franz Rosenthal's introduction to his translation of the *Muqaddimah*: "Much of its value lies in the light it sheds upon details in Ibn Khaldûn's political, sociological, economic and philosophic thinking."[22] These terms are exactly what distinguishes Ibn Khaldûn from his predecessors[23] and, unfortunately, also from his successors. Before him, and also after him, there was not a single Muslim historian to whom these terms could rightly be applied. If earlier historiographers *had* any comprehensive point of view, any focal approach to the history they recorded, it was the religious ideology of Islam, its position in the world they described, its development, its theological and philosophic problems and the way they were solved, and the attitudes of the various rulers or groups toward it. None of them—even, up to a point, the philosophers—attempted to understand the *processes* at work in forming their Muslim society, let alone society in the abstract; none pondered the factors that made a society grow and expand or that caused it to decay. They wrote about the ancient people and recorded their ascent, the height of their power, their decline and fall; but not until Ibn Khaldûn wrote this book did anyone (and not only any Muslim scholar) ponder the *causes* of these phenomena. That is what Ibn Khaldûn's genius achieved.

Before he began the chronicling of world history, Ibn Khaldûn thought deeply about the reasons for the coming and going of (what he termed) *dawlah*, "dynasty," that is, the appearance of powerful nations and their disappearance from the world scene, sometimes entirely, sometimes with some vestiges left, but without retaining any power. In analyzing the problem and in searching for its answer, he recognized several decisive factors for this development: environment (including climate and geographical conditions), *esprit de corps* (Ibn Khaldûn's *ʿaṣabîyah*, Rosenthal's "group consciousness," Issawi's[24] "social solidarity"), and *ʿumrân*, "the sum-total of its life-style, its history and its culture," usually translated by "civilization." The latter, in fact, was the starting point of his inquiry. In Ibn Khaldûn's view, *ʿumrân*, civilization, can exist only under favorable circumstances, of which climate is the most important. Only in the moderate zone of the earth, the one that is neither too hot nor too cold, can all the factors that constitute civilization, for example, agriculture, arts, sciences, and religion, develop.

The second necessary condition is social organization. Its noblest representative in Ibn Khaldûn's view is what he called "Bedouin" society, a term which denoted for him tribal, though sedentary, not nomad, society, in contrast to *ḥaḍârah*, the "urban" (literally "settled") one. *ʿAṣabîyah,* "consciousness of belonging to and supporting one's own group," becoming gradually "consciousness of belonging to an elite group," exists most strongly with the Bedouin; therefore, Bedouin society is the precondition for the growth of a strong aristocracy which becomes the nucleus for the formation of a *dawlah*, "state." This term is usually translated, in this context, as "dynasty," but as understood by Ibn Khaldûn, it denotes the corepower arround which the whole organization of a specific society evolves. Supported by *ʿaṣabîyah*, the *dawlah* retains its vitality as long as it keeps to the original virtues on which it rested: ability to perform the tasks necessary for the satisfaction of its needs, from defending itself against outsiders to producing the foodstuffs and the manifold artifacts needed to maintain the material environment. But with the growing affluence of individual members of the *ʿaṣabîyah* group, demands for luxury goods increase, and division of skills and labor sets in; in its wake, individual and collective independence diminish, and the need to rely on the services of others to provide these goods becomes paramount. Thus, the cohesion of the society, its *ʿaṣabîyah*, is weakened; and while other groups with their own *ʿaṣabîyah* are in ascendancy and begin to form a new *dawlah*, the earlier group loses its power; weakened also in physical strength, it has to depend on professional defenders, often hired from outside their groups, and eventually has to give up its superiority to the new *ʿaṣabîyah* group. Thus, a new *dawlah,* "dynasty," with a new virile *esprit de corps* arises, supplanting the aging one. This process repeats itself again and again, in a cycle lasting three generations.

This is the core of Ibn Khaldûn's social philosophy. But it does not exhaust either the contents of the *Muqaddimah* or its brilliant and novel ideas. Though Ibn Khaldûn never doubts the basic tenets of Islam, he subjects them to a searching and critical analysis, the like of which one will not find in any other work by a Muslim author (not even in modern times). To give an example: he does not *tell* the story of the Prophet, in the usual manner of a *sîrah*; he investigates what *constitutes* prophethood and what *distinguishes* the prophet—any prophet—from the ordinary human being. He examines the various religous "sciences" (*Ḥadîth*, *Fiqh*, etc.) and the schools that propagate them and views them in the light of his findings on "man's ability to think"; he also submits the natural sciences to a critical analysis. To quote Franz Rosenthal once more, in summing up this short analysis of the *Muqaddimah*: "[Ibn Khaldûn] was right when he claimed that the *Muqaddimah* was profoundly original and constituted a new departure in scholarly research. Its originality in the intellectual sense is obvious. The *Muqaddimah* reëvaluates, in an altogether unprecedented way, practically every single manifestation of a great and highly developed civilization. It accomplishes this both comprehensively and in detail in the light of one fundamental and sound insight, namely, by considering everything as a function of man and human social organization."[25]

It is regrettable that Ibn Khaldûn, in the purely historical parts of the *ʿIbar* (which he may have considered his main objective), does not follow his own insights as propounded in the *Muqaddimah*. The parts of his work containing the history of the peoples of the world are composed on the principles generally prevailing in Muslim historiography. As Professor Rosenthal points out,[26] Ibn Khaldûn lectured on his *Muqaddimah*; this shows his own appreciation of its importance and of the novelty of its approach and his conviction that he presented in fact a new "science" of historical writing and interpretation of history. The question thus arises: Why did he fail to apply his insight into the historical processes and the laws of historical development to his actual historiographic work? Obviously, it could not have been due to lack of intellectual ability; it seems rather to have been due to reluctance to offend traditional attitudes toward sacred personalities and sacrosanct values, though in the *Muqaddimah* he was not afraid of speaking out freely and critically, even on traditional beliefs. Perhaps he dared to reveal his unusual thoughts and sharp analyses of traditional concepts to the circle of disciples and intimate friends while he did not feel free to offer them to a general audience. He would not have been alone in such an attitude; the feeling that only an intellectual elite was able to understand, and should receive, true knowledge was an accepted doctrine of classical and medieval intellectuals.

To write a world history was also the task that Abu'l-Ḥasan ʿAlî al-Masʿûdî (died 356 A.H./956 A.D.) had set himself. His *Murûj al-Dhahab wa-Maʿâdin al-Jawhar*, "Meadows of Gold and Mines of Gems,"[27] the surviving work of this polyhistor, traveler, and raconteur, is constructed on two principles: to give an account of what really happened, and also to collect all the *mirabilia* and legends surrounding the localities, personalities, and sacred and profane history and events. Of his many writings, apart from some minor essays, only one, his major opus, the much-read and much-quoted *Murûj al-Dhahab*, has come down to us. Though even in the form in which it survived it fills nine volumes in the French edition (with translation), it is itself only an abridgment of a much larger work, as the author mentions himself. It is full of serious information on history, geography (often based on his own travels), and scientific subjects, such as astronomy; but it is also a treasure trove of folklore and legends on the people and places of ancient and his own times. Al-Masʿûdî's work is, in fact, more representative of the so-called *adab* literature than of historiography in its true sense.

CHAPTER 4

The Religious Literature of Islam

I Sunnah *and* Ḥadîth

With the Prophet's death Revelation had come to an end. To this day, in the mind of the pious Muslim, except for the Aḥmadîyah, a modern minority sect, Muhammad was the last prophet ever to emerge and the Koran the last, definite, irrevocable, and unsurpassable Revelation for all times to come.[1] However, this conviction did not save the Muslim community from change and growth, beginning with the geographical expansion and the ever increasing numbers of Believers in the wake of the Conquest. In addition, the diversity in the character of the original cultural and religious environment of the newcomers, often more sophisticated than that of the Arabs, made itself felt. Only the most basic elements of the new faith were embedded in the Koran; their implications for the day-to-day life and problems of an ever growing community had to be worked out. Thus, a twofold task awaited the Muslims. First, they had to evolve a specifically Muslim way of life and thought, involving religious usage as well as law; second, they were forced to cope with philosophic and dogmatic questions that went far beyond the scope of the problems consciously faced by the Prophet and his *ummah* during his lifetime, as reflected in the Koran. In fact, many of the most disturbing questions occupying the minds of later generations might, on the basis of Koranic pronouncements, be answered in opposing, or at least in varying, ways.

The Muslims solved this twofold task in a fashion that was almost unique. In theory, the evolving Muslim faith was based on two authorities—and on these only—the Word of God and the Prophetic *Ḥadîth,* (literally: tale, but as a technical term Tradition) the only comparable process to the latter possibly to be found in the Talmudic records of the debates of the post-Exilic Jewish Rabbis. But even though similarities may be detected between the forms of the Muslim *Ḥadîth* and the Talmud,[2] and though the latter may possibly have exerted some influence on the former, there are characteristics inherent in the *Ḥadîth* that are not found in the Talmud. The latter is strictly and avowedly the record of the Rabbis' debates on, and interpretation of, law and ritual, duties and obligations of the Jewish community and individuals and their eventual decision based on the authoritative standing of the debaters in the community of their peers. This last element prevailed in the end to some extent also within the Muslim sphere. But since every *ḥadîth* claims to go back to the divinely inspired Prophet, or a contemporary witness to his acts or decisions, all the pronouncements made in his name were supposed to have divine sanction and were eventually considered to be unalterable law binding for all times. Thus, most of the similarity between Talmud and *Ḥadîth* rests on their external form, especially the enumeration of the transmitting authorities that preceded each *ḥadîth* (the so-called *isnâd,* "chain of supporting authorities") and which also often accompanies, though usually with fewer links, the record of the rabbinical debate. In addition, it can be shown that a number of Islamic Traditions (the conventional translation of the term *Ḥadîth*) have parallels in the Talmud, from which they may have been derived[3]—almost unavoidably, because of the proximity of the localities where they developed, for example, in Iraq where there were famous rabbinical schools, if not in time (the Talmud developed much earlier, having been recorded since the second to third century A.D.).

Sunnah, the "Way of the Prophet," and *Ḥadîth* dominated Muslim religious and secular life as well as its philosophy and theology through the centuries, and even modern Muslim thinkers must still contemplate (and debate) the role they should play in contemporary Islam. Their impact and peculiar method can be understood only from the situation in which the Muslim community found itself in the early decades after Muhammad's death.

Every aspect of its life as an Islamic community, as well as the personal behavior of its individual members as Muslims, had to be established and defined on the basis of a new morality (this, in particular, for its Arab members whose social and moral attitudes were based on the tribal organization of their life) and on the direction toward a new central ideology. Policital elements played a role, too; but for many, if not most, of the converts to Islam the fundamental reorientation concerned their religious concepts. It is frequently asserted that Islam struck a familiar note for Near Eastern men because of the many Jewish and Christian elements in the Koran; even so, Muhammad's reinterpretation of these provoked antagonistic criticism in Jewish as well as in Christian circles, for it demanded from those who converted to Islam an adjustment of many of their ancient beliefs to the new Muslim interpretation: for the Christian, for example, the Muslim concept of Jesus as a prophet, but not as the Son of God; for both Jews and Christians, the central cult of the Kaʿbah. For the pagan or sectarian Near Easterner and the Iranian Zoroastrian, the strict monotheism of the Koran, for one, meant an utter renunciation of the dualism inherent in their ancient beliefs.

Yet, in spite of these difficulties, Islam succeeded in creating, in the course of a few centuries, a unified faith, through the method of *Ḥadîth,* though sometimes interpreted, but on an *Islamic* fundament, in various ways, as for example, in Shîʿism or Ṣûfism.

Basically, *ḥadîth,* in this context, means a report on an action of the Prophet's, or lack of it, an order or prohibition, a recommendation or disapproval by him of an act or attitude, originally related by an eyewitness and transmitted from generation to generation by trustworthy scholars or teachers. On the basis of these tales—the word *ḥadîth* literally means exactly that—the Prophet's own judgment about the righteousness, or the inadmissibility, of a Muslim's action or a theological position was inferred. Gradually a system of rights or wrongs, *more Islamico*, evolved, based on what was supposed to have been the Prophet's way of life or thought. This is what the oft-quoted term *Sunnah* implies: the Prophet's alleged actions and reactions in historic or assumed situations, or toward problems presumed to have arisen in his time.

While in the first generation after the Prophet's death genuine eyewitnesses were still available and for another generation or two secondhand oral transmitters could relate true traditions on the basis of eyewitness reports, the line of trustworthy communication became increasingly tenuous, and tendentious stories gradually were substituted for less and less available reliable testimony. Thus only a relatively small core of genuine Prophetic *Ḥadîth* may safely be presumed to have existed. However, in the course of a few centuries, the amount of alleged Traditions grew, and the scholars, on their travels through Muslim lands "in search of learning" (as the saying went) are reported to have gathered camel-loads of notes which they themselves were wary of considering authoritative without further critical scrutiny. Their criticism was based on an exhaustive investigation of the chain of authorities on which the report rested; the individual scholars' reputation in the world of scholarship, their trustworthiness in the eyes of their peers, and the range of their knowledge, in particular the course of their studies and their travels, were examined closely in order to establish an unbroken chain of immediate transmission from generation to generation going back eventually to the Prophet's own time. Any interruption in this supporting chain of evidence, the so-called *isnâd*, any "weak," that is, unreliable, link made the report unacceptable. References to a vague source (as, for example, "a man of great knowledge," or "a sheikh from his family") which in the early time of developing *Ḥadîth* tradition were quite common and frequently encountered in such honored early works as Ibn Isḥâq's *Sîrat an-Nabî* "Biography of the Prophet," or Muḥammad ibn Ḥabîb's (died 245 A.H./859 A.D.) *Kitâb al-Muḥabbar,* "The Gilt Book," discredited not only the *isnâd* but made the report itself suspect and untrustworthy.

This instinctive distrust, indeed the acknowledgment of possible falsification, was sound; but it developed that the least authentic *Ḥadîths*—those that were patently invented for a definite purpose—carried at their head irreproachably "sound" *isnâd*, blatantly made up to show perfection. What should have been scrutinized was the *matn,* the "contents" of the *Ḥadîth* itself; but eventually even the most unlikely tradition was accepted when it served its purpose of supporting a dogma, a philosophic or theological position, or a legal decision, as long as the *isnâd* was "sound."

From this, there was but a short step to the use of *Ḥadîth* as a weapon in the dogmatic conflicts that arose between theological and philosophic schools of thought. *Ḥadîth* was used to support the most conflicting and contradictory ideologies. Problems that never could have arisen during the Prophet's lifetime were tried to be solved by alleged pronouncements of his which were invented *ad hoc.* The opponents similarly produced counter-*Ḥadîths* which just as obviously were not genuine. Yet, as long as the *isnâd* was considered "sound," the contents of the tale could be accepted as genuine.

This method, fraudulent as it may appear to us, was accepted by all sides and used in arguments for and against a dogmatic position by representatives of all schools of thought. They all knew that it was, at the worst, a *pia fraus*, at best, a method, possibly the only one, of solving contemporary problems in accordance with Islamic concepts by projecting them back into the Prophet's time, so to speak, to decide them the way the Prophet would have done had he been confronted with them, and thus to insure continuity, an "identity in change." The result was a vast amount of *Ḥadîth* that had to be sorted out, evaluated, collected, and made available to scholars in a systematic and organized form, if it was to become, as indeed it did, the accepted fundament for the creation of canon law (*fiqh*) and civil law *(sharîᶜah)* as well as the arbiter for the correctness of theological and philosophical concepts.

The next logical step to be taken by Islamic scholarship was therefore the definition of acceptable and, in contrast, unacceptable tradition. While in the early phase of this process *raʾy*, "individual, considered opinion," and *ijtihâd*, "personal study and decision," were used, and held to be admissible and valid ways of coming to a decision, they gradually became discredited as being too subjective and open to prejudice and influence by personal or group interests. Instead, the so-called *ijmâᶜ*, "the consensus of the community as represented by its scholars," became a highly acceptable criterion for making a decision binding as being in accordance with the Prophet's *Sunnah* and God's Word, the Koran.

With the establishment of these binding criteria, the collection of those traditions that resulted in accepted definitions of what constituted the Prophet's *Sunnah*—that is, Islamic usage—became possible, if not an outright and unavoidable necessity. In this context, the term *Ḥadîth*—frequently used in combination with *Sunnah* ("*Ḥadîth* and *Sunnah*")—acquired the function of a Muslim technical term, distinguished from the historical *ḥadîth* "tale, report" which is the basis for Muslim historiography.

By the third century of the *Hijrah*, corresponding to the ninth century A.D., six collections of *Ḥadîth* had acquired such prominence that they became universally accepted in Sunnî Islam, gradually being looked upon as binding and usually referred to as "The Six Canonical *Ḥadîth* Works."[4]

Two of these works, by al-Bukhârî (died 256 A.H./870 A.D.) and Muslim (died 261 A.H./875 A.D.), respectively, were held in highest esteem and are referred to as the "Two Sound Ones" from their title *al-Jâmiᶜ al-Ṣaḥîḥ*, "The Sound Comprehensive Work." This characterization refers to the strictness with which their authors scrutinized the "soundness" not only of the credentials of the authorities supporting the *Ḥadîth* but also of the concepts of behavior implied in the texts and the rules of Muslim conduct to be based on them. Al-Bukhârî is said to have collected an immense amount of Traditions during his extensive travels in search of them; but he reportedly discarded a great many of them as "unsound." Still, his is a voluminous work. Many of the *Ḥadîth* works were arranged according to the *isnâd* supporting each *Ḥadîth*, and are therefore characterized as being "*musnad*" "arranged according to the *isnâd*," while the six canonical works are arranged on the basis of the contents of the texts "*muṣannaf*."

The remaining four canonical works were composed by Ibn Mâjâ (died 273 A.H./886 A.D.), Abû Dâ'ûd (died 275 A.H./888 A.D.), al-Tirmîdhî (died 279 A.H./892 A.D.), and al-Nasâ'î (died 303 A.H./915 A.D.).

These works deal with the laws regulating the *form* of Muslim life, the permissible or prescribed ways of behavior in all situations and walks of life. What to eat and drink (and vice versa, what not to eat or drink), how to dress, when and where to pray and how to observe the prescribed ablutions, how to keep the fast or to perform the pilgrimage, the way to conclude a contract or to enter into matrimony, the laws of ritual purity or impurity, how to bury the dead—all the myriads of human needs, endeavors, and situations were dealt with in all their aspects and actions were declared *ḥalâl*, "allowed," or *ḥarâm*, "forbidden," on the basis of prophetic precedent or prescription. Thus, the alleged *Sunnah* of the Prophet encompasses and regulates to this day a Muslim's life to the last minute detail.

II *Canon Law* (Fiqh *and* Sharî'ah)

The *Sunnah,* in the narrower sense of the term as discussed in the preceding chapter, affected mainly the private and individual obligations of Muslim ritual and behavior. The sphere of social interrelations and public affairs, too, demanded new forms based on Islamic tenets which had to be evolved, and a comprehensive legal system remained therefore to be formed.

The traditional Muslim opinion avers that Islamic jurisprudence[5] (*fiqh*) was created in the generation of the Prophet's Companions; but this assertion does not tally with historical facts. Instead, it evolved slowly out of a continuing demand for decisions on problems of a legal nature as they occured in a growing community whose daily life became increasingly sophisticated and complex.

In Muhammad's own lifetime, legal problems demanding immediate. consideration were brought to his attention, and his decisions, which he himself, in profound sincerity, considered to be revelations from Allâh, are recorded in the Koran; being sacrosanct, they became the basis on which later generations tried to evolve an intricate legal system. An example for this procedure is his decision on behalf of a widow and her daughters left destitute by the death of their husband and father that women should inherit from their father half of the amount that a son would receive. The Koranic laws, as far as they went, besides cult and ritual, covered mainly some aspects of marriage and divorce, of inheritance, slavery, the prohibition of usury (*ribâ*); that is, they dealt with personal relations of an ethical nature. For instance, the Koran considered slavery a normal feature of Arabian society but frequently recommended the freeing of a slave as morally superior and enjoined it as an act of expiation. Holy Writ also decreed freedom of conscience; no one should be converted to Islam by force: "there is no unwillingness [forced conversion] in Islam" (*lâ ikrâha fi-l-Islâm*) (Sûrah 2,v.257). However, even where the Koran offered some detailed precepts, as in these fields, real-life situations demanded far more specific rules to be applicable in practice.

In the early decades of Islam, customary law, both of pre-Islamic Arabia and that governing the conquered regions, continued to be followed, but the need for establishing Islamic legal practices made itself increasingly felt. These concerned especially criminal law, economic and socio-political problems, and community development. Further problems to be solved by laws based on characteristically Islamic principles included the status of minorities—in the Muslim context the so-called *Ahl al-Kitâb*, "People of the Book" (also called *dhimmîs*, "protected people"), both terms affecting essentially the Jews and Christians within the Muslim Empire; laws governing the conquered territories, the *Dâr al-Islâm*, "Region of Islam," where Islam was sovereign, and the relations with and attitudes toward the *Dâr al-Ḥarb*, "Region of War," that is, the non-Muslim world. Economic problems, *zakât*, "taxation," of the Muslims, the *kharâj*, the "land tax" imposed on the conquered regions, and the *jizyah*, "poll tax," levied on the *dhimmîs* were among the urgent problems to be solved. Gradually, toward the turn of the first and the beginning of the second century of the *Hijrah*, scholars in the centers of Muslim learning began to search for solutions to these legal questions, attempting to base them on the moral, ethical, and social principles of the new faith, and to set up guidelines by which to pronounce judgment and to make binding decisions in litigations. Turning to the source of all Islamic thought, the Koran, they could find in it only a few definite statements of a legal character, and even these were not specific enough to cover all possible exigencies of social, communal, and political life. Even such Koranic pronouncements as did exist needed further implementation. For instance, the Koranic law of inheritance, revealed in answer to a specific emergency, required further elucidation, which eventually culminated in the establishment of an intricate system of legal claimants to an estate and their proportionate share in it.[6]

The consecutive steps taken in evolving a Muslim code of law (though this term has to be used with a grain of salt) are closely related to those effective in the development of the religious Tradition. Individual scholars propounded their views on the basis of *raʾy* and *ijtihâd*, leaning heavily also on *istiḥsân*, "preference," and *iṣṭilâḥ*, "consideration of general welfare"; laws were established by decisions of a *qâḍî*, "judge." Thus, individual reflection played a considerable role. *Qiyâs*, "following a precedent," by way of analogy, was established only comparatively late as a valid legal principle, while *raʾy* and *ijtihâd* came to be considered too subjective and too much reflecting the personality of the individual judge or scholar. In the end, only *qiyâs* and *ijmâʿ*, "consensus," together with the Koran and *Sunnah* remained, throughout the centuries, the *uṣûl al-fiqh*, "the fundamental principles of canon law."

We can follow this development by looking at the emergence of the four *madhâhib*, "schools of legal thought" (often referred to as "rites"), still in existence. In the early period of this process groups formed when scholars of a congenial type of mind joined and established a common trend of legal thinking by way of *ijmâʿ*. Thus, a number of "schools" emerged, or, rather, circles of disciples gathered around a scholar whose decisions and teachings they accepted and passed on to their disciples. These "schools" differed only slightly from one another and eventually merged into larger ones. Within these schools—as for example, those of ʿIraq (centered in Kûfah), Syria (in Damascus), and the Ḥijâz (in Medînah)—the decisions and opinions of predecessors were cited, in the well-known form of *isnâd* and *ḥadîth*, in order to lend added authority to interpretation and decision. Only gradually was it considered necessary to evoke in the *isnâd* the testimony of a Companion to root law firmly in the earliest time of Islam. This trend culminated in the work of the famous legal scholar al-Shâfiʿî (150–204 A.H./767–819 A.D.), who considered only those decisions as valid whose authenticity was allegedly attested to by the Prophet himself.

The debates on the correct handling of issues are recorded in the familiar form of *Ḥadîth* with its *isnâd* and *matn*; these constitute the theoretical aspects of *fiqh*, "Islamic canon law." The oldest extant *fiqh* work is the *Muwaṭṭaʾ*, "The Levelled Path," by Mâlik ibn Anas (90 or 95–179 A.H./ca.713–795 A.D.), one of the earliest scholars of Islamic law. He represents the legal tradition of Medînah where the custom of the prophetic era made itself felt through the descendants of the Companions still surviving; in other words, his views were based on the idealized customs of the early Muslim community.[7] He was a practicing judge who had to adjudicate actual cases, in contrast to Abû Ḥanîfah (died 150 A.H./768 A.D.), the leading spirit of the ʿIraqi school, who did not hold such office.[8] The latter's ideas found theoretical expression and suggested practical application in the *Kitâb al-Kharâj*, "Book of Land Tax," which his disciple Abû Yûsuf (died 182 A.H./798 A.D.) composed for the caliph Hârûn al-Rashîd and which covered a far larger range of legal and administrative topics than its title suggests. While Abû Ḥanîfah considered *raʾy* and *istiḥsân* valid principles for legal decisions, Mâlik emphasized *ijmâʿ*, the consensus of scholars, which for him meant those of Medînah.[9] Mâlik's *Muwaṭṭaʾ* is not a code in the strict sense of the word (in fact, none of the *fiqh* works could rightly be called that), but a collection of some 1700 Traditions dealing with legal problems, arranged according to topics, followed by Mâlik's comment based on his own views in the matter and stressing the Medinian usage. Only when he could not produce either tradition or custom did he allow himself a decision according to his own judgment, a method later entirely discarded as unacceptable and innovatory.

Al-Shâfiʿî, the third in the group of founders of *fiqh* schools that still survive, lived and taught for a long time in Egypt, where his tomb in Cairo is still a venerated sanctuary. He must be credited with establishing the overruling authority of decisions based directly on alleged prophetic action over those based on *raʾy*, *istiḥsân*, or *ijtihâd*; from his time dates the exclusive definition of the four *uṣûl*, "foundations," of *fiqh*, namely, the Koran, the Prophetic Sunnah, *ijmâʿ*, "consensus of the community, as expressed by its scholars," and *qiyâs*, "analogy," that is, conclusions derived by precedence through the first three foundations.[10] He left a considerable body of writings (*rasâʾil*, "essays"), most of which were collected by his disciples in the *Kitâb al-Umm*; many of them are cast into the form of questions and answers, and dialogues with opponents.

Aḥmad ibn Ḥanbal (died 241 A.H./855 A.D.), considered to be the founder of the last of the four orthodox (Sunnî) *madhâhib*, "rites, legal schools," lent his name to that *madhhab* that rejected any human reasoning in legal decisions and relied wholly on the Koran and *Sunnah*. His teachings were collected by his adherents in the so-called *Musnad* of Ibn Ḥanbal, which comprised some 28,000 traditions attributed to him. *Qiyâs* and *raʾy*, as well as *istiḥsân* and *istiṣlâḥ*, "taking the common weal into consideration," are rejected as inferior principles, leading to *bidʿah*, "innovation." Ibn Ḥanbal himself was a man of character whose personal tragic history assures him deep respect. Subjected to torture by the caliph al-Maʾmûn's *miḥnah*, "inquisition," he refused to abandon his convictions. Twice in later centuries his strict teachings were reiterated and even intensified, in the thirteenth century by Ibn Taimîyah (died 682 A.H./1283A.D.) and in the eighteenth century by Muḥammad ibn ʿAbd al-Wahhâb (died 1301 A.H./1787 A.D.), the eponym of the Wahhâbîs of Saʿûdi Arabia.

Modern Islamic law, as far as it is still effective, if not in secular, civil affairs, at least in religious matters and disputes, is still built upon these four ancient *madhâhib*. They are considered equally "orthodox," or one should more correctly say, all belong to the Sunnî concept of Islam. Shîʿism, which differed in its interpretation of the caliphate and in the position it accorded ʿAlî and the veneration if offered him, developed a legal tradition and a *Sunnah* of its own. One of the best known differences between Sunnî and Shîʿî law is the prohibition of the so-called *mutʿah* marriage (marriage for a specified term) in Sunnî Islam and its recognition by the Shîʿah (though modern Shîʿite states have begun to withdraw legitimacy from that form of "temporary" marriage). However, under the influence of the so-called modernist movement and, even more, of Western rule over Islamic peoples, interpretation of canon law, for example, in the sphere of "personal law" (that governing marriage, divorce, inheritance, etc.) on the basis of Western legal principles and procedure has modified Islamic legal practice to a certain extent, so that one may speak nowadays of Muslim law as practiced in India, Northwest Africa, Indonesia, and so on.[11]

One word may be added regarding the use of the terms *sharîʿah* and *fiqh*. Though not entirely identical, they are not strictly distinguished in actual use and are often employed interchangeably. However, one may say that *fiqh*, on the whole, designates the theory of law, jurisprudence, whereas *sharîʿah* is used largely for its practice, jurisdiction.

III *Dogma and Philosophy*

The *Sunnah,* insofar as it represented the Muslim Way of Life, developed gradually, almost unconsciously, through the desire of the individual Muslim to follow the Prophet's example, and through the necessity for the Muslim community to formulate guidelines and norms for its communal life. On the whole, this development proceeded without undue difficulties and with only minor conflicts when the scholars discussed topics such as the attitude toward luxury in contrast to asceticism, or toward life within the world as against withdrawal into solitude.

However, far more intricate problems remained to be solved besides those of ritual and law, questions of a theological and philosophical nature that cut deeply into the fundaments of faith.[12] As was the case with regard to laws, the Koran did not contain precise pronouncements on which theological and philosophical dogmas could be based without arousing controversy. True, there was one tenet that was uttered and restated in unequivocal terms in the Holy Book: the Oneness of God, the utter absence of any deity equal to Him—but even that proved not enough. This fundamental belief seemed to be shaken by such expressions as "God is knowing," "God is merciful," "God is forgiving," "God is all-powerful,"—all, and many more phrases of this kind, found in the Koran itself. Thus, the question arose whether, if God was eternal, these "attributes" were not eternally coexistent with Him, or whether these qualities possibly existed as entities outside of God? If that were so, that would be *shirk*, "association of other eternal things with God," that is, *the* fundamental sin of polytheism.

The more the pious thinkers of Islam pondered over God's nature and tried to penetrate into the secrets of His essence, the deeper the conflicts became. And that was not solely due to external influences, of Greek philosophy in particular, strong as it proved to be, but was inherent in religious questioning itself.

Therefore, from the early second century of the *Hijrah* on, the scholars, theologians as well as philosophers of Islam (and not infrequently they were one and the same person) turned not only to the task of establishing Muslim norms of conduct (as laid down in the *Sunnah*) but also to discussing the fundaments of Islamic theology and dogma. As in their efforts to establish principles of religious practice, they turned to prophetic authority by way of *Ḥadîth*.

The most disquieting problem—not only in Islam, but to this day for every sensitive religious mind—was the existence of evil in the world. God is by definition good and intended the world to be good, and therefore could not desire, or even allow, evil. How was it possible, then, that evil was found in the world? Its evident existence was a problem that loomed large in the minds of the early Muslim generations; moreover, it had not only theological, but also political implications. The Umaiyad caliphs, confronted with the task of creating a unified, governable political entity out of a diffuse variety of elements, were not deeply concerned with the niceties of Islamic conduct, nor with theological dogmas. With the exception of ʿUmar ibn ʿAbd al-ʿAzîz (ruled 717–20 A.D.), they were rather worldly in their private lives and pragmatic in their way of governing. Nevertheless, by virtue of their adherence to the *Shahâdah*, "Confession of Faith," their claim to being true Muslims could not be disputed. They could not be relegated outright into the category of sinners who would forever be denied entry into Paradise, but, nonetheless, the orthodox would not accept them fully as ideal Muslims.

The way out of this dilemma was found by deferring judgment and leaving the decision to Allâh Himself on Judgment Day. Those who proclaimed this opinion were called *Murjiʾites*, "Delayers"; politically, they were thus able to justify the legitimacy of Umaiyad rule; with regard to religion, they would stress *imân*, "faith," over *ʿamal*, "acts." This position was in strong contrast to the opinion held by the *Khârijites*, "Secessionists," who denied the possibility of repentance, atonement, and redemption, and took a firm stand that "once a sinner, always a sinner." On the other hand, the Khârijîyah did not limit the right to the caliphate to any particular group, tribe, or faction; any Muslim, within their definition of that term, could become caliph "were he even an 'Ethiopian' [black] slave." This stand was politically directed against the Shîʿî as well as the Sunnî legitimists. Their religious dogma survived into modern times only in small splinter groups, the so-called ʿIbâdîs (ʿAbâdîs), in Northwest Africa, Zanzibar, and Oman; in the Middle Ages, their hand could be found in various uprisings and revolts, almost invariably of a social character.

Closely connected was the problem of free will versus predestination. When the Muslim turned to the Koran, he would not find there an unequivocal answer to this question. In many of His verses, Allâh would lay the burden of decision between the Path of the Righteous and the road that led to sin on the shoulder of man himself; but in others He declared that every soul, since its creation, was allotted an unalterable destiny. The orthodox would believe that God knew the fate of every creature even before being created. However, God was also, by definition, just; but where was His justice, if a man was predestined, even before he was born, to become a sinner and be condemned to the Fire, or to be one of the Righteous and enter Paradise and eternal bliss?

Another disturbing problem was the character of the Koran itself. To the Muslim, it is not the recorded echo of one man's inner religious experience, but the Word of God Himself as revealed to His Prophet Muhammad and announced to the world by using him as His Messenger. This, however, posed several problems: Was the Koran itself created, that is, ephemeral, or uncreated and eternal? Or was only the *Umm al-Kitâb* eternal, the "Mother of the Book," that is, the original Revelation ("*Ur-Offenbarung*") which rested at Allâh's throne and of which all Revelation—Torah and Evangelion, as well as the Koran—is an earthly counterpart? And were the copies of the Holy Book that were in the hands of the Koran readers, or its recitation in the mosques throughout the world, created or uncreated? Grave questions these, and attempted to be solved in various ways according to the basic philosophic-theological position of the Muslim thinkers.

This is not the place to go into the intricate details of the debates or the solutions offered. Here it must suffice to say that two great opposing groups emerged, the orthodox, traditionalist theologian and the rationalistic "freethinking" "philosopher." The former clung to the literal formulations of the Koran, with all its anthropomorphic references to God's hands, His feet, His face, His eye, His thigh; some went so far as to demonstrate their literal understanding of these terms by pointing to their own body or by performing the actions mentioned in the verses of the Koran. The fundamentalists maintained that the Koran, in whatever form, whether as *Umm al-Kitâb*, as recitation, or as a book "between the two covers," was eternal and uncreated, a position strongly opposed by the rationalist *Muʿtazilah* movement. As for the problem of man's freedom of will, his fate was determined even before he was created; he would be righteous and enter Paradise, or he would be evil and condemned to eternal hellfire. Only later a "mediating" interpretation solved the problem of the attributes ("God is knowing," etc.) by defining them as existing but as having no describable quality, that they were "*Bi-lâ-Kayf*," "without a how-ness."

Not so the second group of thinkers, known as the Muʿtazilites, philosophically by far the more sophisticated and fruitful one, which grew out of an earlier trend of thought called the *Qadarîyah*. In contrast to the so-called *Jabarîyah* movement which proclaimed the blind working of fate (*jabar* = "decree"), the Qadarîyah *denied* the inevitability of *qadar*, "preordained fate," and averred that man has some command over his actions; the word *qadar* with them indicates their *denial* of the invincible power of fate and, by way of contrast, a sense of its limitation.

The Muʿtazilites were not satisfied with the simplistic answers of the traditionalist theologians. For them, the basic criterion for any solution was whether it could stand up to the demands of rational thought. *ʿAql*, "reason," had to come into its rightful place. They "discussed" (*takallama*) the problems—and were hence known also as *mutakallimûn*, "those who discussed [issues rationally]"—using dialectic methods which became their trademark through the term *kalâm* (literally, "speech," but used specifically in the sense of "dialectics"). To them, doubt was far more valuable than blind belief: "Fifty doubts are better than one certainty," or "The essential precondition of knowledge is doubt," a Cartesian position centuries before Descartes.

Their most urgent problem concerned that of freedom of will. God, by definition, was just: thus, He could not justly condemn man to eternal hellfire even before he was created. Their answer was that God laid the burden of *choice* upon the conscience of the individual; He showed him both paths, that of good and that of evil. Man then decided: but God in His omniscience had known what his choice would be. Furthermore, since God is, also by definition, wise, He can only do what is beneficial to the common weal: thus, the Muʿtazilites emphasize God's care for the well-being of mankind, His *maṣlaḥah*.

In a similar vein, the irksome problem of the attributes was solved rationally. Since monotheism denied any eternal existence beside God, any phrase such as "God is wise, just, merciful," or any similar statement meant simply "God is [i.e., exists]" and then just "God." Because of their insistence on God's unity and His justness, the Muʿtazilites were known as the *Ahl al-ʿadl wa-l-tawḥîd*, "the People of Justice and Unity." As for the problem of the createdness or uncreatedness of the Koran, they held that only the *Umm al-Kitâb* was eternal, but that the copy in the hand of the Koran reader and his recitation of its *sûrahs* did not partake of this exalted status.

For some decades, from 202 to 234 A.H., the position of the Muʿtazilah enjoyed official recognition by two caliphs, al-Maʾmûn and al-Muʿtaṣim. Al-Maʾmûn proclaimed it as the official concept of the state and instituted a *miḥnah*, "inquisition," against those who adhered to the fundamentalist doctrines; among its prominent victims was Aḥmad ibn Ḥanbal. It was rescinded only by al-Mutawakkil, who reinstated orthodoxy.

A reaction against the extreme position of both orthodoxy and rationalism was bound to set in. It took the form of a mediating theology symbolized by the name of al-Ashʿarî (died 324 A.H./935 A.D.) and al-Mâturidî (died 333 A.H./944 A.D.). In reality, as the former's treatise called *al-Ibânah ʿan Uṣûl al-Diyânah*, "Elucidation of the Foundations of Faith,"[13] shows, al-Ashʿarî upholds firmly the literal orthodoxy of Aḥmad ibn Ḥanbal, as he proclaims explicitly at the outset of this treatise. However, the work of the Muʿtazilites, especially their dialectic method, exerted a deep influence on the thought processes of the thinkers of the orthodox schools, and al-Ashʿarî's disciples accepted and used some of its methods for their own purpose. This is particularly evident in their use of rationalization and adoption of *kalâm*, "dialectics," and their acceptance of *naẓar*, "speculation," instead of *taqlîd*, "blind imitation," as well as employing *taʾwîl*, "figurative interpretation," in order to avoid anthropomorphism, and consequently *shirk*.

Thus, in spite of the polemics of their master al-Ashʿarî against the Muʿtazilite rationalism, his disciples took over its methods, in particular its *kalâm;* the term *mutakallimûn,* in fact, gradually applied particularly to these defenders of orthodoxy. In consequence, the conflict between rationalism and tradition remained unresolved and still exists in our own time.

An entirely different approach to solving the problems of the character of God and His relation to His creation is based not on rational thought—ultimately rooted in Aristotle—but on the Idealism of Plato as interpreted by Plotinus (204–70 A.D.). Neither the philosophy of Islam nor its theology can be understood unless one realizes that they stood on the shoulders of these great philosophers. The Muʿtazilites as well as their opponents were influenced in their definitions of Allâh by the speculations on the Absolute of Plato and Aristotle; the Muslims, however, did not know them in their original form but as transmitted and interpreted through Plotinus.[14]

It is not possible, in the present essay on Arabic literature, to analyse in detail the complex combination of Aristotelian and Platonic thought that resulted, via Plotinus, in the so-called neo-Platonism. Both Plato and Aristotle were searching for a definition of the absolute. For the idealist Plato, that reality, the *ontos on*, was the ideas; for the realist Aristotle, the absolute was the Prime Mover from whom all being stems. This fitted well with the basic Muslim concept of the Oneness of God and His being the source of all life. However, the relation of His transcendence to the material world of created things had still to be established. Neo-Platonism seemed to some of the Muslim philosophers to offer a solution to this problem, through its doctrine of emanation, that is, the transition from the ideal realm of the True Being (the *On*) or the True One (the *Hen*) by way of the intellect—that is, the creative principle—to the soul as the vital principle in the universe, and from there to nature which joins form and matter.

Neo-Platonism dominated the philosophy of several of the most famous medieval Muslim thinkers. These philosophers, too, were concerned with defining God and His relation to Creation in all its various forms—minerals, animals, plants, human beings, and heavenly bodies. The neo-Platonic approach was first introduced into Islamic theology and philosophy by Abû Yaʿqûb ibn Isḥâq al-Kindî (of Kûfa, died ca. 260 A.H./874 A.D.), who, by the way, was the only Muslim philosopher of Arab stock, as his tribal name *al-Kindî* indicates. Its greatest and most famous exponents were Abû Naṣr al-Fârâbî (died 339 A.H./950 A.D.) and Abû ʿAlî al-Ḥusayn ibn ʿAbd Allâh Ibn Sînâ (370–428 A.H./980–1037 A.D.), known to the West as Avicenna. They accepted the neo-Platonic doctrine of emanation, propagated by Plotinus, translated into Islamic terms, amalgamating basic Muslim dogmas, especially that of the Oneness of Allâh, with neo-Platonic concepts.

The theory of emanation first became known to the Muslim philosophers by way of the so-called *Theology of Aristotle,* a ninth-century Arabic pseudonymous work attributed to Aristotle but in reality a translation of parts of Plotinus' *Ennead.* Following the doctrine of emanation, al-Kindî, and after him al-Fârâbî, accepted the theory of the descending scale of creation from God, the All-One (*Ur-Eine*) by way of reason, soul, ideal matter, to the sphere of realities, and the ascending scale from stone to plant, to animal, to man, to prophet and philosopher, to angel, and back to God.

But as Muslims, they had to bring this theory into harmony with the Koranic basic principle of monotheism and with the dogma of the finite ephemeral creation by the infinite, eternal Creator, Allâh. In accordance with neo-Platonism, they considered the Creator of all things to be the Prime Mover, the creative *Nûs*, in Arabic *al-ʿAql al-Faʿʿâl*, from Whom all other "existences," *mawjûdât*, emanated in a descending order. Al-Fârâbî distinguishes six levels constituting the "principles of existence," *mabâdiʾ al-mawjûdât*. These are, in descending order: (1) the First Cause, (2) the spheres (=secondary causes), (3) creative reason (*al-ʿaql al-faʿʿâl* = *Nûs*), (4) the soul (or World Soul), (5) form, and (6) matter. Since the First Cause can only be one, it is identified with God. The secondary Causes are identified with spirits or angels; the creative *ʿaql* leads man to the highest perfection within his grasp, that is, for him, the highest happiness is to reach the stage of creative reason. The Muslim neo-Platonists regard Islam as the finest actual example of this theory.

Though al-Kindî was a prolific writer—the titles of 265 essays of his have been recorded, including, by the way, also studies on music—very few of his works are known to exist at present. Al-Fârâbî's *oeuvre*, on the other hand, is well known. Besides extensive studies of Greek, in particular Aristotelian, philosophy, as such titles as *The Harmony between Plato and Aristotle* and *Essay on the Ideas of Aristotle's Metaphysics*[15] show, his most famous works are his thoughts on the Muslim state as expounded in two studies entitled *Arâ' ahli'l-madînah al-fâḍilah,* "Opinions of the Inhabitants of the Ideal State," and *Fî mabâdî'-l-mawjûdât,* "The Principles of Existence."[16] These are at the same time most important for the study of the Islamic theory of state, one of the problems discussed intensely by modern Muslims and Islamists. For al-Fârâbî, the organization of human society finds its counterpart in the human body, which is regulated by a central and dominating organ, the heart. This, projected onto human society, is equated with the leader of the state. Just as there are other organs subordinated to the heart, the "body politic" needs subordinate officials who look after the proper execution of the leader's commands, the observation of the laws, and the proper conduct of the members of the community. Above all, there is the Supreme Ruler. The complex physiological functions of the organs of the body need to be regulated and coordinated from a supreme source. Human society, likewise, needs a supreme regulator who is above every other authority and from whom all the impulses emanate. For the Muslim al-Fârâbî this supreme—and at the same time, infinite—leader is Allâh, Whose commands and intentions are imparted (or revealed) to the Prophet. The latter, in turn, passes Allâh's commands on to his subalterns and so down the line to each individual member of the *ummah*, "community." States that do not follow that organization are "evil states"; again, as befits a Muslim, the "Ideal State," the *Madînah al-Fâḍilah*, for al-Fârâbî, can be only a Muslim state.

Far apart from the philosophers, of all shades of convictions, were the mystics. They were called Ṣûfîs, from the woolen garment that was their distinctive garb. Another derivation of the Arabic term *ṣûfîya* from the Greek *sophos* has been rejected by many scholars. But recently, in 1969, the French scholar Henri Corbin again defended this etymological connection, saying ironically that "it was too good to be true" to be accepted, and supporting it by referring to al-Bêrûnî (tenth century) and by the inner evidence of the Ṣûfî being "the sage-prophet."[17]

The philosopher attempted to define the essence of God by way of rational thought processes and in logical terms, or tried to describe the relation between God and the world of creation in terms of emanation, as did the Muslim neo-Platonists. None of these speculations satisfied the mystics' desire to establish the closest possible relationship between the individual human being and God. Only by losing one's own identity in God and by utterly merging one's own self with Him could this be achieved. With one of their earliest representatives they defined their aim as the "apprehension of Divine realities and renunciation of human possessions." With the Koran, they felt Him to be as close to man "as his jugular vein" (Sûrah 50,v.15; see also Sûrahs 2,v.18; 5,vv.20f.), the answer the Prophet himself had given to those of his Meccan contemporaries who questioned him about the essence of God. His own anxiety at the difficulty to comprehend and define God except in terms of subjective certainty and the realization of the impossibility of conveying this to others may possibly have inspired Muhammad to formulate his answer in this manner.

The Ṣûfîs searched for means by which to achieve that perfect understanding that could not come by way of philosophic definitions or theories of emanation. Only immersion of one's whole being in the all-embracing Being of God could bring this goal near; they called the means to its attainment "Love." As Professor Nicholson described it: "The whole of Sûfism rests on the belief that when the individual self is lost, the Universal Self is found, or, in religious language, that ecstasy affords the only means by which the soul can directly communicate and become united with God. Ascetism, purification, love, gnosis, saintship—all the leading ideas of Sûfism—are developed from this cardinal principle."[18]

To express their experience of ecstasy and of total union with the "Beloved," as they called God, the Ṣûfîs used terms such as "love" and "drunkenness" commonly applied to human sensations. Their poetry therefore could be taken, or rather mistaken, for love and wine poetry. To quote here, as an illustration, a few lines by Ibn ʿArabî, in Nicholson's translation, which might have been composed by a pre-Islamic poet such as Imraʾ al-Qais:

Oh, her beauty—the tender maid! Its brilliance gives light like lamps to one travelling in the dark.
She is a pearl hidden in a shell of hair as black as jet
A pearl for which Thought dives and remains unceasingly in the deeps of that ocean.

He who looks upon her deems her to be a gazelle of the sand hills, because of her shapely neck and the loveliness of her gestures.[19]

But these poems must be understood entirely as allegories, describing in human terms the spiritual ecstasy of a mystic that otherwise would defy verbal expression.

As Arabic was the literary language for Muslim poets, writers, and scholars of the most diverse ethnic origins, it was also the vehicle for the expression of their philosophic thought. Yet not all of their work was composed in Arabic. Most of the greatest Ṣûfîs were Persians and wrote in their native language, for example, Ḥâfiẓ, whose poetry seems to be in praise of love and wine, and Jalâl al-Din Rûmî. Only few of the mystics were Arabs or wrote in that language. One of the greatest was the martyr al-Ḥallâj al-Ḥusayn ibn Manṣûr (born ca. 857 A.D., executed 309 A.H./922 A.D.).[20] His martyrdom was caused by his assertion that he had reached the state of *fanà*, the total unification with the Truth, that is, God. By exclaiming *Anâ al-Ḥaqq*, "I am the Truth," he had violated, in the eyes of the orthodox traditionalists and the uninitiated, the fundamental, and most rigorously asserted, creed of Islam, namely that there could be no Associate to God; he had transgressed the boundaries that separate the Creator from the created. For that he was cruelly executed by the caliph al-Muqtadir; but his martyrdom was also the result of less exalted motives, rooted in theological rivalries and political expediency.

Egypt was the native land of two great Ṣûfîs, Dhû'l-Nûn al-Miṣrî (died 246 A.H./860 A.D.), one of the earliest of the mystics, who probably was a Copt or a Nubian, and Sharaf al-Dîn ʿUmar ibn al-Fâriḍ, who lived and died in Cairo (577–633 A.H./1181–1235 A.D.). His poetic style reflects the fact that he was a pure Arab. Two of his poems became most famous, a hymn in praise of divine love called *Naẓm al-Sulûk*, "The Path of the Wanderer," on account of which he was accused of adhering to the doctrine of *Ḥulûl*, "incarnation [of God in human beings]," and a poem ostensibly in praise of wine called *al-Khamrîya*, "Ode to Wine"; both poems must, however, be understood in the manner of Ṣûfî allegory.

The greatest mystic of Arab stock undoubtedly was Muḥyî ad-Dîn ibn ʿArabî, who was born in Murcia, Spain, in 560 A.H./1165 A.D., and died in Damascus in 638 A.H./1240 A.D.[21] His greatness is attested to by the epithet *al-Sheikh al-Akbar*, "The Great Master," which his disciples bestowed unto him and by which he is known to generations of his adherents to this day. In his great work, *al-Futûḥât al-Mekkîyah*, "The Meccan Revelations," he established a complete system of mystical science based on his mystic experience. He asserted to have seen the Prophet Muhammad himself who bade him expound on the divine mysteries. This he did in his work *Fuṣûl al-Ḥikmah*, "Gems of Wisdom," in which he meditated on the twenty-seven prophets from Adam to Muhammad. Another time, while he was making the sacred circuit around the Kaʿbah, a beautiful youth appeared to him who, in reality being a celestial spirit, revealed to him divine mysteries and bade him write down what he had seen in his visions. In Mecca, too, he met his "Beatrice," the woman who for him represented Divine Wisdom, a young girl by name of Niẓâm ʿAyn al-Shams waʾl-Bahâʾ, "Harmony, Eye of the Sun and Beauty." To her he devoted a *dîwân* of poetry in which he poured the sacred mysteries of "love" into profane phrases, but which he reminded his readers were not to be taken in their literal, but in an esoteric, sense, as symbols of spiritual, mystic experiences. Ibn ʿArabî, too, strove toward and attained the supreme goal of the Ṣûfî, the mystic union (*fanà*) with the deity.

Among the medieval Muslim philosophical works there are a few that merit individual mention because of their unusual character. For in these works the authors' philosophic thoughts and arguments appear in a literary garb and even attain artistic heights. The very rarity of this fact—we shall later see that even Arabic belles-lettres, the so-called *adab* literature, did not serve *l'art pour l'art* purposes, but frequently had didactic aims—makes an analysis the more relevant. Among them are found such illustrious names of medieval Islam as Ibn Sînâ, al-Ghazâlî (died 505 A.H./1111 A.D.), and Ibn Ṭufayl (born ca. 506 A.H./1110 A.D., died 581 A.H./1186 A.D.); they are joined by a group of anonymous thinkers and writers of the fourth A.H./tenth A.D. century known by their fraternal name of *Ikhwân al-Ṣafâʾ*, "Brethren of Purity."[22]

Not much is known about this latter group except that they were adherents of the Fâṭimides, who laid down their philosophy in a series of essays preserved under the title *Rasâʾil Ikhwân al-Ṣafâʾ*, "Epistles of the Brethren of Purity." These studies (fifty or fifty-one in number) contain the essence of their neo-Platonic ideas on nature and its relation to the deity, mixed with Pythagoraean speculations on numbers. However, one of these epistles is a charming allegorical tale in which Man and Beasts are contending before the tribunal of the King of Jinns for supremacy. The various animals, from the lowly cicada to the mighty lion, the king of beasts, accuse Man of arrogance and cruelty, of assuming domination and power over them; the accusers are trying to show their own physical as well as moral and ethical superiority over Man. As each genus of the animal world, of wild and domesticated animals, including fish and birds, send their speakers to plead their cause before the court of the King of Jinns, and Man answers their accusations, they express and elaborate the theological dogmas as well as the philosophical Weltanschauung of the Ikhwân al-Ṣafâ'.[23]

This is not the only example in Arabic literature of a philosophic idea cast into literary, or as it might possibly better be called, allegorical, form. Ibn Sînâ was the first to create the figure of Ḥayy ibn Yaqẓân, "The Living One, the Son of the Awaker [Vigilans, Wakeful]." For Ibn Sînâ he was the symbol of the eternal sage, at once youthful and ancient, seeker and guide. In this latter capacity, he discourses with the author (Ibn Sînâ) and his companions on the knowledge he has gathered and reveals to them its esoteric meaning. The essay is, in its intent as well as in its contents, the vehicle for conveying Ibn Sînâ's Ṣûfic philosophy, intensely permeated with Gnostic ideas.[24]

Ibn Ṭufayl's Ḥayy ibn Yaqẓân differs from Ibn Sînâ's in character as well as in concept. Far from being the young-old sage who guides the ignorant from the pinnacle of his wisdom, Ibn Ṭufayl's Ḥayy is himself the seeker and, beyond that, the self-taught sage—precursor, by centuries, of Rousseau's Émile. Brought up since his birth by a doe, far from any human contact, his only companions being animals, he develops, through his own insights and experiences and without any external guidance, the most complicated philosophic ideas and deepest religious concepts. Entirely on his own, he reiterates the evolutionary course of humanity, is victor in the physical fight for survival, and overcomes the age-old doubts and conflicts of attempted solutions to the emotional, philosophic, and religious problems known to mankind. Only after having attained, through his innate intellectual powers, the height of philosophic understanding and of religious certainty does Ḥayy meet with another human being. The first encounter with a creature of his own kind, who, like him, turns out to be a philosopher, confirms the results of his own intellectual journey and philosophic search.[25]

Somewhat different in character is the third work, which merits special attention from the point of view of literature. It is al-Ghazâlî's autobiographical work *Munqidh min al-Ḍalâl*, "The Deliverer from Error." Though he, too, was dealing with philosophic problems, he was writing of his own personal conflicts, struggles, and doubts, and the way in which he overcame them. Such a personal approach is rare in Arabic literature. In most works, the author's personality is concealed; only occasionally, in a sentence or two, can personal emotions be glimpsed. In fact, al-Ghazâlî is almost the only classical Muslim writer who emerges from his work as a personality in his own right, with a distinct character which does not remain hidden behind his work. There were others whose fate is known to us, often moving or tragic, like Aḥmad ibn Ḥanbal's, who fell victim to al-Ma'mûn's inquisition, or that of the martyred al-Ḥallaj. But we know of their suffering mainly through the reports of their biographers or by contemporary witnesses, not from their own words. Al-Ghazâlî did speak about his own path in search of truth and his emotional conflicts before finding it. This is the reason why he moves us, so many centuries later, as he stirred his contemporaries and the generations of Muslims following him who acclaimed him as *Muḥyî ud-Dîn,* "Reviver of the Faith."

This title was richly deserved. For al-Ghazâlî, probably more than any other Muslim thinker, may be credited with the restoration of vitality to philosophic thought combined with religious emotion in Islam. The positions of theology as well as of philosophy had hardened into dogmas of warring parties, each believing to represent truest Islam and to be closest to the intentions of its Prophet. The result was rigid, tradition-bound, lifeless orthodoxy. Ṣûfism was the only way to escape from its stifling fetters. But Ṣûfism threatened Islam with a danger of a different kind. The Ṣûfî, though often living in fraternal orders and following the instructions and way of life and thought of a master, was basically a lonely man who satisfied his own emotional needs and strove by and for himself to reach his personal goal of *fanà.* This could only be attained in solitude and was granted only to a few select men, in effect an elite. Thus, Ṣûfism ran counter to the very basic concept of Islam of being a community in which individual well-being and common weal were, to say the least, interdependent.

In his pre-Ṣûfic career, al-Ghazâlî himself took part in the propagation of orthodox thought in his capacity of teacher at the Niẓâmîyah academy in Baghdâd and as the author of many works on Muslim philosophy and theology. But as the result of what must have been an intensely personal struggle, he repudiated not only the work of generations of thinkers before him but also his own in a book aptly entitled *Tahâfut al-Falâsifa,* "The Collapse of the Philosophers." It was directed against Muslim theologians and their attempts at saving religious beliefs by casuistry and dialectics. In destroying their premises as well as their results, he became, for a time, a full-fledged skeptic. But the deeply religious core of his personality led him to spending a decade as a Ṣûfî in search of spiritual fulfillment. This period of withdrawal resulted in the conviction that personal feeling was as essential a factor in religion as was the strict adherence to the letter of the law. Returning from his retreat into contemplation to active participation in the community—for a time he even resumed his position at the Niẓâmîyah academy—he wrote his great work of reconciliation between philosophy and faith called *Iḥyâ' 'Ulûm al-Dîn*, "The Revival of Religious Sciences." In stressing the relevance of what he called "acts of the heart," he assured *imân*, "faith," its righteous place by the side of *fi'l*, "acts," in Islam, thus extricating it from merely being a body of laws and prohibitions, of "do's" and don'ts," and molding it into the deeply personal, passionate profession of faith that it has remained until this day. By emphasizing at the same time the validity of the traditional concepts, though stripped of the sophistry and distortion of extremist interpreters of all types, he led Ṣûfism away from its isolation back into the mainstream of Islam.

Al-Ghazâlî's *Collapse of the Philosophers* did not remain unchallenged. He was severely criticized by Abu'l-Walîd Muḥammad ibn Aḥmad ibn Muḥammad ibn Rushd (born in Córdoba 520 A.H./1126 A.D., died in Morocco 595 A.H./1198 A.D.), in his *Tahâfut al-Tahâfut*, "Collapse of the Collapse." One of the most outstanding personalities of his time, known to the West as Averroës, Ibn Rushd influenced, more than any other Muslim thinker, the development of Western Scholasticism through his famous commentaries on Aristotle.

The diversity of faiths, Muslim and non-Muslim ones, and the variety of interpretation of their fundamental tenets expressed through the great number of sects and philosophical groups aroused the interest of two great scholars, one a Spaniard, the other from Khurâsân, who lived within a century of each other. Both called their works *Kitâb al-Milal wa'l-Nihal*, "Book of Philosophic and Religious Sects." 'Alî ibn Aḥmad ibn Ḥazm (died 456 A.H./ 1064 A.D.) of Córdoba was an outstanding and somewhat rigorous representative of the Ẓâhirite school of the interpretation of the Koran and Tradition. This led him to a rather narrow-minded position with regard to some of the constructive principles in the creation of *Sunnah*, rejecting *qiyâs* as well as *ra'y*. In view of this orthodoxy, it is somewhat amazing that he should write what Sir Hamilton Gibb called "the first work on Comparative Religion."[26] In it he analyzed the beliefs of various religions according to their views on the origin of the world and on prophethood and refuted them from the point of view of Islam; he also discussed the various Muslim sects and philosophical schools and finally gave an exposé of his own theological views.

The second work with the same title, written almost a century later, was composed by Abu'l-Fatḥ Muhammad ibn ʿAbd al-Karîm al Shahristânî (died 528 A.H./1153 A.D.), who hailed from Khurâsân. His book is one of the best sources for the many religious groups in the East, including Judaism and Christianity and their heresies, Greek and Indian philosophy and the early Church Fathers. His account is objective and fair, in spite of his own orthodox Muslim belief.

Finally, mention may be made of a rather interesting type of literary work that at one time seems to have been in vogue, possibly reflecting, at least up to a point, a predilection for discussion on religious problems which still exists among Muslims. In the centers of Islam, Jewish and Christian communities lived in close proximity to their more numerous Muslim neighbors, and Jewish and Christian scholarship flourished, sometimes vying, sometimes collaborating, with their Muslim contemporaries in science and philosophy. It seems quite natural that the discussion often turned to the relative merits of their religions. The political and social problems involved, the questions of *dhimmî*, "protected people," and *jizyah* "head tax," even that of conversion, fall outside this essay; but these discussions created a special genre of literature, that of disputations.

These writings generally follow a pattern: a representative of the Jewish faith, a Christian, and a Muslim discuss the tenets of their respective religions, the superiority (or inferiority) over one another, and the merits of their "prophets." Often these discussions were alleged to have taken place at the caliph's court or in the presence of an assembly of learned men of all faiths; sometimes they may actually have been held in the caliph's presence, as was reportedly the case in al-Maʾmûn's time, who, in fact, was deeply concerned with philosophic and theological problems. One of the main issues in the debate concerned the sacrifice of Ibrâhîm's son demanded by Allâh. While the Bible explicitly gives his name, Isaac, the Koran, in the decisive passage, does not mention his name at all (Sûrah 37,vv.100f.—in verse 112 Isaac is called "a prophet among the righteous"). But it became a dogma for the Muslims that the *Dhabîḥ*, "the Sacrifice," was Ishmael (Ismâʿîl) not Isaac (Isḥâq) as asserted by the Jews on the strength of their Scripture. As was explained earlier in this essay, Ibrâhîm and Ismâʿîl are cornerstones in Muhammad's edifice of

Islam, as *ḥanîfs*, "prerevelation monotheists," through whom the rites of the Kaʿbah could gain acceptance into the strictly monotheistic new faith. Lesser issues stressed the ethical superiority of Islam over the other religions; others were disputes over their moral demands from their adherents.

A number of literary polemical pamphlets have survived, some written by Jewish or Christian converts to Islam, others by men who were born to that faith, sometimes inviting a non-Muslim to accept Islam. At least one work of this kind, of a high literary and philosophic order, was composed by a Jew, as an apology for his faith, written in Arabic and conforming to the style of these disputations. Though not strictly speaking *Arabic* literature, and though by far the greater part of the work is an exposé of medieval Jewish thought, however deeply permeated with ideas also essential in medieval Islam, this work by the Spanish-Jewish physician, poet, and philosopher Judah ben Samuel Hallevi (ca. 1085-ca. 1140 A.D.) may stand here as a literary example of this type of medieval philosophic thought. It is chosen not because in this work Judaism happens to be triumphant, but because it towers over the other possible examples as a philosophic and literary work of high caliber.

It is cast in a framework with a factual historical background, namely, the conversion to Judaism of the Khazars. Before their king took that step, he invited—says the author—a Greek philosopher, a Muslim theologian, a Christian scholastic, and a Jewish rabbi to expound to him the tenets of their respective philosophies, so that he could decide to which religion he should adhere. Through these representatives, Judah Hallevi analyzes the various philosophic positions of the Greeks, Christian doctrines, and Muslim philosophic theology; in the end, the representation of the Jewish faith and its religious expressions prevails, and the king accepts Judaism as his religion and that of his people. However, in the course of this work, Judah Hallevi reveals himself as a true fellow thinker of his contemporary al-Ghazâlî, with whom he agrees in emphasizing the ultimate superiority of the "acts of the heart" over the tyranny of religious dogma.[27]

CHAPTER 5

The Secular (Non-Religious) Literature

I *Scientific Literature*

Philology, Grammar, Dictionaries

The Muslims' thirst for knowledge and for understanding all facets of the world they lived in did not end with their historical, theological, and philosophic studies. They extended their investigation into philology, geography, and the natural sciences.

In the wake of their endeavors to solve the many-sided problems involved in determining the religious tenets of Islam and its philosophic positions, they created a variety of auxiliary sciences. As scholars, bent on establishing firm fundaments on which to rest their findings and their decisions, they explored all avenues that might lead to irrefutable, authoritative bases for a normative Islam, their primary goal. To establish the philosophical positions discussed in the preceding chapter, they had recourse, as we have seen, to *Sunnah* and *Ḥadîth.*

However, in view of the many definitions of what was right or wrong, they needed standards by which to assess the validity of the divergent assertions and the trustworthiness of their supporters. Among the ensuing research, two disciplines are specifically associated with Koran interpretation and *Ḥadîth* work, the main interests of Muslim religious scholarship. They are grammar and dictionaries and biographies of scholars and authorities. (The latter have already been discussed in a previous chapter.) Biographical data were needed to establish the acceptibility of a *Ḥadîth* on the evidence of the authorities on which it depended. Knowledge of *naḥw,* "grammar," which included what could be called philology, was necessary for the correct reading of the Koran and for understanding its true meaning.

Even the philosophers often had recourse to the differences in interpretation offered by the structure of the Arabic language in which minute changes in vocalization could produce a major change in meaning. Linguistic, philological, and grammatical studies were therefore no idle pastimes but essential and meaningful factors in serious research.

At an early time scholars began their investigations into the intricacies of the Arabic language. Two groups developed and often engaged in controversies with each other. The earliest school was established in Başra under the leadership of its alleged founder, Abu'l-Aswad al-Du'alî, who died at the turn of the first century of the *Hijrah*. Some of the most renowned scholars belonged to that school, among others Abû ʿUbaidah and al-Aşmaʿî, the authorities on pre-Islamic times whose works have already been discussed, and Ibn Durayd (223–323 A.H./837–934 A.D.), the author of *al-Jamharah fi'l-Lughah,* a comprehensive Arabic dictionary. The school of Başra could boast of counting among its members the Persian *mawlà* Sîbawayhi (136–77 A.H./753–93 A.D.) whose great work on grammar became famous as *al-Kitâb,* "The Book," par excellence. Another member was Khalîl ibn Aḥmad (100–182 A.H./718–98 A.D.), Sîbawayhi's teacher, who is credited with the invention of the metric system of Arabic poetry. His *Kitâb al-ʿAyn,* "Book on (the letter) ʿAyn," is supposed to have been the first Arabic dictionary. It should be reemphasized that most of these Muslim scholars did not restrict themselves to one field of scholarship, though their fame often rested on one or another specialty.

A competitor to the school of Başra grew up in the newly founded military settlement of Kûfa on the Euphrates. At first an amicable exchange of ideas was carried on among the two groups, but soon rivalry and differences of opinion and approach arose between the two schools. The men of Başra upheld stricter standards with regard to grammatical and philological purity and were regarded more reliable as historians and transmitters of ancient lore. However, the school of Kûfa, too, could take pride in its representatives, such as al-Kisâ'î, the authority on prophetic legends, and al-Mufaḍḍal al-Ḍabbî (died ca. 170 A.H./ca. 786 A.D.), the compiler of one of the most outstanding collections of Arabic poetry, called after him *al-Mufaḍḍalîyât*. The polemics between these two schools is discussed in detail in a work by the Kûfan scholar Abu'l-Barakât al-Anbârî (272–328 A.H./885–939 A.D.), *Kitâb al-Inṣâf fî masâ'il al-Khilâf bayn al-naḥwîyîn al-Baṣrîyîn wa'l-Kûfîyîn*[1], "An Impartial Discussion of the Conflicts between the Grammarians of Başra and Kûfa."

In the third century of the *Hijrah,* however, both schools lost their importance. With the shift of political power from Damascus to Baghdâd, these early centers had to cede their preeminence to the new capital, which developed into a new focus for scholarship, and the differences between the views of the ancient schools disappeared. Ibn

Qutaiba, the author of the *ʿUyûn al-Akhbâr,* "Choice Histories" (see below p. 111), and a well-known dissertation on poets and poetry called *Kitâb al-Shiʿr waʾl-Shuʿarâʾ*, "Book of Poetry and Poets", is one of the outstanding representatives of the Baghdâd school. Scholars of Iranian origin gradually became preeminent, as is evidenced by the fame gained by al-Zamakhsharî (467–538 A.H./ 1074–1143 A.D.), the author of a Koran commentary and of the grammatical work *Kitâb al-Mufaṣṣal,* "Book of Detailed Analysis." These non-Arab scholars used their philological studies as one more weapon in the struggle between Arab pride and Shuʿûbite anti-Arab feeling. Ibn Durayd, of South Arabian origin, the compiler of the *Jamharah fiʾl-Lughah*, was one of the defenders of Arabism against the Shuʿûbîyah; his *Kitâb al-Ishtiqâq,* "Book of Etymology," dealing with the etymology of Arab tribal names and incidentally also with tribal lore, served the purpose of enhancing Arab pride and fending off the non-Arabs' attacks on the Arabs.

Through the concerted efforts of the scholars of these three leading schools, Arabic grammar—syntax as well as morphology—was put on a firm basis. It has been asserted that foreign, in particular Greek, influence had been brought to bear in creating that system; yet it has remained valid, and almost unchallenged, to this day in the Arab world and is also still not entirely disregarded in Western Arabist circles. For instance, Ibn Mâlik's (died 672 A.H./1273 A.D.) *Alfîyah,* a versified grammar, and the *Âjurrûmîyah* by al-Ṣanhâjî (died 723 A.H./1323 A.D.), a compendium on grammar, are still being used as textbooks on Arab philology in Muslim schools.

In the first chapter of this essay, the difficulties inherent in the Arabic language itself were discussed. As regards the Koran, difficulties of new terminology, often expressed in words of foreign origin, were added. The Koranic language also offers peculiarities in style and grammatical forms, even in syntax, which the Muslim grammarians tried to explain and to integrate into their grammatical system. Thus, it was not only the unfamiliar and provocative religious ideas contained in the revelations of the Koran that made further interpretation necessary, but the very language in which they were couched was not that of Arab everyday life. In fact, it is held by both Muslim and Western scholarship that the language of the Koran represents a special type, based largely on that in vogue, in the Prophet's time, in Mecca.

The methods used by the philologians in these, as in other, fields could pass muster by the standards of modern scholarship. They tried to establish rules, explored the reasons for linguistic developments, and investigated the irregularities and divergences from the norms. They brought order and system into the mass of material that had accumulated as a result of their diligent efforts. In their search for supporting evidence, they turned to ancient Arabic poetry for expressions which had either fallen into disuse or were employed only by certain tribes or poetic schools. The context in which these words appeared in the verses served as interpretation and to establish specific meanings. These verses were then incorporated as so-called *shawâhid,* "evidence" (literally, "witnesses"), into the discussions of the basic roots from which the expression was thought to be derived. These quotations of often otherwise unknown or forgotten verses attributed frequently to unknown poets are in themselves of considerable value,[3] since they supplement our knowledge of Arab poets and their poetry.

In the course of these studies the need for dictionaries made itself felt. The earliest compilation, which however remained unfinished, was Khalîl's *Kitâb al-ʿAyn,* so called because it began with the letter *ʿayn* and ended with *yâʾ*. It was thus not arranged in the usual order of the Arabic alphabet, but on phonetic principles which are thought to have been derived from Indian linguistics.

The arrangement of these dictionaries strictly followed the principles of "radicals" of the Arabic language, that is, any word, whether noun or verb or adjective, and so on, was listed under its three (or, more rarely, four) radicals in their alphabetical order and in the order of their "derived" forms with their modifications.[4] Each entry contained an often quite lengthy explanation of its meaning in various contexts, a discussion of its morphology, phrases in which it was used, and other linguistic, philological, and intellectual discussions. *Shawâhid* verses, of a familiar or unfamiliar kind, were richly interspersed to confirm the philological analysis and in order to show the actual application of the word under discussion.

The overall organization of these dictionaries is somewhat uncommon and deserves special mention to avoid bewilderment for the user. Besides their usefulness for the Koran scholar of old, they were also intended to be of use to the poet who had to find fitting words with the final letter required for the ending syllable of the verses of their odes.[5] Therefore, the ancient dictionaries were arranged in the alphabetical order of the final (usually the third) radical; that is, if we take, following Arab usage, the root *FʿL (faʿala)* as a pattern, any word with this basic root would be entered, and have to be looked up, in the volume dealing with roots *ending* in *Lâm,* not *beginning* with *Fâʾ*. Within this volume, however, the arrangement follows the customary order of the Arabic alphabet.

This system was used for the first time in the lexicographical work called *al-Ṣiḥâḥ,* "The Authentic Compendium," by al-Jawharî (died ca. 399 A.H./1008 A.D.) and was accepted as the norm by the later lexicographers whose works are indispensable to this day for anyone trying to understand classical Arab literature. The *Lisân al-ʿArab,* "Tongue of the Arabs," by Ibn Mukarram (died 711 A.H./1311 A.D.), which in the old Bûlâq edition comprises twenty volumes, the later *Tâj al-ʿArûs,* "Crown of the Bride"—ten volumes in the Bûlâq edition—by Murtaḍâ al-Zabîdî (died 1205 A.H./1790 A.D.), justify the title *Qâmûs,* "Ocean," which al-Fîrûzâbâdî (died 817 A.H./1414 A.D.) bestowed upon his work, upon which the *Tâj al-ʿArûs* was based. In addition to these general lexica, a number of special works in dictionary form on special problems were composed, such as *al-Muʿarrab,* "Arabic Words of Foreign Origin" by al-Jawâlîqî (died 465 A.H./1072 A.D.) or Ibn al-Athîr's (died 608 A.H./1209 A.D.) *al-Nihâya fî gharîb al-Ḥadîth,* "The Definite (Work) on the Terminology of *Ḥadîth,*" a special dictionary for *Ḥadîth* works.

The modern student of Arabic literature and culture has at his disposal a variety of lexica and dictionaries. Of greatest value, and the most frequently consulted among these, is that compiled by the English scholar Edward Lane (1801–76), but unfortunately left incomplete by the death of its author. He based his work on the original ancient dictionaries and used, with English translation, their explanations and the examples of usage given by the classical authors.

Travel and Geography

The very vastness of the Muslim Empire and, even more so, the concentration of political power as well as of cultural activities in a few, yet widely separated, centers—at the courts of the caliphs and of the viceroys who became increasingly independent from the caliphs and who founded academic centers of their own—forced mobility on those eager to increase their knowledge as well as to find new opportunities for gaining fame and fortune. A *Pax Islamica* reigned for centuries over a vast territory in Asia and extended westward into large parts of Africa (the so-called Maghrib) and at times into European countries of the western Mediterranean; as a result, the uninhibited movement of men and merchandise and, through them, the spread of ideas, was greatly facilitated. Hence, Muslim scholars left their native lands to travel throughout the realm of Islam *fî ṭalab al-ʿilm,* "in search of knowledge."

This constant movement of scholars from one center of learning to another—a fact that is confirmed in the biographies of almost all the outstanding scholars of all kinds—is reflected in the interdependence of their literary works. It makes it almost impossible to distinguish their writings according to the provenance of their authors. In all the main branches of "Arabic" literature which have been dealt with in this essay, it is impossible to classify their *oeuvre* according to the authors' native lands; such a distinction would, indeed, be unrealistic. They were influenced by the great teachers in their special field of interest, regardless of the happenstance of locality; every region of the vast empire made its contribution to the sum total of knowledge, be it Spain and the Maghrib or the farthest part of Iran and northern India.

A prime factor in this mobility was the participation of the inhabitants of the Muslim regions in the commerce between East and Central Asia, as far east as China, and Europe and Africa, via the so-called Middle East. Muslim traders (who were joined by European as well as by Oriental Jews) could traverse the far-flung empire and the adjoining lands without restraint. How far afield they went and how far their trade was carried is shown by the large number of Arab coins found in northern Russia and in Bulgaria, as far north as Finland, Sweden, and Norway, and even in Britain and Iceland in the west. However, it is evident from the geographical writings that these coins reached the last-named lands through intermediary, not Muslim, merchants.[6]

An anonymous work called *Silsilat al-Tawârikh,* "Chain of Histories," written in 851 A.D. gives us the first Arabic account of China and of the coastal regions of India, attributed in this work to a merchant called Sulaymân from al-Sîrâf on the Persian Gulf. Seven decades later, in 921 A.D., Aḥmad ibn Faḍlân ibn Ḥammâd, the emissary of the caliph al-Muqtadir to the king of the Bulgars, for the first time reports reliably on Russia; his account formed the basis of the entries on that country found in Yâqût's *Muʿjam al-Buldân,* "Geographical Dictionary."

These Muslim traders, travelers, and geographers (often these categories were combined in one person) continued a tradition established from antiquity. Already in Ptolemaic times and before, seafarers plied the seas, charted the sea lanes, and established a short cut from the Mediterranean to the Indian Ocean via a canal roughly equivalent to the modern Suez Canal, which had already existed in ancient Egypt in the Twelfth Dynasty (ca. 2000–1788 B.C.). The spice trade through Arabia and the silk route from China through Central Asia and the northern tier of the Islamic Empire antedated the latter's foundation by many centuries. Equally ancient was the effort to set down the experiences of the sailors and the wayfarers in writing for the benefit of other travelers, often embellished by fanciful stories and legends for the entertainment of their readers. Among the ancient writers on the region we may mention the Greek Strabo (died 24 A.D.) and the anonymous author of the *Periplus of the Erythraean Sea* (50–60 A.D.).

A third incentive to the geographical exploration and description of the lands visited within and adjacent to the Muslim Empire was the need for effective administration of its far-flung provinces separated from its capital by a journey of many days or even weeks. The Umaiyads had already created a courier system for the purpose of communication with the outlying posts; this *barîd,* "mail," required exact knowledge of the roads and inns, the mountains, rivers and deserts, the settlements, large or small, encountered en route and the distances between them, the possibility of replenishing the provisions for the caravans from the products of the country including the availability of fresh pack animals, in particular, camels. Though the *barîd* was intended to serve only the caliph and his administrators and governors, it also provided information and assistance for the ordinary Muslim who wished to fulfill one of the "pillars" of his faith, the Pilgrimage to Mecca. The *Ḥajj* itself, in fact, constituted one more factor in the movement of large numbers of the populace.

All these factors combined to produce an imposing number of geographical works, the scope of which gradually widened to include, beside the physical description of the regions, detailed data about what we would call today their social structure and economic conditions. Included were statistical figures on the various products, notes on soil conditions, rainfall and climate, agricultural methods and irrigation, the principal crafts and industries found in the area. The works discussed the composition of its inhabitants and their relationship with neighboring groups or cities, observations on the outstanding personalities, the various religious denominations found there and the number of their adherents, and, last but not least, the history of the province or city or village under scrutiny. Thus, whenever the author either reports findings based on his personal observations or where he relies on those of predecessors who themselves wrote trustworthy firsthand reports, the resulting works of the Muslim travelers and geographers are a treasure house of social, economic, and historical information on the conditions prevailing in the flourishing Muslim Empire. The earliest of these, entitled *Kitâb al-Masâlik waʾl-Mamâlik,* "Book of Roads and Realms," by Ibn Khurdâdhbih (died ca. 300 A.H./912 A.D.), emphasized the topography of the lands visited. As head of the *barîd,* he had access to a great deal of information, and his work, written ca. 232 A.H./846 A.D., became the source used by a number of later writers.

From these records which are founded on eyewitness reports must be separated those writings that deal with tales of legendary lands and islands, such as the mysterious al-Wâqwâq, the speculations about the mythical mountain *Kâf,*[7] or the *majmaʿ al-baḥrayn,* "confluence of the two seas," which do not belong in the sphere of scientific geography but to the realm of half-mythological, half-folkloristic "tall tales." The best known representatives of this genre are the fanciful adventures encountered by Sindbâd the Seafarer which eventually found their way into the *Arabian Nights.* This fairly late collection of travel romances is partly based on real travels of Oriental sailors but also draws its inspiration from various non-Arab sources, including Greek ("Homeric") poetry and ancient Indian and Persian adventure stories, such as are found in al-Qazwînî's (died 682 A.H./1283 A.D.) *ʿAjâʾib al-Makhlûqât,* "Marvels of Creation," and Ibn al-Wardî's (died 749 or 750 A.H./1348 A.D.) *Kharîdat al-ʿAjâʾib wa-Farîdat al-Gharâʾib,* "Precious Pearls of Marvels and Strange Things."

A word may be added here on the general geographic and cosmographic concepts of the Muslims. Ancient cosmological ideas survived in the Koran, such as that of the two seas that are separated by an insurmountable barrier (Sûrah 25, v. 55; 55, vv. 19f.) and their confluence (Sûrah 18, vv. 59f.). They were taken to be actual geographic features, the location of which was the object of much investigation and speculation. The earth was supposed to be surrounded by an ocean, *al-Muḥîṭ,* "The Surrounding One," a term still used for ocean.[8] Then there was the mythical mountain *Kâf* held to be located in the farthest East in an inaccessible place. On the authority of the Prophet's Companions, the earth was described as looking like a bird, and even al-Muqaddasî still heard the Indian Ocean described as shaped like a mantle or a bird, before he could get a more accurate description of its features and its shape. From time immemorial stems the idea of the Navel of the Earth, the Omphalos, thought by the representatives of different cultures to be located in various places, among others in Jerusalem, in Mecca, or somewhere in

India.[9] In the tenth century A.D., the century of scholarly geographers and travelers, description of the earth emerged from imagination to attempts at factual data derived from personal observation or reliable reportage based on such observation. Al-Masʿûdî (died 345 A.H./956 A.D.), who spent a large part of his life as a world traveler, combined in his voluminous books both aspects, recording the legends and myths, often at great length, but adding critical evaluation and factual history based on accurate and trustworthy sources or on his own notes and research.

The serious scholarly geographical literature developed under the influence of Ptolemy's *Geography,* which was translated from the Greek into Arabic in the ninth century A.D., the time when the Greek philosophic and scientific works began to be translated into Arabic, directly or via Syriac or Hebrew. This served as a model for the first original Arab work of this kind by Muhammad ibn Mûsà al-Khwârizmî (164–ca. 236 A.H./780–ca. 850 A.D.), called *Ṣûrat al-Arḍ,* "Image of the Earth." This work remained the model for generations of later geographers. Its most distinguished feature was the inclusion of a map of the world and of the sky, the earliest map in an Islamic work, which al-Masʿûdî still consulted but which no longer exists. This work remained admired and influential until as late as the fourteenth century A.D.

This emphasis on maps was continued in particular by the tenth-century author al-Iṣṭakhrî (died 339 A.H./950 A.D.), who added colored maps to each country he described in his work *Masâlik al-Mamâlik,* "Roads of the Realms," in which he concentrated his main interest on the regions within the Islamic world. Iṣṭakhrî himself was stimulated by Abû Zayd al-Balkhî (died 323 A.H./934 A.D.), an earlier tenth-century geographer whose work, however, has not survived. Iṣṭakhrî requested Ibn Ḥawqal (fl. 332–367 A.H./943–977 A.D.) to revise his maps and the text of his book and to enlarge its scope. Ibn Ḥawqal traveled as far as Spain, rewrote al-Iṣṭakhrî's book, and republished it as his own with the title *al-Masâlik waʾl-Mamâlik,* "Roads and Realms." Far more original than Ibn Ḥawqal's is the work of his contemporary al-Muqaddasî (or al-Maqdisî), who spent twenty years of his life traveling through most of the Muslim countries. He described his travels in the lively manner of one who relives his experiences, in the book entitled *Aḥsan al-Taqâsim fî Maʿrifat al-Aqâlim,* "The Finest Classification on the Knowledge of the Regions" (in 387 A.H./985–86 A.D.).

The sum total of geographical knowledge thus gained was made available to the scholarly world in an easily usable form in a number of geographical works which were arranged in alphabetical order, in the form of dictionaries, with the names of the localities, rivers, or regions discussed as headings. Again, Yâqût (ca. 575–626 A.H./ca. 1179–1229 A.D.), the former slave of Greek origin, is outstanding. His *Muʿjam al-Buldân,* "Geographical Dictionary," systematized all the accumulated information in this manner. Historical memorabilia of the places treated, famous men born or living there, their topography and social conditions, and any other information available, even verses in which the locality was mentioned, are collected in this voluminous work. Another earlier work of this kind was compiled by Abû ʿUbaid Allâh ibn ʿAbd Allâh ibn ʿAbd al-ʿAzîz al-Bakrî, a Spanish scholar (died 487 A.H./1094 A.D. in Córdoba).

Almost all these authors added occasional remarks on their personal experiences to their notes on statistics and factual figures, such as encounters with saints and scholars, or other travelers or with humble men whom they met on the road. But the reader feels that such passages were interspersed to enliven the dryness of the report; they were not the main purpose of the work. Distinct from these—one might almost call them academic—reports are those of a few men who traveled for the sake of the enjoyment and thrill inherent in visiting foreign countries and out-of-the-way places. Outstanding among these were two men from the Maghrib, the Spaniard Abu'l-Ḥusayn Muhammad ibn Aḥmad ibn Jubayr (born in Valencia in 540 A.H./1145 A.D., died in Alexandria in 614 A.H./1217 A.D.) and Muhammad ibn ʿAbd Allâh ibn Baṭṭûṭah (born in Tangier in 704 A.H./1304 A.D., died in Marrakesh 779 A.H./ 1377 A.D.).

The former kept a diary of his travels in which the detailed description of the rites of the pilgrimage to Mecca is outstanding. Ibn Baṭṭûṭah's work is probably the most delightful travelogue to have come to us about those distant ages and faraway lands. After his first pilgrimage to Mecca in 726 A.H./1325 A.D., this wanderer by choice traveled throughout the Muslim world and beyond to Ceylon and the Maldive Islands, undertaking four extended journeys in the course of his life. The account of his travels is vivid, full of his own personal experiences, which included contacts with high-ranking personalities in the countries visited; these used him as emissary to other dignitaries and as representative to foreign courts, as he used them to further his own travel plans. His reminiscences of these journeys, which carried him also to Africa and to the steppes of Russia, were written from memory since his notes were lost in the course of his journey. Both as a contribution to knowledge and as a literary work of the genre, the *Travels of Ibn*

Baṭṭûṭa—through the accomplished translation of Sir Hamilton Gibb—have taken their place in the ranks of world-famous travelogues in the series of famous travels published by the Hakluyt Society, in itself a not inconsiderable accolade.

Medicine and the Natural Sciences

Arabic science reached its summit in the field of medicine and related sciences. The Muslim physicians and scientists followed in the footsteps of the great Greek physicians, above all Galen and Hippocrates, just as philosophy was guided by the Greeks; but they also made important original contributions to medical knowledge. The Muslims thus became the teachers of the West in this field, as they were in the sphere of explorations and travels and by transmitting the heritage of the Greek philosophers. Representatives of the many ethnic strains that constituted the population of the Muslim Empire and of the many religions they professed cooperated in this work; this was one of the most striking achievements of that era and its most enduring value, and, next to the creation of Islam itself, the greatest glory of the medieval Muslim world. Syriac Christians of all denominations, especially the Nestorians, "Ṣabians" from the Ḥarrân (in North Syria), Jews, Zoroastrians, and Muslims, descendants of Greeks, Persians and Arabs —all pooled their intellectual abilities in this common endeavor. Indeed, quite a few works of the great Greek philosophers, physicians, and mathematicians (e.g., Euclid) owe their preservation to the translations into Hebrew, Syriac, or Arabic;[10] often they were first translated into one of these languages from which retranslations into the others were made, though this process sometimes resulted in a garbled text. Many then were retranslated in the West into Latin and passed on from generation to generation in this language while the Greek original remains lost. In fact, until the Renaissance men raised the cry *Ad Fontes,* "To the Sources," the West knew the Greek authors only in their Oriental garb; the originals became known in the West only through the tomes which the Greek scholars who fled Constantinople after its conquest by the Turks (1453) carried with them to the West.

The present study was written at a time of strife and dissension in the area, and one can only look back with deep regret and nostalgia to the time when all the best minds of the age and the region, regardless of their cultural origin, religious faith, or ethnic background were working together in the common task of preserving a precious heritage for the common good of mankind.

While scholarship was cultivated in Egypt during the Hellenistic era, in the Academy of Alexandria,[11] from the third Christian century onward its standard bearers were mainly Syrian Christians, in particular the Nestorians. Founded in Constantinople two centuries before Islam, they established their center first in Edessa and then transferred it to Nisibis, in Mesopotamia; in the sixth century, the Nestorian scholars migrated from there to Jundêshâpûr, the Sassanian seat of learning in southwest Iran. There they met with Greek savants who had come from Athens as a result of the closing of the Greek schools by Justinian in 529 A.D. Scholarship in Jundêshâpûr was also enriched by contact with Indian learning. With the rise of Islamic power, it shifted back to the coreland of the medieval Near East where new academies were founded. In Baghdâd, al-Ma'mûn established a *Bayt al-Ḥikmah,* "House of Wisdom" (ca. 215 A.H./830 A.D.), with a library which was said to have contained some twenty thousand volumes, but of which no trace was left. Later, the Seljûk vizier Niẓâm al-Mulk founded the Niẓâmîyah academy of al-Ghazâlî fame in Baghdâd (458 A.H./1065–67 A.D.).

These academies were full-fledged universities, devoted to all branches of scholarship. It was there that philosophical and theological studies were pursued, disputations held, and legal and religious problems discussed. Students and teachers lived on the premises, often receiving a stipend or a salary and free lodging and food; libraries contained the books to be studied. A survival of these academies in our own time is the well-known al-Azhar in Cairo, which was founded in 362 A.H./972 A.D. by the Fâṭimide vizier Jawhar and which is still the most renowned theological university in the Islamic world. Though even now basically devoted to the study of religious Tradition and law, in the four great representative *madhhabs,* "rites," it has, in the last few decades, added secular training and the study of modern secular subjects to its curriculum. Yet, as in the old days, its fame throughout the Muslim and non-Muslim world still rests on the cultivation of traditional Islam and as an authoritative voice in decisions on problems of Islam.

From the modern point of view, the original contributions these academies made to widen the scope of medical knowledge were of equal importance with the preservation of ancient texts and the knowledge of the ancients through their translation. Connected with them were hospitals (*Bîmâristân,* as they were called with a Persian word) where students were trained and patients treated; they offered the scholars opportunities for observation and the study of illnesses and their treatment and remedies for them. As in Europe, dissection was not yet practiced; even in Europe the first official dissection took place only toward the end of the sixteenth century in Bologna.

The patients treated in these hospitals provided the physicians with rich case material, especially in those illnesses which were endemic to the Near and Middle East, as many of them still are. Thus, it is not too amazing that smallpox and measles, *al-Judarî wa'l-Ḥaṣbah,* were first described by Abû Bakr Muhammad ibn Zakarîyâ' al-Râzî, the great physician of Persian lineage (251–313 A.H./865–925 A.D.) and that ophthalmology occupied a high rank in medieval medicine. As an outgrowth of practical necessity, pharmacology became another field in which Muslim medieval science excelled.

The results of these studies were embedded in many works, some of which were comprehensive, "all-including" works on all aspects known to the physicians of the times. The most famous example of this kind is al-Râzî's manual, which is called *al-Ḥâwî,* "The Comprehensive Book." The *Ḥâwî* was a compendium, in some twenty-odd volumes, of the knowledge of his time based on his own research as well as on that contained in the works of his Greek and Syrian or Arab predecessors. In reality, only the first ten of these volumes are by al-Râzî, for the work was completed only after his death by his disciples. In its Latin translation, made in 1279 by a Sicilian Jewish physician by the name of Faraj ibn Sâlim ("Farragut") of Girgenti, it gained preeminence in Europe, as the *Liber Continens,* which it retained for several centuries. Besides this comprehensive work, al-Râzî himself, as did other leading scholars of the medieval medical schools, wrote monographs on specific diseases, such as the above-mentioned dissertation on smallpox and measles and on their treatment, on kidney diseases, on ophthalmology, and even on psychological aspects of illness and "bedside manner."

Another equally prominent physician, who has already found his place in this essay as an outstanding philosopher, was Ibn Sînâ (Avicenna). His fame as a physician rests on two great works, his *Kitâb al-Shifâ'*, "Book of Healing," and his *al-Qânûn fi'l-Ṭibb,* "The Canon on Medicine." The latter was another compendium containing the sum total of Greek and Muslim medical knowledge. It deals in an encyclopedic fashion with all aspects relating to medical theory and practice, discussing general medicine, drugs, diseases of all parts of the body, pathology, and pharmacopeia. This work, too, found entrance and acceptance in the West in the Latin translation made by Gerard of Cremona in the twelfth century. Its influence in the West endured into the seventeenth century; it is still studied and used as an authority in the East.

The need for finding remedies for the many diseases led the medieval physicians to an intensive study of drugs and the minerals and plants from which to derive them. This included scientific investigation of their qualities and their application in the treatment of specific diseases; in turn, this led to the composition of works on alchemy as well as on what may rightly be called chemistry. Again al-Râzî was the leader in this field, in particular because his work was based on scientific observation and was free from the mystical approach of his predecessors who were searching for the magical properties of the drugs. In this connection, the *Rasâʾil,* "Epistles," of the *Ikhwân al-Ṣafâʾ* may be mentioned once more. They contain, *inter alia,* discussions on the formation of minerals, on meteorology and on the elements explained in relation to the celestial bodies and systematized in accordance with the general neo-Platonic ideas of this brotherhood.

The pseudo-science of medieval alchemy is especially connected with a man by the name of Jâbir ibn Ḥayyân whose identity is somewhat obscure. A Ṣûfî of this name is known to have lived in Kûfah in the late eighth century A.D. In the West, he was famous as "Geber." A large number of writings on alchemy was attributed to him which, however, can be proved to be of far later, tenth century, date. According to Max Meyerhof, "the author [Jâbir] recognized more clearly, and stated more definitely, the importance of experiment than any other early alchemist. Thus he was enabled to make noteworthy advances in both the theory and practice of the subject. His influence can be traced throughout the whole historic course of European alchemy and chemistry."[12] Among the achievements that may be credited to Jâbir are the invention of methods for evaporation, melting, crystallization, and other basic chemical processes.

The activities of the scientists in the Muslim Empire extended into other branches of the natural sciences as well. Mineralogy created a whole genre of scientific literature, the so-called *Lapidaries;* the search for remedies led to treatises on drugs, and the interest in nature created studies on animals and plants. Works on the camel (we are reminded of its description as part of the pre-Islamic *Qaṣîdah*), the horse, the palm tree, and the like led to a type of writing that was literature rather than science. Books like al-Aṣmâʿî's *Kitâb al-Khayl,* "Book of Horses," or Ibn al-Kalbî's *Nasab al-Khayl fiʾl-Jâhilîyah,* "Genealogy of the Horses in Pre-Islamic Times," and Ibn al-ʿArabî's *Asmâʾ Khayl al-ʿArab,* "Names of the Horses of the Arabs" recount the exploits of famous horses and the story of their owners and describe and praise their physical characteristics. In the same way, the famous *Kitâb al-Ḥayawân,* "Book of Animals," by Abû ʿUthmân ʿAmr ibn Baḥr al-Jâḥiẓ (died 255 A.H./868–69 A.D.), contains folkloristic and mythological tales rather than scientific zoology. The same is true of two later books of this kind, one by the Persian al-Qazwînî (died 682 A.H./1283 A.D.), the other by an Egyptian, al-Dâmîrî (died 808 A.H./1405 A.D.); all these books, by the way, offered Muslim artists welcome opportunities for fine illustrations, and, as a result, there exists a number of illuminated manuscripts of these works with exquisite miniatures. Another noteworthy work of pseudo-science is the so-called *al-Falâḥah al-Nabaṭîyah,* "Nabataean Agriculture," by Ibn Waḥshîyah (third century A.H./tenth century A.D.), a spurious work, of Shuʿûbiyah tendencies, alleged to be a translation of an ancient "Nabataean" (here implying Chaldaean or Babylonian) work.

Muslims also made important contributions to mathematics, astronomy, and physics. To this day, the term "Arabic numerals" is used for the way our figures are written, though the Arabs used the term *ḥurûf hindîyah,* "Indian figures"; another important improvement, the *Zero,* called in Arabic *ṣifr,* "empty" (from which the word "cipher" is derived), was introduced in a tenth-century Arabic work called *Mafâtîḥ al-ʿUlûm,* "Keys to the Sciences," two and a half centuries before it found its way into Western arithmetic. The Iranian al-Khwârizmî (164–ca. 236 A.H./780–ca. 850 A.D.) compiled the oldest astronomical tables and the oldest work on algebra, *Ḥisâb al-Jabr wa'l- Muqâbalah,* "Calculation of Integration and Equation." This work, too, was translated into Latin by Gerard of Cremona in the twelfth century, but its original is lost. ʿUmar al-Khayyâm (died 517 A.H./1123–24 A.D. in Nîshapûr) whose (Persian) *Quatrains* are world famous, was primarily a mathematician and astronomer. Both algebra and astronomy, besides being cultivated as sciences, were essential for practical religious purposes: the former in particular in connection with the intricate Muslim laws of inheritance, for calculating the exact share of the heirs according to their degree of kinship with the deceased; the latter to establish the exact *Qiblah,* "Direction toward Mecca," and the times of the beginning and end of the fast of Rumaḍân.

For astronomical and astrological calculations, the Muslims made use of the astrolabe, originally an invention of the Greeks. This instrument was also an invaluable help for making nautical observations. The surviving early Muslim astrolabes, preserved in various museum collections, are of fine workmanship and rank among the precious Muslim works of art.

One of the greatest Muslim mathematicians and astronomers was al-Bîrûnî (363–440 A.H./973–1048 A.D.), who came from Afghanistan and who is equally outstanding as a scientist and as a historian. In this double capacity we owe to him a work on the calendars and the chronology of the ancient peoples called *al-Athâr al-Bâqîyah ʿan al-Qurûn al-Khâlîyah,* "Remaining Traces of the Eras of the Past," and also a work on India. His main contribution to science is a discussion of the earth's rotation on its axis and the exact determination of latitudes and longitudes; he also determined the specific weight of eighteen precious stones and metals.

It is impossible to mention all, or even most, of the men who contributed to the high state of scientific research achieved by their concerted efforts in all parts of the medieval Muslim world. Spain and the Maghrib as well as its easternmost lands contributed to the results. We have only to consult the special biographical works compiled by Ibn al-Nadîm (*Fihrist al-ʿUlûm* "Index of Sciences"; 378 A.H./988 A.D.), Ibn Abî Uṣaybîyah of Cairo (died 669 A.H./1270 A.D.), and Ibn al-Qifṭî (who died in Damascus in 646 A.H./1248 A.D.), to realize their large number, the extent of their studies, their interest in all branches of the sciences, and the high standard of quality of their work.

II *Adab "Belles-Lettres"*

Later Poetry

Side by side with the intense religious emotions, fostered by the circles of theologians of all shades of conviction, which often led men and women to asceticism or to withdrawal into contemplative Ṣûfism, life was conducted on a very worldly plane, especially at the courts of the caliphs and in the entourage of their governors and the rulers of the outlying provinces. This influenced the development of Arabic literature in many of its branches, not least in its poetry and in the emergence of popular entertainment literature.

Already in pre-Islamic times, the court of the Lakhmides at al-Ḥîrah, the rulers of the buffer state on the Euphrates created by the Sassanians against Arab incursions into Persian territory, was a center of royal patronage to which the poets flocked, where they would flatter the king in expectation of praise and remuneration, or try to gain his ear, through their poems, to procure help for their tribe and its causes. In the same way, the Ghassanides, the dependents of the Byzantine rulers to the north of Arabia, granted their patronage to pre-Islamic Arab poets who dedicated their poems to them. In the post-Muhammad era, the

Umaiyad palace at Damascus, and later that of the ʿAbbâssides in Baghdâd and Sâmarrâ, became the focus for the activities of the literati and poets. When the caliphs' power was waning, the courts of the upstart *sulṭâns,* for example, that of the Hamdânides in Aleppo, took over that role.

This shift from the desert of Arabia to the settlements and cities was accompanied by a change in the ways of life and caused an entirely fresh approach to morals and manners. No longer was the poet a Bedouin wandering through the desert in search of pasture for his camels; he entered the circles of high society and was in contact with the finest minds of his time that were concerned with solving the most subtle problems of theology and metaphysics. Thus, the obligatory themes of ancient poetry, the plaint at the deserted camp sites, the strain of desert travel, the feuds and battles of the tribes (though these continued in their new settlements) lost their meaning for the new poets. True, the pedantic philologians, at the same time the collectors and the critical judges of poetry, decreed that only those who would produce poems in the old style were worthy of the name of poet, though in fact only the so-called *muḥaḍramûn,* bards who had lived at least part of their life in the Jâhilîyah, could lay claim to that honor.

Almost the only survival of genuine expression of ancient sentiments were the *Naqâʾiḍ*, "Poetic Slander," which the Umaiyad poets Jarîr and al-Farazdaq (and al-Akhtal, who took al-Farazdaq's part) hurled at each other and which gave vent to feelings of rivalry amounting to hatred. Living at the time of the caliph ʿAbd al-Malik, they were still keenly aware of their ancient tribal feuds and of the prowess of their ancestors. Al-Farazdaq, in particular, took pride in his grandfather al-Ṣaʿṣaʿah, who was renowned for redeeming female infants doomed to be buried alive. Using the fame of one's ancestor to enhance one's own stature was entirely in the tradition of the Jâhilîyah poetry, as was the attack on one's adversary by taunting him with his forefathers' misdeeds. Both Jarîr and al-Farazdaq died in 110 A.H./728 A.D.

But the rising generation of poets had different experiences, far away from the desert, dominated by the exciting new life in the city. Thus, we find in their poetry, for the first time in Arab lands, the echo of personal attitudes, of human problems expressed in original ways, identifiable through their individual language as the poetry of a specific poet. Their poems were no longer interchangeable because of their near-identical form, style, and thought, as they had been in the Jâhilîyah, when verses, indeed, were frequently attributed to more than one poet, or whole poems disputed as to authorship. The style, the ideas, the metaphors, and the imagery of the outstanding poets of these later times have a recognizable cachet of their own; for the first time individuality made its appearance in Arabic poetry and was deeply appreciated.

In Medînah, ʿUmar ibn Abî Rabîʿah shocked the emerging pietistic circles of theologians and ascetics by enjoying the high life of Medinian society and by pouring out his love songs to his many ladyloves, some of high rank, in the very center of the new Muslim aristocracy. He still hinted off and on at motifs of ancient love poetry; but his poems expressed personal feelings, often only thinly disguising the identity of the woman to whom they were addressed.

The most renowned of the later poets among the Arabs of his own and of later times was al-Mutanabbî, "He who pretends to be a prophet" (303–54 A.H./915–65 A.D.). His real name, by which he is rarely cited, was Abu'l-Ṭaiyib Aḥmad b. Ḥusayn. His poetic style and his eloquence were equally admired by his contemporaries and by modern Arabs. Many of his poems were addressed to Sayf al-Dawlah, the Hamdânide ruler of Aleppo whose friendship he enjoyed for almost a decade and whom he eulogized extravagantly in brilliant verses, in an Arabic style which was considered first rate and inimitable by his contemporaries. But even then they needed commentaries to be appreciated and understood. Later he addressed his panegyrics to the Ikhshidide Kâfûr in Egypt. An admiring fellow poet confessed at one time his inability, try as he might, to improve on a somewhat unsatisfactory phrase in one of al-Mutanabbî's poems. But the poet also found a severe critic in al-Thaʿâlibî (350–430 A.H./961–1038 A.D.), who objected to his use of obscure language and unfamiliar words and to his excessive affectation and exaggeration, a criticism echoed by modern scholars. However, al-Thaʿâlibî also had high praise for those features that show the poet's skill, his inventiveness in endowing traditional motifs with new imagery, his finesse in introducing new ways into the old *fakhr* forms and new styles into the poetic art of expression in general.

Close contact with the high life of the aristocracy provided Abû Nuwâs (died 188 A.H./803 A.D. or 195 A.H./810 A.D.) with the motifs of his poetry for which he is mostly renowned. He was the boon companion of Hârûn al-Rashîd, of half-Persian origin, who openly despised the Arabs, his paternal ancestors. Though he also composed poems with the traditional themes of love, satire, and the chase, and though he even wrote religious poetry, he became famous mainly for his wine-songs. Because of them, and of his poems in praise of the beauty of young boys, he was considered immoral, blasphemous, and a drunkard, and it is recorded that Hârûn al-Rashîd tried in vain to banish him from his entourage.

In severe contrast to Abû Nuwâs' disdain of morality and piety are two other celebrated poets, one his contemporary, the other living some two centuries later. Unlike the lighhearted Abû Nuwâs, both Abu'l-ʿAtâhîyah (131–211 A.H./748–ca. 825 A.D.) and al-Maʿarrî (363–449 A.H./973–1057 A.D.) were deeply religious, disturbed by the shallowness of life and uncertainties of the times. Of Bedouin origin, Abu'l-ʿAtâhîyah turned from the frivolities of court life to that of an ascetic and devoted his gift of poetry to meditations on the mortality of man and other religious reflections. By disregarding the formal obligations of Islam, he incurred the reputation of being a heretic in spite of his donning the garb of a *zuhdî*, "ascetic"; his poems are of a philosophic character in which there are echoes of Manichaean views, though for the most part they reflect the doctrines current in Islamic philosophy.

Almost two centuries later, the blind poet Abu'l-ʿAlâ' al-Maʿarrî spoke of the world and its enticements in even more deprecating terms. The world was but a prison—more so for him than for other men because of his blindness—and death the ultimate goal and the end of all existence. This denial of the beyond in itself was utterly opposed to the outlook of Islam, which, in the last analysis, is positive and optimistic; moreover, he did not grant any religion preference over any other, if, indeed, he believed in divine revelation at all. "Ḥanîfs are stumbling, Christians all astray/Jews wildered, Magians far on error's way/We mortals are composed of two great schools—/Enlightened knaves or else religious fools.[13] As a poet, he was inventive and often forced his ideas into the straitjacket of artificial forms, as in his famous philosophic work *Luzûm mâ lâ yalzam*, "The Necessity of what is not necessary," usually referred to as *Luzûmîyât*. But the predominating theme of his poetry was the expression of his philosophic ideas about his own faith and those of other religions, in which pessimism, ascetism, and fatalism predominate. In his artistic style, he, like Abû Nuwâs and al-Mutanabbî, did not follow the restrictive rules of the philologians; he disdained to speak of fictitious loves he had never felt or battles he had not fought. He himself avers that his work is "moral poetry."

Instruction and Entertainment

Polite society was also fertile ground for nurturing that branch of Arab literature that the Arabs themselves called *adab* and which is usually translated by the Western term of belles-lettres. The term *adab* itself is of somewhat obscure origin. This writer would venture to suggest very tentatively that it might have come from the Sumerian term *é-dub-ba-a*, "school" or "university," which occurs in a tablet of ca. 2000 B.C.[14] In the context of Arabic literature, and as used by the ancient scholars themselves, *adab* literature comprises belles-lettres in the European sense, that is, works written for the purpose of mere entertainment; but it also applies to works that provided the educated with easily accessible information on various intellectual and literary fields. The novel, in Europe belles-lettres par excellence, is absent from classical Arabic literature, as is also drama, and only developed in modern times entirely under European influence. Another important aspect of *adab* literature was to serve the educated as a source for the requisite material for the formal style in which their official correspondence as well as their private forms of social affairs has to be conducted. It often also served didactic purposes, including teaching moral, ethical, and socially acceptable forms of behavior.

There were two types of *adab* works. The first were the numerous collections of pre-Islamic poetry, most often accompanied by full commentaries. The poems were assembled, either in *dîwâns*, which brought together the *oeuvre* of individual poets, or in anthologies, frequently compiled for the benefit, or by order, of a caliph or other ranking patron, as well as in arrangements of poems selected from a specific point of view. The first group, the *dîwâns*, were mainly "published" by later scholars (such as al-Sukkarî [275 or 290 A.H. /888 or 902 A.D.]) on the basis of the usual oral tradition through the *râwîs*; so were the anthologies. The latter were often bulky compilations, especially since they were mostly provided by the compiler with extensive commentaries. The best known, and most often quoted, example of this type is the *Kitâb al-Aghânî* by Abu'l-Faraj al-Iṣfahânî (357 A.H./967 A.D.). This "Book of Songs" was based on an earlier one compiled for the caliph Hârûn al-Rashîd, who had ordered an anthology of one hundred of the best poems to be assembled. Abu'l-Faraj extended this collection by adding a description of their tunes and the manner these were played and by writing full biographies of their authors. This led him on to narrate the events of their times and to comment on the contents of the poems, adducing more explanatory poetry by other poets, which, in turn, provoked an account of the events alluded to in the latter. The result was a huge work that fills twenty volumes in the old Bûlâq print (with another volume of indices) and even more in a modern annotated edition. It is a treasure house of information quoted extensively by his native successors and used frequently by modern Arabists.

Other collections of this type were the *Mufaḍḍalîyât,* called thus after their compiler al-Mufaḍḍal al-Ḍabbî (died 170 A.H./786 A.D.); the *Ḥamâsah* of Abû Tammâm (died ca. 236 A.H./850 A.D.), so called after its first chapter on "Bravery"; another collection of the same title by al-Buḥturî (died 284 A.H./897 A.D.); and collections of ancient proverbs by al-Maydânî (died 518 A.H./1124 A.D.) and al-Mufaḍḍal al-Ḍabbî. Abû Tammâm's *Ḥamâsah* is especially noteworthy; it was already famous in its own time; but for the modern Arabist its value lies in the large number of poems and fragments of poetry not found elsewhere in our sources. These are assembled according to their main contents in ten "books": *Ḥamâsah,* "Bravery"; *Marâthi,* "Dirges"; *Adab,* "Manners"; *Nasîb,* "Love"; *Hijâʾ,* "Satire"; *Aḍyâf wa-Madîḥ,* "Hospitality and Praise"; *Ṣifât,* "Descriptions"; *as-Sayr waʾl-Nuʿâs.* "Wanderings and Fatigue"; *Mulaḥ,* "Pleasantries"; and *Mudhammat an-Nisâʾ,* "Annoyance over Women."

The second type of *adab* works was composed for instruction, as handbooks for the use of the *Kâtib,* "Secretary" and as encyclopedic guides for polite forms and erudite or elegant conversation. Outstanding among these are two works by Ibn Qutaybah, the author also of various works on Arabic poetry, one called *ʿUyûn al-Akhbâr,* "Choice Histories," and the other *Adab al-Kâtib,* "Accomplishments of the Secretary." The latter is a manual on style, orthography, and lexicography, especially composed to help the "Secretaries" in the drafting of official letters and documents which had to be composed in conventional forms. The former is addressed to the aristocracy to give them advice and direction for the conduct of official, social, and private affairs. These are provided in the form of anecdotes, moralistic tales, and alleged historic examples of actions by prominent men and women and their success or failure.

These works are intended to serve as patterns for the ruler to decide on a path of action in situations that resembled those recorded in the anecdotes. Problems of government and war, but also personal dilemmas and moralistic attitudes were the topics discussed in this didactic, but at the same time entertaining, manner. The material for these works was borrowed from many sources, including in particular Indian and Persian ones, but containing also Greek and Jewish elements. Other works of the genre were composed by al-Jâḥiẓ (died 251 A.H./865 A.D.) and al-Bayḥaqî (tenth century A.D.).

Pure entertainment for the masses as well as for a more sophisticated audience formed an important part of the *adab* literature. The two outstanding examples of works addressed to the latter were the so-called *maqâmât,* a literary term usually translated as "assemblies" or "séances." Full of wit and learned allusions, they presupposed a knowledgeable audience that could appreciate them. The creator of this art form—for it was art and not instruction that the author had in mind—was Badî' al-Zamân, "Wonder of the Age," al-Hamadhânî (359–99 A.H./969–1008 A.D.). The leading character of his work was Abu'l-Fatḥ of Alexandria, the wandering scholar, the Muslim counterpart of the *Fahrende Schüler* or *Vagans Clericus* of medieval Europe, who lived by his wits roving through the land. The narrator of the *Maqâmât* pretends to have encountered this character wherever he went and entertained his audience with Abu'l-Fatḥ's erudition and the anecdotes he told.

The *Maqâmât* were composed in a style characteristic for this art form. They were cast into the ancient form of *saj'*, "rhymed prose" (the form, as will be remembered, in which the Koran was revealed). Each *maqâmah* dealt with a separate topic, the whole being unified by the persons of the narrator and the traveler, Abu'l-Fatḥ in al-Hamadhânî's *Maqâmât,* Abû Zayd of Sarûj in those by the later al-Ḥarîrî (446–516 A.H./1054–1122 A.D.). This style enabled the authors to display all the brilliancy of their erudition, their rhetoric, and their wit. The *maqâmât* became almost the best known and most highly appreciated literary works of later times among the Arabs; in particular, al-Ḥarîrî's *Maqâmât* were praised highly and remained a favorite in the Muslim world. They found imitators all over its sphere of influence, including, in Spain, the *Maqâmât* of the Jewish thinker al-Ḥarîzî (thirteenth century).

The masses had yet another form of entertainment. Like the ancient *quṣṣâṣ* reciting the "tales of the prophets," *qiṣaṣ al-anbiyâ'*, the storytellers in the streets and coffeehouses of Baghdâd, Damascus, and Cairo wove a web of fantasies around heroes and caliphs, fabulous travelers and scholars. Taking their material from whatever source they could find, these stories were assembled in the course of time into the world-famous *Alf Laylah wa-Laylah,* "A Thousand and One Nights"; the *Sîrat 'Antar,* "Life of 'Antar"; and the Abû Zayd cycle. The 'Antar romance centers around the pre-Islamic hero and poet 'Antarah ibn Shaddâd. Already in the ancient *aiyâm* tales, this black slave was described as strong yet magnanimous; his alleged heroic deeds and his generous acts are retold to this day in the coffeehouses of Arab cities and villages, and the modern littérateur, educator, and political leader Ṭaha Ḥusayn (1889–1973) recalls in his autobiography *Al-Aiyâm* how he listened as a child to the voice of the storyteller who recited the exploits of these ancient heroes.

Modern scholars studied the development of the *Alf Laylah wa-Laylah* from oral storytelling into the literary form in which they eventually were recorded and transmitted. Persia contributed greatly, to the *Nights,* through an ancient work called *Hazâr Afsân,* "A Thousand Tales," which in its turn had drawn on Indian sources. This foreign origin was already recognized by the ancient native scholars, as witnessed by an entry on the *Alf Laylah* made by Ibn al-Nadîm in his *Fihrist,* the catalogue of his collection of books, tracing it back to the ancient Persians, the Parthian kings, and the Sassanian epoch. Greek, and later on in Egypt, Jewish, motifs were adopted and became an integral part of the *Nights,* until in about the twelfth century A.D. they merged into the form in which they have survived and become known in the West, where they still remain the best known literary product of Arabian culture next to the Koran. A small fragment of a manuscript dated in the ninth century A.D., bearing the title *Alf Laylah,* "A Thousand Nights" (without the added "One Night"), discovered and published by Nabia Abbot,[15] confirms that a collection by that title was known at this early date.

The *Alf Laylah* stories were assembled under a framework already found in the Persian *Hazâr Afsân* source. A certain Persian king finds himself betrayed by his wife. He forswears marriage and instead orders his vizier to bring him each day a virgin whom he kills after having spent one night with her. The vizier's daughter Shahrazâd volunteers to attend the king; but by telling him a story in which she slyly alludes to another even more thrilling one and leaving both unfinished at the break of day, she fascinates her listener so much that he delays her execution and spends another night with her. Again the storyteller applies her wily stratagem by continuing the story she had begun the night before and again alluding to another, even more intriguing, tale, and leaving it unfinished at dawn. The king succumbs to her ruse a second time. In this manner, a thousand and one nights pass, in the course of which all stories are eventually fully told. By that time, the king had forgotten his original aggravation and made Shahrazâd, who in the meantime had borne him a son, his queen.

The character of the *Alf Laylah wa-Laylah* stories varies. They may be fanciful and romantic—tales of love at first sight or at the mere sound of a woman's voice abound—adventurous, roguish, and bawdy. Hârûn al-Rashîd and his city of Baghdâd form the center of one set of tales. Even philosophy takes its place within the ranks of the *Nights'* topics, showing at the same time the variety of the audiences that might listen to the storyteller and of their interests. In one of the *Nights* tales, the slave-girl Tawaddud vies with scholars, philosophers, and theologians to show the depth of her knowledge of all the refinements of theology, law, and philosophy. The heroes and heroines recite poetry which they attribute to famous ancient poets. But according to modern research only very few can be verified and accepted as genuine products of the alleged author.[16] The best known stories in the West are the "Fisherman and the Jinnî," "ʿAlî Bâba and the Forty Thieves," "Sindbâd the Sailor." The last named story, incidentally, was originally an independent collection of Indian origin and was incorporated into the *Arabian Nights* comparatively late. Since the first translation into a European language in the seventeenth century by the Frenchman Antoine Galland (1646–1715), they have become part and parcel of Western literary tradition and, in simplified form, are part of the literary treasures of European childhood from the nursery on.

Since beauty of expression, correctness of grammar, variety of contents, and refinement of style were valued highly, it is not amazing to find works dealing especially with these aspects of literary composition. Al-Thaʿâlibî's criticism of al-Mutanabbî in his *Yâtimat al-Dahr* has already been cited. The works on *ʿIlm al-Balâgha,* "Rhetoric," discuss the permissible or inadmissible in style and topics, the ways in which each specific branch of literature may or may not be treated, and the best manner in which to express one's ideas.

From the earliest times the Koran had been thought to be the ideal work in the Arabic language and, being the Word of Allâh, inimitable; its stylistic forms as well as its vocabulary were subjected to intense scrutiny. The results were works on the marvelous language of the Koran, including also essays on its *gharâʾib,* "strange [or foreign] expressions." Foremost among the works discussing this subject is the *Iʿjâz al-Qurʾân,* "Eloquence of the Koran," by Abû Bakr Muhammad ibn al-Ṭaiyib al-Bâqillânî (died 497 A.H./1103 A.D. in Baghdâd), in which he analyzes the Holy Book in comparison with a critical examination of outstanding ancient poems.[17]

Adab literature was intensely subject to foreign influence. Persian, Indian, and Greek elements are clearly discernible in it; indeed, many of the most outstanding *adab* works are directly derived from non-Arab prototypes. Ibn al-Muqaffaʿ (died ca. 143 A.H./760 A.D.), a Persian, translated Persian works into Arabic—among them the famous book of *Kalîlah wa-Dimnah,* a collection of fables, folk tales, and legends which is itself derived from the Sanscrit *Fables of Bidpai.* He is frequently quoted, by name or anonymously as "a Persian author," in Ibn Qutaybah's *'Uyûn al-Akhbâr* and other *adab* works.

The dividing line between *adab* and other literary genres is not always sharply drawn. Elements of *adab* character penetrated into historical writing, and historical facts and events were used (often fancifully elaborated and adorned or otherwise distorted) in works of pure entertainment, as witness, for example, the Hârûn al-Rashîd stories in the *Arabian Nights.* Modern Arab purists relegate in particular the *Alf Laylah* into the category of "folk literature" and therefore consider its style inferior and the whole genre of such tales second rate, both in contents and with regard to style and language. To the folklorist as well as the cultural historian and sociologist, however, they offer an invaluable mirror of the life of the masses, the customs of the aristocracy (even though probably exaggerated), and the ideas, dreams, hopes, and ideals of medieval Arab society as a whole. Nor do they deserve harsh judgment as literature; indeed, they bring a measure of naturalness and freedom in language as well as in form into the only too often stylized and schematized art forms of Arab literature.

CHAPTER 6

Retrospect and Outlook

From the preceding chapters emerges the picture of a diversified, brilliant, sophisticated literature equally concerned with artistic form as with variety and discernment in contents. Poetry and prose, philosophy and science, moralistic and ethical studies vied with each other; critical appraisal and discussion of content, ideology, and form were applied to the individual works. The height of medieval achievement reached by the Muslim writers, poets, and thinkers makes the ensuing stagnation—beginning roughly speaking in the late Middle Ages and contemporary with the European Renaissance—the more amazing. Granted that much of the brilliance of thought and of the forms in which it was expressed was owed to foreign influences—Greek, Roman, Indian, Iranian, and Jewish—these were assimilated and integrated in a manner that resulted in what must be called Islamic culture, with a character of its own, with a style of life and art forms (both in literature and in "fine arts") recognizably Muslim, different from other Western or Oriental art forms, however much these, too, may have been developed under the same influences.

The inevitable question arises why after such vitality, such daring probing into philosophical and religious problems and discussion of their effect on Muslim life and thought, intellectual and artistic creativity ceased. For centuries, into our own time, the endeavor of Muslim scholars was directed not toward finding new solutions for age-old, and still unsolved, problems, especially those of theology, but only toward refining the presentations given by their medieval predecessors. For centuries, no works appeared dealing *creatively* with the questions of free will and predestination, the essence of God, and the problems of His attributes, no fresh insights were offered. On the contrary, any attempt at *ijtihâd*, "free investigation," or any new approach was condemned as *bid'ah,* "innovation," and rejected as unacceptable. Thus, from approximately the fourteenth or fifteenth century on, Muslim literature is characterized by innumerable commentaries and supercommentaries; authors of *tafsîr* and *ḥadîth* works saw their task in reiterating the comments of the ancient authorities and in assembling in their "new" works the discussions previously dispersed in separate works. In poetry, too, the ancient themes had to be repeated according to the rules set up by the scholars.

Two factors prevented the later generations of Muslims (including many of our own contemporaries) from undertaking a "new look" at old established dogmas. The most cogent reason was the acceptance of the Koran as incontrovertible Revelation; if there had seemed to be contradictions in it, they had been debated and resolved in the disputations of the forefathers. Their struggles and conflicts had been settled, one way or the other, in these ancient discussions; their refutation or acceptance had decided the problems for all times, the decision then reached became established dogma, allowing no further controversy. *Bid'ah,* originally looked upon as either "good," that is, acceptable and fruitful, or "bad," unacceptable because considered damaging for the community, became, in principle, invidious. For that reason, the *bâb al-ijtihâd,* "gate of free investigation," was declared closed; ever since, decisions had to be made on the basis of the established canon, "by the book," so to speak, not through fresh interpretations of Koran and *Sunnah.* The *mujtahid* became an investigator of precedence through the canonical books, not, as the term would imply, an innovator, a searcher for fresh insight. Philosophy, too, ceased to be creative and froze into a kind of scholasticism.

However, under the impact of "Westernization," the need was felt to counteract its influence on Muslim youth. The critical studies of Western Orientalists, too, had to be met by modern Muslim apologists; thus, we find now leading Muslim educators and writers, in Egypt as well as elsewhere in the Muslim world, trying to interpret the religious tenets in modern (Western) rationalistic terms. This is especially evident in Muhammad Ḥusayn Haykal's biography of the Prophet, written for the expressed purpose of providing doubting and critical Muslim youth with a "scientific" analysis of the phenomenon of divine inspiration and the inner workings of the prophetic mind. The result, *Ḥayyât Muḥammad*, "Life of Muhammad," is, however, in fact a rewriting of the ancient *Sîrah*, with all the traditional factors accepted, the reality of revelation unquestioned; it is only a not-too-successful attempt at interpreting the miraculous and mysterious processes leading to the emergence of the Prophet in terms of modern psychology. Muhammad 'Abduh, too, though he urges acceptance of modern science and its application to the interpretation of the Koran, is only another apologist. For he uses the results of modern scientific research merely to justify and explain Koranic cosmology and its concepts of the natural phenomena through modern terms, without ever doubting the divine truth of the Koranic concept of Creation.

Whether writing in Arabic or using secular (Western or Eastern) languages, the majority of modern Muslim authors uphold the authority of the Koran and support the validity of the traditional interpretations and ordinances for all times. Thus, in the main, modern works on religious problems and issues in Islam are apologetic, conservative, and, on the whole, devoid of the creative spirit that characterized the works of classical Muslim thinkers. This judgment holds good, with very rare exceptions, in all quarters of the Muslim world. Even Muhammad Iqbal, one of the most forward-looking, seminal Muslim thinkers of modern times, returns in the end to his starting point, the inviolability of Revelation.

The two other fields in which the medieval Muslim mind excelled were poetry and the sciences. In the course of the centuries, science became, in principle, dissociated from religion. The exact sciences, those based on scientific observation of natural phenomena (the movement of stars, or the functions of the human body) or on mathematical laws, had, even in the Middle Ages, enjoyed some degree of intellectual freedom (though, of course, one must not forget the ordeal of the Christian Galileo and the mentality that caused it). Thus, the emancipated, liberal scientist of our day who happens to be a Muslim, could, if he wished, be as unfettered in his research by religious dogma as is his non-Muslim colleague. But in common with the fundamentalists of any other denomination, the orthodox modern Muslim scientist feels obliged to bring his scientific insight into harmony with orthodox beliefs based essentially on those of the Koran. That is the reason why so many articles and books by Muslims are written in an attempt to reconcile religion with science. This was essentially also Muhammad ʿAbduh's intention.

In the field of Arabic belles-lettres, the religious element was not a predominant or controversial factor. Poets and writers could, therefore, in principle, freely develop their art. However, even in this field, a certain amount of struggle has crept in. Conservative elements demanded from the modern writer that he adhere strictly to the classical language and forms. It was so daring a step for Haykal to write his novel *Zaynab*, with a contemporary theme, in the modern *naḥwî* idiom (with even some colloquial passages) that he dared to admit his authorship publicly only in its second edition, after it had been successful and had gained public and critical acclaim. Other writers adhered to the classical style, the famous littérateur and scholar Ṭaha Ḥusayn almost excessively so. But more and more, especially in poetry, the Arab freed himself from the fetters of classicism; both form and topics became modernized.

Drama, as we have seen, never was an important art form in Arabic literature. What has emerged in modern times is entirely derived from Western models and is, at least so far, of no great artistic merit.

What, then, will be our evaluation of the past achievements and the hopes for a revival of Arabic literature and of the ability of future writers and scholars to emulate the high quality of their ancient predecessors? The works of the past are accorded high praise by Western critics as well as by Eastern admirers; the former apply impartial criteria and weigh their judgment by both Western and Eastern standards. The Arabs value their classical heritage highly. However, while praising it, perhaps excessively, they have rested on their ancient laurels and so far have failed to create new masterpieces. Standing in awe of tradition, they resented even the most moderate expression of criticism and attacked any such utterance, even when it came from within their own ranks. Thus, bound by tradition, they obstructed the path to new creativity. This is not to assert that no new writers have arisen in the Arab/Muslim world, only that they have not yet founded a genuine new Arab/Muslim literature rooted in its own soil. Much modern writing deals with topical questions, such as politics. social problems, education, and nationalism, but these works can hardly claim to be art, nor do many of them reach the intellectual refinement of their medieval counterparts.

Two contemporary scholars, Sir Hamilton Gibb (died 1971) and G. E. von Grunebaum (died 1972), may be singled out to show the high degree of empathy into the Muslim mind achieved by Western scholarship, based on thorough knowledge of classical and modern Muslim thought and its literary expression. Both hold it in high esteem, though they are not unaware of limitations in the ancient works, due to their being dominated by acceptance of revelation as the final argument and arbiter. Both analyzed modern literature as attempts at "self-interpretation" (Grunebaum's term), as conveyor of ideas, and evaluated modern Arab belles-lettres by applying artistic criteria. If Arab/Muslim literature is ever again to reach the heights it attained in medieval times, Muslim thinkers and writers could do worse than to contemplate the ideas expressed by these two great Arabists in their many essays and analyses. On the other hand, there is no reason to believe that goal to be unattainable.

So far, however, if we want to find a measure of real creativity, the use of Muslim ideas in new artistic forms of expression (though rarely new approaches to the age-old basic problems of Islam), we have to turn to the non-Arab-speaking Muslim world. Iran and the Indo-Pakistan subcontinent have continued to bring forth poets who created exquisite poetry with free use of ancient symbols and imaginative artistry; but they wrote mainly in their own languages and therefore fall outside the scope of this essay.

Notes and References

Chapter 1

1. Sûrah 2, v. 257.
2. Sûrah 12, v. 2; 16, 105; 26, 192–5; cf. 41, 44.
3. See Ibn Ḥabîb, *Kitâb al-Muḥabbar,* pp. 246ff.
4. I. Goldziher, *Muhammedanische Studien,* vol. I, pp. 76ff.; see especially p. 78 (English translation, pp. 77ff.; especially p. 78).
5. See e.g., *Naqâ'iḍ,* ed. Bevan, pp. 83ff.
6. See Ibn Ḥabîb, *Muḥabbar,* pp. 263ff.
7. See Henri Frankfort, *Kingship and the Gods,* Chicago (1948), chap. 6, especially p. 85 and figs. 25 and 26. The interpretation of certain rites of the pilgrimage to Mecca merits a separate investigation.
8. W. W. Barthold, "Der Koran und das Meer," in *ZDMG,* vol. 83, pp. 37ff.; but cf. the author's article "Origins and Interpretation of Some Qur'ânic Symbols," in *Studi Orientalistici . . . Giorgio Levi Della Vida* (hereafter cited as *Studi LDV.*), vol. II, pp. 70ff.

Chapter 2

1. I. Lichtenstadter, "Das *Nasîb* der altarabischen *Qaṣîde,*" in *Islamica,* vol. V, pp. 88ff.; cf. Paul Haupt, *Biblische Liebeslieder,* Leipzig, 1907.
2. See. I. Goldziher, *Muh. Stud.,* vol. I, p. 43ff., especially 47f. (English translation pp. 48ff., especially p. 51).
3. N. Rhodokanakis, *al-Ḫansâ' und ihre Trauerlieder, SBWA,* 147,4; Wien, 1904.
4. See I. Lichtenstadter, *Nasîb,* pp. 63ff.
5. Cf. Georg Jacob, *Schanfarà Studien, SKBAW.,* philos.-philol. & hist. Kl., 1914–15.
6. For the following discussion consult I. Goldziher, *Muh. Stud.,* vol. I, chaps. IV and V.
7. For an analysis of the *aiyâm al-ʿArab* as an art form, see W. Caskel, "Aijâm al-ʿarab, Studien zur altarabischen Epik," in *Islamica,* III, Supplement. Cf. also E. Mittwoch, *Proelia Arabum Paganorum quomodo litteris tradita sint,* Berlin, 1908.
8. G. Rothstein, *Die Dynastie der Lachmiden in al-Ḥîra,* Berlin, 1899. Theodor Noeldeke, *Die Ghassanischen Fürsten aus dem Hause Ghafna's,* Berlin, 1887 (Abh. K.Pr.Akad. Wissensch.). E. Bräunlich, *Bisṭâm ibn Qais, ein vor-islamischer Beduinenfürst und Held,* Leipzig, 1923.

9. Cf. F. Rosenthal, *A History of Muslim Historiography*, Leiden, 1952 (2nd ed., 1968), chap. I.

10. For editions of Arabic texts, see Bibliography.

11. See I. Lichtenstadter, "Folklore and Fairy-tale Motifs in Early Arabic Literature," in *Folk-Lore*, vol. LI, Edinburgh, 1940, pp. 195ff.

12. See Bibliography.

Chapter 3

1. See A. J. Wensinck, *Navel of the Earth*, passim.

2. For books on the Koran, the life of the Prophet, etc., consult the Bibliography.

3. The writer was happy to find this conviction of hers supported by A. J. Arberry in the preface to the second volume of his *The Koran Intrepreted.*

4. The following discussion was published separately in slightly different form with full notes added, in a volume dedicated to the memory of Arthur Upham Pope, by The Asia Institute, in Shiraz, Iran, as "A Note on the Biblical Stories in the Korân", 1974.

5. J. Horovitz, *Koranische Untersuchungen*, pp. 10ff.

6. *Ibid.*, pp. 12, 130 (*s.v.* Firʿawn).

7. *Studi LDV.; Arabic and Islamic Studies in Honor of Hamilton A. R. Gibb*, edited by George Makdisi, Leiden, 1965, pp. 426ff.

8. See Bibliography, *s.v.* Koran.

9. For a full translation see Ibn Isḥâq, *Sîrah*, . . . translated by A. Guillaume, pp. 231ff.

10. J. Horovitz, "Die poetischen Einlagen der Sîra," in *Islamica*, vol. II, pp. 308–12. Leipzig, 1926.

11. Ibn Hishâm, *Sîrah*, 4 vols. Cairo, 1355/1936, vol. III, pp. 96ff.; trans. by A. Guillaume, *loc. cit.*, pp. 231ff.

12. I. Goldziher, *Muh. Stud.*, vol. II, pp. 10ff. (English trans. pp. 23f.)

13. J. Horovitz, "The earliest Biographies of the Prophet and their Authors," in *Islamic Culture*, Hyderabad, 1927, vol. I, pp. 535ff.; 1928, vol. II, pp. 22ff.; 164ff., 495ff.

14. J. Horovitz, *De Waqidii Libro*, Berlin, 1898; J. Wellhausen, *Muhammed in Medinah*, Berlin, 1882.

15. See Bibliography, *s.v.* Texts and Editions.

16. The most comprehensive and penetrating analysis of this field of Arabic literature is Franz Rosenthal's *A History of Muslim Historiography*, Leiden, 1952 (2nd ed., 1968).

17. See R. A. Nicholson, *Literary History of the Arabs*, London, 1907, pp. 355f.

18. See S. D. Goitein's Introduction to vol. V of the Jerusalem edition (cf. Bibliography).

19. For a thorough discussion of these conflicts consult J. Wellhausen, *Das Arabische Reich und sein Sturz*, 2nd ed., Berlin, 1960.

20. Cf. Introduction to Franz Rosenthal's translation of the *Muqaddimah* (see Bibliography).

21. Translated by McGuckin de Slane, as *Histoire des Berbères et des dynasties musulmanes de l'Afrique septentrionale,* ed. Paul Casanova, 2 vols., Paris, 1925–27.

22. See F. Rosenthal, *loc. cit.,* vol. I, p. lxi.

23. For a discussion of this question, cf. *ibid.,* pp. lxxxivff., cf. also pp. lxxivf.

24. Charles Issawi, *An Arab Philosophy of History,* London, 1950, *passim.*

25. F. Rosenthal, *loc. cit.,* pp. lxxxvif.

26. *Ibid.,* pp. ixf.

27. See Bibliography, *s.v.* Texts and Editions.

Chapter 4

1. For this chapter in general, consult I. Goldziher, *Muhammedanische Studien,* vol. II. (English translation, London, 1971.)

2. Cf. J. Horovitz, article "Islam," in *Encyclopedia Judaica,* vol. VIII, cols. 566–88, Berlin, 1931.

3. *Ibid.,* cols. 573ff.

4. See especially I. Goldziher, *loc. cit.,* pp. 248ff., English trans., pp. 228ff.

5. Consult Joseph Schacht, *The Origins of Muhammadan Jurisprudence,* Oxford, 1950, and *An Introduction to Islamic Law,* Oxford, 1964; see also Bibliography.

6. See *Encycl. Islam,* 1st. ed. *s.v. Farâ'iḍ.*

7. See J. Schacht, *Introduction,* p. 43.

8. *Ibid.,* p. 44.

9. *Ibid.,* pp. 60ff.

10. *Ibid.,* p. 60.

11. Cf., e.g., A. A. A. Fyzee, *Outlines of Muhammedan Law,* Calcutta, 1949.

12. For this discussion, consult in general I. Goldziher, *Vorlesungen über den Islam,* Heidelberg, 1910.

13. Translated by Walter C. Klein, New Haven, 1940.

14. For the following discussion, consult F. Dieterici's editions and translations of al-Fârâbî's works and his introductory discussions of Greek and Muslim philosophy (see Bibliography).

15. Discussed and translated by F. Dieterici (see Bibliography).

16. Edited and translated by F. Dieterici (see Bibliography). Professor Richard Walzer of Oxford University is preparing a new edition of this work.

17. See Henri Corbin, *Creative Imagination in the Ṣûfism of Ibn ʿArabî,* p. 30, n. 5. Princeton, 1969.

18. R. A. Nicholson, *The Mystics of Islam,* London, 1963, p. 59.

19. *Ibid.,* pp. 102f.

20. See Bibliography (al-Ḥallâj).

21. See above, n. 17.

22. I. Goldziher, *Muh. Stud.*, vol. I, p. 9, n. 1, translates this term as "Die Getreuen," the English translation, p. 18, "The Faithful Ones." The usual German translation is "Die Lauteren Brüder," in English, "Brethren of Purity." F. Rosenthal translates it as "Die Treuen Freunde" (*Fortleben der Antike*, p. 81).

23. See Bibliography. An English translation by L. E. Goodman is in preparation.

24. See Henri Corbin, *Avicenna and the Visionary Recital*, New York, 1960.

25. Translated by Lenn E. Goodman, New York, 1972 (see Bibliography for further references).

26. See H. A. R. Gibb, *Arabic Literature*, 2nd ed., Oxford, 1963, p. 114.

27. See Moritz Steinschneider, *Die Polemische und Apologetische Litteratur der Juden*, Leipzig, 1877.

Chapter 5

1. Gotthold Weil, *Die grammatischen Streitfragen der Basrer und Kufer, herausgegeben, erklärt und eingeleitet von G. Weil*, 1913.

2. Edited by M. J. De Goje, Leiden, 1904.

3. August Fischer & Erich Bräunlich, *Schawâhid-Indices*, Leipzig-Wiesbaden, 1934–45.

4. See Chapter 1, p. 8f.

5. See Chapter 2, p. 26f.

6. Cf. in general the chapters on geography, in *Legacy of Islam*, and in P. K. Hitti, *History of the Arabs*, pp. 49, 373ff., and see Bibliography.

7. See A. J. Wensinck, *Tree and Bird*, p. 42; I. Lichtenstadter, in *Studi LDV.*, vol. II, p. 68.

8. See A. J. Wensinck, *The Ocean in the Literature of the Western Semites*, Amsterdam, 1918.

9. *Idem, Ideas of the Western Semites concerning the Navel of the Earth*, Amsterdam, 1916.

10. Consult in general M. Meyerhof, in *Legacy of Islam*: see Bibliography.

11. Cf. Max Meyerhof, *Von Alexandrien nach Bagdad*, Berlin, 1930.

12. Cf. *idem*, in *Legacy of Islam*, pp. 315; 326–29; this quotation is on p. 327.

13. See R. A. Nicholson, *Literary History*, p. 318.

14. See S. N. Kramer, "Schooldays: A Sumerian Composition relating to the Education of a Scribe," in *Journal of the American Oriental Society*, vol. LXIX, pp. 199ff.

15. Nabia Abbott, "A Ninth-Century Fragment of the 'Thousand Nights'. New Light on the Early History of the Arabian Nights," in *Journal of Near Eastern Studies*, vol. VIII, Chicago, 1949, pp. 129ff.

16. Cf. J. Horovitz, "Poetische Zitate in Tausend und eine Nacht," in *Festschrift für Eduard Sachau*, Berlin, 1915, pp. 375–79.

17. See the excerpts from this work, no. 19, in Part II.

Bibliography

ʿABDUH, MUHAMMAD. See: Koran.

ABÛ YÛSUF YAʿQÛB. See: Fagnan, E.

ANDRAE, TOR. *Mohammad, sein Leben und sein Glaube.* Translated as *Mohammed, the Man and His Faith* by Theophil Menzel. New York, 1936, 1955; paper, 1960.

———. *Die Person Muhammeds in Lehre und Glauben seiner Gemeinde.* (Archives d'Etudes Orientales no. 16). Leipzig/Paris/Petrograd, 1917.

ARBERRY, A.J. *Avicenna on Theology.* London, 1951. (The Wisdom of the East Series.)

———. *Modern Arabic Poetry: An Anthology* with English verse translations. London, 1950.

———. See also: Koran

AL-ASHʿARÎ ABU'L-ḤASAN ʿALÎ ISMÂʿÎL. *Al-Ibânah ʿan Uṣûl ad-Diyânah* (The Elucidation of Islâm's Foundation). A translation with introduction and notes by Walter C. Klein. New Haven, Conn., 1940. (American Oriental Series, vol. 19.)

AVICENNA. See: Arberry, A.J.; Corbin, Henri.

AZAD, ABU-L-KALAM. See: Koran

AL-BALÂDHURÎ, AḤMAD IBN YAḤYÀ. *The Ansâb al-Ashrâf.* Published for the first time by the Institute of Asian and African Studies, Hebrew University, Jerusalem. Vol. V, ed. S. D. Goitein, 1936; vol. IV B, ed. Max Schloessinger, 1938; vol. IV A, ed. Max Schloessinger, revised and annotated by M. J. Kister, 1971.

———. See also: Levi Della Vida, Giorgio.

BALJON, J.M.S. *Modern Muslim Koran Interpretation (1880–1960).* Leiden, 1961.

BEVAN, ANTHONY ASHLEY. See: List of texts and editions, *s.v. al-Mufaḍḍalîyât* and *Naqâ'iḍ.*

AL-BÎRÛNÎ, See: Sachau, Eduard.

BISHAI, WILSON B. *Islamic History of the Middle East.* Boston, 1969.

BLACHÈRE, R. *Histoire de la littérature arabe.* Paris, 1952–56. 3 vols.

BROADHURST, R. J. C. See: Ibn Jubayr.

BROCKELMANN, CARL. *Geschichte der Arabischen Litteratur.* 2nd ed., vols. I, II, Leiden 1943–49; Suppl. I–III, Leiden, 1937–42.

———. *Grundriss der vergleichenden Grammatik der semitischen Sprachen.* 2 vols. Berlin, 1908–13.

BURDACH, KONRAD· *Die älteste Gestalt des West-östlichen Divans.* Berlin, 1904. (Sber. K.Pr. Ak. Wissensch. philos.-hist. Classe, xxvii.)

BÜRGEL, J. CHRISTOPH. *Die ekphrastischen Epigramme des Abû Ṭâlib al-Ma'mûnî.* Göttingen, 1966. (Nachr. Gött. Akad. d. Wissensch. I, Philol. Hist. Kl. 1965, no. 14.)

CAETANI, LEONE. *Annali dell' Islam,* Milano, 1905–26.

CASKEL, WERNER. *Das Schicksal in der altarabischen Poesie. Beiträge zur arabischen Literatur- und zur allgemeinen Religionsgeschichte.* (Morgenländische Forschungen und Texte vol. 1, 5.) Leipzig. 1926.

———. "Aijâm al-ʿarab, Studien zur altarabischen Epik," *Islamica,* vol. III, Suppl. Leipzig, 1929.

———. *Ǧamharat an-Nasab. Das genealogische Werk des Hišâm ibn al-Kalbî.* 2 vols. Leiden, 1966.

CHWOLSOHN, D. *Die Ssabier und der Ssabismus.* St. Petersburg, 1856.

CORBIN, HENRI. *Avicenna and the Visionary Recital.* Translated from the French by Willard R. Trask. New York, 1960. (Bollingen Series LXVI.)

———. *Creative Imagination in the Ṣûfism of Ibn ʿArabî.* Translated from the French by Ralph Manheim. Princeton, 1969. (Bollingen Series XCI.)

COULSON, N. J. *A History of Islamic Law.* Edinburgh, 1964. (Islamic Surveys, 2.)

DIETERICI, FRIEDRICH. See: al-Fârâbî; al-Mutanabbî.

ETTINGHAUSEN, RICHARD. *Studies in Muslim Iconography. I: The Unicorn.* (Freer Gallery of Art, Occasional Papers, vol. I, no. 3.) Washington, 1950.

FAGNAN, E. *Les Statuts gouvernementaux ou règles de droit public et administratif.* Traduits et annotés par E. Fagnan. Alger, 1915.

———. *Kitâb al-Kharâj. Le livre de l'impôt foncier* par Abou Yousuf Yaʿḳoub, traduit et annoté par E. Fagnan. Paris, 1921.

AL-FÂRÂBÎ. *Al-Fârâbî's Der Musterstaat,* aus Londoner und Oxforder Handschriften hrsg. von Dr. Friedrich Dieterici. Leiden, 1895. Photomech. Nachdruck, Leiden, 1964.

———. *Der Musterstaat.* Aus dem Arabischen übertragen von Dr. Friedrich Dieterici. Voran geht die Abhandlung: "Über den Zusammenhang der Arabischen und Griechischen Philosophie." Leiden, 1900.

———. *Die Staatsleitung von al-Fârâbî. Eine metaphysische . . . Studie . . .* Aus dem Nachlasse . . . F. Dieterici herausg. . . . von Dr. Paul Brönnle. Leiden, 1904.

———. *Al-Fârâbî's Philosophische Abhandlungen, aus dem Arabischen übersetzt,* von Fr. Dieterici. Leiden, 1892.

———. Angel Gonzáles Paléncia, *Alfarabi Catálogo de las Ciencias.* Madrid: Edición y traducción Castellana, 1932.
See also: Mahdi, Muhsin.

FARIS, NABIH AMIN, ED. *The Arab Heritage.* Princeton, 1944.

FAZLUR RAHMAN. *Islam.* London, 1966.

———. *Prophecy in Islam.* London, 1958.

FISCHEL, WALTER J. *Ibn Khaldûn and Tamerlane, Their Historic Meeting in Damascus,* A.D. *1401 (803* A.H.*).* Berkeley and Los Angeles, 1952.

FYZEE, A. A. A. *Outlines of Muhammadan Law.* Oxford, 1949, 3rd ed., London, 1964.

———. *A Modern Approach to Islam.* New York, 1963.

GÄTJE HELMUT, *Koran und Koranexegese.* Zürich und Stuttgart, 1971. (Die Bibliothek des Morgenlandes.)

GIBB, HAMILTON A. R. *Arabic Literature.* Oxford, 1926; 2nd ed., Oxford, 1963.

———. *Modern Trends in Islam.* Chicago, 1947.

———. *Mohammedanism, an Historical Survey.* Oxford, 1949. Also paper.

———. *Studies on the Civilization of Islam.* S. J. Shaw and W. R. Polk, eds. Boston, 1962.

———. *Arabic and Islamic Studies in Honor of Hamilton A. R. Gibb.* George Makdisi, ed. Leyden, 1965.

———.Trans. Ibn Baṭṭûṭa, *Travels in Asia and Africa.* London, 1929. (The Broadway Travellers.)

———. Trans. Ibn Baṭṭûṭa, *The Travels of Ibn Baṭṭûṭa,* A.D. *1325–1354.* Cambridge, 1958–. (Hakluyt Society, Works, 2nd Series, no. 110.)

———. and Jacob M. Landau. *Arabische Literaturgeschichte.* Zürich und Stuttgart, 1968. (Die Bibliothek des Morgenlandes.)

———. and Kramers, eds. *Shorter Encyclopedia of Islam.* Leiden, 1953.

GOICHON, AMÉLIE MARIE. *Lexique de la langue philosophique d'Ibn Sînâ.* Paris, 1938.

GOITEIN, S. D. *Jews and Arabs. Their Contact through the Ages.* New York: Schocken, 1974.

———. See also: al-Balâdhûrî.

GOLDZIHER, IGNAZ. *Muhammedanische Studien.* 2 vols. Halle, 1889–90. Photomech. reprint in 1 vol., Hildesheim, 1961. Translated as *Muslim Studies,* by C. R. Barber and S. M. Stern, 2 vols. London, 1966, 1971.

———. *Vorlesungen über den Islam.* Heidelberg, 1910.

———. *Die Ẓâhiriten, ihr Lehrsystem und ihre Geschichte.* Leipzig, 1884.

———. *Die Richtungen der Islamischen Koranauslegung.* Leiden, 1920. Photomech. reprint, Leiden, 1952.

———. *Streitschrift des Gazâlî gegen die Bâṭinîja-Sekte.* Leiden, 1916; reprinted 1956. (Veröffentl. der De Goje-Stiftung, n° 3.)

GONZÁLES PALÉNCIA, ANGEL. See: al-Fârâbî.

GOODMAN, LENN EVAN. *Ibn Tufayl's Hayy Ibn Yaqzân, a philosophical tale.* Translated with introduction and notes. New York, 1972. (Library of Classical Arabic Literature, vol. I.)

GRUNEBAUM, G. E. von. *Die Wirklichkeitweite der früharabischen Dichtung.* Wien, 1937. (Beihefte zur WZKM., Heft 3.)

———. *Medieval Islam. A Study in Cultural Orientation.* Chicago, 1946; 4th ed., 1954.

———. *Islam. Essays in the Nature and Growth of a Cultural Tradition.* Menashe, Wisconsin, 1955.

———. *Der Islam* (in Propyläen-Weltgeschichte, vol. v, pp. 23–179.) 1963.

———. Ed. *Studies in Islamic Cultural History.* Menashe, Wisconsin, 1954.

———. Ed. *Arabic Poetry; Theory and Development.* Wiesbaden, 1973.

———. For full bibliography to 1969, see *Studien zum Kulturbild und Selbst-*

verständnis des Islam (Collected writings in German translation.) Zürich und Stuttgart, 1969.

GUILLAUME, ALFRED. *The Traditions of Islam.* An introduction to the study of the Hadith literature. Beirut, 1966.

———. Ed. *The Legacy of Islam.* Oxford, many editions.

———. See also: Prophet, Life of the.

AL-ḤALLÂJ. See: Massignon, Louis; Mason, Herbert; Schimmel, Annemarie.

HAMIDULLAH, M. "Influence of Roman Law on Muslim Law." Madras, 1943. (Reprint from the *Journal of the Hyderabad Academy* Studies no. 6.)

———. *Le Prophète de l'Islam.* 2 vols. Paris, 1959.

HAMMER-PURGSTALL, JOSEPH VON. *Literaturgeschichte der Araber.* 7 vols. Wien, 1850–56.

HARTNER, WILLY. *Oriens-Occidens.* Ausgewählte Schriften zur Wissenschafts- und Kulturgeschichte. Hildesheim, 1968. (Collectanea, III.)

HITTI, PHILIP K. *History of the Arabs.* 3rd ed. London, 1946 (also later eds.).

———. *Islam, a Way of Life.* Minneapolis, 1970.

———. *Makers of Arab History.* London, 1968.

HOROVITZ, JOSEF. "The Earliest Biographies of the Prophet and Their Authors" in *Islamic Culture.* Hyderabad, India: vol. I, 1927,; vol. II, 1928.

———. *Die Hâšimijjât des Kumait,* herausgegeben, übersetzt und erläutert. Leiden, 1904.

———. *Koranische Untersuchungen.* Berlin-Leipzig, 1926.

IBN ʿARABÎ. See: Corbin, Henri.

IBN BAṬṬÛṬA. See: Gibb, Hamilton A. R.

IBN ḤABÎB, MUḤAMMAD. See: Lichtenstadter, Ilse.

IBN ISḤÂQ, MUḤAMMAD. See: Prophet, Life of the.

IBN IYÂS. *Histoire des Mamlouks.* See: Wiet, Gaston.

IBN JUBAYR. *The Travels.* Ed. and trans. R. J. C. Broadhurst. London, 1952.

IBN KHALDÛN. See: Fischel, Walter J.; Rosenthal, Franz.

IBN ṬUFAYL, ABÛ BEKR. See: Goodman, Lenn Evan.

JACOB, GEORG. *Altarabisches Beduinenleben.* Berlin, 1897.

———. *Schanfarà-Studien.* 1. Teil: Der Wortschatz der Lâmîja nebst Übersetzung und beigefügtem Text (SKBAW. philos.-philolog. u. hist. Klasse, Jahrg. 1914, 8. Abh.), München, 1914. 2. Teil: Parallelen und Kommentar zur *Lâmîja;* Schanfarà-Bibliographie (SKBAW... Jahrg. 1915, 4. Abh.), München, 1915.

JACOBI, RENATE. *Studien zur Poetik der altarabischen Qaṣîde.* (Akademie der Wissenschaften und Kultur, Veröffentlichungen der Orientalischen Kommission, Band XXIV.) Wiesbaden, 1971.

JEFFERY, ARTHUR. *Islam, Muhammad and His Religion.* New York, 1958.

———. *A Reader on Islam.* The Hague, 1962.

KHOURY, RAIF GEORGES. *Wahb b. Munabbih,* Teil I: Der Heidelberger Papyrus PSR Heid Arab 23; Leben und Werk des Dichters. Teil II: Faksimiletafeln. 2 vols. Wiesbaden, 1972. (Codices Arabici Antiqui, Band I.)

KISTER, M. J. "Al-Ḥîra. Some notes on its relations with Arabia," in *Arabica, Revue d'Etudes Arabes*, vol. XV, 2. Leiden, 1968.

———. See also: al-Balâdhûrî.

KLEIN, WALTER J. See: al-Ashʿarî.

KORAN. Koran verses are given according to Fluegel's edition of the text.

(ʿABDUH, MUHAMMAD) RASHÎD RIḌÂ. *Tafsîr al-Manâr*. Cairo, 1926–34. Cf. J. Jomier, *Le commentaire coranique du Manâr*. Paris, 1954.

AZAD, ABU-L-KALAM. *The Tarjumân al-Qur'ân*, ed. and rendered into English by Syed Abdu'l Latif, 2 vols. Bombay, 1962, 1967.

ARBERRY, A. J. *The Koran Interpreted*. 2 vols. London, 1955.

HENNING, MAX. *Der Koran*. Einleitung und Anmerkungen von Annemarie Schimmel. Stuttgart, 1966.

PICKTHALL, MARMADUKE. *The Meaning of the Glorious Koran*. London, 1930.

KOWALSKI, T. *Der Dîwân des Ḳais Ibn al-Ḫaṭîm*, hrsg.... mit einer Einleitung versehen. Leipzig, 1914.

LANDAU, JACOB. See: Gibb, Hamilton A. R.

LEVI DELLA VIDA, GIORGIO. *Les "Livres des Chevaux" de Hišâm Ibn al-Kalbî et Muḥammad Ibn al-Aʿrâbî*. (Publications de la Fondation "De Goje," n° VIII.) Leiden, 1928.

———. *Les Sémites et leur rôle dans l'histoire religieuse*. Trois leçons au Collège de France. (Annales du Musée Guimet, 53.) Paris, 1938.

——— and Pinto, Olga. *Il Califfo Muʿâwiya I, secondo il "Kitâb Ansâb al-Ashrâf*... traduzione annotata dal testo inedito. Rome, 1938.

———. *Studi Orientalistici in Onore di Giorgio Levi Della Vida*. 2 vols. Rome, 1956.

LEVY, REUBEN. *The Social Structure of Islam*, being the second edition of *The Sociology of Islam*. Cambridge, 1957.

LICHTENSTADTER, ILSE. "Das Nasîb der altarabischen Qaṣîde," in *Islamica*, vol. V, pp. 17ff. Leipzig, 1931.

———. *Women in the Aiyâm al-ʿArab*. (Royal Asiatic Society, Prize Publication vol. XIV.) London, 1935.

———. "Origin and Interpretation of Some Qur'ânic Symbols," in *Studi Orientalistici... G. Levi Della Vida*, vol. II, pp. 58ff. Rome, 1956.

———. "Origin and Interpretation of Some Koranic Symbols," in G. Makdisi (ed.), *Arabic and Islamic Studies in Honor of Hamilton A. R. Gibb*. Leiden, 1965.

———. "A Note on the Biblical Stories in the Koran," in volume in memory of Arthur Upham Pope. Shiraz. Tokyo, 1974.

———. "From Particularism to Unity: Race, Nationality and Minorities in the Early Muslim Empire," in *Islamic Culture*, vol. XXIII, pp. 30ff. Hyderabad, India, 1959.

———. "A Note on the *Gharânîq* and Related Koranic Problems," in *Israel Oriental Studies*, vol. V, Tel Aviv, 1975.

———. "Muḥammad ibn Ḥabîb and his *Kitâb al-Muḥabbar*," in *Journal of the Royal Asiatic Society* (1939) 1ff.

———. Ed. Muḥammad ibn Ḥabîb, *Kitâb al-Muḥabbar (Dâ'irat al-Ma'ârif).* Hyderabad, India, 1942.

LYALL, CHARLES. *The Dîwâns of 'Abîd Ibn al-Abraṣ of Asad and 'Âmir Ibn aṭ-Ṭufail, of 'Âmir ibn Ṣa'ṣa'ah.* Edited with a translation and notes. (Gibb Memorial Series, vol. XXI.) London/Leyden, 1913.

———. Ed. *The Mufaḍḍaliyât.* Vol. I: Text: Vol. II: translation and notes; vol. III: Indexes by A. A. Bevan. Oxford, 1921, 1918; London, 1924.

———. *Translations of Ancient Arabian Poetry, Chiefly Pre-Islamic.* With an introduction and notes. New York, 1930.

MACDONALD, DUNCAN B. *Development of Muslim Theology, Jurisprudence and Constitutional Theory.* New York, 1903.

MAHDI, MUHSIN S. *Ibn Khaldûn's Philosophy of History.* Chicago, 1964.

———. *Al-Farabi's Philosophy of Plato and Aristotle.* Trans. with an introduction. Ithaca, New York, 1962; rev. ed., 1969.

MAKDISI, GEORGE. See: Gibb, Hamilton A. R.

———. et Grosjean, Jean. "Al Moutanabbi: Tranquilles sont les espions sur tes visites nocturnes. Remarques," *La Nouvelle Revue Française* 220 (Avril 1971).

MASON, HERBERT. See also: Massignon, Louis.

———. *Two Statesmen of Mediaeval Islam: Vizir Ibn Hubayra (499–560 A.H./1105–1165 A.D.) and Caliph an-Nâṣir li-Dîn Allâh (553–622 A.H./1158–1225 A.D.).* The Hague/Paris, 1972.

MASSIGNON, LOUIS. *La Passion d'al-Hosayn ibn Mansour al-Hallaj, martyr mystique de l'Islam.* 2 vols. Paris, 1922. [A new ed. in English is being prepared by Herbert Mason, under the auspices of the Bollingen Foundation, in Princeton, New Jersey.]

———. *Diwan.* Traduit et présenté. Paris, 1955.

MA'ṢÛMI, M. ṢAGHÎR ḤASAN. *Imâm Râzî's 'Ilm al-Akhlâq.* English translation of his *Kitâb al-Nafs wa' l-Rûḥ wa Sharḥ Quwâhumâ.* Islamabad, Pakistan: Islamic Research Institute, 1969.

AL-MAWARDÎ, ABÛ'L-ḤASAN. See: Fagnan, E.

MEYERHOF, MAX. *Von Alexandrien nach Bagdad. Ein Beitrag zur Geschichte des Philosophischen und Medizinischen Unterrichts bei den Arabern.* (Abh. K. Pr. Akad. Wissnsch., Phil.-hist. Klasse, xxiii.) Berlin, 1930.

———. "Science and Medicine" in *Legacy of Islam.* Oxford, 1931.

AL-MUTANABBÎ. *Carmina cum commentario Wâḥidii primum edidit* . . . Fr. Dieterici. Berlin, 1861.

NICHOLSON, R. A. *A Literary History of the Arabs.* London, 1907; 2nd ed., Cambridge, 1930; now also in paperback.

———. *Eastern Poetry and Prose.* Cambridge, 1922.

———. *The Mystics of Islam.* New York, 1975.

———. *Studies in Islamic Poetry.* Cambridge, 1921; repr., 1969.

NIELSEN, DITLEF. *Handbuch der Altarabischen Altertumskunde.* Copenhagen, 1927.

NOELDEKE, THEODOR. *Die Ghassanischen Fürsten aus dem Hause Ghafna's,* in Abh. Pr. Akad. Wissensch., Berlin, 1887.

——— *Beiträge zur Kenntniss der Poesie der alten Araber.* Hannover, 1864.
——— *Fünf Moʿallaqât übersetzt und erklärt,* in SBWA. (Phil. hist. Klasse, vol. CXL, vii, CXLII, v, CXLIV, i). Wien, 1899–1901.

NOELDEKE, THEODOR and SCHWALLY, F. *Geschichte des Qorans.* 2nd ed., Leipzig, 1908–38: repr., Hildesheim, 1961.
———. Full bibliography in the *Orientalische Studien Th. N. . . . gewidmet* and "Nachtrag zu dem Verzeichnis der Schriften Th. N.," in F. Rosenthal, *Die Aramäistische Forschung,* q.v.

PARET, RUDI. *Die legendäre Maghâzi Literatur.* Arabische Dichtungen über die muslimischen Kriegszüge zu Mohammads Zeit. Tübingen, 1930.
——— *Der Ritterroman von ʿUmar an-Nuʿmân und seine Stellung zur Sammlung von 1001 Nacht.* Tübingen, 1927.
———. *Sîrat Saif ibn Dhî Jazân.* Ein arabischer Volksroman. Hannover, 1924.

PERLMANN, MOSHE. *Ibn Kammuna's Examination of the Three Faiths,* a 13th century essay in the comparative study of religion, trans. with an introduction and notes. Los Angeles, 1972.
———. "A Late Muslim Jewish Disputation," *Proceedings of the American Academy for Jewish Research,* vol. XII. New York, 1942.

PHILBY, H. ST. JOHN B. P. *The Background of Islam, being a Sketch of Arabian History in Pre-Islamic Times.* Alexandria, 1947.
———. *The Empty Quarter.* London, 1933.
———. *Sheba's Daughter . . .* with an appendix on the rock inscriptions by A. F. L. Beeston. London, 1939.

PHILLIPS, WENDELL. *Qataban and Sheba,* exploring the ancient kingdoms on the biblical spice routes of Arabia. London, 1953.

PINTO, OLGA. See: Levi Della Vida, Giorgio.

POLK, W. R. See: Gibb, Hamilton A. R.

PROPHET, LIFE OF THE

(a) *ARABIC*

al-Sîrah al-Nabawîya li-Ibn Hishâm. 4 vols. Cairo, 1936ff.

Das Leben Muḥammeds nach Muḥammed ibn Isḥâḳ . . . ed. F. Wüstenfeld. 2 vols. Göttingen, 1858–1860; 2nd pr., Leipzig, 1901.

(b) *TRANSLATIONS*

Sîrah . . . , The Life of Muhammad. Trans. A. Guillaume. Oxford, 1958.

Das Leben Muhammeds . . . übersetzt v. G. Weil. Stuttgart, 1864.

(c) LIFE OF MUHAMMAD

MUIR, W. *The Life of Mahomet and History of Islam.* 4 vols. London, 1858–61.

SPRENGER, A. *Das Leben u. die Lehre Mohammeds.* 3 vols. 2nd ed., Berlin, 1869.

BUHL, FRANTS. *Das Leben Muhammeds.* Trans. from the Danish by H. H. Schaeder. Leipzig, 1930.

QAYS IBN AL-KHAṬÎM. See: Kowalski, T.

RAHMAN, F. See: Fazlur Rahman.

RIḌÂ, RASHÎD. See: Koran.

AR-RÂZÎ. See Maʿṣûmî, M. S. H.

ROSENTHAL, ERWIN I. J. *Ibn Khaldun's Gedanken über den Staat: Ein Beitrag zur Geschichte der mittelalterlichen Staatslehre.* Berlin und München, 1932.

ROSENTHAL, FRANZ. *Die Aramäistische Forschung seit Theodor Noeldeke's Veröffentlichungen.* Leiden, 1964. (Photo-mech. Nachdruck.)

———. *History of Muslim Historiography.* Leiden, 1952; 2nd ed., 1968.

———. *Ibn Khaldûn, the Muqaddimah. An Introduction to History.* Trans. from Arabic. 3 vols. New York, 1958. (Bollingen Series, XLIII.)

———. *The Herb. Hashish versus Medieval Muslim Society.* Leiden, 1971.

———. *Das Fortleben der Antike im Islam.* Zürich und Stuttgart, 1965. (Die Bibliothek des Morgenlandes.)

RÜCKERT, FRIEDRICH. *Hamasa oder die ältesten arabischen Volkslieder,* gesammelt von Abu Temmâm, übsersetzt und erläutert. Stuttgart, 1846.

———. *Orientalische Dichtung in der Übersetzung Friedrich Rückerts.* Herausgegeben und eingeleitet von Annemarie Schimmel. Bremen, 1963.

SACHAU, EDUARD, Ed. *Alberuni's India, an account of the religion, philosophy, literature, chronology, astronomy, customs, laws and astrology of India about 1030.* London, 1887. English ed. with notes and indices, London, 1888, 2 vols.

SCHACHT, JOSEPH. *An Introduction to Islamic Law.* Oxford, 1964.

The Origins of Muhammadan Jurisprudence. Oxford, 1950.

SCHIMMEL, ANNEMARIE. See also: Koran; Rückert, Friedrich.

———. *Al-Halladsch, Märtyrer der Gottesliebe.* Leben und Legende, ausgewählt, übersetzt und eingeleitet. Köln, 1968.

———. *Die Bildersprache Dschelaladdin Rumis.* (Beiträge zur Sprach- u. Kulturgeschichte des Orients, Heft 2.) Walldorf, 1949.

———. *Islamic Calligraphy.* (Iconography of Religions, Section xxii: Islam, fasc. i.) Leiden, 1970.

SCHLOESSINGER, MAX. See: al-Balâdhûrî.

SCHROEDER, ERIC. *Muhammad's People. A Tale by Anthology,* Portland, Maine, 1955.

AL-SHANFARÀ. See: Jacob, Georg.

SHAW, STANFORD J. See: Gibb, Hamilton A. R.

SNOUCK HURGRONJE, C. *Mekka.* 2 vols. The Hague, 1888, 1889.

STEINSCHNEIDER, MORITZ. *Die arabischen Übersetzungen aus dem Griechischen.* 1889, 1891, 1893, 1896. (Reprinted collectively in Graz, 1960.)

———. *Die arabische Literatur der Juden.* Frankfurt a/M., 1902.

———. *Hebräische Übersetzungen des Mittelalters.* Berlin, 1893.

———. *Europäische Übersetzungen aus dem Arabischen.* Wien, 1904.

———. *Polemische und apologetische Literatur in Arabischer Sprache zwischen Muslimen, Christen und Juden,* nebst Anhängen verwandten Inhalts. (Abhandlungen für die Kunde des Morgenlandes, VI, 3.) Leipzig, 1877.

AL-ṬABARÎ, ABÛ JAʿFAR MUḤAMMAD B. JARÎR. *The Reign of al-Muʿtaṣim* (833–842). Transl. and annotated by Elma Marin. (American Oriental Series, vol. 35.) New Haven, Connecticut, 1951.

WALZER, RICHARD. *Greek into Arabic*. Oxford, 1962.

WATT, W. MONTGOMERY. *Bell's Introduction to the Koran*. (Islamic Surveys, No. 8.) Edinburgh, 1970.

———. *Muhammad at Mecca*. Oxford, 1953.

———. *Muhammad at Medinah*. Oxford, 1956.

———. *The Faith and Practice of al-Ghazālī*. London, 1967.

———. *Der Islam* (from Propyläen-Weltgeschichte, vol. 16, pp. 243–86).

WELLHAUSEN, JULIUS. *Das Arabische Reich und sein Sturz*. Berlin, 1902; photomech. reprint, 1960. English trans. by Margaret G. Weir: *The Arab Kingdom and Its Fall*. Calcutta, 1927.

———. *Reste Arabischen Heidentums*. 2nd. ed. Berlin, 1897.

———. *Medinah vor dem Islam*. (Skizzen und Vorarbeiten IV, 1.) Berlin, 1889.

———. *Muhammads Schreiben und die Gesandtschaften an ihn*. (Skizzen und Vorarbeiten IV, 3.) Berlin, 1889.

———. *Die Lieder der Hudhailiten*. See: *Hudhaylî Dîwân*.

———. *Muhammad in Medinah*. Berlin, 1882.

WENSINCK, A. J. *A Handbook of Early Muhammadan Tradition*, alphabetically arranged. Leiden, 1927.

———. *The Ideas of the Western Semites concerning the Navel of the Earth*. Amsterdam, 1916. *The Ocean in the Literature of the Western Semites*. Amsterdam, 1918. *Tree and Bird as Cosmological Symbols in Western Asia*. Amsterdam, 1921. (Verhand. der Koninkl. Akad. van Wetensch. te Amsterdam, Afd. Letterkunde, N. R. deel XI, 2; XVII, 1; XXII, 1.)

WIET, GASTON. *Journal d'un Bourgeois du Caire. Ibn Iyâs, Histoire des Mamlouks*. Traduit et annoté par Gaston Wiet. (Bibliothèque Générale de l'Ecole Pratique des Hautes Etudes, viᵉ Section.) Paris, 1955.

WILLIAMS, JOHN ALDEN. *Islam*. New York, 1963; paperback.

———. *Themes of Islamic Civilization*. Berkeley, 1971.

WÜSTENFELD, FERDINAND. *Genealogische Tabellen der Arabischen Stämme und Familien*. Göttingen, 1852. Register . . . Göttingen, 1853.

———. *Vergleichungstabellen der muhammedanischen und christlichen Zeitrechnung* . . . Leipzig, 1844. Fortsetzung . . . bis 1500, von E. Mahler, Leipzig, 1887. [continued by B. Spuler.]

———. *Die Geschichtsschreiber der Araber und ihre Werke*. (Abh. Kgl.Ges. d. Wiss., vols. XXVII & XXIX) Göttingen, 1882.

See also: Prophet, Life of the.

Select List of Texts and Editions

AHLWARDT. *The Divans of the six ancient Arabic poets*, Ennābigha, ʿAntara, Tharafa, Zuhair, ʿAlqama and Imruulqais. London, 1870.

Kitâb al-Aghânî, by Abuʾl-Faraj al-Iṣfahânî. New ed., Cairo, 1927ff.; old ed., Bulaq, in 20 vols.

Hudhaylî Dîwân: The Hudsailian poems... ed. in Arabic and trans. J. G. L. Kosegarten. London, 1854. *Letzter Theil der Lieder der Hudhailiten,* arabisch und deutsch, von J. Wellhausen. (Skizzen und Vorarbeiten, 1. Heft.) Berlin, 1884.

IBN ABI UṢAYBIYA *ʿUyûn al-Anbâʾ fî Ṭabaqât al-Aṭibbâʾ* herausg. von August Müller, Königsberg. 1884.

IBN QUTAYBA, *Shiʿr wa-Shuʿarâʾ:* Ibn Qotaiba Liber poesis et poetarum, ed. M. J. De Goje. Leiden, 1904.

———. *ʿUyûn al-Akhbâr.* 4 vols. Cairo, 1925.

MASʿÛDÎ, MAÇOUDI. *Les Prairies d'or.* Texte et traduction par C. Barbier de Meynard et Parvet de Courteille. 9 vols. Paris, 1861–77.

MAYDÂNÎ. *Majmaʿ al-Amthâl:* Arabum Proverbia, vocalibus instruxit, latine vertit, commentario illustravit G. G. Freytag. 3 vols. Bonn, 1838ff.

al-Mufaḍḍalîyât, ed. C. J. Lyall. Vol. I: Text; Vol. II: translation and notes, Oxford, 1918–21; vol. III: indexes, by A. A. Bevan, London/Leiden, 1924. (Gibb Memorial Series, n.s. vol. III.)

Naqâʾiḍ. The Naḳâʾiḍ of Jarîr and al-Farazdak. Ed. A. A. Bevan. vols. I & II: text; vol. III: indices and glossary. Leiden, 1905–1912.

Kitâb al-Ṭabaqât al-Kabîr: Ibn Saad, *Biographien Muhammeds, seiner Gefährten und der späteren Träger des Islams,* bis zum Jahre 230 der Flucht... herausg. von Eduard Sachau. Leiden, 1905ff.

AL-ṬABARÎ. *Kitâb al-Taʾrîkh; Annales,* auctore Abu Djafar Mohammed ibn Djarîr aṭ-Ṭabarî quos ed.... M. J. De Goje. Leiden, 1879–1901.

ABÛ TAMMÂM. *Hamasae carmina*... edidit... versione latina... G. G. Freytag. 2 vols. Bonn, 1828–47.

———. *Hamasa oder die ältesten arabischen Volkslieder... übersetzt*... von Friedrich Rückert. 2 vols. Stuttgart, 1846.

List of Abbreviations

E. I. Encyclopedia of Islam

SBWA. Sitzungsberichte der Wiener Akademie der Wissenschaften

ZDMG. Zeitschrift der Deutschen Morgenländischen Gesellschaft

SKBAW. Sitzungsberichte der Königlich-Bayrischen Akademie der Wissenschaften

Abh.K.Pr.Akad.Wissensch. Abhandlungen der Königlich-Preussischen Akademie der Wissenschaften

Sber.K.Pr.Ak.Wissensch. Sitszungsberichte der Königlich-Preussischen Akademie der Wissenschaften

JRAS Journal of the Royal Asiatic Society of Great Britain and Ireland, London

JAOS Journal of the American Oriental Society, New Haven, Conn.

Gött. Akad. Wissensch. Akademie der Wissenschaften in Göttingen

Nachr. Nachrichten

Abh. Abhandlungen

Index

[The article *al-* and words like *fî*, *min*, etc. are disregarded in establishing the alphabetical order.]

Index of Sûrahs Quoted

PART II

Selections from Arabic Literature

1

ʿAMR IBN KULTHÛM *

Muʿallaqah

'Up, maiden! Fetch the morning-drink and spare not
The wine of Andarîn,
Clear wine that takes a saffron hue when water
Is mingled warm therein.
The lover tasting it forgets his passion,
His heart is eased of pain;
The stingy miser, as he lifts the goblet,
Regardeth not his gain.

Pass round from left to right! Why let'st thou, maiden,
Me and my comrades thirst?
Yet am I, whom thou wilt not serve this morning,
Of us three not the worst!
Many a cup in Baalbec and Damascus
And Qâsirîn I drained,
Howbeit we, ordained to death, shall one day
Meet death, to us ordained.

And oh, my love and yearning when at nightfall
I saw her camels haste,
Until sharp peaks uptowered like serried sword-blades,
And me Yamâma faced!
Such grief no mother-camel feels, bemoaning
Her young one lost, nor she,
The grey-haired woman whose hard fate hath left her
Of nine sons graves thrice three.'

Translated by R. A. Nicholson

*Sixth century A.D. Author of one of the Muʿallaqât. Killed ʿAmr b. al-Mundhir, king of al-Ḥîrah, in revenge for insulting his mother, in 568 or 569 A.D.

ASH-SHANFARÂ *

Lâmîyat al-ʿArab

"And somewhere the noble find a refuge afar from scathe,
The outlaw a lonely spot where no kin with hatred burn.
Oh, never a prudent man, night-faring in hope or fear,
Hard pressed on the face of earth, but still he hath room to
turn.

To me now, in your default, are comrades a wolf untired,
A sleek leopard, and a fell hyena with shaggy mane
True comrades: they ne'er let out the secret in trust with them,
Nor basely forsake their friend because that he brought them
bane.

And each is a gallant heart and ready at honour's call,
Yet I, when the foremost charge, am bravest of all the brave;
But if they with hands outstretched are seizing the booty won,
The slowest am I whenas most quick is the greedy knave.

By naught save my generous will I reach to the height of worth
Above them, and sure the best is he with the will to give.
Yea, well I am rid of those who pay not a kindness back,
Of whom I have no delight though neighbours to me they live.

Enow are companions three at last: an intrepid soul,
A glittering trenchant blade, a tough bow of ample size,
Loud-twanging, the sides thereof smooth-polished, a handsome
bow
Hung down from the shoulder-belt by thongs in a comely wise,
That groans, when the arrow slips away, like a woman crushed
By losses, bereaved of all her children, who wails and cries."

Translated by R. A. Nicholson

*Sixth century A.D. Famous outlaw poet.

2

IMRA' AL-QAYS *

"*Rain*"

1. Torrential rain with clouds like trains of garments
 cover the face of the land and drench it.
2. You can see al-Wadd[1] when it relents; but the darkening
 clouds, heavy again, conceal it.
3. You can see the lizard, light and swift, bend its paws
 now rid of their cover of dust.
4. When the downpour is strongest you can see clumps of trees
 and they look as if headless but covered with veils,
5. for a while; then heavy rain lashes out and beats down
 in a downpour and cloudburst like flapping wings.
6. At dusk, the eastwind drives the rain, then it shifts,
 and southern stormshowers begin to flow,
7. without let-up, until the flood has narrowed
 the lands of Khaym and Khufâf and Yusur.

*Died in 540 A.D. Son of al-Ḥujr, king of the B. Kindah whose death he set out to avenge. He died by donning a poisoned gift robe.

---

[1] A mountain

3

The Day of Waqîṭ *

Abû ʿUbaida said: Firâs b. Ḥandaq gave us the following report about this day:

The Lahâzim—that is the tribes of Qais, Taim Allâh b. Thaʿlaba b. ʿUkâba, and ʿIjl b. Lujaym, and ʿAbtara b. Asad b. Rabîʿa b. Nizâr—assembled to attack the B. Tamîm who were themselves engaged in a raid. Nâshib b. Bashâma al-ʿAnbarî, al-Aʿwar, a prisoner of the B. Saʿd b. Mâlik b. Dubayʿa b. Qais b. Thaʿlaba, saw that and said to them: "Allow me to send a messenger to my family whom I can entrust with some desire of mine." The B. Saʿd who had bought him from the B. Abî Rabîʿa b. Dhuhl b. Shaybân said to him: "You may send one, but (you may talk to him) only while we are present." This they did for fear lest he should send a warning to his people. He said: "That's alright." and they brought a slave who was born amongst them. Nâshib said: "You brought me a block-head", but the slave said: "no, I am no blockhead". Nâshib al-Aʿwar said: "I think you are out of your mind", but the slave said: "no, by Allâh, I am not out of my mind". Then Nâshib asked: "Are the sun and the moon bigger or are the stars?" the slave answered: "the stars, for they are far more." Al-Aʿwar said: "You are a big block-head; I can't think of using you as a messenger!" The slave retorted: "On the contrary, I shall report everything that you say." Then al-Aʿwar filled his hand with sand and asked him: "How much sand have I got in my hand?" He answered: "I don't know, it is much too much for me to count." Then al-Aʿwar pointed with his hand to the sun and asked: "What is that?" He answered: "That is the sun." Then al-Aʿwar said: "Now I see that you are clever and intelligent. Go to my people and bring them news of my good health and my greetings. Tell them they should treat their prisoner well and with honor, for I am with people who treat me well and honorably (Ḥanẓala b. Ṭufayl al-Marthadî was in the hands of the

*Pre-Islamic, date uncertain.

B. al-ʿAnbar). Tell them further, they should not saddle my red camel, but rather ride on my grey-haired camel; and that they should take care of the little sons of Mâlik. Tell them further that the *ʿAwsaj*-shrub has already sprouted leaves, and that the women are preparing leather bottles. Further, they should not obey Hammân b. Bashâma, for he is ill-fated (lit. a bad omen) and unlucky; they should rather obey Hudhayl b. al-Akhnas, for he is firm and lucky." The B. Qais said to al-Aʿwar: "Who are the little sons of Mâlik?" He answered: "The sons of my brother".—They also told another version of this story, namely, that Nâshib b. Bashâma saw a rider and asked him: "Where are you bound?" The rider answered: "To such and such a place." Thereupon he said to the B. Saʿd b. Mâlik: "That route leads to my people; will you let me give him a message for them, to entrust Ḥanẓala to their care?" They said: "Only when we can hear the message." He said: "You can hear it alright." They gave him permission to talk to the rider while he was with them. He told him: "When you come to Umm Qudâma, tell her: You have mistreated my red camel and have exhausted it by hard riding; now treat it better. You must treat my reddish camel al-ʿAfîya better when you ride her." When the rider told that to Umm Qudâma, she said to her sons: "He is ordering you to ride into the Dahnâ and to leave al-Ṣammân."—Now the story goes back to the original report.—The messenger came to them and reported everything; but the B. ʿAmr b. Tamîm did not understand what al-Aʿwar was trying to tell them and they said: "We do not understand this talk; al-Aʿwar must be a little 'off his rocker'! for we do not know of any she-camel nor any other camel of his that looks as he describes it; as far as we can see, he has only one kind of camel." However, Hudhayl b. al-Akhnas said to the messenger: "Do tell me the whole story once more." Then he repeated what al-Aʿwar had said and what he had answered from beginning to end. Hudhayl said: "Give him my greetings, when you come back to him and tell him we shall take care of everything he has asked us to do." The messenger then left. Hudhayl exclaimed: "You ʿAnbar people, your companion (i.e., I) will now explain to you (what the message meant). By the sand which he took into his hand, he wished to inform you that an innumerable horde of people will come to you; by pointing to the sun, he wished to tell you that this was clearer than the sun. His red camel refers to al-Ṣammân: he is ordering you to move away from there, and his ash-grey she-camel means al-Dahnâ, he orders you to seek refuge there. The small sons of Mâlik means that he orders you to warn them and to make an alliance between them and you. That the *ʿAwsaj* shrubs are having leaves means that the people have already put on their weapons, and by speaking of the women's making leather bags, he wants to inform you that they have already prepared the leather bottles, i.e., they are sewing the leather water-skins and vessels which they take along on their raids." The historian goes on in his report: The ʿAmr b. Tamîm took these precautions and rode into the Dahnâ and informed the B. Mâlik b. Ḥanẓala b. Zayd Manât of the impending raid. However the latter said: "We do not know what the B. al-Jaʿrâʾ (that is the B. al-ʿAnbar) are talking about—we will not move to where your leader told us." The historian adds: The Lahâzin came to the B. Ḥanẓala but found that ʿAmr had struck camp and left.

4

Reckless Men of the Jâhilîyah *

The story of Ḥanẓala b. ʿUthmân b. ʿAmr b. Fâtik b. al-Qulayb b. ʿAmr b. Asad is as follows:

Ḥanẓala used to wander about among the Arabs because of his criminal deeds, for he was a reckless man and the Arabs were well aware of his recklessness. He was one of the most handsome people and therefore used to veil his face for fear of the people's envy. Once, on one of his wanderings, he stayed with the B. ʿAbd Manât b. Bekr b. Saʿd b. Ḍabba with a *bint ʿamm* of his [his wife] who had her small children with her; he also had with him a great many camels and their herdsmen. The B. Ḍabba said: 'Ḥanẓala is a most treacherous and most wicked man, and if any one could be at peace with him, it would be his own people, his own brothers. But whenever any persons granted him protection, adversity befell them. Therefore, apportion his possessions (to our people), kill him and give his wife to some one who has none.' They agreed, and began to cast arrows to distribute his property, until, one day, Ḥanẓala violently beat his wife. Next morning, he went away on some business of his. One of her neighbors came to her and finding her weeping, asked her: 'Why are you crying?' She answered: 'This wicked man has beaten me and I can't bear him any more' (lit. my companionship is spoiled). The neighbor said to her: 'Don't cry, for they will only wait until the holy month is past; then they will kill him. There are only four or five more days left, and then they will give you to one of their men of noblest descent, and most honoured reputation and with the most handsome face, for they are the ones who have cast arrows over his fortune.'

Ḥanẓala's wife saw that she gloated over her story. When Ḥanẓala returned later in the day, she told him the story. He got a slaughtering-camel and killed it, and brought its meat into his tents, except for its head. In the evening, when it was cooked completely, he dug a hole in his house, spread a rug over it and placed a divan next to it. At night-

*Pre-Islamic, date uncertain.

fall, he sent one of his small daughters to the B. Ḍabba, one by one, so that none knew that the others were also invited. It was the custom of the people in the Jâhilîyah, on being invited to a meal, to ask: for what purpose is it? and thus the little girl would answer every one who asked her that question: 'because of the head.' Each of the invited accepted thinking it to be a special invitation from her father. Ḥanẓala girded his sword and as soon as any one came to him, he grabbed him suddenly just as he sat down, struck his neck and threw him into that hole. When he had done so with seven of their warriors, there remained only an old blind man whose son led him on his camel. Ḥanẓala had sent to him last of all and when he arrived, Ḥanẓala jumped at him and killed him. Then he left his tent pitched, a barking dog bound to it and also a young camel from his herd with its tendon cut. He himself drove away his camels and fled with his family. When it became late and the old man had not come home, his son began to inquire what had happened and people began to miss their friends. They came to Ḥanẓala's tent and found the murdered men and saw that he had gone.—There are many more stories about his recklessness.

The story of Thumâma b. al-Mustanîr al-Sulamî, also al-Ẓafarî, and Muʿâwîya b. al-Ḥâritha al-Jushamî runs as follows:

Thumâma was a very shrewd Arab, hard-boiled and reckless. He used to make his raids unmounted. Whoever intended to go out on a raid with him had to comply with this condition: 'I won't obey any order from you and you must not obey me in anything that I may order you to do.' Therefore no one who ever went out on a raid with him returned, but all were killed; in the end, there was nothing left for him but to undertake his raids alone.

After a while, Muʿâwiya b. al-Ḥârith al-Jushamî, one of the B. Jusham b. Muʿâwiya, came to Thumâma and said: 'I should like to go out on raids with you.' Thumâma answered: 'As it happens, it is just time for my raid; but to undertake one with me is exacting and I would suggest to you something better than that.' Muʿâwiya asked: 'What would that be?' Thumâma replied: 'I shall give you some of my camels so that you will be rich and may return to your family.' Muʿâwiya retorted: 'Just because I fled from them do I want to go out on a raid with you.' Thumâma said: 'But whoever does that must never obey me, even, if it would mean his death, nor shall I ever obey him, though it be my death.' Muʿâwiya said: 'Agreed!'

Thus they went forth unmounted and came to the country of Bajîla where they spent a day. They intended to start their raid in the evening and then return with their booty. But while they were waiting for the night to come, they suddenly saw a man standing on top of a hill giving the alarm. They said: 'Did you see him? he knows our intention!' Many people began to gather round the guard, watching and listening. When quite a crowd had gathered, the watchman said: 'Listen, I have followed the traces of two men crossing the wâdî al-Bâriḥa, and I believe them to be those of Thumâma b. al-Mustanîr and a companion of his. Watch out for yourselves and your herds and don't let them graze without guards; let no one go out alone until you are sure that that villain has left your country. Now disperse!' They did so.

Thumâma said to his companion: 'Have you ever seen a man so sure of himself and giving such strict orders?' Muʿâwiya answered: 'I have never seen any one like him.' Thereupon Thumâma said: 'Go and bring him to me!' His friend exclaimed: 'What does that mean! How can I bring him to you? By Allâh, there is none like him among the Arabs.' But Thumâma insisted and said: 'That's that, of course you must bring him to me, and if you had been the first to tell me to bring him to you, I should have done so or would have died in the attempt.' Muʿâwiya left the cave, took his sword and went off. When he had almost reached the tribe's camp, he hid his sword in a ditch between himself and the tribe. Then he walked on slowly, entered the tent area and asked for that of their *saiyid*. They led him to the house of the man who had warned the tribe. He sat down with him and said: 'I am a man of the B. Juhaim of Quḍâʿa, I have with me my old father, my old mother, and a sister, and we brought along all our possessions and wish to ask for protection in your tribe, therefore do grant it to us.' The *saiyid* said: 'I grant you my protection.' However, Muʿâwiya asked: 'Give me a holy pledge!' He passed him some dates and Muʿâwiya ate some. Then he said: 'My father won't believe and won't trust my word; would you mind coming along with me so that he may see you?' The other answered: 'I will.' He went with Muʿâwiya; but when they came to the ditch where Muʿâwiya had hidden the sword, he picked it up and said: 'By Allâh, I shall knock off your head, if you won't go wherever I lead you.' The *saiyid* submitted and Muʿâwiya brought him to the cave. He bade him enter and sit down next to Thumâma and said to the latter: 'Here he is!' The man of Bajîla said: 'But you are Thumâma!' He answered: 'Yes, indeed, I am Thumâma.' The other man said: 'I thought to warn my people and here I have myself fallen into your hand!' Thumâma said: 'Redeem yourself.' He answered: 'Alright, you shall have seventy she-camels.' Thumâma retorted: 'Promise us to have them all together by the time when we shall return to you, and give us a safe conduct until we leave your country and when we return to you.' He said: 'Allâh be your witness for that.' Then they left the cave.

The two brigands went on raids in different directions and made much booty. Later they returned, passed by the Bajîlî to get the seventy she-camels from him and then they left the territory of the Bajîla taking their spoil with them.—Meanwhile Ḥurâḍa b. al-Ḥârith al-Jushamî, a brother of Muʿâwiya who was on the raid with Thumâma, left his family and stopped as a guest at Thumâma's house and asked for his brother. They told him: 'He has gone away with Thumâma, and by Allâh, every one who has ever gone out raiding with Thumâma was killed.' He bided his time, but in the evening he attacked Thumâma's brother and killed him. Then he left. Meanwhile, Thumâma and his companion were approaching their home with their booty. When they entered the country of the B. Sulaym, Thumâma said to Muʿâwiya: 'You are now safe, you may now drive on slowly with the camels.' Thumâma himself mounted a she-camel and hurried to his home. When his family saw him, they began to cry and he asked: 'What's your trouble?' They said: 'The brother of that Jushamî who was with you killed your brother', and they told him the story. Thumâma said: 'Be quiet; but let no one leave the precincts of the tribe.' He then returned on the spot to his companion, the Jushamî and the camels, intending to kill him. When Muʿâwiya saw him he called: 'Stop! don't come near! What is the matter? and what has brought you back?' He answered: 'I have come to my tribe and found them well, but I was afraid lest some fool among the tribe insult you; so I came back to you so that we might be seen together.' Muʿâwiya said: 'By Allâh, this is not what brought you back, for, indeed, you left with one face, and now you are coming back with quite a different one! Allâh knows that you are here only because of some justified grievance which I can guess (lit. know).' He answered: 'Let there be no lie between us! Your brother killed mine.' Muʿâwiya said: 'And now you have come to kill me. Give me a pledge not to kill me and then come on and we can talk the matter over.' He gave the pledge and they proceeded to divide the camels with the Jushamî agreeing that he would leave the country and go back to his own. While they were busy doing that, Thumâma said: 'Do you see that she-camel among your share of the booty which the stallion covered last night? You'll have to hand over to me what is in her belly.' Then the Jushamî (i.e., Muʿâwiya) returned with his spoil to his brother and reproached him with what he had done.

When the time came for the she-camel to give birth, Muʿâwiya said to his brother: 'O Ḥurâḍa, by Allâh, I believe Thumâma will soon call for the camel, for I am pledged to give him the calf at its birth, and I am sure that Thumâma has calculated the time when the camel will be born.' Thumâma and his brother, in turn, left their home and stopped in a near-by wâdî; from there, they kept watch. But Muʿâwiya and his brother, too, kept guard in their home by night. Muʿâwiya was to sleep during the first part of the night, while Ḥurâḍa should watch; but before long Ḥurâḍa fell asleep. Thumâma had watched them and said to his brother: 'Stay where you are.' He himself advanced cautiously passing by Ḥurâḍa who was sleeping. He entered the tent and hit Muʿâwiya with his sword right in the breast (lit., middle); then he rushed back to his brother and called: 'Flee, for I have just slain that man!' But Muʿâwiya said to his brother after the sword had hit him: 'Run along the wâdî and leave me alone.' Ḥurâḍa ran away; but Muʿâwiya took his sword and crept towards the tent door, hoping that Thumâma would come back. Thumâma's brother saw Ḥurâḍa running along the wâdî and said: 'By Allâh, I don't think you have killed that man, for I see his brother running along the wâdî: he certainly wants to bring help. I think you have only wounded him; therefore return, for you have not killed him. Now be steady and finish him off.' Thumâma went back, while Muʿâwiya was sitting with his last breath holding his sword, hoping for Thumâma's return. When Thumâma entered the tent, Muʿâwiya struck and threw him to the floor. Thumâma exclaimed: 'Your brother is a lazybones, and my brother is a villain. Let my brother be your *jâr,* and ask your people to bury me and you together in one tomb.'

5

The Day of Shiʿb Jabala *

The Day of Shiʿb Jabala, to which Jarîr refers in the line "ʿAmr and his tribe did not destroy us", was one of the most violent warfares of the Arabs. These were three in number: the Day of Kulâb, the Day of Dhû Qâr, fought by the Rabîʿa, and the Day of Shiʿb Jabala (the Ravine of Jabala).

The cause for the Day of Shiʿb Jabala was that the Banû ʿAbs b. Baghîḍ, fleeing from the B. Dhubyân b. Baghîḍ with whom they were fighting, were wandering hither and thither (asking for help). When they came to ar-Rabîʿ b. Ziyâd al-ʿAbsî, he said: 'By Allâh, I shall throw stones at these Arabs, turn to the B. ʿÂmir!' So they went on until they stopped at a summer camp of the B. ʿÂmir; then (their leader) said: 'Stay here!' Rabîʿ and ʿUmâra the sons of Ziyâd, and al-Ḥârith b. Khulayf set forth and halted at the house of Rabîʿa b. Shakal b. Kaʿb b. al-Ḥarîsh, for there existed an alliance between the B. ʿÂmir and the B. Kaʿb b. Rabîʿa, while the leadership was with B. Kilâb b. Rabîʿa. Rabîʿb. Shakal said: 'You B. ʿAbs, your affair is important and the hatred induced in you is strong; however, by Allâh, I know very well that this war will be the most violent that the Arabs have ever fought. But, by Allâh, there is absolutely no escape from the B. Kilâb; therefore give me time until I have consulted the opinion of my people.'

He set forth with a troup of riders of the B. Kaʿb and came to the B. Kilâb. ʿAuf b. al-Aḥwaṣ met them and said: 'You people, obey me in handling this group of the Ghaṭafân and kill them and take booty from them, for the Ghaṭafân will never be successful afterwards, and you will continue to fatten and defend them; better become enemies of their tribe.' But they refused to obey him, and they went on until they came to al-Aḥwaṣ b. Jaʿfar and submitted their problem to him. Al-Aḥwaṣ said to Rabiʿ b. Shakal: 'Did you grant them your protection and offer them your food?' He said: 'Yes, I did.' Al-Aḥwaṣ

*Ca. 552 A.D.; according to other sources, ca. 570 A.D. Celebrated decisive battle in the wars between the B.ʿÂmir b. Ṣaʿṣaʿah and the B. Tamîm, during which the famous poet ʿÂmir b. al-Ṭufayl was born.

said: 'Then, by Allâh, you have made these people your wards (*jâr*).' Thereupon they let the people enter into the midst of their camp.

Bishr b. ʿAbdallâh b. Ḥayyân al-Kilâbî mentioned that when the ʿAbs were fighting against their tribe, they came to the B. ʿÂmir wishing that ʿAbdallâh b. Jaʿda and Ibn al-Ḥarîsh would become their allies against the B. Kilâb. Qays b. Zuhayr, too, proceeded to the B. Jaʿfar together with ar-Rabîʿ; they reached al-Aḥwaṣ sitting before his house. Qays said to ar-Rabîʿ: 'There won't be any alliance nor any trust if I do not approach this *shaykh*.' So Qays approached him and touched his waist from behind and said: 'I am in the situation of one who is taking refuge with you: You have killed my father, but I did not take any bloodmoney for him nor did I kill any one in revenge for him; now I have come to you asking you to protect us.' Al-Aḥwaṣ said: 'Yes, I shall protect you from whatever I would protect myself.'

ʿAuf b. al-Aḥwaṣ, however, was not present at this conversation and when he heard of this, he came to al-Aḥwaṣ while the B. Jaʿfar were still with him and said: 'You people of Jaʿfar, obey me to-day and do not oppose me even if by Allâh you will never again obey me in the future. By Allâh, if they had met the B. Dhubyân, they would have turned the points of their lances against you, while they were breathing soft talk with their mouths. Make a start with these people and kill them and make them like a flea whose brain is in its blood.' But they refused and allied themselves with them. ʿAuf exclaimed: 'I shall never enter into this alliance.' The narrator said: The B. Dhubyân found out where they had settled down and mustered their troups and prepared for battle. Ḥiṣn b. Ḥudhayfa b. Badr, and with him his two allies Asad and Dhubyân who were seeking revenge for the blood of Ḥudhayfa b. Badr, went out against them and with them advanced Muʿâwiya b. Shuraḥbîl b. Akhḍar b. al-Jawn (al-Jawn 'the Black' was Muʿâwiya who was called that because he was pitch black) b. Âkil al-Murâr al-Kindî with a troup of Kinda. The B. Ḥanẓala b. Mâlik advanced also, led by Laqîṭ b. Zurâra, who was seeking revenge for the blood of Maʿbad b. Zurâra and of Yathribî b. ʿUdus. Ḥassân b. ʿAmr b. al-Jawn advanced with a strong troup of Kinda and others and the Waḍâʾiʿs, the troups that used to be in al-Ḥîra with the Lakhmide kings. Among these Ribâb [collective name for these groups] was one of their noble men called an-Nuʿmân b. Qahwas al-Taymî who was carrying the standard of those who went to Jabala and who was one of the 'Horsemen of the Arabs'. Dukhtanûs, the daughter of Laqîṭ composed about him on this Day the following verses:

1. Ibn Qahwas, the bold one, fled though in his hand was a strong lance ready to strike
2. They attacked with it the firm flesh as if he were the cub of a hyena-wolf with slender thighs.
3. You are from the Taym, so leave the Ghaṭafân alone, whether they march or rest.
4. Their multitude does not affect you, nor does it concern you whether they perish or are abased
5. Like the glory of a whore in the litter of her mistress when the people make light of her, who does not ride in the litter, nor is there shelter in it for some one bent on sinning.
6. However, I have seen your father among the people tying kids or gathering dung
7. Wearing the rope of the kid, as if it were an iron collar round his neck.

The narrator continued in his story: Among the leaders of the B. Tamîm who were with them were Ḥâjib b. Zurâra, Laqîṭ b. Zurâra, ʿAmr b. ʿAmr and ʿUtayba b. al-Ḥârith b. Shihâb; further some rabble and common people who wanted to gain booty. They gathered an army larger than any that had ever existed in the Jâhilîya and the Arabs did not doubt that the B. ʿÂmir would perish. They marched until they passed by the B. Saʿd b. Zayd Manât and said to them: 'March with us against the B. ʿÂmir'. But the B. Saʿd answered: "We are not inclined to march with you, because we believe that ʿÂmir b. Ṣaʿṣaʿa the son of Saʿd b. Zayd Manât (is praiseworthy or they belong to us).[1]" They said: 'If you decline to march with us, then at least refrain from turning against us.' The B. Saʿd said: 'As far as that is concerned, that's alright.'

When the B. ʿÂmir heard of their march, they convened at al-Aḥwaṣ b. Jaʿfar's for consultation. He was at that time an old man whose eyebrows fell over his eyes and had given up raids, except for giving advice to his people. He was experienced, resolute and of a happy disposition. They told him the story and al-Aḥwaṣ said to them: 'I am an old man and I cannot come to a firm decision, for my power of thinking has gone from me. But when I hear your ideas, then I can understand; so gather your opinions, then sleep over them through tonight; then in the morning come to me and submit your views.'

---

[1] The parenthesis is in Bevan's text.

They did that. When it was morning, they came back to him; a mantle was spread out for him in his yard on which he sat down. He held back his eyebrows from his eyes with a ribbon and then asked: 'Now bring me your ideas.' Qays b. Zuhayr al-ʿAbsî said: 'There are a hundred plans in my quiver.' But al-Aḥwaṣ answered: 'One firm effective proposal would be enough for me. Come on and empty your quiver.' So he began to submit to him every proposal that he had thought out, until he had exhausted them; but al-Aḥwaṣ said: 'I do not think that there was in your quiver even one acceptable idea.' Then the other people submitted their plans until they had exhausted them all; but he said: 'I have not heard anything worthwhile; but you have come to me for advice, so pack your possessions and gather your weak people.' They did that. Then he said: 'Now pack your women,' and they put them in the litters. Then he said: 'Get going! (lit.: ride!)' They rode off, putting him into a litter; then he said: 'Go on until you ascend into Yemen and if some one meets you, attack him and when you have weakened them then go on.'

The people travelled until they came early in the morning to the Wâdî Biḥâr; but all of a sudden they came back one by one and al-Aḥwaṣ exclaimed: 'What is the matter?' He was told: 'This ʿAmr b. ʿAbdallâh b. Jaʿda and some young men of the B. ʿÂmir hold back those that want to pass by them and cut off the saddle-pillows of the women.' Al-Aḥwaṣ said: 'Bring me there.' They took him there and he stood before them and asked: 'What are you doing?'. ʿAmr answered: 'You wish to put us to shame and drive us from our land as refugees! Yet we are the mightiest of the Arabs, the most numerous and strongest and have the sharpest weapons! You want to make us *mawlàs* among the Arabs, since you are running away with us!' Al-Aḥwaṣ asked: 'But how can I do otherwise since there arose a situation over which we have no power, nor is there any other counsel!' ʿAmr answered: 'Let us return to the ravine of Jabala and concentrate the women and children and the weak people and the herds at its upper end and we will be in its middle, for there is space and water enough for the camp, and when any one comes towards you from below, they will be without water, so that they cannot stay there, and when they try to ascend, then you fight against them from above their heads with rocks. You will be protected, while they will be unprotected and you will be more powerful in fighting them than they will be against you.' Al-Aḥwaṣ exclaimed: 'That is by Allâh the right proposal—but where was it when I consulted the people?' He said: 'It just came into my mind.' Al-Aḥwaṣ told the people to turn back and they did so. Nâbigha of the B. Jaʿda composed these verses in connection with this episode:

1. We restrained the tribes ʿAbs and ʿÂmir for Ḥassân and Ibn al-Jawn when they were told: proceed
2. When their women had ascended from Dhû Biḥâr like the rising of eagles who do not desire to settle down.
3. We turned towards them like a biting she-camel and they chanced to find strength and refuge from the red hill.

They entered the ravine of Jabala—Jabala is a red hill between al-Shurayf and al-Sharaf, (al-Shurayf is a waterhole belonging to the B. Numayr, and al-Sharaf is a waterhole of the B. Kilâb) and Jabala is a high mountain with a steep wide ravine and one has access to the mountain only from the ravine. The ravine itself has a narrow entrance, but its interior is spacious; to-day the B. ʿUrayna of Bajîla dwell in it. The B. ʿÂmir occupied a part of the ravine called Musalliḥ, kept the women and the children and their chattel in a camp on top of the mountain, drove the camels away from the waterholes and divided the ravine up (amongst the people) by casting arrows, and its rocky parts were also allotted by casting lots.

The B. Numayr, with whom were on this day as allies the Bâriq, a tribe of al-Azd (Bâriq is Saʿd b. ʿAds b. Ḥâritha b. ʿAmr Muzayqiyâ b. ʿÂmir Mâʾ as-Samâʾ) left and occupied al-Khalîf (which was a connecting road between the two ravines) because their arrows disagreed [about the place where they should camp]. About this fact Muʿaqqir b. Aus b. Ḥimâr al-Bâriqî composed this verse:

We are the lucky ones of the B. Numayr, for the mountain road runs in our part before them.

(The narrator) said: Muʿaqqir was on that day an old, blind man with whom was a daughter of his to lead his camel. He began to ask her: 'What kind of people are moving in down there?' and she would tell him, and he would say: 'these are the Banû So-and-so.' When they were all assembled in the ravine, he said: 'get down, for the ravine will continue to be defended for the rest of the day'—and the people settled down.—Kabsha bint ʿUrwa ar-Raḥḥâl b. ʿUtba b. Jaʿfar b. Kilâb was at that time pregnant with ʿÂmir b. al-Ṭufayl. She said: 'Oh you B. ʿÂmir, bring me up to the mountain top, for in my womb is the strength of the B. ʿÂmir.' They put their bows on their shoulders and carried her up until they put her down on the top of the mountain; it is thought that she gave birth to ʿÂmir on the day when the people stopped fighting. [Here follows a list of the participants in the battle of Shiʿb Jabala; they were said to have numbered 30,000 men.]

However, the situation became precarious for the B. ʿÂmir and they began to wonder what the approach of the people from far away meant, for the B. Tamîm and Dhubyân and Asad and their allies advanced towards Jabala. These met Karib b. Ṣafwân b. Shijn b. ʿUṭârid b. Zayd Manât and asked him: 'Where are you going? Do you want to warn the B. ʿÂmir about us?' He answered: 'No.' They said: 'Give us a firm promise and binding treaty that you won't do that.' He gave it to them and they let him go. Then he hurried on, on an Arab horse of his, until when he saw the assembled B. ʿÂmir, among whom was al-Aḥwaṣ, he stopped under a tree where they could see him. They sent some one to him to invite him to join them but he said: 'I can't do that; but come to my house when I have got off, for there I shall give you the report.' When he had stopped, they came to his place and there he had dust in a purse and a thorn with a broken-off point and with split-open side; also a coloquinth lay there and a hose with milk in it was hanging there. Al-Aḥwaṣ said: 'This man has given promises to some one that he would not talk; but he is telling us that people, numerous like dust are coming whose weapons are blunt and who are dispersed. That means, the B. Ḥanẓala are coming to you. Now look what is in the milk hose.' They poured it out, and the milk in it had curdled and become sour. Then he said: 'The people are as far away from you as the time it takes for fresh milk to become sour.' A man of the B. Yarbûʿ (or it is said, Dukhtanûs bint Laqîṭ) spoke the following verses:

1. Karib b. Ṣafwân b. Shijna does not leave any one from Dârim or from Nahshal in the lurch
2. You have taken Yarbûʿ for a *qawrati dâʾirin* (?)[2] while you have solemnly sworn by Allâh that you would not do it.

and the following are verses that ʿÂmir b. Ṭufayl[3] composed some time after Jabala:

1. Bring this message to the assembly of Saʿd: Rest assured that we will awake you sleepers.
2. You decided to keep away (from the battle) and did not help (the enemy) against us—you were indeed noble!

---

[2] cp. Bevan's Glossary where it is untranslated.

[3] See Dîwân II, p. 100 verse 30–32, trsl. p. 97.

3. But if you had joined with Ibn al-Jawn, you would have been like those who perished and became shameful.

When the B. ʿÂmir had thus become certain of the approach of their enemies, they went up in the ravine; al-Aḥwaṣ ordered every camel which had been kept thirsty before this to be fettered with two ropes on its forelegs. Next morning, Laqîṭ and the people with him gathered —Laqîṭ had command over them—when a scabby, old, bald and crooked camel came up to them baring its teeth. The soothsayers of the B. Asad said: 'Slaughter it!' But Laqîṭ said: 'Oh no, by Allâh, it won't be slaughtered until it will become the stallion of my camels, as I vow' (for that camel was of the ʿAṣâfir breed of al-Mundhir which Qurra b. Hubayra b. ʿÂmir b. Salama b. Qushayr had taken. ʿAṣâfir camels were a noble breed for kings.) Then Muʿâwiya b. ʿUbâda b. ʿUqayl who was left-handed came up to them and said:

'I am the left-handed youth/ in me is good and evil/ but evil in me is more.'

The B. Asad took that as an evil omen said 'Turn back from them and obey us'. The B. Asad left and did not participate at Jabala with Laqîṭ, except for a small unimportant group amongst whom were the poet Sha'ʾs b. Abî Bulaiy Abû ʿAmr, and Maʿqil b. ʿÂmir b. Mawʾala al-Mâlikî.

The people said to Laqîṭ: 'What do you think?' Laqîṭ answered: 'I think you should go up the ravine after the B. ʿÂmir.' But Sha'ʾs said: 'Don't enter the ravine against the B. ʿÂmir. I know the people amongst them very well, for I have fought against them and they have fought against me, and I have driven them to flight and they have driven me to flight. But I have never seen people more restless in their camping grounds than the B. ʿÂmir, and by Allâh, I can't find a better comparison for them than the *Shujâʿ* snake which does not remain in its hiding place either because of its restlessness. They will certainly come out against you, and by Allâh, if you remain here this night, you will find for sure that they will come down against you.' But Laqîṭ said: 'By Allâh, we *will* go against them.' Thus, Laqîṭ and his men came to the B. ʿÂmir; but the latter had taken their precautions and al-Aḥwaṣ had put his son Shurayḥ in command of the battlelines of his people. Laqîṭ and his companions over-confidently advanced and climbed up the hill at sunrise and he ascended with his men to occupy both sides of the ravine. The B. ʿÂmir said to al-Aḥwaṣ: 'There they come'. He said: 'Let them come!' But when they had come halfway up the mountain and had spread out there, al-Aḥwaṣ said: 'Now loosen the ropes of the animals and drive them against the enemy and follow after them and let every man of you throw two or three rocks after his camel.' Then the men shouted at the camels and rushed only after the camels that needed water and pasture and they began to throw rocks and shoot arrows at them. The camels rushed forward breaking everything in their path, and they began to roll down rocks with their feet hither and thither. Laqîṭ and his men were (at first) making fun of what the B. ʿÂmir were doing with their camels. A man of the B. Asad said:

1. You thought that the caravans would not fight/ 2. verily when the saddles rattle/ 3. and the Indian swords and the pointed lances clash/ 4. and the heroes say: who will come forward to fight?/ 5. verily, in that there is value and favour.

The people ran down the mountain in flight until they reached low ground, and when they reached the plain, no one had any other aim but to run on his own. But the B. ʿÂmir began to kill them and to knock them down with their swords wherever they were and to drive them along in wild flight.

A man of the B. ʿÂmir began to recite *Rajaz* verses:

1. I never saw a "day" like the Day of Jabala/ 2. the day on which Asad and Ḥanẓala came against us/ 3. and Ghatafân and all the kings/ 4. whom we beat down with sharp excellent swords/ 5. which had only just been polished/ until we drove them as one drives pack camels.

ʿAql b. ʿÂmir also said these *Rajaz* verses:

1. We are the protectors of the Ravine on the Day of Jabala/ on the day when Asad and Ḥanẓala came against us
3. And Ghaṭafân and all the kings/ whom we beat down with sharp, excellent swords
5. Which have only just been polished until we drove them as one drives pack camels.

And Maʿqil b. ʿÂmir began to say these *Rajaz* verses, too:

1. We are the protectors of the Ravine on the Day of Jabala/ with every cutting sabre and arrows with long iron
3. and with strong horses of high built

(*al-miʿbala* is a broad arrow).

The B. Numayr came forth from the mountain road on their horses, driving the people back. Shurayḥ b. al-Aḥwaṣ was cut off with some horsemen when he reached the muddy river bank and many people were killed in a violent massacre. Laqîṭ who on that day was at the river bank on a heavy-footed pack animal of his, dressed in brocade given to him by Kisrà—he was the first Arab to be clad in silk—began to say:

1. I have known you—and tears flow from my eye—because of a horseman whom you have destroyed and who cannot be replaced
2. For he (always offered) roast meat and boiled meat and round bread and beautiful singers and fresh cups (of wine)
3. And the best from the cooking vessel and offerings of food to the lance-bearing horsemen while the horses were marching steadily.

Then he did not let any one of the (fleeing) army pass by without saying to him: 'By Allâh, you have killed us and offended us,' and he said:

1. Oh ye people, you have burned me with blame/ but I did not fight against the ʿÂmir before this day
3. But to-day, when I am fighting against them, there is no blame/ so, advance, and put me at the head of the army.
5. How different is this! (and its reward will be) embrace and sleep/ and the cool bed in the shade of a *Dawm*-palm.

Shaʾs b. Abî Bulaiy answered him:

I, however, have fought them before this day:/ if only my order had not been disobeyed among the people!

Then Laqîṭ began to call: 'Whoever will return to battle will get fifty camels!' then he recited:

They all urged on their horse with cries of 'get-going'/but you see him only as impending fate/ leading an army and as an outstanding leader.

And he said further:

'You ruddy horse if you do not advance, you will get your throat slit/ and if you shy away from the tumult of battle, you will be slaughtered.'

Then he repeated:

'Roast meat and boiled meat and round bread.'

Shurayḫ b. al-Aḫwaṣ answered him:

1. 'If you are a real fighter then drive it down to the riverbank
2. and bring close the reddish horse so that you can recognize
3. our faces—for we are the noble sons with glittering swords.'

Between him and Shurayḫ and Laqîṭ was the forbidding river bed; but Laqîṭ beat his horse and drove it against him towards the river. Shurayḫ hurled his lance against him and he fell. However, some people disagree with that and state that the one who threw the lance was Jazʾ b. Khâlid b. Jaʿfar, and the B. Jaʿfar maintain that ʿAuf b. al-Muntafiq al-ʿUqaylî killed him on that day. He began to recite:

1. My wife continuously blamed me because she lacked knowledge—yet last night you were still kind—
2. Since you have killed my young camel and its rider—but I healed my soul with his sword
3. I killed him in the Ravine, the first horseman, before the sun had advanced in the east.

The people maintain that this ʿAuf killed on that day six men; his son was killed, and so was a nephew of his; but the scholars do not doubt that Shurayḫ killed Laqîṭ and that he was carried wounded from the battle field with lances still stuck in him; he lingered on thus for another day, then he died. While he was dying Laqîṭ began to recite the following poem:

1. Would that I knew, oh Dukhtanûs/ 2. when the secret news reaches you/
3. Whether you'll cut off your tresses or whether you'll boast/
4. but no, she will boast, for she is a bride.

(Dukhtanûs was the daughter of Laqîṭ and she was the wife of ʿAmr b. ʿAmr b. ʿUdus). The B. ʿAbs began to beat him though he was already dead.

Dukhtanûs spoke the following verses:

1. Oh the disgrace for her, the disgrace of one who wept because the B. ʿAbs beat Laqîṭ when he had already expired
2. They hit a face on which there was already the awe of death—and deaf stones do not care about one who has already fallen
3. But if you had met Laqîṭ early in the morning (when he was still alive), you would have had to endure lances and spears
4. You acted treacherously, for you were like ostriches that the hunter meets at the side of al-Sharâ

5. And there is no ransom for him among you—for his ransom was already Shurayḥ—for the lances struck him and he was hurled down.
6. And when the Days of ʿÂmir follow one another, there will be a firebrand over them which cannot be stopped when it is attacking
7. So that he should pay with twofold killing for one killing, for there is no deception for the blood of Ḥums, oh, Mâlik.
8. If the B. Ghâlib had killed us, killing them would be a greater duty for us than inflicting on their noblemen the disgrace of cutting off their nose.

Dukhtanûs said further:

1. By my life, even if the troubled Dârim had encountered any evil, their blows would have rendered Ḥamîd ineffective
2. They were fainthearted in the Ravine when Rabîʿa persisted against them, while their Kaʿb and Kilâb tribes were called on (for help)
3. They struck with their Indian swords and the deadly battlefields were filled with tumult where the ravens were not flying (i.e., were settling down because of the many dead)
4. The lions of the plains met the lions of the thicket, their Median mail (covering) their thick lion's necks.

And she said further:

1. The death-news of the flower of Khindif came in the morning, of their old men and their youth
2. And of their most noble men when their (aristocratic) origin is recounted
3. The B. Asad fled like the flight of birds away from their nests.
4. Not caring for their noble descent nor having regard for the shadow of their standard.

On that day Qurayẓ b. Maʿbad b. Zurâra and Zayd b. ʿAmr b. ʿUdus were killed (al-Ḥârith b. al-Abraṣ b. Rabîʿa b. ʿÂmir b. ʿUqayl killed the latter); killed, too, were al-Falatân b. al-Mundhir b. Salmà b. Jandal b. Nahshal, and Ibn Iyâs b. Ḥarmala b. al-ʿAjlân b. Ḥashwara b. ʿAjab b. Thaʿlaba b. Saʿd b. Dhubyân.

The latter said on that Day:

1. Come forth oh Qaṭîb [name of a horse] for they are the B. ʿAbs
2. The Ḥilla-group within a Ḥums people

(*gloss:* The Ḥums are Quraysh and those born among the tribes of the Arabs who were firm in their (ancient) faith, and the Ḥilla were not.)

ʿAmr b. Ḥasḥâs b. Wahb b. Aʿyâʾ b. Ṭarîf al-Asadî was encircled by attackers and Maʿqil b. ʿÂmir b. Mawʾala saved and nursed and clothed him. About this event Maʿqil said:

1. I have extended help to Ibn Ḥasḥâs b. Wahb at the plain of Dhu-l-Jidhât with a noble hand
2. I held back from him the horse al-Dahmâʾ when I was present while any friend of his was far away
3. But if I had wanted, I could have been as far away from him as are the Farqadân stars of Ursa Minor
4. I told him that his wound was only a light one and that 'you are carried on a strong indefatigable horse'.
5. I remember the conversation of the young men one day—and that blame is attached only to the blameworthy.

Muʿâwiya b. Badr b. Fazâra attacked and took Kabsha the daughter of al-Ḥajjâj b. Muʿâwîya b. Qushayr, who was the wife of Mâlik b. Khafâja b. ʿAmr b. ʿUqayl prisoner; and Muʿâwiya b. Khafâja, the brother of Mâlik, attacked Muʿâwiya b. Badr and killed him, and thus retrieved Kabsha from him, and he said: 'Oh you B. ʿÂmir, they will die!' (Aḥmad [a commentator frequently quoted in one of the manuscripts] quotes another version: he said, they will not die!).

Ḥassân b. ʿAmr b. al-Jawn came down from the hillside and shouted: 'Come on, you Kinda!' Shurayḥ b. al-Aḥwaṣ attacked him, but a man from Kinda, whose name was Ḥawshab, put himself before Ibn al-Jawn and Shurayḥ b. al-Aḥwaṣ hit him over the head and the sword broke in him. The man ran away with the broken piece of the sword stuck in him and this condition frightened the people. Ṭufayl b. Mâlik b. Jaʿfar set upon al-Ḥassân b. al-Jawn and took him prisoner, and ʿAwf b. al-Aḥwaṣ set upon Muʿâwiya b. al-Jawn and took him prisoner, but cut off his forelock and set him free against a ransom. But the B. ʿAbs met him and Qays b. Zuhayr attacked and killed him. ʿAwf came to them and said: 'You have killed my freed-man; either bring him back to life, or give me a king like him.' Then the B. ʿAbs feared evil from him, for he was frightening and they exclaimed: 'Take it easy!' (lit.: treat us gently). They went off to Abû Barâʾ ʿÂmir b. Mâlik b. Jaʿfar asking him for help against ʿAwf. Abû Barâʾ said: 'Your only hope (*dûnakum*) is Salmà b. Mâlik, for he was his boon companion and friend; they were much alike, both were red and ruddy, with big noses and Salmà has a sense of shame.' Thus they came to him and he said: 'I shall certainly speak for you to Ṭufayl that he should take his brother (and give him up in blood revenge), for nothing else would save you from ʿAwf's revenge—and by Allâh, he will come to a miser!' They went to Ṭufayl who said: 'I have already heard why you have come: you want to get Ibn al-Jawn from me to kill him in revenge for ʿAwf—take him!' He gave him to them and they brought him to ʿAwf who cut off his forelock and set him free. ʿAwf was thenceforth nicknamed al-Jazzâz (The "Cutter-offer"). This episode is dealt with in the verse of Nâfiʿ b. al-Khanjar b. al-Ḥakam b. ʿUqayl b. Ṭufayl b. Mâlik in Islamic times:

> 'We have settled the blood debt with the ʿAbs but the fate of Maʿbad amongst us was to starve.'

The narrator continues: Labîd b. Rabîʿa b. Mâlik b. Jaʿfar, too, witnessed the battle of Shiʿb Jabala at the age of nine years, but some say, he was in his teens. ʿÂmir b. Mâlik would say to him: 'To-day you were orphaned on your father's side, for your paternal uncles were killed.' Zuhayr b. ʿAmr b. Muʿâwiya, too, was killed on that day; he was found slain amongst the B. ʿÂmir in a place where the battle had not reached (that Muʿâwiya was al-Dibâb b. Kilâb). His brother Ḥuṣayn said about his slayer:

1. You hairy hyena, do not pretend to be friendly,/ when you have eaten up the flesh of the exhausted foal
2. I swear by Allâh to whom the B. Ballî make the pilgrimage/ and whom the B. Ghanî exalt over al-ʿUzzà
3. I have sworn at the place of the sacrificial animals/ that I shall offer you only the edges of Mashrafî swords,
4. There is no one like me (to avenge) Zuhayr on the B. Ghanî/ for he was brave and eloquent and sage.
5. A determined horseman, highminded and haughty/ carrying his burden (bearing his responsibility) when he was staying with me.

The scholars reported that Ṭufayl b. Mâlik said, when he saw the battle on the Day of Jabala: 'Woe be to you, where are the camels of all these people?' He raided the camels of ʿAmr and his brothers who were part of the B. ʿAbdallah b. Ghaṭafân and also of the B. al-Tharmâʾ; he drove a thousand camels away. ʿUbayda b. Mâlik b. Jaʿfar met him and asked him for a share, and he gave him one hundred camels. Then Ṭufayl said: 'I have a feeling that you will meet Ẓabyân b. Murra b. Khâlid and that he will say to you: he gave you only one hundred camels out of one thousand? and you will get angry.' ʿUbayda did meet Ẓabyân who asked him 'How many did he give you?' and he answered: 'one hundred'. Ẓabyân asked: 'one hundred out of a thousand!' ʿUbayda got angry. The story is then that ʿUbayda rushed into battle on that day though his brothers ʿÂmir and Ṭufayl had forbidden him to do so until he would see a favourable opportunity for fighting. But he disobeyed them and rushed forward. A man hurled his lance into his shoulder until it came out over his breast and the iron end of the lance remained stuck in him. He came to Ṭufayl and said to him: 'please, pull it out!' But Ṭufayl refused out of anger about what he had done; so he came to ʿÂmir and said: 'please, pull it out!' He, too, angrily refused to do it. So he came to Salmà b. Mâlik, who pulled it out. Then he was brought wounded together with other wounded men to the women until the battle would be over. On that day the B. ʿÂmir killed eighty uncircumcised young men of the B. Tamîm.[4]

As for Ḥâjib b. Zurâra he fled and the Two Zahdams, i.e., Zahdam and Qays, the sons of Ḥazn b. Wahb b. ʿUwayr b. Rawâḥa of ʿAbs, ran after Ḥâjib and called 'Surrender', for they had gotten hold of him. But he said: 'Who are you two?' They answered, 'the two Zahdams'. He exclaimed: 'I shall never surrender to two freedmen.' But while they were bickering, Mâlik Dhu-l-Ruqayba b. Salama b. Qushayr came to them and said to Ḥâjib 'surrender'. Ḥâjib said, 'and who are you,' and he answered, 'I am Mâlik Dhu-l-Ruqayba'. Then Ḥâjib said: 'I'll do that, but, by my life, you did not get hold of me until I was to become a slave anyhow.' Then he thrust his spear against him; but Zahdam got him by his neck and threw him down from his horse. Then Ḥâjib shouted 'Help! Help!' His sword dropped and Zahdam tried to get hold of its handle. Mâlik got down and pulled Zahdam away from Ḥâjib. Thereupon Zahdam and his brother Qays went to Qays b. Zuhayr and said: 'Mâlik has taken our prisoner out of our hands.' Qays asked, 'and who is your prisoner?' They said: 'Ḥâjib'. Qays went out, passing through the crowd and raising his voice using verses of Ḥanẓala b. al-Sharqî al-Qaynî, that is Abû al-Ṭamaḥân:

1. Did the ancestor of the B. al-Sharqî intend to injure me (by saying): ask a man for protection, and though he is strong, he will betray you
2. If I would say 'I shall fulfil my promise' (I shall always do so), but caprice comes over him, and, oh you driver of protected men, I may fail you by mistake.

[4] Bevan: some of the B. Tamîm were Zoroastrians.

until he stopped at the B. ʿÂmir and said: 'Your companion has grabbed our prisoner.' They asked, 'who was that?' He answered: 'Mâlik b. Salama, he took Ḥâjib away from the two Zahdams.' Mâlik, however, came to them and said: 'I have not taken any one from them, but he surrendered to me and he left them both.' They did not cease to argue until they decided to leave the decision to Ḥâjib himself, who was in the house of Dhu-l-Ruqayba. They asked him: 'Who took you prisoner, oh, Ḥâjib?' 'Those who kept me from carrying out my intention and prevented me from saving myself and saw my weak spot, but neglected it, that were the two Zahdams, but the one to whom I surrendered, that was Mâlik. Now leave the decision about myself to me.' They said: 'We leave the decision to you.' Then Ḥâjib said: 'Mâlik shall get one thousand camels and the two Zahdams will receive one hundred camels.' Thereafter there was anger between the Zahdams and Qays. Qays composed these verses:

1. The two Zahdams granted me a bad reward, while I am a man who is rewarded with honour
2. (For instance), I came to the help of the B. Qurṭ—as the Maʿadd know—and of their uncle Qudâma
3. I rode with them on the road to get their right, until I won for them thereby compensation for a hundred wrongs.

Jarîr said in relation to this Day:

1. On the Day of the Ravine, they left Laqîṭ, as if he was wearing a purple cloak
2. And Ḥâjib was fettered for a year in Shamâm and he decided in favour of Dhu-l-Ruqayba, for he was kind.

... The historian said: The Day of Jabala took place fifty-seven years before the coming of Islam, seventeen years before the birth of the Prophet, Peace be on Him; the Prophet was born in the year of the Elephant; after forty years he received the Revelation, and he died when he was sixty-three years of age. ʿÂmir b. al-Ṭufayl came to him in the year he died, at the time when ʿÂmir was eighty years old.

6

ʿADÎ IBN ZAYD *

The Poet of Al-Ḥîra

ʿAdî ibn Zayd had two brothers ʿAmmâr, called Ubey, and ʿAmr, called Sumey; on the mother's side they had also a brother ʿAdî ibn Ḥanẓala of Ṭaʾy. Ubey used to be with Kisrà; they were Christians of a respected house, who were with the Kisràs, had their maintenance with them and stood in high esteem; they also had assigned them fiefs and given them rich presents. When al-Mundhir became king of al-Ḥîra he placed his son al-Nuʿmân under the guardianship of ʿAdî, whose family brought him up. Al-Mundhir had yet another son, al-Aswad, whose mother, Mâriya bint al-Ḥârith ibn Julhum was of the Banû Teym al-Rabâb. A group of some people of al-Ḥîra, who were called Banû Marînâ, and who derived their pedigree from the Lakhm and were nobly born, educated him. Besides these two al-Mundhir had ten other children. His children were called al-Ashâhib—*i.e.* the Brilliant ones, on account of their beauty. Al-Aʿshâ says of them:

> ʿAnd the sons of Al-Mundhir, the brilliant ones, in al-Ḥîra, they go forth in the morning like gleaming swords.'

Al-Nuʿmân, however, had a reddish freckled skin, was small of stature; his mother was Salmà the daughter of Wâʾil ibn ʿAṭiya, the goldsmith of Fadak. Before his death al-Mundhir confided his ten—according to others, thirteen—sons to Iyâs ibn Qabîsa al-Ṭâʾi and appointed him king until Kisrà should make his decision. When Kisrà ibn Hurmuz found no man who seemed suitable to him he grew irritable and said: 'I will send 120,000 horsemen to al-Ḥîra, put in a Persian as King and order him to break into the houses of the Arabs and take away from them their property and their women.' However, when after that ʿAdî came to him, he asked him: 'Who is left of the family of al-Mundhir, and is there one among them in whom there is any good?' He said: 'Yes glorious king; in all his descendants there is good.' Thereupon he ordered him to have them summoned, where-

*Fl. *ca.* 580 A.D. Christian poet of al-Ḥîrah, was influential at its court and that of the Persian Chosroës (Sassanian emperors). He was imprisoned by al-Nuʿmân b. al-Mundhir of al-Ḥîrah and murdered in captivity.

upon ʿAdî went to al-Ḥîra, spoke with them, gave them his instructions and went with them to Kisrà. When they had alighted at ʿAdî's house he sent word to al-Nuʿmân: 'I will not make king any one but thee; and let it not distress thee if I show more favour to thy brothers for thereby I shall but beguile them.' Thereafter he gave them greater hospitable entertainment and made them think that he thought ill of al-Nuʿmân and did not wish that the succession should fall to him. Then he remained alone with one after the other and said: 'When I bring you to the king, then put on your finest and most beautiful clothes. Should he invite you to a meal, then be languid, make the morsels small and eat little. If he then says: "Will you be able to manage the Arabs for me?" say: "Yes." Should he then say: "Even if one of you breaks away and rebels?" answer "No, none of us can do anything against the others," this in order that he may fear you, may not wish to divide you and may know that the Arabs possess power of resistance and strength.' They accepted his advice; but he remained alone with al-Nuʿmân and said to him: 'Put on thy travelling clothes, gird thyself with thy sword; when thou sittest down to the meal, take big mouthfuls, chew and swallow quickly; eat much and appear hungry beforehand, for much eating pleases Kisrà, especially in the case of Arabs; for he thinks that there is nothing good in an Arab if he is not a greedy eater, especially when he sees something which is not his accustomed food and of which he does not know the nature. If he then asks thee: "Wilt thou master the Arabs for me?" say: "Yes," If he then asks: "But who will master thy brothers for me?" say "If I am too weak for them then I shall certainly be so for the others."' When after that Ibn Marînâ was alone with al-Aswad, asked concerning ʿAdî's advice and was informed of it, he said: 'By the Cross and Baptism! he hath deceived thee, and has not advised thee rightly; if thou obey me, then thou wilt do the opposite of all that he advised thee, then thou wilt be appointed king. Should you disobey me, then al-Nuʿmân will be appointed king. Be not misled by the honour and the precedence over al-Nuʿmân with which he has favoured thee, for that is only slyness and guile, as these Maʿadd are never free from guile and slyness.' He, however, replied: 'ʿAdî has advised me well and knows Kisrà better than thou; if I disobey him, he will turn against me and be prejudiced against me; he has brought us here and praised us, and Kisrà is guided by his word.' When Ibn Marînâ had given up hope that he would take his warning, he said: 'Thou wilt learn.' The Kisrà had them summoned and when they came into his presence their beauty and their perfection pleased him and he saw that they were men the like of whom he seldom met. Then he invited them to a meal and they did as ʿAdî had advised them: he, however, looked at al-Nuʿmân, who sat between them, and observed the way he ate. Then he said to ʿAdî in Persian: 'If there is any good in one of them, it is in this one.' When they had washed their hands he summoned one after another and said: 'Canst thou master the Arabs for me?' Whereupon the other answered: 'All except my brothers.' When last of them all al-Nuʿmân came he said to him also: 'Canst thou master the Arabs for me' 'Yes.' 'All?' 'Yes.' 'Even thy brothers?' 'If I am too weak for them, then I am too weak for all.' So he appointed him king, gave him a robe of honour and invested him with a crown adorned with pearls and gold worth 60,000 Dirhams. Then when al-Nuʿmân came forth after his coronation, Ibn Marînâ said to al-Aswad: 'Here thou hast the result of thy disobedience against me.' After that ʿAdî prepared a feast in a church and sent to Ibn Marînâ, saying: 'Come to me with whom thou wilt; I have a matter to settle.' So he came with a number of his people and they had their breakfast in the church. ʿAdî said to him: 'People like thee must know better than any one else how it is proper to act and must blame no one for so doing. I know thou wouldst rather that al-Aswad had been king and not al-Nuʿmân; but blame me not for a thing that thou wouldst have done just the same. I would that thou take not ill from me what thou wouldst have done hadst thou been able, and I would that thou vouchsafe to me what I vouchsafe to thee; for I have no more interest in this matter than thou hast.' Then he went into the church and swore that he would aim no satirical verse against him, nor plan any hurt for him, nor withhold any good from him. When ʿAdî ibn Zayd had ended, ʿAdî ibn Marînâ rose and swore that he would not cease to write satirical verse against him and to cause him harm as long as he lived. Al-Nuʿmân betook himself to the home of his father in al-Ḥîra. ʿAdî ibn Marînâ, however, said to ʿAdî ibn Zayd:

'Up, Make mention of ʿAdî to ʿAdî, and be not anguished though thy snares wear out,
'Our churches are beneficent for those not poor, so that thou mayest earn praise, or thy wealth may become perfect.
'If thou winnest now, thou winnest not praiseworthily; if thou fallest, then we wish others than thee to remain near us (in death).
'Thou wast rueful as the Kusaʿî[1] when thine eyes saw what thy hands had done.'

[1] Proverbial phrase.

Then ʿAdî ibn Marînâ said to al-Aswad: 'If thou hast not won, still be not so weak as not to take vengeance on this Maʿaddî who has used thee so. I always told thee that the intrigues of Maʿadd never sleep, and advised thee not to follow him. But thou didst act against my counsel.' He then said: 'What willst thou then?' He replied: 'that you hand over all the revenues of your wealth and landed property to me for management.' And that he did. Ibn Marînâ, however, was himself already rich in wealth and landed property. Not a day passed now without a present from Ibn Marînâ appearing at al-Nuʿmân's gate. In that way he acquired the greatest influence with him, and he gave no judgment as prince except according to the direction of Ibn Marînâ. If anyone now spoke of ʿAdî ibn Zayd before him, he praised him much and spoke highly of his virtues, adding however, 'a true Maʿaddite is, of course, never without guile and deceit.' Now when the people in al-Nuʿmân's entourage saw what influence Ibn Marînâ had over him, they adhered closely to him. Then he said occasionally to his most trusted allies: 'When you hear how I praise ʿAdî ibn Zayd in the king's presence, say: Of course he is as thou sayest, but he leaves no one unmolested; he maintains forsooth that the king (*i.e.* al-Nuʿmân) is only a governor and that he invested him with the office.' They said so continually till they made him hateful to the king. Then they wrote a letter in the name of ʿAdî to one of his agents and caused the letter to be seized and taken to al-Nuʿmân. When the latter read it he was very much incensed and sent to ʿAdî, saying: 'I pray thee, why dost thou not visit me? I long much to see thee once again.' ʿAdî was with Kisrà; he asked him at once for leave, obtained it and went to al-Nuʿmân. The latter however, hardly saw him, for he was at once put in a place of imprisonment where no one might visit him. Here, in the prison, ʿAdî ibn Zayd made many poems. The first that he composed there runs:

'Oh, that I knew but something of the prince! Nevertheless continual asking will bring thee sure tidings of him.

'What has our stake of property and life availed us, at the time when they formed up for battle on the day of guile?

'And at the time when I, at thy side, did shoot with the people for the prize; they shot and so did I, and none of us did his part badly.

'And I obtained what thou wouldst without guile, and I inflicted on them yet more hurt continually.

'Oh, that I had but grasped death with my own hands and had not had to suffer the kind of death which is assigned to enemies.

'They have uttered their calumnies in order to destroy us in this year, and they have let the handmill fall upon the leather pad beneath it.'

And in like manner he made several poems. Whenever al-Nuʿmân learnt of a poem of ʿAdî or heard talk of him, he felt remorse. He also sent to him often and made him all kinds of promises, but was afraid to set him free, lest ʿAdî then should seek to do him injury. ʿAdî said further, while he was imprisoned:

'I was sleepless on account of a thick cloud, wherein were lightning flashes, which rose above the summit of Shîb.
'The Mashrafite sword flashed above its summit, and the sides of the new well-guarded mantle gleamed.
'The foes haste all around, forsaking not the evil against me, by the Lord of Mekka and of the Cross.
'They wish that thou shouldst have naught to do with ʿAdî so that he may be kept imprisoned or plunged in the well.
'It was I who held fast to thy foes without fleeing after they had pressed thee hard on a hot day.
'Oft speak I unto them, but keep each secret hidden like that which lies between the bark and stem
'And I did gain thy crown, despite them, when we forgathered, even as the arrow (in the Meysir game) attains the prize.
'Neither was my purpose to bespatter merit, but that which hath befallen me is astounding.
'Who will send al-Nuʿmân word for me? Oft good advice is offered in secret.
'Is my lot to be the chain, the fetter and the yoke? Plain speech is with the wise.
'The news hath come to thee that my imprisonment hath lasted long. Feelest thou no reluctance for the suffering of a prisoner, robbed of his wealth?
'And my house is empty, only widowed women are therein, laid low with wailing
'They shed tears for ʿAdî, like a waterskin which the slaves have patched badly
'They fear those who slander ʿAdî and the sins which they have committed against him
'If I have failed in aught or done wrong, full oft doth one who dealeth uprightly commit a fault against a friend.

'If I do wrong, then thou hast punished me; but if wrong befalleth me, then such is my fate.
'If I die, then thou wilt feel my loss and be forsaken when the spear-points clash together in the battle.
'Wouldst thou acquire that which we possess, so that thou mayst not neglect good advice?
'I, however, have this day resigned my cause unto a Lord who is nigh and heareth prayer.'

And in the same connection he says further:

'This night has been long for us, and close, and I am as one, who in the early morning takes a vow, engaged in night-discourse.
'Because of the secret care which abides with me far more than that which I make known and that which I keep secret.
'And the night is long, as if there were therein a further night, and yet, of old, shortness was ascribed to night.
'I have not closed mine eyes throughout its length till it was ended, wishing that I could see the morning gleam.
'Not love has ravaged me of sleep and made me wakeful, but something that came near during the night.'

In the same poem he then continues:

'Convey to al-Nuʿmân a message from me, the word of one who fears suspicion and would clear himself.
'I am, by Allâh—accept my oath!—a monk, who, when he prays, lifts up his voice.
'One whose soul shivers in a cloister, one who has fair locks and flowing hair.
'I have not borrowed hatred from thy foes; God hath the knowledge of that which is kept hid.
'Be not as one who heals his bone by art of medicine till, when the bone is healed, he aims at weakening it, if he tries to use it in walking, then it breaks.
'And remember the kindness which in my troubles I shall not forget of thee, since only slaves are thankless.'

Further he said:

'Let a message reach al-Nuʿmân from me, that for me my durance lasts too long, and my waiting.
'Were my throat reddened with something other than water, then would I swallow the food with water, like unto one choking.

'O that I knew something about an interloper, who invents lies if he observes aught of my day or my night.
'I sit still, their spreading abroad (lies) troubles my soul, but my place of imprisonment is inaccessible, also my constancy.
'For the sake of a good deed, which the first among you multiplied, because I had come near to you and had become allied to you by marriage
'We give help when thou demandest it, and defend thee with large hands.'

Further he said:

'Verily long are the nights and the day'

And many other poems, which he composed and sent to him in writing, though it helped him not at all with al-Nuʿmân. When he then grew weary of imploring al-Nuʿmân, he made poems wherein he reminded him of death and represented to him how many kings had died before him; for instance:

'Departeth he at eventide or in the morning?'

And many other poems.

When the imprisonment of ʿAdî had lasted a long time, he wrote to his son, ʿAmr ibn ʿAdî, who stood in favour with Kisra:[2]

'Unto whom is a night long and fearful for the sake of a prisoner, because an inward grief oppresses him,
'What is the crime of a man who bears a long chain round his neck and fetters on his legs?
'Thy mother, O ʿAmr, may be robbed of thee after my death; dost thou sit still or leap up because I am not set free?
'Doth it not grieve thee that thy father is captive while thou holdest aloof? May the ghouls run away with thee!
'The daughter of al-Qayn ibn Jasr sings to thee, and wine is thy companion in thy madness.
'Wert thou the captive—mayest thou not be so!—then all Maʿadd would know what I say.
'If I fall, well, I have conferred upon my people benefits, which all are good and fair;

---

[2] This letter of ʿAdî to ʿAmr and the poem which he addressed to him are quoted only in al-Yaʿqûbî (*Tarîkh*, ed. Houtsma Vol. I, 244).

'Nor have I faltered in the strife for noble deeds whether the fate of death befall me soon, or whether it be long to wait.'

After that his brother wrote to him:[3]

'If fate hath cheated thee, still thou hast been no weak, deedless one, no whining wretch.
'And by God, if some dark-coloured, grinding (host) with flashing swords,
'A din striding through the whirlpool of death, with undamaged, padded coats of mail
'Had caught thee in its midst, then had I come in haste, be sure of that, when I heard thy cry for help.
'Or had money been asked of me for thee, then had I withheld neither inherited nor garnered wealth for any object whatsoever.
'Or wert thou in a land to which I could, by any means, have come, then neither distance nor danger would have deterred me.
'If I must miss you, know, as deeply-anguished friend, by God, there is naught that can compensate for thee so far as falls the autumn rain.
'Since thou art far from me, the might of this age and the command are with the enemies.
'Aye, by my life, if at last I hold myself in patience, yet few there are like thee, far though I roam around.'

All the scholars say: After he had read ʿAdî's letter, Ubey went before Kisrà and spoke with him of the matter. Then the latter wrote a letter in which he ordered al-Nuʿmân to set ʿAdî at liberty, and dispatched at the same time an envoy. But Nuʿmân's agent, too, sent word to him that the king had written to him. Then came ʿAdî's enemies of the race of Buqeyla of the tribe of Ghassân and said: 'Slay him at once', but he was unwilling. As for the man who then arrived, ʿAdi's brother had bribed him beforehand and charged him to go first to ʿAdî, who was a prisoner in the castle of Sinnîn, and hear his wishes. When the envoy came in to ʿAdî, he said: 'I bring thy deliverance; what do I get for that?' He replied: 'A reward such as thou wishest' and made him promises, but added: 'Leave me not, but give me the letter that I may send it on to him, for, by God, if thou leavest me, I shall be murdered.' But he answered: 'I must absolutely present the letter in my proper

[3] Agh. vol. II, p. 119 line 3.

person to the king.' Meanwhile, someone went to al-Nuʿmân to inform him of the matter, and said: 'Kisrà's envoy has gone to ʿAdî and will take him with him. If he does so, then ʿAdî will spare none of us.' Then al-Nuʿmân sent his enemies, who strangled him and buried him. When after that the envoy of the Kisrà presented the letter to him, he said: 'Certainly, it's a command.' Thereupon al-Nuʿmân caused 4,000 *mithqâl* and a girl slave to be given to him and said: 'Tomorrow morning early go to him and thyself bring him out.' When he, however, rode up on the following morning and entered the prison, the warders told him: 'He has already been dead some days, only we dared not announce this to the king out of fear of him, because we know how little he wished for his death.' Thereupon the envoy returned to al-Nuʿmân and said: 'I was with him yesterday and he was still alive: today however, when I came there, the guards informed me that he has been dead for days.' But al-Nuʿmân replied: 'The King sends thee to me and thou goest first to him? Thou liest, thou wishest only to obtain bribes and shameful payment!' Thus he first intimidated him, but then gave him further gifts and honours and bound him by an oath to inform the Kisrà that ʿAdî had died before he came to him. So the envoy said on his return to Kisrà: "ʿAdî was already dead before I came to him.'

Translated by Josef Horovitz

7

Qais Ibn Al-Khaṭîm *

The story of Khâṭib, a strong, noble man, with great power among his tribe, the Banû ʿAmr b. ʿAuf, is as follows:

He befriended (lit. protected) a man of the Banû Thaʿlaba ibn Saʿd and received him hospitably. This guest (Arab.: *jâr*) of his went to the fair of the Banû Qainuqâʿ, where a man from the Banû al-Ḥârith b. al-Khazraj ordered one of the Jews to hit him on his buttock. The Thaʿlabî cried: 'Oh, my protector! I was beaten up!' Khâṭib came in fury and killed the Jew; later he was told that the Khazrajî had ordered the insult. Therefore he turned against the Khazrajî and killed him; then he left. The story reached the B. al-Ḥârith and they immediately went off until they reached Khâṭib among the B. Muʿâwiya and killed him. His friend among them was Yazîd b. al-Ḥârith (he is the one who is called Yazîd b. Fusḥum). War broke out between the Aus and the Khazraj and each of the parties gathered and prepared for the fight. They marched against each other and met in the river bed of Buṭḥân—which is a *wâdî* in al-Medînah—where they fought bitterly (violently). That day turned against the Aus, for the B. al-Ḥârith were at that time (lit. on that day) the strongest group of the Khazraj, dauntless in battle. The leader of the Khazraj on that Day was ʿAmr b. al-Iṭnâbah, the leader of the Aus on that Day was Ḥuḍayr b. Simâk.

Yazîd b. Fusḥum composed in this context the poem that begins:

The phantom of Umayma came to us by night, and I did not close my eyes all night because of sleeplessness.
We pounded them in both battlegrounds and Qais became like a woman bereaved of children and helpless.

Qais b. al-Khaṭîm composed [the following poem] about Khâṭib and the Buʿâth War:

*Died before the Hijrah 622 A.D. Participated, on the side of the B. Aws, in the fratricidal wars in Yathrib between the Aws and the Khazraj. He was assassinated before the Hijrah.

[no. IV.]

1. Do you recognize the traces, resembling the sequence of golden letters, of ʿAmra's deserted camp, no longer the resting place of a horseman?
2. The homesteads of her who nearly stopped us when we were passing by Minà, had the riding camels not been rushing on.
3. She appeared to us like the sun under a cloud, one brow of hers appeared, but she begrudged the other brow.
4. I saw her only on the three days of Minà, while my tryst (lit. contract) with her was that of a virgin with curly hair (lit. curls on her forehead).
5. Yet many a woman such as you have I beguiled, but none who was an in-law or a *jâra* or the wife of a friend.
6. I called on the Banû ʿAuf to prevent bloodshed, but when they refused to heed my plea, I participated in the Khâṭib war,
7. For I am a man who does not provoke unjust war, but when they refused my offer, I kindled the fire of war on all sides.
8. I tried to prevent the war until I saw that instead of preventing, this would only increase the possibility of its outbreak (lit.: its coming closer).
9. And since there is no defense against the finality of death, let it be welcome, since it has always been welcome (with us in a good cause).
10. And when I realized this war to be a war with naked swords (lit. drawn) I put the garment of a warrior over the two striped *burdas:*
11. a double armor long enough to cover the fingertips, whose two pairs of nail-heads look like the eyes of locusts.
12. Then came the troops of the two (Jewish) *Kâhin* tribes, and also the two "Excellent Tribes", Mâlik and Thaʿlaba of the clan of Ibn Ghâlib.
13. Men who, when called to a fight until death, would rush headlong towards it as untractable camels would rush on.
14. When they are fearful lest the unsteady lines of the attacked tribe (would not hold firm) they rush to their aid with vigorous support like the towering wave of a foaming torrent.
15. Then you would see the splinters of the spears blown about as if they were yard-long palmbranch pieces in the hand of the women that strip them.

16. Early in the morning we stormed with them the forts around Muzâhim, the tops of our foremost line of helmets shining like stars;
17. our helmets [so smooth] if you would throw coloquinths over them they would roll down from their tightly-welded tops.
18. Whenever we might seem to be fleeing, the worst of our flight amounted only to averting our cheeks and turning our shoulders away.
19. Averting only our cheeks while our lances remain intertwined and our feet still hold firm in the brawl.
20. If our swords are too short, our steps will bring them close to our enemies, by drawing near to them.
21. I fought them on the Day of al-Ḥadîqa without armor, provoking them as if my hand with the sword were like the twisted kerchief of a *mikhrâq*[1] player.
22. And on the Day of Buʿâth our swords made us worthy to enter the shining lineage of the ranks of Ghassân.
23. They were white when drawn from their sheaths, but when we hit our enemy, they were red when replaced into the scabbard, honed thin at the edges where they had struck.
24. The Banû ʿAuf obeyed a leader who kept them away from keeping peace, until he was the first to be killed.
25. I felt pity for the ʿAuf when their women, while defending themselves by shooting at us, were exclaiming "Would that we had not begun to fight!"
26. We attacked them in early morning, clad in shimmering armor with iron helmets that revealed (by their reflexion) the anklets of the fleeing women.
27. Our swords hit the back of a noble man* and only the sons of wood-gathering slavewomen were spared (*or: a white-faced man).
29. I was pleased when they did not dare to come out of their holes to look for their far-away cattle except with a companion (for fear of being attacked).
30. Had it not been for the tops of the forts—as you know well— and the defection of al-Faḍâ, you would have had to share the full-bosomed women (with us).

---

[1] a game resembling 'Blind Man's Buff'.

31. For you could not defend against us a place of refuge of yours which we coveted, except for the terraces of its upper stories.
32. Why were you not steadfast against our attacks in the continuous warfare?—however, misfortune is an untractable steed.
33. We have abased you with our shining swords until you have become lower then male camel-foals among milk camels.
28. Among us is the one who swore off wine for thirty days until he would have 'visited' you with his squadrons.
34. For when we entered al-Ḥartha, our leader said: 'Wine be forbidden to us as long as we have not fought'.
35. Then the noblest men among us complied willingly and continued to abstain from wine until drinking was lawful again.
36. Would that Suwaid had seen which one of you was led away (to captivity) and who fled when the victor drove them like foreign slaves* (*or: like camel caravans).
37. Then we returned to our sons and our women; but he whom we left behind at Buʿâth will never return.
38. (Unfortunately), I was kept away from a Day when my kinsfolk called upon me by my *kunya* (to help them)—yet the Day of Buʿâth was indeed a day of hot contest.

[no. XVI.]

1. Has Laylâ filled you with longing
 departing admidst her tribe?
 yes, indeed, and the tears come flooding
 in streams over my breast.
2. He wept at traces of a woman's camp
 who had travelled to far-away lands:
 she did not delay her departure
 unmoved by the suffering and mourning
 of a sad and lovelorn man.
3. From early morning to nightfall
 and all through the night did he mourn,
 and all of his sorrows [and sighing]
 overwhelmed him again and again.
4. He said to himself: 'do consider
 that love remains firmly attached
 and comes back to mind as of yore,
 though the beloved no longer dwells nigh.'

5. I saddle my strong she-camel
   spurring her on
   till she dashes along
o'er forbidding and dangerous paths.
6. Racing in competition
   with riding camels that cast
their sunken eyes around
   afraid of the cracks of the whip.
7. And when the worth of the people
   is weighed, you will find us among
those counted as generous people
   and coming from noble stock.
8. We guard our reputation
   among our kinfolk and clan
by helping impoverished members
   to attain their rightful claims.
9. To wit, the blind man whom we guided
   charitably along on his way,
or the quarrelsome intruder persisting
   in mischief whom we put in his place.
10. We marched to hand-to-hand combat
   the way stubborn camels would march,
wherever you looked there was death
   lurking and threatening us.
11. With silent warriors covered
   by armor, the color of honey,
protected by helmets of iron
   bright like the color of stars.
12. Beneath their armor, courageous,
   hitting with all might and main,
they fought as if they were lions
   with their swords drawn.
13. Their strongholds on days of misfortune
   are sharply-honed, trustworthy swords,
whose quality is famous,
   enhanced by steadfastness of men.
14. You weakened before the attackers
   who drove deep into your compounds,
until the defenders were pushed back
   by the mere use of fingertips.
15. They rammed the gates open and clambered

into the forts and pursued
the tribe and their riding camels
that fled with Qurayẓa's troups.

[no. XVII]

1. The phantom of Layla Umm ʿAmr came to us by night—for only one reason did it visit us.
2. My beloved in the litter said at her departure: 'Do you abandon what you have gathered with a maimed lung (i.e., in despair)?'
3. But I answered her: 'Leave me alone, for when I have vanquished them, my fortune will come back, be it evening or night.'
4. I would not be the son of a chaste woman, if you had not seen us fighting as if we had drunk wine (i.e., like mad).
5. The Quraysh will carry on for us the war against the enemies until their fingertips will look as if they had been crushing ripe dates (i.e., red and sticky with blood).
6. They will attain full revenge among the Khazraj, putting to shame the two *Kâhin* tribes (i.e., the Banû Qurayẓa and Banû an-Naḍîr) and shaming ʿAmr.
7. We yelled at the date palms and at the forts, until, when they did not join us when we were yelling,
8. We decided to break up, and travelled the way Ḥudhayfa, the Valiant, the son of Badr, travelled.
9. We inherited fame—as Maʿadd knows well—we were never vanquished nor surpassed in taking revenge.
10. When you meet the men of Aus, you meet men in garments of snakes and panther skins (i.e., well armored).
11. We fight valiantly in the morning, when we meet the foe, even if the morning fight would be like fiery coals.
12. Send a message (lit. a messenger) to the Banû Ẓafar: We were never despised in Yathrib except for that one month
13. when we were forsaken, when the clients betrayed us, the pure-blooded allies left us in the lurch without real need.
14. We put to shame (i.e., vanquished) the mailed warriors, the way our *yamânî* swords had shamed the Banû Saʿd b. Bakr.

15. And when we reach Abraha, the Yamânî, and Nuʿmân and ʿAmr, who will honor us,
16. And when we dismount at Kurz, the man of valour, we will find with him abundant drink (lit. not paltry—i.e., welcome and help)
17. He has two buckets: one bucket full of pure wine, and another bucket filled with rain water mixed with old wine.
18. We shall fend off whatever they intend, nor will any one be allowed to remain entrenched in the camp amidst violence.
19. And when in the morning the Ghaṭafân join us, we shall make the Khazrajite women ride behind us (as captives) and shall kill every falcon.
20. We shall settle down, whatever our fate, and shall occupy every frontier.

[The commentator adds the following note:]

But ʿAbdallâh ibn Rawâḥa answered him this way:

"You are lying—for you were already held in contempt there, in Yathrib; you still stay there in contempt, and you fled by night."

8

MUḤAMMAD IBN ISḤÂQ *

Sîrat Rasûl Allâh

NEGOTIATIONS BETWEEN THE APOSTLE AND THE LEADERS OF QURAYSH AND AN EXPLANATION OF THE SŪRA OF THE CAVE

Islam began to spread in Mecca among men and women of the tribes of Quraysh, though Quraysh were imprisoning and seducing as many of the Muslims as they could. A traditionist told me from Saʿīd b. Jubayr and from ʿIkrima, freedman of ʿAbdullah b. ʿAbbās, that the leading men of every clan of Quraysh—ʿUtba b. Rabīʿa, and Shayba his brother, and Abū Sufyān b. Ḥarb, and al-Naḍr b. al-Ḥārith, brother of the Banū Abduʾl-Dār, and Abuʾl-Bakhtarī b. Hishām, and al-Aswad b. al-Muṭṭalib b. Asad and Zamaʿa b. al-Aswad, and al-Walīd b. al-Mughīra, and Abū Jahl b. Hishām, and ʿAbdullah b. Abū Umayya, and al-ʿAṣ b. Wāʾil, and Nubayh and Munabbih, the sons of al-Ḥajjāj, both of Sahm, and Umayya b. Khalaf and possibly others—gathered together after sunset outside the Kaʿba. They decided to send for Muhammad and.to negotiate and argue with him so that they could not be held to blame on his account in the future. When they sent for him the apostle came quickly because he thought that what he had said to them had made an impression, for he was most zealous for their welfare, and their wicked way of life pained him. When he came and sat down with them, they explained that they had sent for him in order that they could talk together. No Arab had ever treated his tribe as Muhammad had treated them, and they repeated the charges which have been mentioned on several occasions. If it was money he wanted, they would make him the richest of them all; if it was honour, he should be their prince; if it was sovereignty, they would make him king; if it was a spirit which had got possession of him (they used to call the familiar spirit of the jinn *raʾīy*), then they would exhaust their means in finding medicine to cure him. The apostle replied that he had no such intention.

*Died 768 A.D. (See Index, s.v.)

He sought not money, nor honour, nor sovereignty, but God had sent him as an apostle, and revealed a book to him, and commanded him to become an announcer and a warner. He had brought them the messages of his Lord, and given them good advice. If they took it then they would have a portion in this world and the next; if they rejected it, he could only patiently await the issue until God decided between them, or words to that effect. 'Well, Muhammad,' they said, 'if you won't accept any of our propositions, you know that no people are more short of land and water, and live a harder life than we, so ask your Lord, who has sent you, to remove for us these mountains which shut us in, and to straighten out our country for us, and to open up in it rivers like those of Syria and Iraq, and to resurrect for us our forefathers, and let there be among those that are resurrected for us Quṣayy b. Kilāb, for he was a true shaikh, so that we may ask them whether what you say is true or false. If they say you are speaking the truth, and you do what we have asked you, we will believe in you, and we shall know what your position with God is, and that He has actually sent you as an apostle as you say.' He replied that he had not been sent to them with such an object. He had conveyed to them God's message, and they could either accept it with advantage, or reject it and await God's judgement. They said that if he would not do that for them, let him do something for himself. Ask God to send an angel with him to confirm what he said and to contradict them; to make him gardens and castles, and treasures of gold and silver to satisfy his obvious wants. He stood in the streets as they did, and he sought a livelihood as they did. If he could do this, they would recognize his merit and position with God, if he were an apostle as he claimed to be. He replied that he would not do it, and would not ask for such things, for he was not sent to do so, and he repeated what he had said before. They said, 'Then let the heavens be dropped on us in pieces,[1] as you assert that your Lord could do if He wished, for we will not believe you unless you do so.' The apostle replied that this was a matter for God; if He wanted to do it with them, He would do it. They said, 'Did not your Lord know that we would sit with you, and ask you these questions, so that He might come to you and instruct you how to answer us, and tell you what He was going to do with us, if we did not receive your message? Information has reached us that you are taught by this fellow in al-Yamāma, called al-Raḥmān, and by God

[1] Cf. Sūra 17.94.

we will never believe in the Raḥmān. Our conscience is clear. By God, we will not leave you and our treatment of you, until either we destroy you or you destroy us.' Some said, 'We worship the angels, who are the daughters of Allah.' Others said, 'We will not believe in you until you come to us with God and the angels as a surety.'

When they said this the apostle got up and left them. ʿAbdullah b. Abū Umayya b. al-Mughīra b. ʿAbdullah b. ʿUmar b. Makhzūm (who was the son of his aunt ʿAtika d. of ʿAbduʾl-Muṭṭalib) got up with him and said to him, 'O Muhammad, your people have made you certain propositions, which you have rejected; first they asked you things for themselves that they might know that your position with God is what you say it is so that they might believe in you and follow you, and you did nothing; then they asked you to take something for yourself, by which they might know your superiority over them and your standing with God, and you would not do it; then they asked you to hasten some of the punishment with which you were frightening them, and you did not do it', or words to that effect, 'and by God, I will never believe in you until you get a ladder to the sky, and mount up it until you come to it, while I am looking on, and until four angels shall come with you, testifying that you are speaking the truth, and by God, even if you did that I do not think I should believe you.' Then he went away, and the apostle went to his family, sad and grieving, because his hope that they had called him to accept his preaching was vain, and because of their estrangement from him. When the apostle had gone Abū Jahl spoke, making the usual charges against him, and saying, 'I call God to witness that I will wait for him tomorrow with a stone which I can hardly lift,' or words to that effect, 'and when he prostrates himself in prayer I will split his skull with it. Betray me or defend me, let the B. ʿAbdu Manāf do what they like after that.' They said that they would never betray him on any account, and he could carry on with his project. When morning came Abū Jahl took a stone and sat in wait for the apostle, who behaved as usual that morning. While he was in Mecca he faced Syria in prayer, and when he prayed, he prayed between the southern corner and the black stone, putting the Kaʿba between himself and Syria. The apostle rose to pray while Quraysh sat in their meeting, waiting for what Abū Jahl was to do. When the apostle prostrated himself, Abū Jahl took up the stone and went towards him, until when he got near him, he turned back in flight, pale with terror, and his hand had withered upon the stone, so that he cast the stone from his hand. The Quraysh asked him what had happened, and he replied that when he got near him a camel's stallion got in his way. 'By God', he said, 'I have never seen anything like his head, shoulders, and teeth on any stallion before, and he made as though he would eat me.'

I was told that the apostle said, 'That was Gabriel. If he had come near, he would have seized him.'

When Abū Jahl said that to them, al-Naḍr b. al-Ḥārith b. Kalada b. ʿAlqama b. Abdu Manāf b. Abdu'l-Dār b. Quṣayy got up and said: 'O Quraysh, a situation has arisen which you cannot deal with. Muhammad was a young man most liked among you, most truthful in speech, and most trustworthy, until, when you saw grey hairs on his temple, and he brought you his message, you said he was a sorcerer, but he is not, for we have seen such people and their spitting and their knots; you said, a diviner, but we have seen such people and their behaviour, and we have heard their rhymes; and you said a poet, but he is not a poet, for we have heard all kinds of poetry; you said he was possessed, but he is not, for we have seen the possessed, and he shows no signs of their gasping and whispering and delirium. Ye men of Quraysh, look to your affairs, for by God, a serious thing has befallen you.' Now al-Naḍr b. al-Ḥārith was one of the satans of Quraysh; he used to insult the apostle and show him enmity. He had been to al-Ḥīra and learnt there the tales of the kings of Persia, the tales of Rustum and Isbandiyār. When the apostle had held a meeting in which he reminded them of God, and warned his people of what had happened to bygone generations as a result of God's vengeance, al-Naḍr got up when he sat down, and said, 'I can tell a better story than he, come to me.' Then he began to tell them about the kings of Persia, Rustum and Isbandiyār, and then he would say, 'In what respect is Muhammad a better story-teller than I?'

Ibn ʿAbbās, according to my information, used to say eight verses of the Qurān came down in reference to him, 'When our verses are read to him, he says fairy tales of the ancients';[2] and all those passages in the Qurān in which 'fairy tales' are mentioned.

When al-Naḍr said that to them, they sent him and ʿUqba b. Abū Muʿayṭ to the Jewish rabbis in Medina and said to them, 'Ask them about Muhammad; describe him to them and tell them what he says, for they are the first people of the scriptures and have knowledge which we do not possess about the prophets.' They carried out their instructions, and said to the rabbis, 'You are the people of the Taurāt, and we have come to you so that you can tell us how to deal with this

[2] Sūra 68. 15.

tribesman of ours.' The rabbis said, 'Ask him about three things of which we will instruct you; if he gives you the right answer then he is an authentic prophet, but if he does not, then the man is a rogue, so form your own opinion about him. Ask him what happened to the young men who disappeared in ancient days, for they have a marvellous story. Ask him about the mighty traveller who reached the confines of both East and West. Ask him what the spirit is. If he can give you the answer, then follow him, for he is a prophet. If he cannot, then he is a forger and treat him as you will.' The two men returned to Quraysh at Mecca and told them that they had a decisive way of dealing with Muhammad, and they told them about the three questions.

They came to the apostle and called upon him to answer these questions. He said to them, 'I will give you your answer tomorrow,' but he did not say, 'if God will.' So they went away; and the apostle, so they say, waited for fifteen days without a revelation from God on the matter, nor did Gabriel come to him, so that the people of Mecca began to spread evil reports, saying, 'Muhammad promised us an answer on the morrow, and today is the fifteenth day we have remained without an answer.' This delay caused the apostle great sorrow, until Gabriel brought him the Chapter of The Cave, in which he reproaches him for his sadness, and told him the answers of their questions, the youths, the mighty traveller, and the spirit.

I was told that the apostle said to Gabriel when he came, 'You have shut yourself off from me, Gabriel, so that I became apprehensive.' He answered, 'We descend only by God's command, whose is what lies before us, behind us, and what lies between, and thy Lord does not forget.'[3]

He began the Sūra with His own praise, and mentioning (Muhammad's) prophethood and apostolate and their denial thereof, and He said, 'Glory belongs to God, who has revealed the book to His servant,'[4] meaning Muhammad.

'Verily thou art an apostle from Me,' i.e. confirming what they ask about thy prophethood. 'He hath not made therein crookedness, it is straight,' i.e. it is level, without any difference. 'To warn of a severe punishment from Him,' that is, His immediate judgement in this world. 'And a painful judgement in the next,' that is, from thy Lord, who has sent thee as an apostle. 'To give those who believe, who do good works,

---

[3] Sūra 19.65.

[4] Sūra 18.

the good news that they will have a glorious reward, enjoying it everlastingly,' i.e. the eternal abode. 'They shall not die therein,' i.e. those who have accepted your message as true, though others have denied it, and have done the works that you have ordered them to do. 'And to warn those who say God has taken a son.' He means the Quraysh when they say, 'We worship the angels who are the daughters of Allah.' 'They have no knowledge about it, nor had their forefathers', who take hardly your leaving them and shaming their religion. 'Dreadful is the word that proceedeth from their mouth' when they say the angels are God's daughters. 'They say nothing but a lie, and it may be that thou wilt destroy thyself,' O Muhammad. 'In grief over their course if they believe not this saying,' i.e. because of his sorrow when he was disappointed of his hope of them; i.e. thou shalt not do it. 'Verily We have made that which is upon the earth an ornament to it to try them which of them will behave the best,' i.e. which of them will follow My commandment and act in obedience to Me. 'And verily we will make that which is upon it a barren mound,' i.e. the earth and what is upon it will perish and pass away, for all must return to Me that I may reward them according to their deeds, so do not despair nor let what you hear and see therein grieve you.

Then comes the story of what they asked him about the young men, and God said: 'Have you considered that the dwellers in the Cave and al-Raqīm were wonders from our signs?' i.e. there were still more wonderful signs in the proofs I have given to men. Then God said: 'When the young men took refuge in the Cave they said, O Lord, show us kindness and give us guidance by Your command, so We sealed up their hearing in the Cave for many years. Then We brought them to life again that We might know which of the two parties would best calculate the time that they had been there.' Then He said; 'We will tell you the true account of them; they were young men who believed in their Lord, and We gave them further guidance, and We strengthened their hearts. Then they stood and said, Our Lord is the Lord of heaven and earth. We will pray to no other god but Him. If we were to say otherwise we should speak blasphemy,' i.e. they did not associate anyone with Me as you have associated with Me what you know nothing about. 'These people of ours have chosen gods in addition to Him, though they bring no plain authority for them,' i.e. a clear proof. 'Who is more wicked than he who invents a lie against God? When you withdraw from them and what they worship instead of God, then take refuge in the Cave; your Lord will spread for you by His mercy and prepare a pillow for you in your plight. You might see the sun when it rises move away from their Cave towards the right, and when it sets it would go past them to the left, while they were in a cleft of the Cave.' 'That was one of the signs of God', i.e. for a proof against those of the people of the scriptures who knew their story and who ordered those men to ask you about them concerning the truth of your prophecy in giving a true account of them. 'Whom God guides is rightly guided, and for him whom He leads astray you will find no friend to direct. And you would think they were awake while they were sleeping, and we would turn them over to the right and the left, while their dog was lying with its forepaws on the threshold.' 'If you observed them closely you would turn your backs on them fleeing, and be afraid of them' up to the words 'those who gained their point said,' i.e. the people of power and dominion among them. 'Let us build a mosque above them; they will say,' i.e. the Jewish rabbis who ordered them to ask these questions. 'Three, their dog being the fourth of them, and some say five, their sixth being the dog, guessing in the dark,' i.e. they know nothing about it, 'and they say seven and their dog the eighth. Say: My Lord knows best about their number; none knows them save a few, so do not contend with them except with an open contention,' i.e. do not be proud with them. 'And do not ask anyone information about them,' for they know nothing about it. 'And do not say of anything I will do it tomorrow unless you say, If God will. And mention your Lord if you have forgotten and say, Perhaps my Lord will guide me to a nearer way of truth than this,' i.e. do not say about anything which they ask you what you said about this, viz. I will tell you tomorrow, and make God's will the condition, and remember Him when you have forgotten to do so and say, Perhaps my Lord will guide me to what is better than what they ask of me in guidance, for you do not know what I am doing about it. 'And they remained in their Cave three hundred years and they added nine,' i.e. they will say this. 'Say: Your Lord knows best how long they stayed there. The secrets of heaven and earth are with Him. How wonderfully He sees and hears. They have no friend but Him, and He allows none in His dominion as a partner,' i.e. nothing of what they ask you is hidden from Him.

And He said about what they asked him in regard to the mighty traveller, 'And they will ask you about Dhū'l-Qarnayn; say, I will recite to you a remembrance of him. Verily We gave him power in the earth, and We gave to him every road and he followed it'; so far as the end of his story.

It is said that he attained what no other mortal attained. Roads were stretched out before him until he traversed the whole earth, east and west. He was given power over every land he trod on until he reached the farthest confines of creation.

A man who used to purvey stories of the foreigners[5], which were handed down among them, told me that Dhū'l-Qarnayn was an Egyptian, whose name was Marzubān b. Mardhaba, the Greek, descended from Yunān b. Yāfith b. Nūḥ.

Thaur b. Yazīd from Khālid b. Maʿdān al-Kalāʿī, who was a man who reached Islamic times, told me that the apostle was asked about Dhū'l-Qarnayn, and he said, 'He is an angel who measured the earth beneath by ropes.'

Khālid said, "Umar heard a man calling someone Dhū'l-Qarnayn, and he said, "God pardon you, are you not satisfied to use the names of the prophets for your children that you must now name them after the angels?"' God knows the truth of the matter, whether the apostle said that or not. If he said it, then what he said was true.

God said concerning what they asked him about the Spirit, 'They will ask you about the Spirit, say, the Spirit is a matter for my Lord, and you have only a little knowledge about it.'[6]

I was told on the authority of Ibn ʿAbbās that he said, When the apostle came to Medina, the Jewish rabbis said, 'When you said, "And you have only a little knowledge about it," did you mean us or your own people?' He said, 'Both of you.' They said, 'Yet you will read in what you brought that we were given the Taurāt in which is an exposition of everything.' He replied that in reference to God's knowledge that was little, but in it there was enough for them if they carried it out. God revealed concerning what they asked him about that 'If all the trees in the world were pens and the ocean were ink, though the seven seas reinforced it, the words of God would not be exhausted. Verily God is mighty and wise,'[7] i.e. the Taurāt compared with God's knowledge is little. And God revealed to him concerning what his people asked him for themselves, namely, removing the mountains, and cutting the earth, and raising their forefathers from the dead, 'If there were a Qurān by which mountains could be moved, or the earth split, or the dead spoken to [it would be this one], but to God belongs the disposition of all things,' i.e. I will not do anything of the kind unless I choose. And He revealed to him concerning their saying,

[5] Or 'the Persians.'
[6] Sūra 17.87.
[7] Sūra 31.26.

'Take for yourself', meaning that He should make for him gardens, and castles, and treasures, and should send an angel with him to confirm what he said, and to defend him. 'And they said, "What is this apostle doing, eating food, and walking in the markets? Unless an angel were sent to him to be a warner with him, or he were given a treasure or a garden from which he might eat [we would not believe]"; and the evildoers say, "You follow only a man bewitched". See how they have coined proverbs of thee, and have gone astray and cannot find the way. Blessed is He, who if He willed, could make for thee something better than that,' i.e. than that you should walk in the marketplaces, seeking a livelihood. 'Gardens beneath which run rivers, and make for thee castles.'[8]

And He revealed to him concerning their saying, 'When We sent messengers before thee they did eat and walk in the markets, and we made some of you a test for others, whether you would be steadfast, and your Lord is looking on,'[9] i.e. I made some of you a test for others that you might be steadfast. Had I wanted to make the world side with my apostles, so that they would not oppose them, I would have done so.

And he revealed to him concerning what ʿAbdullah b. Umayya said, 'And they said, "We will not believe in thee until fountains burst forth for us from the earth, or you have a garden of dates and grapes and make the rivers within it burst forth copiously, or make the heavens fall upon us in fragments as you assert, or bring God and the angels as a surety, or you get a house of gold, or mount up to heaven, we will not believe in thy ascent until you bring down to us a book which we can read." Say: exalted be my Lord, am I aught but a mortal messenger'[10]

He revealed to him with reference to their saying 'We have heard that a man in al-Yamāma called al-Raḥmān teaches you. We will never believe in him.' 'Thus did We send you to a people before whom other peoples had passed away that you might read to them that which We have revealed to thee, while they disbelieved in the Raḥmān. Say, He is my Lord, there is no other God but He. In Him I trust and unto Him is the return.[11]

And He revealed to him concerning what Abū Jahl said and in-

[8] Sūra 25.8.
[9] Sūra 25.22.
[10] Sūra 17.92.
[11] Sūra 13.29.

tended: 'Have you seen him who prohibited a servant when he prayed, have you seen if he was rightly guided or gave orders in the fear of God, have you seen if he lied and turned his back; does he not know that Allah sees everything? If he does not cease we will drag him by the forelock, the lying sinful forelock; let him call his gang, we will call the guards of hell. Thou shalt certainly not obey him, prostrate thyself and draw near to God'.[11a]

And God revealed concerning what they proposed to him in regard to their money, 'Say, I ask no reward of you, it is yours; my reward is God's concern alone and He witnesses everything.'[12] When the apostle brought to them what they knew was the truth so that they recognized his truthfulness and his position as a prophet in bringing them tidings of the unseen when they asked him about it, envy prevented them from admitting his truth, and they became insolent against God and openly forsook his commandments and took refuge in their polytheism. One of them said, 'Do not listen to this Qurān; treat it as nonsense and false; and treat him as a mere raver—you will probably get the better of him, whereas if you argue or debate with him any time he will get the better of you.'

Abū Jahl, when he was mocking the apostle and his message one day, said: 'Muhammad pretends that God's troops who will punish you in hell and imprison you there, are nineteen only, while you have a large population. Can it be that every hundred of you is unequal to one man of them?' In reference to that God revealed, 'We have made the guardians of hell angels, and We have made the number of them a trial to those who disbelieve', to the end of the passage.[13] Whereupon when the apostle recited the Qurān loudly as he was praying, they began to disperse and refused to listen to him. If anyone of them wanted to hear what he was reciting as he prayed, he had to listen stealthily for fear of Quraysh; and if he saw that they knew that he was listening to it, he went away for fear of punishment and listened no more. If the apostle lowered his voice, then the man who was listening thought that they would not listen to any part of the reading, while he himself heard something which they could not hear, by giving all his attention to the words.

Dā'ūd b. al-Ḥuṣayn freedman of ʿAmr b. ʿUthmān told me that ʿIkrima freedman of Ibn ʿAbbās had told them that ʿAbdullah b. ʿAbbās had told them that the verse, 'Don't speak loudly in thy prayer

[11a] [Sūra 96. 9ff.]
[12] Sūra 34. 46.
[13] Sūra 74. 31.

and don't be silent; adopt a middle course,'[14] was revealed because of those people. He said, 'Don't speak loudly in thy prayer' so that they may go away from you, and 'Don't be silent' so that he who wants to hear, of those who listen stealthily, cannot hear; perhaps he will give heed to some of it and profit thereby.

QURAYSH PREPARE TO GO TO BADR

The men prepared quickly, saying, 'Do Muhammad and his companions think this is going to be like the caravan of Ibn Ḥaḍramī? By God, they will soon know that it is not so.' Every man of them either went himself or sent someone in his place. So all went; not one of their nobles remained behind except Abū Lahab. He sent in his place al-ʿĀṣ b. Hishām b. al-Mughīra who owed him four thousand dirhams which he could not pay. So he hired him with them on the condition that he should be cleared of his debt. So he went on his behalf and Abū Lahab stayed behind.

ʿAbdullah b. Abū Najīḥ told me that Umayya b. Khalaf had decided to stay at home. He was a stately old man, corpulent and heavy. ʿUqba b. Abū Muʿayṭ came to him as he was sitting in the mosque among his companions, carrying a censer burning with scented wood. He put it in front of him and said, 'Scent yourself with that, for you belong to the women!' 'God curse you and what you have brought,' he said, and then got ready and went out with the rest. When they had finished their preparations and decided to start, they remembered the quarrel there was between them and B. Bakr b. ʿAbdu Manāt b. Kināna, and were afraid that they would attack them in the rear.

The cause of the war between Quraysh and B. Bakr, according to what one of B. ʿĀmir b. Luʾayy from Muhammad b. Saʿīd b. al-Musayyab told me, was a son of Ḥafṣ b. al-Akhyaf, one of the B. Maʿīṣ b. ʿĀmir b. Luʾayy. He had gone out seeking a lost camel of his in Ḍajnān. He was a youngster with flowing locks on his head, wearing a robe, a good-looking, clean youth. He passed by ʿĀmir b. Yazīd b. ʿĀmir b. al-Mulawwiḥ, one of B. Yaʿmar b. ʿAuf b. Kaʿb b. ʿĀmir b. Layth b. Bakr b. ʿAbdu Manāt b. Kināna in Ḍajnān, he being the chief of B. Bakr at that time. When he saw him he liked him and asked him who he was. When he told him, and had gone away, he called his tribesmen, and asked them if there was any blood outstanding with Quraysh, and when they said there was, he said,

[14] Sūra 17. 110.

'Any man who kills this youngster in revenge for one of his tribe will have exacted the blood due to him.' So one of them followed him and killed him in revenge for the blood Quraysh had shed. When Quraysh discussed the matter, ʿĀmir b. Yazīd said, 'You owed us blood so what do you want? If you wish pay us what you owe us, and we will pay you what we owe. If you want only blood, man for man, then ignore your claims and we will ignore ours'; and since this youth was of no great importance to this clan of Quraysh, they said, 'All right, man for man', and ignored his death and sought no compensation for it.

Now while his brother Mikraz was travelling in Marr al-Ẓahrān he saw ʿĀmir on a camel, and as soon as he saw him ʿĀmir went up to him and made his camel kneel beside him. ʿĀmir was wearing a sword, and Mikraz brought his sword down on him and killed him. Then he twirled his sword about in his belly, and brought it back to Mecca and hung it overnight among the curtains of the Kaʿba. When morning came Quraysh saw ʿĀmir's sword hanging among the curtains of the Kaʿba and recognized it. They said, 'This is ʿĀmir's sword; Mikraz has attacked and killed him.' This is what happened, and while this vendetta was going on, Islam intervened between men, and they occupied themselves with that, until when Quraysh decided to go to Badr they remembered the vendetta with B. Bakr and were afraid of them.

Mikraz b. Ḥafṣ said about his killing ʿĀmir:

> When I saw that it was ʿĀmir I remembered the fleshless corpse of my dear brother.
> I said to myself, it is ʿĀmir, fear not my soul and look to what you do.
> I was certain that as soon as I got in a shrewd blow with the sword, it would be the end of him.
> I swooped down on him, on a brave, experienced man, with a sharp sword.
> When we came to grips I did not show myself a son of ignoble parents,
> I slaked my vengeance, forgetting not revenge which only weaklings forgo.

Yazīd b. Rūmān from ʿUrwa b. al-Zubayr told me that when Quraysh were ready to set off they remembered their quarrel with B. Bakr and it almost deterred them from starting. However, Iblīs appeared to them in the form of Surāqa b. Mālik b. Juʿtham al-Mudlijī who was one of the chiefs of B. Kināna saying, 'I will guarantee that Kināna will not attack you in the rear,' so they went off speedily.

The apostle set out in the month of Ramaḍān. He gave the flag to Mūṣ'ab b. 'Umayr b. Hāshim b. 'Abdu Manāf b. 'Abdu'l-Dār. The apostle was preceded by two black flags, one with 'Alī called al-'Uqāb and the other with one of the Anṣār. His companions had seventy camels on which men rode in turns: the apostle with 'Alī and Marthad b. Abū Marthad al-Ghanawī one camel; Ḥamza and Zayd b. Ḥāritha and Abū Kabsha and Anasa freedmen of the apostle one camel; and Abū Bakr, and 'Umar, and 'Abdu'l-Raḥmān b. 'Auf one camel. The apostle put over the rearguard Qays b. Abū Ṣa'ṣa'a brother of B. Māzin b. al-Najjār.

He took the road to Mecca by the upper route from Medina, then by al-'Aqīq, Dhū'l-Ḥulayfa, and Ūlātu'l-Jaysh. Then he passed Turbān, Malal, Ghamīsu'l-Ḥamām, Ṣukhayrātu'l-Yamām, and Sayāla; then by the ravine of al-Rauḥā' to Shanūka, which is the direct route, until at 'Irqu'l-Ẓabya he met a nomad. He asked him about the Quraysh party, but found that he had no news. The people said, 'Salute God's apostle.' He said, 'Have you got God's apostle with you?' and when they said that they had, he said, 'If you are God's apostle, then tell me what is in the belly of my she-camel here.' Salama b. Salāma said to him, 'Don't question God's apostle; but come to me and I will tell you about it. You leapt upon her and she has in her belly a little goat from you!' The apostle said, 'Enough! You have spoken obscenely to the man.' Then he turned away from Salama.

The apostle stopped at Sajsaj which is the well of al-Rauḥā'; then went on to al-Munṣaraf, leaving the Meccan road on the left, and went to the right to al-Nāziya making for Badr. Arrived in its neighbourhood he crossed a wadi called Ruḥqān between al-Nāziya and the pass of al-Ṣafrā'; then along the pass; then he debouched from it until when near al-Ṣafrā' he sent Basbas b. 'Amr al-Juhanī, an ally of B. Sā'ida, and 'Adīy b. Abū Zaghbā' al-Juhanî, ally of B. al-Najjār, to Badr to scout for news about Abū Sufyān and his caravan. Having sent them on ahead he moved off and when he got to al-Ṣafrā', which is a village between two mountains, he asked what their names were. He was told that they were Musliḥ and Mukhri'. He asked about their inhabitants and was told that they were B. al-Nār and B. Ḥurāq, two clans of B. Ghifār. The apostle drew an ill omen from their names and so disliked them that he refused to pass between them, so he left them and al-Ṣafrā' on his left and went to the right to a wadi called Dhafirān which he crossed and then halted.

News came to him that Quraysh had set out to protect their caravan, and he told the people of this and asked their advice. Abū Bakr and then ʿUmar got up and spoke well. Then al-Miqdād got up and said, 'O apostle of God, go where God tells you for we are with you. We will not say as the children of Israel said to Moses, "You and your Lord go and fight and we will stay at home,"[15] but you and your Lord go and fight, and we will fight with you. By God if you were to take us to Bark al-Ghimād, we would fight resolutely with you against its defenders until you gained it.' The apostle thanked him and blessed him. Then he said, 'Give me advice, O Men,' by which he meant the Anṣār. This is because they formed the majority, and because when they had paid homage to him in al-ʿAqaba they stipulated that they were not responsible for his safety until he entered their territory, and that when he was there they would protect him as they did their wives and children. So the apostle was afraid that the Anṣār would not feel obliged to help him unless he was attacked by an enemy in Medina, and that they would not feel it incumbent upon them to go with him against an enemy outside their territory. When he spoke these words Saʿd b. Muʿādh said, 'It seems as if you mean us,' and when he said that he did, Saʿd said, 'We believe in you, we declare your truth, and we witness that what you have brought is the truth, and we have given you our word and agreement to hear and obey; so go where you wish, we are with you; and by God, if you were to ask us to cross this sea and you plunged into it, we would plunge into it with you; not a man would stay behind. We do not dislike the idea of meeting your enemy tomorrow. We are experienced in war, trustworthy in combat. It may well be that God will let us show you something which will bring you joy, so take us along with God's blessing.' The apostle was delighted at Saʿd's words which greatly encouraged him. Then he said, 'Forward in good heart, for God has promised me one of the two parties,[16] and by God, it is as though I now saw the enemy lying prostrate.' Then the apostle journeyed from Dhafrān and went over passes called Aṣāfir. Then he dropped down from them to a town called al-Dabba and left al-Ḥannān on the right. This was a huge sandhill like a large mountain. Then he stopped near Badr and he and one of his companions rode on, as Muhammad b. Yaḥyā b. Ḥabbān told me, until he stopped by an old man of the Beduin and inquired about Quraysh and about

[15] Sūra 5. 27.

[16] i.e. the caravan or the army. Cf. Sūra 8. 7.

Muhammad and his companions, and what he had heard about them. The old man said, 'I won't tell you until you tell me which party you belong to.' The apostle said, 'If you tell us we will tell you.' He said, 'Tit for tat?' 'Yes,' he replied. The old man said, 'I have heard that Muhammad and his companions went out on such-and-such a day. If that is true, today they are in such-and-such a place,' referring to the place in which the apostle actually was, 'and I heard that Quraysh went out on such-and-such a day, and if this is true, today they are in such-and-such a place,' meaning the one in which they actually were. When he had finished he said, 'Of whom are you?' The apostle said, 'We are from Māʾ.'[17] Then he left him, while the old man was saying, 'What does "from Māʾ" mean? Is it from the water of Iraq?'

Then the apostle returned to his companions; and when night fell he sent ʿAlī and al-Zubayr b. al-ʿAwwām and Saʿd b. Abū Waqqāṣ with a number of his companions to the well at Badr in quest of news of both parties, according to what Yazīd b. Rūmān from ʿUrwa b. al-Zubayr told me, and they fell in with some water-camels of Quraysh, among whom were Aslam, a slave of B. al-Ḥajjāj, and ʿArīḍ Abū Yasār, a young man of B. al-ʿĀṣ b. Saʿīd, and they brought them along and questioned them while the apostle was standing praying. They said, 'We are the watermen of Quraysh; they sent us to get them water.' The people were displeased at their report, for they had hoped that they would belong to Abū Sufyān, so they beat them, and when they had beaten them soundly, the two men said, 'We belong to Abū Sufyān,' so they let them go. The apostle bowed and prostrated himself twice, and said, 'When they told you the truth you beat them; and when they lied you let them alone. They told the truth; they do belong to Quraysh. Tell me you two about the Quraysh.' They replied, 'They are behind this hill which you see on the farthest side.' (The hill was al-ʿAqanqal.) The apostle asked them how many they were, and when they said, 'Many,' he asked for the number, but they did not know; so he asked them how many beasts they slaughtered every day, and when they said nine or ten, he said, 'The people are between nine hundred and a thousand.' Then he asked how many nobles of Quraysh were among them. They said: "Utba, Shayba, Abūʾl-Bakhtarī, Ḥakīm, Naufal, al-Ḥārith b. ʿĀmir, Ṭuʿayma, al-Naḍr, Zamaʿa, Abū Jahl, Umayya, Nabīh, Munabbih, Suhayl, ʿAmr b. ʿAbdu Wudd.' The apostle went to the people and said, 'This Mecca has thrown to you the pieces of its liver!' (i.e., its best men).

---

[17] i.e. water.

Basbas and ʿAdīy had gone on until they reached Badr, and halted on a hill near the water. Then they took an old skin to fetch water while Majdī b. ʿAmr al-Juhanī was by the water. ʿAdīy and Basbas heard two girls from the village discussing a debt, and one said to the other, 'The caravan will come tomorrow or the day after and I will work for them and then pay you what I owe you.' Majdī said, 'You are right,' and he made arrangements with them. Adīy and Basbas overheard this, and rode off to the apostle and told him what they had overheard.

Abū Sufyān went forward to get in front of the caravan as a precautionary measure until he came down to the water, and asked Majdī if he had noticed anything. He replied that he had seen nothing untoward: merely two riders had stopped on the hill and taken water away in a skin. Abū Sufyān came to the spot where they had halted, picked up some camel dung and broke it in pieces and found that it contained date-stones. 'By God,' he said, 'this is the fodder of Yathrib.' He returned at once to his companions and changed the caravan's direction from the road to the seashore leaving Badr on the left, travelling as quickly as possible.

Quraysh advanced and when they reached al-Juḥfa Juhaym b. al-Ṣalt b. Makhrama b. al-Muṭṭalib saw a vision. He said, 'Between waking and sleeping I saw a man advancing on a horse with a camel, and then he halted and said: "Slain are ʿUtba and Shayba and Abūʾl-Ḥakam and Umayya". (and he went on to enumerate the men who were killed at Badr, all nobles of Quraysh). Then I saw him stab his camel in the chest and send it loose into the camp, and every single tent was bespattered with its blood.' When the story reached Abū Jahl he said, 'Here's another prophet from B. al-Muṭṭalib! He'll know tomorrow if we meet them who is going to be killed!'

When Abū Sufyān saw that he had saved his caravan he sent word to Quraysh, 'Since you came out to save your caravan, your men, and your property, and God has delivered them, go back.' Abū Jahl said, 'By God, we will not go back until we have been to Badr'—Badr was the site of one of the Arab fairs where they used to hold a market every year. 'We will spend three days there, slaughter camels and feast and drink wine, and the girls shall play for us. The Arabs will hear that we have come and gathered together, and will respect us in future. So come on!'

Al-Akhnas b. Sharīq b. ʿAmr b. Wahb al-Thaqafī, an ally of B. Zuhra who were in al-Juḥfa, addressed the latter, saying, 'God has saved you and your property and delivered your companion Makhrama b. Naufal; and as you only came out to protect him and his property, lay any charge of cowardice on me and go back. There is no point in going to war without profit as this man would have us,' meaning Abū Jahl. So they returned and not a single Zuhrite was present at Badr. They obeyed him as he was a man of authority. Every clan of Quraysh was represented except B. ʿAdīy b. Kaʿb: not one of them took part, so with the return of B. Zuhra with al-Akhnas these two tribes were not represented at all. There was some discussion between Ṭālib b. Abū Ṭalib, who was with the army, and some of Quraysh. The latter said, 'We know, O B. Hāshim, that if you have come out with us your heart is with Muhammad.' So Ṭālib and some others returned to Mecca. Ṭālib said:

> O God, if Ṭālib goes forth to war unwillingly
> With one of these squadrons,
> Let him be the plundered not the plunderer,
> The vanquished not the victor.

Quraysh went on until they halted on the farther side of the wadi behind al-ʿAqanqal. The bed of the wadi—Yalyal—was between Badr and al-ʿAqanqal, the hill behind which lay Quraysh, while the wells at Badr were on the side of the wadi bed nearest to Medina. God sent a rain which turned the soft sand of the wadi into a compact surface which did not hinder the apostle's movements, but gravely restricted the movements of Quraysh. The apostle went forth to hasten his men to the water and when he got to the nearest water of Badr he halted.

I was told that men of B. Salama said that al-Ḥubāb b. al-Mundhir b. al-Jamūḥ said to the apostle: 'Is this a place which God has ordered you to occupy, so that we can neither advance nor withdraw from it, or is it a matter of opinion and military tactics?' When he replied that it was the latter he pointed out that it was not the place to stop but that they should go on to the water nearest to the enemy and halt there, stop up the wells beyond it, and construct a cistern so that they would have plenty of water; then they could fight their enemy who would have nothing to drink. The apostle agreed that this was an excellent plan and it was immediately carried out; the wells were stopped; a cistern was built and filled with water from which his men replenished their drinking-vessels.

ʿAbdullah b. Abū Bakr told me that he was informed that Saʿd b. Muʿādh said: 'O prophet of God, let us make a booth (Ṭ. [Ṭabarî] of palmbranches) for you to occupy and have your riding camels standing by; then we will meet the enemy and if God gives us the victory that is what we desire; if the worst occurs you can mount your camels and join our people who are left behind, for they are just as deeply attached to you as we are. Had they thought that you would be fighting they would not have stayed behind. God will protect you by them; they will give you good counsel and fight with you.' The apostle thanked him and blessed him. Then a booth was constructed for the apostle and he remained there.

Quraysh, having marched forth at daybreak, now came on. When the apostle saw them descending from the hill ʿAqanqal into the valley, he cried, 'O God, here come the Quraysh in their vanity and pride, contending with Thee and calling Thy apostle a liar. O God, grant the help which Thou didst promise me. Destroy them this morning!' Before uttering these words he had seen among the enemy ʿUtba b. Rabīʿa, mounted on a red camel of his, and said, 'If there is any good in any one of them, it will be with the man on the red camel: if they obey him, they will take the right way.' Khufāf b. Aimāʾ b. Raḥaḍa, or his father Aimāʾ b. Raḥaḍa al-Ghifārī, had sent to Quraysh, as they passed by, a son of his with some camels for slaughter, which he gave them as a gift, saying, 'If you want us to support you with arms and men, we will do so;' but they sent to him the following message by the mouth of his son—'You have done all that a kinsman ought. If we are fighting only men, we are surely equal to them; and if we are fighting God, as Muhammad alleges, none is able to withstand Him.' And when Quraysh encamped, some of them, among whom was Ḥakīm b. Ḥizām, went to the cistern of the apostle to drink. 'Let them be!' he said; and every man that drank of it on that day was killed, except Ḥakīm, who afterwards became a good Muslim and used to say, when he was earnest in his oath, 'Nay, by Him who saved me on the day of Badr.'

My father, Isḥāq b. Yasār, and other learned men told me on the authority of some elders of the Anṣār that when the enemy had settled in their camp they sent ʿUmayr b. Wahb al-Jumaḥī to estimate the number of Muhammad's followers. He rode on horseback round the camp and on his return said, 'Three hundred men, a little more or less; but wait till I see whether they have any in ambush or support.' He made his way far into the valley but saw nothing. On his return he said, 'I found nothing, but O people of Quraysh, I have seen camels carrying Death—the camels of Yathrib laden with certain death. These men have no defence or refuge but their swords. By God! I do not think that a man of them will be slain till he slay one of you, and if they kill of you a number equal to their own, what is the good of living after that? Consider, then, what you will do.' When Ḥakīm b. Ḥizām heard those words, he went on foot amongst the folk until he came to ʿUtba b. Rabīʿa and said, 'O Abūʾl-Walīd, you are chief and lord of Quraysh and he whom they obey. Do you wish to be remembered with praise among them to the end of time?' ʿUtba said, 'How may that be, O Ḥakīm?' He answered, 'Lead them back and take up the cause of your ally, ʿAmr b. al-Ḥaḍramī.' 'I will do it,' said ʿUtba, 'and you are witness against me (if I break my word): he was under my protection, so it behoves me to pay his bloodwit and what was seized of his wealth (to his kinsmen). Now go you to Ibn al-Ḥanẓalīya, for I do not fear that any one will make trouble except him.' Then ʿUtba rose to speak and said, 'O people of Quraysh! By God, you will gain naught by giving battle to Muhammad and his companions. If you fall upon him, each one of you will always be looking with loathing on the face of another who has slain the son of his paternal or maternal uncle or some man of his kin. Therefore turn back and leave Muhammad to the rest of the Arabs. If they kill him, that is what you want; and if it be otherwise, he will find that you have not tried to do to him what you (in fact) would have liked to do.'

Ḥakīm said: 'I went to Abū Jahl and found him oiling a coat of mail which he had taken out of its bag. I said to him, "O Abūʾl-Ḥakam, ʿUtba has sent me to you with such-and-such a message," and I told him what ʿUtba had said. "By God," he cried, "his lungs became swollen (with fear) when he saw Muhammad and his companions. No, by God, we will not turn back until God will decide between us and Muhammad. ʿUtba does not believe his own words, but he saw that Muhammad and his companions are (in number as) the eaters of one slaughtered camel, and his son is among them, so he is afraid lest you slay him." Then he sent to ʿĀmir b. al-Ḥaḍramī, saying, "This ally of yours is for turning back with the folk at this time when you see your blood-revenge before your eyes. Arise, therefore, and remind them of your covenant and the murder of your brother." ʿĀmir arose and uncovered; then he cried, "Alas for ʿAmr! Alas for ʿAmr!" And war was kindled and all was marred and the folk held stubbornly on their evil course and ʿUtba's advice was wasted on them. When ʿUtba heard how Abū Jahl had taunted him, he said, "He with the befouled garment will find out whose lungs are swollen, mine or his."' Then ʿUtba looked for a helmet to put on his head; but seeing that his head was so big that he could not find in the army a helmet that would contain it, he wound a piece of cloth he had round his head.

Al-Aswad b. ʿAbduʾl-Asad al-Makhzūmī, who was a quarrelsome ill-natured man, stepped forth and said, 'I swear to God that I will drink from their cistern or destroy it or die before reaching it.' Ḥamza

b. ʿAbduʾl-Muṭṭalib came forth against him, and when the two met, Ḥamza smote him and sent his foot and half his shank flying as he was near the cistern. He fell on his back and lay there, blood streaming from his foot towards his comrades. Then he crawled to the cistern and threw himself into it with the purpose of fulfilling his oath, but Ḥamza followed him and smote him and killed him in the cistern.

Then after him ʿUtba b. Rabīʿa stepped forth between his brother Shayba and his son al-Walīd b. ʿUtba, and when he stood clear of the ranks gave the challenge for single combat. Three men of the Anṣār came out against him: ʿAuf and Muʿawwidh the sons of Ḥārith (their mother was ʿAfrā) and another man, said to have been ʿAbdullah b. Rawāḥa. The Quraysh said, 'Who are you?' They answered, 'Some of the Anṣār,' whereupon the three of Quraysh said, 'We have nothing to do with you.' Then the herald of Quraysh shouted, 'O Muhammad! Send forth against us our peers of our own tribe!' The apostle said, 'Arise, O ʿUbayda b. Ḥārith, and arise, O Ḥamza, and arise, O ʿAlī.' And when they arose and approached them, the Quraysh said, 'Who are you?' And having heard each declare his name, they said, 'Yes, these are noble and our peers.' Now ʿUbayda was the eldest of them, and he faced ʿUtba b. Rabīʿa, while Ḥamza faced Shayba b. Rabīʿa and ʿAlī faced al-Walīd b. ʿUtba. It was not long before Ḥamza slew Shayba and ʿAlī slew al-Walīd. ʿUbayda and ʿUtba exchanged two blows with one another and each laid his enemy low. Then Ḥamza and ʿAlī turned on ʿUtba with their swords and dispatched him and bore away their comrade and brought him back to his friends. (Ṭ. 1318. 2. His leg had been cut off and the marrow was oozing from it. When they brought ʿUbayda to the prophet he said, 'Am I not a martyr, O apostle of God?' 'Indeed you are,' he replied. Then ʿUbayda said, 'Were Abū Ṭālib alive he would know that his words

> We will not give him up till we lie dead around him
> And be unmindful of our women and children

are truly realized in me.') ʿĀṣim b. ʿUmar b. Qatāda told me that when the men of the Anṣār declared their lineage, ʿUtba said, 'You are noble and our peers, but we desire men of our own tribe.'

Then they advanced and drew near to one another. The apostle had ordered his companions not to attack until he gave the word, and if the enemy should surround them they were to keep them off with showers of arrows. He himself remained in the hut with Abū Bakr. I was informed by Abū Jaʿfar Muhammad b. al-Ḥusayn that the battle of Badr was fought on Friday morning on the 17th of Ramaḍān. Ḥabbān b. Wāsiʿ b. Ḥabbān told me on the authority of some elders of his tribe that on the day of Badr the apostle dressed the ranks of his companions with an arrow which he held in his hand. As he passed by Sawād b. Ghazīya, an ally of B. ʿAdīy b. al-Najjār, who was standing out of line he pricked him in his belly with the arrow, saying, 'Stand in line, O Sawād!' 'You have hurt me, O apostle of God,' he cried, 'and God has sent you with right and justice so let me retaliate.' The apostle uncovered his belly and said 'Take your retaliation.' Sawād embraced him and kissed his belly. He asked what had made him do this and he replied, 'O apostle of God, you see what is before us and I may not survive the battle and as this is my last time with you I want my skin to touch yours.' The apostle blessed him.

Then the apostle straightened the ranks and returned to the hut and entered it, and none was with him there but Abū Bakr. The apostle was beseeching his Lord for the help which He had promised to him, and among his words were these: 'O God, if this band perish today Thou wilt be worshipped no more.' But Abū Bakr said, 'O prophet of God, your constant entreaty will annoy thy Lord, for surely God will fulfil His promise to thee.' While the apostle was in the hut he slept a light sleep; then he awoke and said, 'Be of good cheer, O Abū Bakr. God's help is come to you. Here is Gabriel holding the rein of a horse and leading it. The dust is upon his front teeth.'

The first Muslim that fell was Mihjaʿ, a freedman of ʿUmar: he was shot by an arrow. Then while Ḥāritha b. Surāqa, one of B. ʿAdīy b. al-Najjār, was drinking from the cistern an arrow pierced his throat and killed him.

Then the apostle went forth to the people and incited them saying, 'By God in whose hand is the soul of Muhammad, no man will be slain this day fighting against them with steadfast courage advancing not retreating but God will cause him to enter Paradise.' ʿUmayr b. al-Ḥumām brother of B. Salima was eating some dates which he had in his hand. 'Fine, Fine!' said he, 'is there nothing between me and my entering Paradise save to be killed by these men?' He flung the dates from his hand, seized his sword, and fought against them till he was slain, [saying the while

> In God's service take no food
> But piety and deeds of good.
> If in God's war you've firmly stood
> You need not fear as others should
> While you are righteous true and good.][18]

---

[18] Māwardī, 67.

ʿĀṣim b. ʿUmar b. Qatāda told me that ʿAuf b. Ḥārith—his mother was ʿAfrāʾ—said 'O apostle of God, what makes the Lord laugh with joy at His servant?' He answered, 'When he plunges into the midst of the enemy without mail.' ʿAuf drew off the mail-coat that was on him and threw it away: then he seized his sword and fought the enemy till he was slain.

Muhammad b. Muslim b. Shihāb al-Zuhrī on the authority of ʿAbdullah b. Thaʿlaba b. Ṣuʿayr al-ʿUdhrī, an ally of B. Zuhra, told me that when the warriors advanced to battle and drew near to one another Abū Jahl cried, 'O God, destroy this morning him that more than any of us hath cut the ties of kinship and wrought that which is not approved.' Thus he condemned himself to death.

Then the apostle took a handful of small pebbles and said, turning towards Quraysh, 'Foul be those faces!' Then he threw the pebbles at them and ordered his companions to charge. The foe was routed. God slew many of their chiefs and made captive many of their nobles. Meanwhile the apostle was in the hut and Saʿd b. Muʿādh was standing at the door of the hut girt with his sword. With him were some of the Anṣār guarding the apostle for fear lest the enemy should come back at him. While the folk were laying hands on the prisoners the apostle, as I have been told, saw displeasure on the face of Saʿd at what they were doing. He said to him, 'You seem to dislike what the people are doing.' 'Yes, by God,' he replied, 'it is the first defeat that God has brought on the infidel and I would rather see them slaughtered than left alive.'

Al-ʿAbbās b. ʿAbdullah b. Maʿbad from one of his family from Ibn ʿAbbās told me that the latter said that the prophet said to his companions that day, 'I know that some of B. Hāshim and others have been forced to come out against their will and have no desire to fight us; so if any of you meet one of B. Hāshim or Abūʾl-Bakhtarī or al-ʿAbbās the apostle's uncle do not kill him, for he has been made to come out against his will.' Abū Ḥudhayfa said: 'Are we to kill our fathers and our sons and our brothers and our families and leave al-ʿAbbās? By God, if I meet him I will flesh my sword in him!'

This saying reached the apostle's ears and he said to ʿUmar, 'O Abū Ḥafṣ'—and ʿUmar said that this was the first time the apostle called him by this honorific—'ought the face of the apostle's uncle to be marked with the sword?' ʿUmar replied, 'Let me off with his head! By God, the man is a false Muslim.' Abū Ḥudhayfa used to say, 'I never felt safe after my words that day. I was always afraid unless martyrdom atoned for them.' He was killed as a martyr in the battle of al-Yamāma.

The reason why the apostle forbade the killing of Abū'l-Bakhtarī was because he had kept back the people in Mecca from the apostle; he never insulted him or did anything offensive; and he took a prominent part in the cancelling of the boycott which Quraysh had written against B. Hāshim and B. al-Muṭṭalib. Now al-Mujadhdhar b. Dhiyād al-Balawī, an ally of the Anṣār, of the clan of B. Sālim b. ʿAuf, fell in with him and told him that the apostle had forbidden them to kill him. Now al-ʿĀṣ Abū'l-Bakhtarī was accompanied by his fellow-rider Junāda b. Mulayḥa d. Zuhayr b. al-Ḥārith b. Asad who was one of B. Layth, and he said, 'And what about my friend here?' 'No, by God,' said al-Mujadhdhar, 'we are not going to spare your friend. The apostle gave us orders about you only.' 'In that case,' he said, 'I will die with him. The women of Mecca shall not say that I forsook my friend to save my own life.' He uttered this *rajaz* as al-Mujadhdhar came at him and he insisted on fighting:

> A son of the free betrays not his friend
> Till he's dead, or sees him safe on his way.

The result was that al-Mujadhdhar killed him and composed these lines thereon:

> Do you not know or have you forgotten?
> Then note well my line is from Balī.
> Those who thrust with Yazanī spears
> Smiting down chiefs and bringing them low.
> Tell Bakhtarī that he's bereaved of his father
> Or tell my son the like of me.
> I am he of whom it is said my origin is in Balī.
> When I thrust in my spear it bends almost double.
> I kill my opponent with a sharp Mashrafī sword,
> I yearn for death like a camel overfull with milk.
> You will not see Mujadhdhar telling a lie.

Then al-Mujadhdhar went to the apostle and told him that he had done his best to take him prisoner and bring him to him but that he had insisted on fighting and the result had been fatal to him.

Yaḥyā b. ʿAbbād b. ʿAbdullah b. al-Zubayr told me on the authority of his father; and ʿAbdullah b. Abū Bakr and others on the authority of ʿAbdu'l-Raḥmān b. ʿAuf told me the same, saying: 'Umayya b. Khalaf was a friend of mine in Mecca and my name was ʿAbdu ʿAmr, but I was called ʿAbdu'l-Raḥmān when I became a Muslim. When we used to meet in Mecca he would say, "Do you dislike the name your parents gave you?" and I would say yes; and he would say,

"As for me, I don't know al-Raḥmān, so adopt a name which I can call you between ourselves. You won't reply to your original name, and I won't use one I don't know." When he said "O ʿAbdu ʿAmr" I wouldn't answer him, and finally I said, "O Abû ʿAlî, call me what you like," and he called me "ʿAbdu'l-Ilāh" and I accepted the name from him. On the day of Badr I passed by him standing with his son ʿAlī holding him by the hand. I was carrying coats of mail which I had looted; and when he saw me he said, "O ʿAbdu ʿAmr," but I would not answer until he said "O ʿAbdu'l-Ilāh." Then he said, "Won't you take me prisoner, for I am more valuable than these coats of mail which you have?" "By God I will," I said. So I threw away the mail and took him and his son by the hand, he saying the while "I never saw a day like this. Have you no use for milk?" Then I walked off with the pair of them.'

ʿAbdu'l-Wāḥid b. Abū ʿAun from Saʿd b. Ibrāhīm from his father ʿAbdū'l-Raḥmān b. ʿAuf told me that the latter said: Umayya said to me as I walked between them holding their hands, 'Who is that man who is wearing an ostrich feather on his breast?' When I told him it was Ḥamza he said that it was he who had done them so much damage. As I was leading them away Bilāl saw him with me. Now it was Umayya who used to torture Bilāl in Mecca to make him abandon Islam, bringing him out to the scorching heat of the sun, laying him on his back, and putting a great stone on his chest, telling him that he could stay there until he gave up the religion of Muhammad, and Bilāl kept saying 'One! One!' As soon as he saw him he said, 'The arch-infidel Umayya b. Khalaf! May I not live if he lives.' I said, '(Would you attack) my prisoners?' But he kept crying out these words in spite of my remonstrances until finally he shouted at the top of his voice, 'O God's Helpers, the arch-infidel Umayya b. Khalaf! May I not live if he lives.' The people formed a ring round us as I was protecting him. Then a man drew his sword and cut off his son's foot so that he fell down and Umayya let out a cry such as I have never heard; and I said to him 'Make your escape' (though he had no chance of escape) 'I can do nothing for you.' They hewed them to pieces with their swords until they were dead. Abdu'l-Raḥmān used to say, 'God have mercy on Bilāl. I lost my coats of mail and he deprived me of my prisoners.'

ʿAbdullah b. Abū Bakr told me he was told as from Ibn ʿAbbās: 'A man of B. Ghifār told me: I and a cousin of mine went up a hill from which we could look down on Badr, we being polytheists waiting to see the result of the battle so that we could join in the looting. And while we were on the hill a cloud came near and we heard the neighing of horses and I heard one saying "Forward, Ḥaysūm!"[19] As for my cousin, his heart burst asunder and he died on the spot; I almost perished, then I pulled myself together.'

ʿAbdullah b. Abū Bakr from one of B. Sāʿida from Abū Usayd Mālik b. Rabīʿa who was present at Badr told him after he had lost his sight: 'If I were in Badr today and had my sight I could show you the glen from which the angels emerged. I have not the slightest doubt on the point.'

My father Isḥāq b. Yasār from men of B. Māzin b. al-Najjār from Abū Dāʾūd al-Māzinī, who was at Badr, told me: 'I was pursuing a polytheist at Badr to smite him, when his head fell off before I could get at him with my sword, and I knew that someone else had killed him.'

One above suspicion from Miqsam, freedman of ʿAbdullah b. al-Ḥārith from ʿAbdullah b. ʿAbbās, told me, 'The sign of the angels at Badr was white turbans flowing behind them: at Ḥunayn they wore red turbans.'

One above suspicion from Miqsam from Ibn ʿAbbās told me: The angels did not fight in any battle but Badr. In the other battles they were there as reinforcements, but they did not fight.

As he was fighting that day Abū Jahl was saying:

> What has fierce war to dislike about me,
> A young he-camel with razor-like teeth?
> For this very purpose did my mother bear me.

When the apostle had finished with the enemy he ordered that Abū Jahl should be looked for among the slain. (Ṭ. He said, 'O God, don't let him escape Thee!') The first man to find him—so Thaur b. Yazīd from ʿIkrima from Ibn ʿAbbās told me; as well as ʿAbdullah b. Abū Bakr who told me the same—was Muʿādh b. ʿAmr b. al-Jamūḥ, brother of B. Salama, whom they reported as saying: I heard the people saying when Abū Jahl was in a sort of thicket, 'Abū'l-Ḥakam cannot be got at'. When I heard that I made it my business, and made for him. When I got within striking distance I fell upon him and fetched him a blow which sent his foot and half his shank flying. I can only liken it to a date-stone flying from the pestle when it is beaten. His son ʿIkrima struck me on the shoulder and severed my arm and it hung by the skin from my side, and the battle compelled me to leave him. I fought the whole of the day dragging my arm behind me and

---

[19] The name of Gabriel's horse.

when it became painful to me I put my foot on it and standing on it I tore it off.' He lived after that into the reign of ʿUthmān.

Muʿawwidh b. ʿAfrāʾ passed Abū Jahl as he lay there helpless and smote him until he left him at his last gasp. He himself went on fighting until he was killed. Then ʿAbdullah b. Masʿūd passed by Abū Jahl when the apostle had ordered that he was to be searched for among the slain. I have heard that the apostle had told them that if he was hidden among the corpses they were to look for the trace of a scar on his knee. When they both were young they had been pressed together at the table of ʿAbdullah b. Judʿān. He was thinner than Abū Jahl and he gave him a push which sent him to his knees and one of them was scratched so deeply that it left a permanent scar. ʿAbdullah b. Masʿūd said that he found him at his last gasp and put his foot on his neck (for he had once clawed at him and punched him in Mecca), and said to him: 'Has God put you to shame, you enemy of God?' He replied 'How has He shamed me? Am I anything more remarkable than a man you have killed? Tell me how the battle went.' He told him that it went in favour of God and His apostle.

Men of B. Makhzûm assert that Ibn Masʿūd used to say: He said to me, 'You have climbed high, you little shepherd.' Then I cut off his head and brought it to the apostle saying, 'This is the head of the enemy of God, Abū Jahl.' He said, 'By God than Whom there is no other, is it?' (This used to be his oath.) 'Yes,' I said, and I threw his head before the apostle and he gave thanks to God.

ʿUkkāsha b. Miḥṣan b. Ḥurthān al-Asadī, ally of B. ʿAbdu Shams, fought at Badr until his sword was broken in his hand. He came to the apostle who gave him a wooden cudgel telling him to fight with that. When he took it he brandished it and it became in his hand a long, strong, gleaming sword, and he fought with it until God gave victory to the Muslims. The sword was called al-ʿAun and he had it with him in all the battles he fought with the apostle until finally he was killed in the rebellion, still holding it. Ṭulayḥa b. Khuwaylid al-Asadī killed him, and this is what he said about it:

> What do you think about a people when you kill them?
> Are they not men though they are not Muslims?
> If camels and women were captured
> You will not get away scatheless after killing Ḥibāl.
> I set Ḥimāla's breast against them—a mare well used to
> The cry of 'Warriors down to the fight!'
> (One day you see her protected and covered,

Another day unencumbered dash to the fray)
The night I left Ibn Aqram lying
And ʿUkkāsha the Ghanamite dead on the field.

When the apostle said, '70,000 of my people shall enter Paradise like the full moon' ʿUkkāsha asked if he could be one of them, and the apostle prayed that he might be one. One of the Anṣār got up and asked that he too might be one of them, and he replied, "ʿUkkāsha has forestalled you and the prayer is cold.'

I have heard from his family that the apostle said: 'Ours is the best horseman among the Arabs,' and when we asked who, he said that it was ʿUkkāsha. When Ḍirār b. al-Azwar al-Asadî said, 'That is a man of ours,' the apostle answered, 'He is not yours but ours through alliance.'

Yazīd b. Rūmān from ʿUrwa b. al-Zubayr from ʿĀʾisha told me that the latter said: 'When the apostle ordered that the dead should be thrown into a pit they were all thrown in except Umayya b. Khalaf whose body had swelled within his armour so that it filled it and when they went to move him his body disintegrated; so they left it where it was and heaped earth and stones upon it. As they threw them into the pit the apostle stood and said: "O people of the pit, have you found that what God threatened is true? For I have found that what my Lord promised me is true." His companions asked: "Are you speaking to dead people?" He replied that they knew that what their Lord had promised them was true.' ʿĀʾisha said: 'People say that he said "They *hear* what I say to them," but what he said was "They *know*".'

Ḥumayd al-Ṭawīl told me that Anas b. Mālik said: 'The apostle's companions heard him saying in the middle of the night "O people of the pit: O ʿUtba, O Shayba, O Umayya, O Abū Jahl," enumerating all who had been thrown into the pit, "Have you found that what God promised you is true? I have found that what my Lord promised me is true." The Muslims said, "Are you calling to dead bodies?" He answered: "You cannot hear what I say better than they, but they cannot answer me."'

A learned person told me that the apostle said that day, 'O people of the pit, you were an evil kinsfolk to your prophet. You called me a liar when others believed me; you cast me out when others took me in; you fought against me when others fought on my side.' Then he added 'Have you found that what your Lord promised you is true?'

Ḥassān b. Thābit said:

I recognize the dwellings of Zaynab on the sandhill
Looking like the writing of revelation on dirty old paper.
Winds blow over them and every dark cloud
Pours down its heavy rain;
Its traces obscured and deserted
Were once the abodes of dearly loved friends.
Abandon this constant remembrance of them,
Quench the heat of the sorrowing breast.
Tell the truth about that in which there is no shame,
Not the tale of a liar,
Of what God did on the day of Badr,
Giving us victory over the polytheists.
The day when their multitude was like Ḥirā᾽
Whose foundations appear at sunset.
We met them with a company
Like lions of the jungle young and old
In defence of Muhammad in the heat of war
Helping him against the enemy.
In their hands were sharp swords
And well-tried shafts with thick knots.
The sons of Aus the leaders, helped by
The sons of al-Najjār in the strong religion.
Abū Jahl we left lying prostrate
And ʿUtba we left on the ground.
Shayba too with others
Of noble name and descent.
The apostle of God called to them
When we cast them into the pit together.
'Have you found that I spoke the truth?
And the command of God takes hold of the heart?'
They spoke not. Had they spoken they would have said,
'Thou wast right and thy judgment was sound.'

When the apostle gave the order for them to be thrown into the pit ʿUtba was dragged to it. I have been told that the apostle looked at the face of his son Abū Ḥudhayfa, and lo he was sad and his colour had changed. He said, 'I fear that you feel deeply the fate of your father' or words to that effect. 'No,' he said, 'I have no misgivings about my father and his death, but I used to know my father as a wise, cultured, and virtuous man and so I hoped that he would be guided to Islam. When I saw what had befallen him and that he had died in unbelief after my hopes for him it saddened me.' The apostle blessed him and spoke kindly to him.

I have been told that the Qurān came down about certain men who were killed at Badr: 'Those whom the angels took who were wronging themselves they asked, What were you (doing)? They said: We were oppressed in the earth. They said: Was not God's earth wide enough that you could have migrated therein? As for them their habitation will be hell—an evil resort.[20] They were: al-Ḥārith b. Zamaᶜa; Abū Qays b. al-Fākih; Abū Qays b. al-Walīd; ᶜAlī b. Umayya; and al-ᶜĀṣ b. Munabbih. These had been Muslims while the apostle was in Mecca. When he migrated to Medina their fathers and families in Mecca shut them up and seduced them and they let themselves be seduced. Then they joined their people in the expedition to Badr and were all killed.

Then the apostle ordered that everything that had been collected in the camp should be brought together, and the Muslims quarrelled about it. Those who had collected it claimed it, and those who had fought and pursued the enemy claimed that had it not been for them there would have been no booty and that had they not engaged the enemy they would not have been able to get anything; while those who were guarding the apostle lest the enemy should attack him claimed that they had an equal right, for they had wanted to fight the enemy, and they had wanted to seize the booty when there was none to defend it, but they were afraid that the enemy might return to the charge and so they kept their position round the apostle.

ᶜAbdu'l-Raḥmān b. al-Ḥārith and others of our friends from Sulaymān b. Mūsā from Makḥūl from Abū Umāma al-Bāhilī said: 'I asked ᶜUbāda b. al-Ṣāmit about the chapter of *al-Anfāl* and he said that it came down concerning those who took part in the battle of Badr when they quarrelled about the booty and showed their evil nature. God took it out of their hands and gave it to the apostle, and he divided it equally among the Muslims.'

ᶜAbdullah b. Abū Bakr told me that Mālik b. Rabīᶜa one of B. Sāᶜida from Abū Usayd al-Sāᶜidī said: 'I got a sword belonging to B. ᶜĀ'idh the Makhzūmites which was called al-Marzubān, and when the apostle ordered everyone to turn in what they had taken I came and threw it into the heap of spoils. Now the apostle never held back anything he was asked for and al-Arqam b. Abū'l-Arqam knew this and asked him for it and the apostle gave it him.'

---

[20] Sūra 4.99.

Then the apostle sent ʿAbdullah b. Rawāḥa with the good news of the victory to the people of Upper Medina, and Zayd b. Ḥāritha to the people of Lower Medina. Usāma b. Zayd said: 'The news came to us as we had heaped earth on Ruqayya the apostle's daughter who was married to ʿUthmān b. ʿAffan, (the apostle having left me behind with ʿUthmān to look after her), that Zayd b. Ḥāritha had come. So I went to him as he was standing in the place of prayer surrounded by the people, and he was saying: "ʿUtba and Shayba and Abū Jahl and Zamaʿa and Abūʾl-Bakhtari and Umayya and Nubayh and Munab-bih have been slain." I said, "Is this true, my father?" and he said, "Yes, by God it is, my son."'

Then the apostle began his return journey to Medina with the unbelieving prisoners, among whom were ʿUqba b. Abū Muʿayṭ and al-Naḍr b. al-Ḥārith. The apostle carried with him the booty that had been taken from the polytheists and put ʿAbdullah b. Kaʿb in charge of it. A *rajaz* poet of the Muslims said:

> Start your camels, O Basbas!
> There's no halting-place in Dhū Ṭalḥ
> Nor in the desert of Ghumayr a pen.
> The people's camels cannot be locked up.
> So to set them on the way is wiser
> God having given victory and Akhnas having fled.

Then the apostle went forward until when he came out of the pass of al-Ṣafrāʾ he halted on the sandhill between the pass and al-Nāziya called Sayar at a tree there and divided the booty which God had granted to the Muslims equally. Then he marched until he reached Rauḥāʾ when the Muslims met him congratulating him and the Muslims on the victory God had given him. Salama b. Salāma—so ʿĀṣim b. ʿUmar b. Qatāda and Yazīd b. Rūmān told me—said, 'What are you congratulating us about? By God, we only met some bald old women like the sacrificial camels who are hobbled, and we slaughtered them!' The apostle smiled and said, 'But, nephew, those were the chiefs'. When the apostle was in al-Ṣafrāʾ, al-Naḍr was killed by ʿAlī, as a learned Meccan told me. When he was in ʿIrquʾl-Ẓabya ʿUqba was killed. He had been captured by ʿAbdullah b. Salima, one of the B. al-ʿAjlān.

When the apostle ordered him to be killed ʿUqba said, 'But who will look after my children, O Muhammad?' 'Hell', he said, and ʿĀṣim b. Thābit b. Abūʾl-Aqlaḥ al-Anṣārī killed him according to what Abū ʿUbayda b. Muhammad b. ʿAmmār b. Yāsir told me.

Abū Hind, freedman of Farwa b. ʿAmr al-Bayāḍī, met the apostle there with a jar full of butter and dates. He had stayed behind from Badr but was present at all the other battles and afterwards became the apostle's cupper. The apostle said, 'Abū Hind is one of the Anṣār; intermarry with him,' and they did so.

The apostle arrived in Medina a day before the prisoners. ʿAbdullah b. Abū Bakr told me that Yaḥyā b. ʿAbdullah b. ʿAbdu'l-Raḥmān b. Asʿad b. Zurāra told him that the prisoners were brought in when Sauda d. Zamaʿa, the wife of the prophet, was with the family of ʿAfrā' when they were bewailing ʿAuf and Muʿawwidh ʿAfrā''s sons, this being before the veil was imposed on them. Sauda said: 'As I was with them, suddenly it was said: "Here are the prisoners" and I returned to my house where the apostle was. And there was Abū Yazīd Suhayl b. ʿAmr in a corner of the room with his hands tied to his neck. I could hardly contain myself when I saw Abū Yazīd in this state and I said, "O Abū Yazīd, you surrendered too readily. You ought to have died a noble death!" Suddenly the prophet's voice startled me: "Sauda, would you stir up trouble against God and his apostle?" I said, "By God, I could hardly contain myself when I saw Abū Yazīd in this state and that is why I said what I did."'

Nubayh b. Wahb brother of B. ʿAbdu'l-Dār told me that the apostle divided the prisoners amongst his companions and said, 'Treat them well.' Now Abū ʿAzīz b. ʿUmayr b. Hāshim, brother of Muṣʿab b. ʿUmayr by the same mother and father, was among the prisoners and he said, 'My brother Muṣʿab passed by me as one of the Anṣār was binding me and he said: "Bind him fast, for his mother is a wealthy woman; perhaps she will redeem him from you." I was with a number of the Anṣār when they brought me from Badr, and when they ate their morning and evening meals they gave me the bread and ate the dates themselves in accordance with the orders that the apostle had given about us. If anyone had a morsel of bread he gave it to me. I felt ashamed and returned it to one of them but he returned it to me untouched.'

The first to come to Mecca with news of the disaster was al-Ḥaysumān b. ʿAbdullah al-Khuzāʿī, and when they asked for news he enumerated all the Quraysh chiefs who had been killed. Ṣafwān who was sitting in the *ḥijr* said, 'This fellow is out of his mind. Ask him about me.' So they said: 'What happened to Ṣafwān b. Umayya?' He answered, 'There he is sitting in the *ḥijr*, and by God I saw his father and his brother when they were killed.'

Ḥusayn b. ʿAbdullah b. ʿUbaydallah b. ʿAbbās from ʿIkrima, freedman of Ibn ʿAbbās, told me that Abū Rāfiʿ, freedman of the apostle, said, 'I used to be a slave of ʿAbbās. Islam had entered among us, the people of the house; ʿAbbās had become a Muslim, and so had Ummuʾl-Faḍl, and so had I. But ʿAbbās was afraid of his people and disliked to go against them, so he hid his faith; he had a great deal of money scattered among the people. Abū Lahab had stayed behind from the Badr expedition sending in his stead al-ʿĀṣ b. Hishām; for that is what they did—any man who stayed behind sent another in his place. And when news came of the Quraysh disaster at Badr God humiliated Abū Lahab and put him to shame while we found ourselves in a position of power and respect. Now I was a weak man and I used to make arrows, sharpening them in the tent of Zamzam, and lo as I was sitting there with Ummuʾl-Faḍl sharpening arrows delighted with the news that had come, up came Abū Lahab dragging his feet in ill temper and sat down at the end of the tent with his back to mine. As he was sitting there people said, "Here is Abū Sufyān b. al-Ḥārith b. ʿAbduʾl-Muṭṭalib just arrived." Abū Lahab said, "Come here, for you have news." So he came and sat with him while the people stood round, and when he asked his nephew for the news he said, "As soon as we met the party we turned our backs and they were killing and capturing us just as they pleased; and by God I don't blame the people for that. We met men in white on piebald horses between heaven and earth, and by God they spared nothing and none could withstand them." So I lifted the rope of the tent and said: "Those were the angels." Abū Lahab struck me violently in the face. I leapt at him, but he knocked me down and knelt on me beating me again and again, for I was a weak man. Ummuʾl-Faḍl went and got one of the supports of the tent and split his head with a blow which left a nasty wound, saying, "You think you can despise him now his master is away!" He got up and turned tail humiliated. He only lived for another week, for God smote him with pustules, from which he died.'

(Ṭ. 1340. 10. His two sons left him unburied for two or three nights so that the house stank (for the Quraysh dread pustules and the like as men dread plague) until finally a man said to them: 'It is disgraceful! Are you not ashamed that your father should stink in his house while you do not cover him from the sight of men?' They replied that they were afraid of those ulcers. He offered to go with them. They did not wash the body but threw water over it from a distance without touching it. Then they took it up and buried it on the high ground above Mecca by a wall and threw stones over it until it was covered.

Ibn Ḥamīd said that Salama b. al-Faḍl said that Muhammad b.

Isḥāq said that al-ʿAbbās b. ʿAbdullah b. Maʿbad from one of his family on the authority of ʿAbdullah b. ʿAbbās said: 'On the night of Badr when the prisoners were safely guarded, the apostle could not sleep during the first part of the night. When his companions asked him the reason he said: "I heard the writhing of al-ʿAbbās in his prison." So they got up and liberated him whereupon the apostle slept soundly.'

On the same authority I heard that Muhammad b. Isḥāq said: 'al-Ḥasan b. ʿUmāra told me from al-Ḥakam b. ʿUtayba from Miqsam from Ibn ʿAbbās: The man who captured al-ʿAbbās was Abūʾl-Yasar Kaʿb b. ʿAmr brother of the B. Salima. Abūʾl-Yasar was a compact little man while al-ʿAbbās was bulky. When the apostle asked the former how he had managed to capture him, he said that a man such as he had never seen before or afterwards had helped him, and when he described him, the apostle said, "A noble angel helped you against him."')

(Ṣuhaylī, ii. 79: In the *riwāya* of Yūnus Ibn Isḥāq recorded that the apostle saw her (Ummuʾl-Faḍl) when she was a baby crawling before him and said, 'If she grows up and I am still alive I will marry her.' But he died before she grew up and Sufyān b. al-Aswad b. ʿAbduʾl-Asad al-Makhzūmī married her and she bore him Rizq and Lubāba.

They did not bury Abū Lahab, but he was put against a wall and stones were thrown upon him from behind the wall until he was covered. It is said that when ʿĀʾisha passed the place she used to veil her face.)

Yaḥyā b. ʿAbbād b. ʿAbdullah b. al-Zubayr from his father ʿAbbād told me that Quraysh bewailed their dead. Then they said, 'Do not do this, for the news will reach Muhammad and his companions and they will rejoice over your misfortune; and do not send messengers about your captives but hold back so that Muhammad and his companions may not demand excessive ransoms.' Al-Aswad b. al-Muṭṭalib had lost three of his sons: Zamaʿa, ʿAqīl, and al-Ḥārith b. Zamaʿa, and he wanted to bewail them. Meanwhile he heard a weeping woman, and as he was blind he told a servant to go and see whether lamentation had been permitted, for if Quraysh were weeping over their dead he might weep for Zamaʿa Abū Ḥakīma, for he was consumed by a burning sorrow. The servant returned to say that it was a woman weeping over a camel she had lost. Thereupon he said:

Does she weep because she has lost a camel?
And does this keep her awake all night?
Weep not over a young camel

But over Badr where hopes were dashed to the ground.
Over Badr the finest of the sons of Huṣayṣ
And Makhzūm and the clan of Abu'l-Walīd.
Weep if you must weep over ʿAqīl,
Weep for Ḥārith the lion of lions,
Weep unweariedly for them all,
For Abū Ḥakīma had no peer.
Now they are dead, men bear rule
Who but for Badr would be of little account.

Among the prisoners was Abū Wadāʿa b. Ḍubayra al-Sahmī. The apostle remarked that in Mecca he had a son who was a shrewd and rich merchant and that he would soon come to redeem his father. When Quraysh counselled delay in redeeming the prisoners so that the ransom should not be extortionate, al-Muṭṭalib b. Abū Wadāʿa—the man the apostle meant—said, 'You are right. Don't be in a hurry.' And he slipped away at night and came to Medina and recovered his father for 4,000 dirhams and took him away.

The Quraysh sent to redeem the prisoners and Mikraz b. Ḥafṣ b. al-Akhyaf came about Suhayl b. ʿAmr who had been captured by Mālik b. al-Dukhshum, brother of the B. Sālim b. ʿAuf, who said:

I captured Suhayl and I would not exchange him
For a prisoner from any other people.
Khindif knows that its hero is Suhayl
When injustice is complained of.
I struck with my keen sword until it bent.
I forced myself to fight this hare-lipped man.

Suhayl was a man whose lower lip was split.

Muhammad b. ʿAmr b. ʿAtāʾ, brother of B. ʿĀmir b. Luʾayy, told me that ʿUmar said to the apostle, 'Let me pull out Suhayl's two front teeth; his tongue will stick out and he will never be able to speak against you again.' He answered, 'I will not mutilate him, otherwise God would mutilate me though I am a prophet.'

I have heard that in this tradition the apostle said to ʿUmar, 'Perhaps he will make a stand for which you will not blame him.'

When Mikraz had spoken about him and finally agreed on terms with them they demanded the money, and he asked that they would hold him as security and let Suhayl go so that he could send his ransom. They did so and imprisoned Mikraz in his stead. Mikraz said:

I redeemed with costly she-camels a captive hero
(The payment is for a true Arab not for clients).
I pledged my person, though money would be easier for me.
But I feared being put to shame.
I said, 'Suhayl is the best of us, so take him back
To our sons so that we may attain our desires'.

(Ṭ. 1344. Ibn Ḥamīd from Salama from Ibn Isḥāq from al-Kalbī from Abū Ṣāliḥ from Ibn ʿAbbās told me that the apostle said to al-ʿAbbās when he was brought to Medina, 'Redeem yourself, O ʿAbbās, and your two nephews ʿAqīl b. Abū Ṭālib and Naufal b. al-Ḥārith and your ally ʿUtba b. ʿAmr b. Jaḥdam brother of the B. al-Ḥārith b. Fihr, for you are a rich man.' He replied, 'I was a Muslim but the people compelled me (to fight).' He answered, 'God knows best about your Islam. If what you say is true God will reward you for it. But to all outward appearance you have been against us, so pay us your ransom.' Now the apostle had taken twenty okes of gold from him and he said, 'O apostle of God, credit me with them in my ransom.' He replied, 'That has nothing to do with it. God took that from you and gave it to us.' He said, 'I have no money.' 'Then where is the money which you left with Ummuʾl-Faḍl d. al-Ḥārith when you left Mecca? You two were alone when you said to her, "If I am killed so much is for al-Faḍl, ʿAbdullah and Qutham and ʿUbaydullah."' 'By him who sent you with the truth,' he exclaimed, 'none but she and I knew of this and now I know that you are God's apostle.' So he redeemed himself and the three men named above.)

ʿAbdullah b. Abū Bakr told me that Abū Sufyān's son ʿAmr whom he had by a daughter of ʿUqba b. Abū Muʿayṭ was a prisoner in the apostle's hands from Badr; and when Abū Sufyān was asked to ransom his son ʿAmr he said, 'Am I to suffer the double loss of my blood and my money? They have killed Ḥanẓala and am I to ransom ʿAmr? Leave him with them. They can keep him as long as they like!'

While he was thus held prisoner in Medina with the apostle Saʿd b. al-Nuʿmān b. Akkāl, brother of B. ʿAmr b. ʿAuf, one of the B. Muʿāwiya, went forth on pilgrimage accompanied by a young wife of his. He was an old man and a Muslim who had sheep in al-Naqīʿ. He left that place on pilgrimage without fear of any untoward events, never thinking that he would be detained in Mecca, as he came as a pilgrim, for he knew that Quraysh did not usually interfere with pilgrims, but treated them well. But Abū Sufyān fell upon him in Mecca and imprisoned him in retaliation for his son ʿAmr. Then Abū Sufyān said:

O family of Ibn Akkāl, answer his plea
May you lose each other! Do not surrender the chief in his prime.
The Banu ʿAmr will be base and contemptible
If they do not release their captive from his fetters.

Ḥassān b. Thābit answered him:

If Saʿd had been free the day he was in Mecca
He would have killed many of you ere he was captured.
With a sharp sword or a bow of *nabʿa* wood
Whose string twangs when the arrow is shot.

The B. ʿAmr b. ʿAuf went to the apostle and told him the news and asked him to give them ʿAmr b. Abū Sufyān so that they could let him go in exchange for their man and the apostle did so. So they sent him to Abū Sufyān and he released Saʿd.

Among the prisoners was Abūʾl-ʿĀṣ b. al-Rabīʿ, son-in-law of the apostle, married to his daughter Zaynab. Abūʾl-ʿĀṣ was one of the important men of Mecca in wealth, respect, and merchandise. His mother was Hāla d. Khuwaylid, and Khadīja was his aunt. Khadīja had asked the apostle to find him a wife. Now the apostle never opposed her—this was before revelation came to him—and so he married him to his daughter. Khadīja used to regard him as her son. When God honoured His apostle with prophecy Khadīja and her daughters believed in him and testified that he had brought the truth and followed his religion, though Abūʾl-ʿĀṣ persisted in his polytheism. Now the apostle had married Ruqayya or Umm Kulthūm to ʿUtba b. Abū Lahab, and when he openly preached to Quraysh the command of God and showed them hostility they reminded one another that they had relieved Muhammad of his care for his daughters and decided to return them so that he should have the responsibility of looking after them himself. They went to Abūʾl-ʿĀṣ and told him to divorce his wife and they would give him any woman he liked. He refused, saying that he did not want any other woman from Quraysh; and I have heard that the apostle used to speak warmly of his action as a son-in-law. Then they went to ʿUtba b. Abū Lahab with the same request and he said that if they would give him the daughter of Abān b. Saʿīd b. al-ʿĀṣ or the daughter of Saʿīd b. al-ʿĀṣ he would divorce his wife, and when they did so he divorced her, not having consummated the marriage. Thus God took her from him to her honour and his shame, and ʿUthmān afterwards married her.

Now the apostle had no power of binding and loosing in Mecca, his circumstances being circumscribed. Islam had made a division between Zaynab and her husband Abū'l-ʿĀṣ, but they lived together, Muslim and unbeliever, until the apostle migrated. Abū'l-ʿĀṣ joined the expedition to Badr and was captured among the prisoners and remained at Medina with the apostle.

Yaḥyā b. ʿAbbād b. ʿAbdullah b. al-Zubayr from his father ʿAbbād told me that ʿĀ'isha said: 'When the Meccans sent to ransom their prisoners, Zaynab sent the money for Abū'l-ʿĀṣ; with it she sent a necklace which Khadīja had given her on her marriage to Abū'l-ʿĀṣ. When the apostle saw it his feelings overcame him and he said: "If you would like to let her have her captive husband back and return her money to her, do so." The people at once agreed and they let him go and sent her money back.'

THE AFFAIR OF AL-ḤUDAYBIYA, A.H. 6. THE WILLING HOMAGE AND THE PEACE BETWEEN THE APOSTLE AND SUHAYL B. ʿAMR

Then the apostle stayed in Medina during the months of Ramaḍān and Shawwāl and went out on the little pilgrimage in Dhū'l-Qaʿda with no intention of making war. He called together the Arabs and neighbouring Bedouin to march with him, fearing that Quraysh would oppose him with arms or prevent him from visiting the temple, as they actually did. Many of the Arabs held back from him, and he went out with the emigrants and Anṣār and such of the Arabs as stuck to him. He took the sacrificial victims with him and donned the pilgrim garb so that all would know that he did not intend war and that his purpose was to visit the temple and to venerate it.

Muhammad b. Muslim b. Shihāb al-Zuhrī from ʿUrwa b. al-Zubayr from Miswar b. Makhrama and Marwān b. al-Ḥakam told me: The apostle went out in the year of al-Ḥudaybiya with peaceful intent meaning to visit the temple, and took with him seventy camels for sacrifice. There were seven hundred men so that each camel was on behalf of ten men. Jābir b. ʿAbdullah, so I have heard, used to say, 'We, the men of al-Ḥudaybiya, were fourteen hundred.'

Al-Zuhrī continued: When the apostle was in ʿUsfān, Bishr b. Sufyān al-Kaʿbī met him and said: 'There are Quraysh who have heard of your coming and have come out with their milch-camels and have put on leopards' skins, and have encamped at Dhū Ṭuwa swearing that you will never enter Mecca in defiance of them. This man Khālid b. al-Walīd is with their cavalry which they have sent in advance to

Kurāʿu'l-Ghamīn.' The apostle said: 'Alas, Quraysh, war has devoured them! What harm would they have suffered if they had left me and the rest of the Arabs to go our own ways? If they should kill me that is what they desire, and if God should give me the victory over them they would enter Islam in flocks. If they do not do that they will fight while they have the strength, so what are Quraysh thinking of? By Allah, I will not cease to fight for the mission with which God has entrusted me until He makes it victorious or I perish.' Then he said, 'Who will take us out by a way in which we shall not meet them?'

ʿAbdullah b. Abū Bakr told me that a man of Aslam volunteered to do so and he took them by a rugged, rocky track between passes which was very hard on the Muslims, and when they emerged from it on to the easy ground at the end of the wadi the apostle said to the men, 'Say, We ask God's forgiveness and we repent towards Him.' They did so and he said, 'That is the "putting away" that was enjoined on the children of Israel; but they did not say the words.'[21]

The apostle ordered the force to turn to the right through the salty growth on the road which leads by the pass of al-Murār to the declivity of al-Ḥudaybiya below Mecca. They did so, and when the Quraysh cavalry saw from the dust of the army that they had turned aside from their path they returned at a gallop to Quraysh. The apostle went as far as the pass of al-Murār and when his camel knelt and the men said, 'The camel won't get up,' he said: 'It has not refused and such is not its nature, but the One who restrained the elephant from Mecca is keeping it back. Today whatever condition Quraysh make in which they ask me to show kindness to kindred I shall agree to.' Then he told the people to dismount. They objected that there was no water there by which they could halt, so he took an arrow from his quiver and gave it to one of his companions and he took it down into one of the waterholes and prodded the middle of it and the water rose until the men's camels were satisfied with drinking and lay down there.

One of the B. Aslam told me that the man who went into the hole with the apostle's arrow was Nājiya b. Jundub b. ʿUmayr b. Yaʿmar b. Dārim b. ʿAmr b. Wāʾila b. Sahm b. Māzin b. Salāmān b. Aslam b. Afṣā b. Abū Ḥāritha who drove the apostle's camels to sacrifice.

A traditionist alleged to me that al-Barāʾ b. ʿĀzib used to say that it was he who went down with the apostle's arrow, and God knows which it was.

The Aslam quoted verses from the lines which Nājiya made. We think that it was he who went down with the arrow. Aslam alleged that

---

[21] Cp. Sūra 2.55 and 7.161.

a slave-girl of the Anṣār came up with her bucket while Nājiya was in the well supplying the people with water and said:

> O you down below, my bucket is here.
> I can hear all our men who wish you good cheer
> Praising the one who draws water here.

Nājiya said as he was in the hole getting the water:

> The Yamanī slave-girl knows
> That I'm Nājiya down below getting water.
> Many a wide bloody wound I've made
> In the breasts of advancing foes.

In his tradition al-Zuhrī said: When the apostle had rested Budayl b. Warqā' al-Khuzā'ī came to him with some men of Khuzā'a and asked him what he had come for. He told them that he had not come for war but to go on pilgrimage and venerate the sacred precincts. Then he said to them what he had said to Bishr b. Sufyān. Then they returned to Quraysh and told them what they had heard; but they suspected them and spoke roughly to them, saying, 'He may have come not wanting war but by Allah he shall never come in here against our will, nor shall the Arabs ever say that we have allowed it.'

Khuzā'a were the apostle's confidants, both their Muslims and their polytheists. They kept him informed of everything that happened in Mecca.

Then Quraysh sent Mikraz b. Ḥafṣ b. al-Akhyaf brother of B. 'Āmir b. Lu'ayy to him. When he saw him approaching the apostle said, 'This is a treacherous fellow!' When he came up and spoke to him the apostle gave him the same reply as he had given Budayl and his companions, and he returned and told the Quraysh what the apostle had said.

Then they sent to him al-Ḥulays b. 'Alqama or Ibn Zabbān, who was at that time chief of the black troops, being one of B. al-Ḥārith b. 'Abdu Manāt b. Kināna. When he saw him the apostle said, 'This is one of the devout people, so send the sacrificial animals to meet him so that he can see them!' When he saw them going past him from the side of the wadi with their festive collars round their necks and how they had eaten their hair because they had been so long kept back from the place of sacrifice, he went back to Quraysh and did not come to the apostle, so greatly was he impressed by what he had seen. When he told them that, they said, 'Sit down! You are only a Bedouin, utterly ignorant.'

ʿAbdullah b. Abū Bakr told me that this enraged al-Ḥulays, who said: 'You men of Quraysh, it was not for this that we made an alliance and agreement with you. Is a man who comes to do honour to God's house to be excluded from it? By him who holds my life in his hand, either you let Muhammad do what he has come to do or I shall take away the black troops to the last man.' They said, 'Be quiet, Ḥulays! until we obtain for ourselves acceptable terms.'

In his narrative al-Zuhrī said: Then they sent ʿUrwa b. Masʿūd al-Thaqafī to the apostle and he said: 'You men of Quraysh, I have seen the harshness and rude words with which you have received those you sent to Muhammad when they returned to you. You know that you are the father and I am the son—for ʿUrwa was the son of Subayʿa d. ʿAbdu Shams—I heard of what befell you and I collected those of my people who obeyed me; then I came to you to help you.' They agreed and said that they did not suspect him. So he came to the apostle and sat before him and said: 'Muhammad, have you collected a mixed people together and then brought them to your own people to destroy them? Quraysh have come out with their milch-camels clad in leopard skins swearing that you shall never enter Mecca by force. By God I think I see you deserted by these people (here) tomorrow.' Now Abū Bakr was sitting behind the apostle and he said, 'Suck al-Lāt's nipples! Should we desert him?' He asked who had spoken, and when he heard it was Ibn Abū Quḥāfa he said, 'By Allah, did I not owe you a favour I would pay you back for that, but now we are quits.' Then he began to take hold of the apostle's beard as he talked to him. Al-Mughīra b. Shuʿba was standing by the apostle's head clad in mail and he began to hit his hand as he held the apostle's beard saying, 'Take your hand away from the apostle's face before you lose it.' ʿUrwa said, 'Confound you, how rough and rude you are!' The apostle smiled and when ʿUrwa asked who the man was he told him that it was his brother's son, al-Mughīra b. Shuʿba and he said, 'O wretch, it was only yesterday that I washed your dirty parts!'

The apostle told him what he had told the others, namely that he had not come out for war. He got up from the apostle's presence having seen how his companions treated him. Whenever he performed his ablutions they ran to get the water he had used; if he spat they ran to it; if a hair of his head fell they ran to pick it up. So he returned to Quraysh and said, 'I have been to Chosroes in his kingdom, and Caesar in his kingdom and the Negus in his kingdom, but never have I seen a king among a people like Muhammad among his companions. I have seen a people who will never abandon him for any reason, so form your own opinion.'

A traditionist told me that the apostle called Khirāsh b. Umayya al-Khuzāʿī and sent him to Quraysh in Mecca, mounting him on one of his camels called al-Thaʿlab to tell their chiefs from him what he had come for. They hamstrung the apostle's camel and wanted to kill the man, but the black troops protected him and let him go his way so that he came back to the apostle.

One whom I do not suspect from ʿIkrima client of Ibn ʿAbbās from the latter told me that Quraysh had sent forty or fifty men with orders to surround the apostle's camp and get hold of one of his companions for them, but they were caught and brought to the apostle, who forgave them and let them go their way. They had attacked the camp with stones and arrows. Then he called ʿUmar to send him to Mecca with the same message, but ʿUmar told him that he feared for his life with Quraysh, because there were none of B. ʿAdīy b. Kaʿb in Mecca to protect him, and Quraysh knew of his enmity and his rough treatment of them. He recommended that a man more prized there than himself should be sent, namely ʿUthmān. The apostle summoned ʿUthmān and sent him to Abū Sufyān and the chiefs of Quraysh to tell them that he had not come for war but merely to visit the house and to venerate its sanctity.

As ʿUthmān entered or was about to enter Mecca Abān b. Saʿīd b. al-ʿĀṣ met him and carried him in front of him. Then he gave him his protection until he could convey the apostle's message to them. Having heard what ʿUthmān had to say, they said: 'If you want to go round the temple, go round it.' He said that he could not do so until Muhammad did so, and Quraysh kept him a prisoner with them. The apostle and the Muslims were informed that ʿUthmān had been killed.

THE WILLING HOMAGE

ʿAbdullah b. Abū Bakr told me that when the apostle heard that ʿUthmān had been killed he said that they would not leave until they fought the enemy, and he summoned the men to give their undertaking. The pledge of al-Riḍwān took place under a tree. Men used to say that the apostle took their pledge unto death. Jābir b. ʿAbdullah used to say that the apostle did not take their pledge unto death, but rather their undertaking that they would not run away. Not one of the Muslims who were present failed to give his hand except al-Jadd b. Qays, brother of B. Salima. Jābir used to say: 'By Allah, I can almost see him now sticking to his camel's side cringing as he tried to hide himself from the men.' Then the apostle heard that the news about ʿUthmān was false.

THE ARMISTICE

Al-Zuhrī said: Then Quraysh sent Suhayl b. ʿAmr brother of B. ʿĀmir b. Luʾayy to the apostle with instructions to make peace with him on condition that he went back this year, so that none of the Arabs could say that he made a forcible entry. When the apostle saw him coming he said, 'The people want to make peace seeing that they have sent this man.' After a long discussion peace was made and nothing remained but to write an agreement. ʿUmar jumped up and went to Abū Bakr saying, 'Is he not God's apostle, and are we not Muslims, and are they not polytheists?' to which Abū Bakr agreed, and he went on: 'Then why should we agree to what is demeaning to our religion?' He replied, 'Stick to what he says, for I testify that he is God's apostle.' ʿUmar said, 'And so do I.' Then he went to the apostle and put the same questions to which the apostle answered, 'I am God's slave and His apostle. I will not go against His commandment and He will not make me the loser.' ʿUmar used to say, 'I have not ceased giving alms and fasting and praying and freeing slaves because of what I did that day out of fear for what I had said, when I hoped that (my plan) would be better.'

Then the apostle summoned ʿAlī and told him to write 'In the name of Allah the Compassionate, the Merciful.' Suhayl said 'I do not recognize this; but write "In thy name, O Allah."' The apostle told him to write the latter and he did so. Then he said: 'Write "This is what Muhammad, the apostle of God has agreed with Suhayl b. ʿAmr."' Suhayl said, 'If I witnessed that you were God's apostle I would not have fought you. Write your own name and the name of your father.' The apostle said: 'Write "This is what Muhammad b. ʿAbdullah has agreed with Suhayl b. ʿAmr: they have agreed to lay aside war for ten years during which men can be safe and refrain from hostilities on condition that if anyone comes to Muhammad without the permission of his guardian he will return him to them; and if anyone of those with Muhammad comes to Quraysh they will not return him to him. We will not show enmity one to another and there shall be no secret reservation or bad faith. He who wishes to enter into a bond and agreement with Muhammad may do so and he who wishes to enter into a bond and agreement with Quraysh may do so."' Here

Khuzāʿa leapt up and said, 'We are in a bond and agreement with Muhammad,' and B. Bakr leapt up and said the same with regard to Quraysh, adding 'You must retire from us this year and not enter Mecca against our will, and next year we will make way for you and you can enter it with your companions, and stay there three nights. You may carry a rider's weapons, the swords in their sheaths. You can bring in nothing more.'

While the apostle and Suhayl were writing the document, suddenly Abū Jandal b. Suhayl appeared walking in fetters, having escaped to the apostle. The apostle's companions had gone out without any doubt of occupying Mecca because of the vision which the apostle had seen, and when they saw the negotiations for peace and a withdrawal going on and what the apostle had taken on himself they felt depressed almost to the point of death. When Suhayl saw Abū Jandal he got up and hit him in the face and took hold of his collar, saying, 'Muhammad, the agreement between us was concluded before this man came to you.' He replied, 'You are right.' He began to pull him roughly by his collar and to drag him away to return him to Quraysh, while Abū Jandal shrieked at the top of his voice, 'Am I to be returned to the polytheists that they may entice me from my religion O Muslims?' and that increased the people's dejection. The apostle said, 'O Abū Jandal, be patient and control yourself, for God will provide relief and a means of escape for you and those of you who are helpless. We have made peace with them and we and they have invoked God in our agreement and we cannot deal falsely with them.' ʿUmar jumped up and walked alongside Abū Jandal saying, 'Be patient for they are only polytheists; the blood of one of them is but the blood of a dog,' and he brought the hilt of his sword close up to him. ʿUmar used to say, 'I hoped that he would take the sword and kill his father with it, but the man spared his father and so the matter ended.'

When the apostle had finished the document he summoned representatives of the Muslims and polytheists to witness to the peace, namely Abū Bakr, ʿUmar, and ʿAbdu'l-Raḥmān b. ʿAuf, ʿAbdullah b. Suhayl b. ʿAmr, and Saʿd b. Abū Waqqāṣ, Maḥmūd b. Maslama, Mikraz b. Ḥafṣ who was a polytheist at the time, and ʿAlī who was the writer of the document.

The apostle was encamped in the profane country, and he used to pray in the sacred area. When the peace was concluded he slaughtered his victims and sat down and shaved his head. I have heard that it was Khirāsh b. Umayya b. al-Faḍl al-Khuzāʿī who shaved him then. When the men saw what the apostle had done they leapt up and did the same.

ʿAbdullah b. Abū Najīḥ from Mujāhid from Ibn ʿAbbās told me, 'Some men shaved their heads on the day of al-Ḥudaybiya while others cut their hair.' The apostle said, 'May God have mercy on the shavers.' They said, 'The cutters, too, O apostle?' Three times they had to put this question until finally he added 'and the cutters'. When they asked him why he had repeatedly confined the invocation of God's mercy to the shavers he replied, 'Because they did not doubt.'

The same authorities told me that the apostle sacrificed in the year of al-Ḥudaybiya among his victims a camel belonging to Abū Jahl which had a silver nose-ring, thus enraging the polytheists.

Zuhrī continued: The apostle then went on his way back and when he was half-way back the *sūra al-Fatḥ* came down: 'We have given you a plain victory that God may forgive you your past sin and the sin which is to come and may complete his favour upon you and guide you on an upright path.'[22] Then the account goes on about him and his companions until he comes to mention the oath of allegiance and He said: 'Those who swear allegiance to you really swear allegiance to God, the hand of God being above their hands; so he who breaks his oath breaks it to his own hurt; while he who is faithful to what he has covenanted with God, to him will He give a great reward.'

Then He mentioned the Bedouin who held back from him. Then He said when he urged them to take the field with him and they procrastinated, 'The Bedouin who were left behind will say to you: Our possessions and our families preoccupied us!' Then follows an account of them until the words 'Those who were left behind will say when you go out to capture spoil, Let us follow you, wishing to change what God has said. Say, You shall not follow us. Thus has God said beforehand.' Then follows an account of them and how it was explained to them that they must fight a people of great prowess.

ʿAbdullah b. Abū Najīḥ from ʿAtāʾ b. Abū Rabāḥ from Ibn ʿAbbās said (That means) Persia. One whom I do not suspect from al-Zuhrī told me that 'a people of great prowess' meant Ḥanīfa with the arch-liar.

Then He said: 'God was pleased with the believers when they swore allegiance to you under the tree and He knew what was in their hearts and He sent down the Sakīna upon them and rewarded them with a recent victory and much spoil which they will take. God is mighty, wise. God has promised you much spoil which you will capture and has given you this in advance, and kept men's hands from you, that

[22] Sūra 48.

it may be a sign to the believers and that He may guide you on an upright path, and other (things) which you have not been able to get. God encompasses them, and God is almighty.'

Then He mentioned how He had kept him away from battle after the victory over them, meaning those He had kept from him. Then He said: 'He it is who has kept their hands from you and your hands from them in the vale of Mecca, after He had given you victory over them. God is a seer of what you do.' Then He said: 'They are those who disbelieved and debarred you from the sacred mosque and the offering from reaching its goal.' 'And had it not been for the believing men and women whom you did not know lest you should tread them under foot and thus incur guilt for them unwittingly.' *Maʿarra* means 'a fine', i.e. lest you should suffer loss for them unwittingly and pay its bloodwit; as for real guilt he did not fear it on their account.

Then he said, 'When those who disbelieve had set in their hearts zealotry, the zealotry of paganism,' i.e. Suhayl b. ʿAmr when he scorned to write 'In the name of Allah the Compassionate the Merciful' and that Muhammad is God's apostle. Then He said 'God sent down Ḥis *sakīna* upon His apostle and the believers and imposed on them the word of piety, for they were meet and worthy of it,' i.e. the declaration of God's unity, the witness that there is no God but Allah and that Muhammad is His slave and His apostle.

Then He said: 'God has fulfilled the vision to His apostle in truth. You shall enter the sacred mosque if God will, safely with heads shaved and hair cut short fearing not. For He knows what you do not know,' i.e. the vision which the apostle saw that he would enter Mecca safely without fear. He says 'with your heads shaved and hair cut short' along with him without fear, for He knows what you do not know of that, and more than that He has wrought a near victory, the peace of al-Ḥudaybiya.

No previous victory in Islam was greater than this. There was nothing but battle when men met; but when there was an armistice and war was abolished and men met in safety and consulted together none talked about Islam intelligently without entering it. In those two years double as many or more than double as many entered Islam as ever before.

THE CASE OF THOSE LEFT HELPLESS AFTER THE PEACE

When the apostle arrived in Medina Abū Baṣīr ʿUtba b. Asīd b. Jāriya, one of those imprisoned in Mecca, came to him. Azhar b. ʿAbdu

ʿAuf b. ʿAbd b. al-Ḥārith b. Zuhra and al-Akhnas b. Sharīq b. ʿAmr b. Wahb al-Thaqafī wrote to the apostle about him, and they sent a man of B. ʿĀmir b. Luʾayy with a freed slave of theirs. When they came to the apostle with the letter he said, 'You know the undertaking we gave these people and it ill becomes us that treachery should enter our religion. God will bring relief and a way of escape to those helpless like you, so go back to your people.' He said, 'Would you return me to the polytheists who will seduce me from my religion?' He said, 'Go, for God will bring relief and a way of escape for you and the helpless ones with you.' So he went with them as far as Dhū'l-Ḥulayfa where he and the two men sat against a wall. Abū Baṣīr said, 'Is your sword sharp, O brother of B. ʿĀmir?' When he said that it was he said that he would like to look at it. 'Look at it if you want to,' he replied. Abū Baṣīr unsheathed it and dealt him a blow that killed him. The freedman ran off to the apostle who was sitting in the mosque, and when the apostle saw him coming he said, 'This man has seen something frightful.' When he came up the apostle said, 'What's the matter, woe to you?' He said: 'Your man has killed my man,' and almost at once Abū Baṣīr came up girt with the sword, and standing by the apostle he said, 'Your obligation is over and God has removed it from you. You duly handed me over to the men and I have protected myself in my religion lest I should be seduced therein or scoffed at.' The apostle said, 'Woe is his mother, he would have kindled a war had there been others with him.'

Then Abu Baṣīr went off until he halted at al-ʿĪṣ in the region of Dhū'l-Marwa by the sea-shore on the road which Quraysh were accustomed to take to Syria. The Muslims who were confined in Mecca heard what the apostle had said of Abū Baṣīr so they went out to join him in al-ʿĪṣ. About seventy men attached themselves to him, and they so harried Quraysh, killing everyone they could get hold of and cutting to pieces every caravan that passed them, that Quraysh wrote to the apostle begging him by the ties of kinship to take these men in, for they had no use for them; so the apostle took them in and they came to him in Medina.

When Suhayl heard that Abū Baṣīr had killed his ʿĀmirī guard he leant his back against the Kaʿba and swore that he would not remove it until this man's bloodwit was paid. Abū Sufyān b. Ḥarb said, 'By God, this is sheer folly. It will not be paid.' Three times he said it.

Mauhab b. Riyāḥ Abū Unays, an ally of B. Zuhra, said:

A brief word from Suhayl reached me
And woke me from my sleep.

If you wish to reproach me
Then reproach me, for you are not far from me.
Would you threaten me when ʿAbdu Manāf is round me
With Makhzūm? Alas, whom are you attacking?
If you put me to the test you will not find me
A weak support in grave misfortunes.
I can rival in birth the best of my people.
When the weak are ill-treated I protect them.
They defend the heights of Mecca without doubt
As far as the valleys and the wadi sides
With every blood mare and fiery horse
Grown thin from long fighting.
Maʿadd know they have in al-Khayf
A pavilion of glory exalted high.

ʿAbdullah b. al-Zibaʿrā answered him:

Mauhab has become like a poor donkey
Braying in a village as he passes through it.
A man like you cannot attack Suhayl.
Vain is your effort. Whom are you attacking?
Shut up, you son of a blacksmith,
And stop talking nonsense in the land.
Don't mention the blame of Abū Yazīd.
There's a great difference between oceans and puddles.

INCIDENTS AT THE OCCUPATION OF MECCA A.H. 8

Abū Sufyān b. al-Ḥārith b. ʿAbduʾl-Muṭṭalib and ʿAbdullah b. Abū Umayya b. al-Mughīra had met the apostle also in Nīquʾl-ʿUqāb between Mecca and Medina and tried to get in to him. Umm Salama spoke to him about them, calling them his cousin and his brother-in-law. He replied: 'I have no use for them. As for my cousin he has wounded my pride; and as for my aunt's son and my brother-in-law he spoke insultingly of me in Mecca.' When this was conveyed to them Abū Sufyān who had his little son with him said, 'By God, he must let me in or I will take this little boy of mine and we will wander through the land until we die of hunger and thirst.' When he heard this the apostle felt sorry for them and let them come in and they accepted Islam. Abū Sufyān recited the following verses about his Islam in which he excused himself for what had gone before:

By thy life when I carried a banner
To give al-Lāl's cavalry the victory over Muhammad

I was like one going astray in the darkness of the night,
But now I am led on the right track.
I could not guide myself, and he who with God overcame me
Was he whom I had driven away with all my might.
I used to do all I could to keep men from Muhammad
And I was called a relative of his, though I did not claim the relation.
They are what they are. He who does not hold with them
Though he be a man of sense is blamed and given the lie.
I wanted to be on good terms with them (Muslims)
But I could not join them while I was not guided.
Say to Thaqīf I do not want to fight them;
Say, too, 'Threaten somebody else!'
I was not in the army that attacked ʿĀmir,
I had no part with hand or tongue.
'Twas tribes that came from a distant land,
Strangers from Sahām and Surdad.

They allege that when he recited his words 'He who with God overcame me was he whom I had driven away with all my might' the apostle punched him in the chest and said, 'You did indeed!'

When the apostle camped at Marr al-Ẓahrān ʿAbbās said, 'Alas, Quraysh, if the apostle enters Mecca by force before they come and ask his protection that will be the end of Quraysh for ever.' I sat upon the apostle's white mule and went out on it until I came to the arak trees, thinking that I might find some woodcutters or milkers or someone who could go to Mecca and tell them where the apostle was so that they could come out and ask for safety before he entered the town by assault. As I was going along with this intent suddenly I heard the sound of Abū Sufyān (Ṭ. and Ḥakīm b. Ḥazām) and Budayl talking together. Abū Sufyān was saying. 'I have never seen such fires and such a camp before.' Budayl was saying, 'These, by God, are (the fires of) Khuzāʿa which war has kindled.' Abū Sufyān was saying, 'Khuzāʿa are too poor and few to have fires and camps like these.' I recognized his voice and called to him and he recognized my voice. I told him that the apostle was here with his army and expressed concern for him and for Quraysh: 'If he takes you he will behead you, so ride on the back of this mule so that I can take you to him and ask for you his protection.' So he rode behind me and his two companions returned. Whenever we passed a Muslim fire we were challenged, and when they saw the apostle's mule with me riding it they said it was the prophet's uncle riding his mule until I passed by ʿUmar's fire. He challenged me and got up and came to me, and when he saw Abū

Sufyān on the back of the beast he cried: 'Abū Sufyān, the enemy of God! Thanks be to God who has delivered you up without agreement or word.' Then he ran towards the apostle and I made the mule gallop, and the mule won by the distance a slow beast will outrun a slow man. I dismounted and went in to the apostle and ʿUmar came in saying the same words and adding, 'Let me take off his head.' I told the apostle that I had promised him my protection; then I sat by him and took hold of his head and said, 'By God, none shall talk confidentially to him this night without my being present'; and when ʿUmar continued to remonstrate I said, 'Gently, ʿUmar! If he had been one of the B. ʿAdīy b. Kaʿb you would not have said this; but you know that he is one of the B. ʿAbdu Manāf.' He replied, 'Gently, ʿAbbās! for by God your Islam the day you accepted it was dearer to me than the Islam of al-Khaṭṭāb would have been had he become a Muslim. One thing I surely know is that your Islam was dearer to the apostle than my father's would have been.' The apostle told me to take him away to my quarters and bring him back in the morning. He stayed the night with me and I took him in to see the apostle early in the morning and when he saw him he said, 'Isn't it time that you should recognize that there is no God but Allah?' He answered, 'You are dearer to me than father and mother. How great is your clemency, honour, and kindness! By God, I thought that had there been another God with God he would have continued to help me.' He said: 'Woe to you, Abū Sufyān, isn't it time that you recognize that I am God's apostle?' He answered, 'As to that I still have some doubt.'

I said to him, 'Submit and testify that there is no God but Allah and that Muhammad is the apostle of God before you lose your head,' so he did so. I pointed out to the apostle that Abū Sufyān was a man who liked to have some cause for pride and asked him to do something for him. He said, 'He who enters Abū Sufyān's house is safe, and he who locks his door is safe, and he who enters the mosque is safe.' When he went off to go back the apostle told me to detain him in the narrow part of the wadi where the mountain projected so that God's armies would pass by and he would see them; so I went and detained him where the prophet had ordered.

The squadrons passed him with their standards, and he asked who they were. When I said Sulaym he would say, 'What have I to do with Sulaym?' and so with Muzayna until all had passed, he asking the same question and making the same response to the reply. Finally the apostle passed with his greenish-black squadron in which were Muhājirs and Anṣār whose eyes alone were visible because of their armour. He said, 'Good heavens, ʿAbbās, who are these?' and when I told him he said that none could withstand them. 'By God, O Abū Faḍl, the authority of your brother's son has become great.' I told him that it was due to his prophetic office, and he said that in that case he had nothing to say against it.

I told him to hurry to his people. When he came to them he cried at the top of his voice: 'O Quraysh, this is Muhammad who has come to you with a force you cannot resist. He who enters Abū Sufyān's house is safe.' Hind d. ʿUtba went up to him, and seizing his moustache cried, 'Kill this fat greasy bladder of lard! What a rotten protector of the people!' He said, 'Woe to you, don't let this woman deceive you, for you cannot resist what has come. He who enters Abū Sufyān's house will be safe.' 'God slay you,' they said, 'what good will your house be to us?' He added, 'And he who shuts his door upon himself will be safe and he who enters the mosque will be safe.' Thereupon the people dispersed to their houses and the mosque.

ʿAbdullah b. Abū Bakr told me that when the apostle came to Dhū Ṭuwā he halted on his beast turbaned with a piece of red Yamanī cloth and that he lowered his head in submission to God, when he saw how God had honoured him with victory, so that his beard almost touched the middle of the saddle.

Yaḥyā b. ʿAbbād b. ʿAbdullah b. al-Zubayr from his father from his grandmother Asmāʾ d. Abū Bakr said: When the apostle stopped in Dhū Ṭuwā Abū Quḥāfa said to a daughter of his, one of his youngest children, 'Take me up to Abū Qubays,' for his sight had almost gone. When they got there he asked her what she could see and she told him 'a mass of black.' 'Those are the horses,' he said. Then she told him that she could see a man running up and down in front of them and he said that that was the adjutant, meaning the man who carries and transmits the orders to the cavalry. Then she said, 'By God, the black mass has spread.' He said, 'In that case the cavalry have been released, so bring me quickly to my house.' She took him down and the cavalry encountered him before he could get to his house. The girl had a silver necklace and a man who met her tore it from her neck. When the apostle came in and entered the mosque Abū Bakr came leading his father. On seeing him the apostle said, 'Why did you not leave the old man in his house so that I could come to him there?' Abū Bakr replied that it was more fitting that he should come to him than vice versa. He made him sit before him and stroked his chest and asked him to accept Islam and he did so. When Abū Bakr brought his father in his head was as white as edelweiss, and the apostle told them to dye it. Then Abū Bakr got up and taking his sister's hand said, 'I ask in the name of God and Islam for my sister's necklace', and none answered him, and he said, 'Sister, regard your necklace as taken by God (and look to Him to requite you) for there is not much honesty among people nowadays.'

ʿAbdullah b. Abū Najīḥ told me that the apostle divided his force at Dhū Ṭuwā ordering al-Zubayr b. al-ʿAwwām to go in with some of the men from Kudā. Al-Zubayr commanded the left wing; Saʿd b. ʿUbāda he ordered to go in with some of the men from Kadāʾ.

Some traditionists allege that when Saʿd started off he said,

> Today is a day of war,
> Sanctuary is no more,

and one of the muhājirs heard him and told the apostle that it was to be feared that he would resort to violence. The apostle ordered ʿAlī to go after him and take the flag from him and enter with it himself.

ʿAbdullah b. Abū Najīḥ in his story told me that the apostle ordered Khālid to enter from al-Līṭ, the lower part of Mecca, with some men. Khālid was in command of the right wing with Aslam, Sulaym, Ghifār, Muzayna, Juhayna, and other Arab tribes. Abū ʿUbayda b. al-Jarrāḥ advanced with the troops pouring into Mecca in front of the apostle who entered from Adhākhir until he halted above Mecca and his tent was pitched there.

ʿAbdullah b. Abū Najīḥ and ʿAbdullah b. Abū Bakr told me that Ṣafwān b. Umayya and ʿIkrima b. Abū Jahl and Suhayl b. ʿAmr had collected some men in al-Khandama to fight. Ḥimas b. Qays b. Khālid brother of B. Bakr was sharpening his sword before the apostle entered Mecca, and his wife asked him why he was doing so. When he told her it was for Muhammad and his companions she said that she did not think that it would do them any harm. He answered that he hoped to give her one of them as a slave and said:

> I have no excuse if today they advance.
> Here is my weapon, a long-bladed lance,
> A two-edged sword in their faces will dance!

Then he went to al-Khandama with Ṣafwān, Suhayl, and ʿIkrima and when the Muslims under Khālid arrived a skirmish followed in which Kurz b. Jābir, one of the B. Muḥārib b. Fihr, and Khunays b. Khālid b. Rabīʿa b. Aṣram, an ally of B. Munqidh, who were in Khālid's cavalry, were killed. They had taken a road of their own apart from Khālid and were killed together. Khunays was killed first and Kurz put him between his feet and fought in his defence until he was slain, saying meanwhile:

> Ṣafrāʾ of the B. Fihr knows
> The pure of face and heart
> That I fight today in defence of Abū Ṣakhr.

Khunays was surnamed Abū Ṣakhr.

Salama b. al-Maylāʾ, one of Khālid's horsemen, was killed, and the polytheists lost about 12 or 13 men; then they took to flight. Ḥimās ran off and went into his house and told his wife to bolt the door. When she asked what had become of his former words he said:

> If you had witnessed the battle of Khandama
> When Ṣafwān and ʿIkrima fled
> And Abū Yazīd was standing like a pillar
> And the Muslims met them with their swords
> Which cut through arms and skulls,
> Only confused cries being heard
> Behind us their cries and groans,
> You would not have uttered the least word of blame

The apostle had instructed his commanders when they entered Mecca only to fight those who resisted them, except a small number who were to be killed even if they were found beneath the curtains of the Kaʿba. Among them was ʿAbdullah b. Saʿd, brother of the B. ʿĀmir b. Luʾayy. The reason he ordered him to be killed was that he had been a Muslim and used to write down revelation; then he apostatized and returned to Quraysh and fled to ʿUthmān b. ʿAffān whose foster-brother he was. The latter hid him until he brought him to the apostle after the situation in Mecca was tranquil, and asked that he might be granted immunity. They allege that the apostle remained silent for a long time till finally he said yes. When ʿUthmān had left he said to his companions who were sitting around him, 'I kept silent so that one of you might get up and strike off his head!' One of the Anṣār said, 'Then why didn't you give me a sign, O apostle of God?' He answered that a prophet does not kill by pointing.

Another was ʿAbdullah b. Khaṭal of B. Taym b. Ghālib. He had become a Muslim and the apostle sent him to collect the poor tax in company with one of the Anṣār. He had with him a freed slave who served him. (He was a Muslim.) When they halted he ordered the latter to kill a goat for him and prepare some food, and went to sleep. When he woke up the man had done nothing, so he attacked and killed him and apostatized. He had two singing-girls Fartanā and her friend who used to sing satirical songs about the apostle, so he ordered that they should be killed with him.

Another was al-Ḥuwayrith b. Nuqaydh b. Wahb b. ʿAbd b. Quṣayy, one of those who used to insult him in Mecca.

Another was Miqyas b. Ḥubāba because he had killed an Anṣārī who had killed his brother accidentally, and returned to Quraysh as a polytheist. And Sāra, freed slave of one of the B. ʿAbduʾl-Muṭṭalib; and ʿIkrima b. Abū Jahl. Sāra had insulted him in Mecca. As for ʿIkrima, he fled to the Yaman. His wife Umm Ḥakīm d. al-Ḥārith b. Hishām became a Muslim and asked immunity for him and the apostle gave it. She went to the Yaman in search of him and brought him to the apostle and he accepted Islam. (Ṭ. ʿIkrima used to relate, according to what they say, that what turned him to Islam when he had gone to the Yaman was that he had determined to cross the sea to Abyssinia and when he found a ship the master said, 'O servant of God, you cannot travel in my ship until you acknowledge that God is one and disavow any rival to Him, for I fear that if you do not do so we should perish.' When I asked if none but such persons was allowed to travel in his ship he replied, 'Yes, and he must be sincere.' So I thought: Why should I leave Muhammad when this is what he has brought us? Truly our God on the sea is our God on the dry land. Thereupon I recognized Islam and it entered into my heart.) ʿAbdullah b. Khaṭal was killed by Saʿīd b. Ḥurayth al-Makhzūmī and Abū Barza al-Aslamī acting together. Miqyas was killed by Numayla b. ʿAbdullah, one of his own people. Miqyas's sister said of his killing:

> By my life, Numayla shamed his people
> And distressed the winter guests when he slew Miqyas.
> Whoever has seen a man like Miqyas
> Who provided food for young mothers in hard times?

As for Ibn Khaṭal's two singing-girls, one was killed and the other ran away until the apostle, asked for immunity, gave it her. Similarly Sāra, who lived until in the time of ʿUmar a mounted soldier trod her down in the valley of Mecca and killed her. Al-Ḥuwayrith was killed by ʿAlī.

Saʿīd b. Abū Hind from Abū Murra, freed slave of ʿAqīl b. Abū Ṭālib, told me that Umm Hāniʾ d. Abū Ṭālib said: When the apostle halted in the upper part of Mecca two of my brothers-in-law from B. Makhzūm fled to me. (She was the wife of Hubayra b. Abū Wahb al-Makhzūmī.) ʿAlī came in swearing that he would kill them, so I bolted the door of my house on them and went to the apostle and found him washing in a large bowl in which was the remains of dough while his daughter Fāṭima was screening him with his garment. When he had washed he took his garment and wrapped himself in it and prayed eight bendings of the morning prayer. Then he came forward and welcomed me and asked me why I had come. When I told him about the two men and ʿAlī he said: 'We give protection to whomsoever you give protection and we give safety to those you protect. He must not kill them.'

Muhammad b. Jaʿfar b. al-Zubayr from ʿUbaydullah b. ʿAbdullah b. Abū Thaur from Ṣafīya d. Shayba told me that the apostle after arriving in Mecca when the populace had settled down went to the temple and encompassed it seven times on his camel touching the black stone with a stick which he had in his hand. This done he summoned ʿUthmān b. Ṭalḥa and took the key of the Kaʿba from him, and when the door was opened for him he went in. There he found a dove made of wood. He broke it in his hands and threw it away. Then he stood by the door of the Kaʿba while the men in the mosque gathered to him.

[I. I. from ʿAbdullah b. Abū Bakr from ʿAlī b. ʿAbdullah b. ʿAbbās: The apostle entered Mecca on the day of the conquest and it contained 360 idols which Iblīs had strengthened with lead. The apostle was standing by them with a stick in his hand, saying, 'The truth has come and falsehood has passed away; verily falsehood is sure to pass away' (Sūra 17. 82). Then he pointed at them with his stick and they collapsed on their backs one after the other.

When the apostle prayed the noon prayer on the day of the conquest he ordered that all the idols which were round the Kaʿba should be collected and burned with fire and broken up. Faḍāla b. al-Mulawwiḥ al-Laythī said commemorating the day of the conquest:

> Had you seen Muhammad and his troops
> The day the idols were smashed when he entered,
> You would have seen God's light become manifest
> And darkness covering the face of idolatry.

I.I. from Ḥakīm b. ʿAbbād b. Ḥanīf and other traditionists: Quraysh had put pictures in the Kaʿba including two of Jesus son of Mary and Mary (on both of whom be peace!). I. Shihāb said: Asmāʾ d. Shaqr said that a woman of Ghassān joined in the pilgrimage of the Arabs and when she saw the picture of Mary in the Kaʿba she said,

'My father and my mother be your ransom! You are surely an Arab woman!' The apostle ordered that the pictures should be erased except those of Jesus and Mary.

A traditionist told me that the apostle stood at the door of the Kaʿba and said: 'There is no God but Allah alone; He has no associate. He has made good His promise and helped His servant. He has put to flight the confederates alone. Every claim of privilege or blood or property are abolished by me except the custody of the temple and the watering of the pilgrims. The unintentionally slain in a quasi-intentional way by club or whip, for him the bloodwit is most severe: a hundred camels, forty of them to be pregnant. O Quraysh, God has taken from you the haughtiness of paganism and its veneration of ancestors. Man springs from Adam and Adam sprang from dust.' Then he read to them this verse: 'O men, We created you from male and female and made you into peoples and tribes that you may know one another: of a truth the most noble of you in God's sight is the most pious' to the end of the passage.[23] Then he added, 'O Quraysh, what do you think that I am about to do with you?' They replied, 'Good. You are a noble brother, son of a noble brother.' He said, 'Go your way for you are the freed ones.'

[Ṭ. Thus the apostle let them go though God had given him power over their lives and they were his spoil. For this reason the Meccans were called 'the freed ones'. Then the populace gathered together in Mecca to do homage to the apostle in Islam. As I have heard, he sat (waiting) for them on al-Ṣafā while ʿUmar remained below him imposing conditions on the people who paid homage to the apostle promising to hear and obey God and His apostle to the best of their ability. This applied to the men; when they had finished he dealt with the women. Among the Quraysh women who came was Hind d. ʿUtba who came veiled and disguised because of what she had done especially in regard to Ḥamza, for she was afraid that the apostle would punish her. According to what I heard, when they approached him he asked if they gave their word not to associate anything with God, and Hind said, 'By God, you lay on us something that you have not laid on the men and we will carry it out.' He said, 'And you shall not steal.' She said, 'By God, I used to take a little of Abū Sufyān's money and I do not know whether that is lawful for me or not.' Abū Sufyān who was present when she said this told her that so far as the

[23] Sūra 49.13.

past was concerned it was lawful. The apostle said, 'Then you are Hind d. ʿUtba?' and she said 'I am; forgive me what is past and God will forgive you.' He said, 'And do not commit adultery.' She answered, 'Does a free woman commit adultery, O apostle of God?' He said, 'And you shall not kill your children.' She said, 'I brought them up when they were little and you killed them on the day of Badr when they were grown up, so you are the one to know about them!' ʿUmar laughed immoderately at her reply. He said, 'You shall not invent slanderous tales.' She said, 'By God, slander is disgraceful, but it is sometimes better to ignore it.' He said, 'You shall not disobey me in carrying out orders to do good.' She said, 'We should not have sat all this time if we wanted to disobey you in such orders.' The apostle said to ʿUmar, 'Accept their troth,' and he asked God's forgiveness for them while ʿUmar accepted their homage on his behalf. The apostle never used to take the women's hands; he did not touch a woman nor did one touch him except one whom God had made lawful to him or was one of his *ḥarīm*. Ibn Isḥāq from Abbān b. Ṣāliḥ said that the women's homage according to what some traditionists had told him was in this wise: a vessel containing water was put in front of the apostle and when he laid the conditions upon them and they accepted them he plunged his hand into the vessel and then withdrew it and the women did the same. Then after that he would impose conditions on them and when they accepted them he said, 'Go, I have accepted your homage,' and added nothing further.]

Then the apostle sat in the mosque and ʿAlī came to him with the key of the Kaʿba in his hand asking him to grant his family the right of guarding the temple as well as the watering of the pilgrims, but the apostle called for ʿUthmān b. Ṭalḥa and said, 'Here is your key; today is a day of good faith.'

Saʿīd b. Abū Sandar al-Aslamī from one of his tribesmen said: We had with us a brave man called Aḥmar Baʾsan. When he slept he snored so loudly that everyone knew where he was. When he spent the night with his clan he slept apart. If the clan was attacked at night they would call his name and he would leap up like a lion and nothing could withstand him. It happened that a party of raiders from Hudhayl came, making for the people at their water; and when they drew near Ibn al-Athwaʿ al-Hudhalī told them not to hurry him until he had looked round; for if Aḥmar was among the group there was no way to get at them. He snored so loudly that one could tell where he was. So he listened and when he heard his snoring he walked up to him and thrust his sword into his breast pressing on it so that he killed him.

Then they rushed upon the party who cried 'Aḥmar!' But they had no Aḥmar.

On the morrow of the conquest of Mecca Ibn al-Athwaʿ came into Mecca to look round and find out what the situation was. Now he was still a polytheist, and Khuzāʿa saw and recognized him, and they surrounded him as he was at the side of one of the walls of Mecca, saying, 'Are you the man who killed Aḥmar?' 'Yes', he said, 'and what about it?' Thereupon Khirāsh b. Umayya advanced on him with drawn sword saying, 'Get away from the man.' We supposed that he wanted to get the people away from him; but when we drew away he ran at him and thrust his sword in his belly. By God, I can almost see him now with his entrails flowing forth from his belly and his eyes two mere slits in his head the while he said, 'Have you done it, you men of Khuzāʿa' until he collapsed and fell. The apostle said, 'Stop this killing, Khuzāʿa; there has been too much killing even if there were profit in it. I will pay the bloodwit for the man you have killed.'

ʿAbduʾl-Raḥmān b. Ḥarmala al-Aslamī from Saʿīd b. al-Musayyib told me that when the apostle heard what Khirāsh had done he said, 'Khirāsh is too prone to kill,' thereby rebuking him.

Saʿīd b. Abū Saʿīd al-Maqburī from Abū Shurayḥ al-Khuzāʿī said: When ʿAmr b. al-Zubayr came to Mecca to fight his brother ʿAbdullah I came to him and said, 'Listen! When we were with the apostle the day after the conquest of Mecca, Khuzāʿa attacked a man of Hudhayl and killed him, he being a polytheist. The apostle arose and addressed us, saying, "God made Mecca holy the day He created heaven and earth, and it is the holy of holies until the resurrection day. It is not lawful for anyone who believes in God and the last day to shed blood therein, nor to cut down trees therein. It was not lawful to anyone before me and it will not be lawful to anyone after me. Indeed, it is not lawful for me except at this time because of (God's) anger against its people. Now it has regained its former holiness. Let those here now tell those that are not here. If anyone should say, The apostle killed men in Mecca, say God permitted His apostle to do so but He does not permit you. Refrain from killing, you men of Khuzāʿa, for there has been too much killing even if there were profit in it. Since you have killed a man I will pay his bloodwit. If anyone is killed after my sojourn here his people have a choice: they can have his killer's life or the blood-money." Then the apostle paid the bloodwit for the man whom Khuzāʿa had slain.' ʿAmr replied, 'Be off with you, old man! We know more about its sanctity than you. It does not protect the shedder of blood, nor the man who casts off his allegiance nor him who withholds tax.' Abū Shurayḥ answered, 'I was there and you were not. The apostle ordered us who were present to tell those who were absent. I have told you and the responsibility now rests with you.'

Muhammad b. Jaʿfar from ʿUrwa b. al-Zubayr told me that Ṣafwān b. Umayya went out to Judda to take ship to the Yaman. ʿUmayr b. Wahb told the prophet that Ṣafwān, who was a chief among his people, had fled from him to cast himself into the sea, and asked him to grant him immunity. The prophet agreed to do so, and ʿUmayr asked him for a sign to prove it, and he gave him the turban with which he had entered Mecca. ʿUmayr took it and overtook Ṣafwān just as he was about to embark. He begged him not to commit suicide and produced the token of his safety. Ṣafwān told him to be off and not to speak to him. He replied, 'My parents be your ransom! He is the most virtuous, most pious, most clement, and best of men, your very cousin. His honour is your honour.' He replied, 'I go in fear of my life because of him.' He answered, 'He is too clement and too honourable to kill you.' So he went back with him to the apostle and told him that ʿUmayr had said that he had promised him immunity. He said that that was true. Ṣafwān asked for two months in which to make up his mind, and he gave him four months.

Al-Zuhrī told me that Umm Ḥakīm d. al-Ḥārith b. Hishām and Fākhita d. al-Walīd (who was married to Ṣafwān, while Umm Ḥakīm's husband was ʿIkrima b. Abū Jahl) had become Muslims. The latter asked immunity for her husband and the apostle granted it and she joined him in the Yaman and brought him back. When ʿIkrima and Ṣafwān became Muslims the apostle confirmed their first marriages.

THE FAREWELL PILGRIMAGE

In the beginning of Dhūʾl-Qaʿda the apostle prepared to make the pilgrimage and ordered the men to get ready.

ʿAbduʾl-Raḥmān b. al-Qāsim from his father al-Qāsim b. Muhammad from ʿĀʾisha the prophet's wife told me that the apostle went on pilgrimage on the 25th Dhūʾl-Qaʿda.

Neither he nor the men spoke of anything but the pilgrimage, until when he was in Sarif and had brought the victims with him as also some dignitaries had done, he ordered the people to remove their pilgrim garments except those who brought victims. That day my menses were upon me and he came in to me as I was weeping and asked me what ailed me, guessing correctly what was the matter. I told him he was right and said I wished to God that I had not come out with him on the journey this year. He said (Ṭ. Don't do that) 'Don't say that, for you can do all that the pilgrims do except go round the temple.' The apostle entered Mecca and everyone who had no sacrificial victim, and his wives, took off the pilgrim garment. When the day of sacrifice came I was sent a lot of beef and it was put in my house. When I asked what it was they said that the apostle had sacrificed cows on behalf of his wives. When the night that the pebbles were thrown duly came the apostle sent me along with my brother ʿAbduʾl-Raḥmān and let me perform the *ʿumra* from al-Tanʿīm in place of the *ʿumra* which I had missed.

Nāfiʿ, client of ʿAbdullah b. ʿUmar from ʿAbdullah, from Ḥafṣa d. ʿUmar, said that when the apostle ordered his wives to remove the pilgrim garments they asked him what prevented him from doing the same and he said: 'I have sent on my victims and have matted my hair, but I shall not be free of the *iḥrām* until I slaughter my victims.'

ʿAbdullah b. Abū Najīḥ told me that the apostle had sent ʿAlī to Najrān and met him in Mecca when he was still in a state of *iḥrām*. He went in to Fāṭima the apostle's daughter and found her dressed in her ordinary clothes. When he asked why, she told him that the apostle had ordered his wives so to do. Then he went to the apostle and reported the result of his journey and he told him to go and circumambulate the temple and remove the pilgrim garb as the others had done. He said that he wanted to slaughter a victim as the apostle did. The apostle again told him to remove the pilgrim garb. He replied: 'I said when I put on the pilgrim garb, "O God, I will invoke thy name over a victim as your prophet and your slave and your apostle Muhammad does."' When he asked him if he had a victim he said that he had not, and the apostle gave him a share in his, so he retained the pilgrim garb with the apostle until both of them had completed the pilgrimage and the apostle slaughtered the victim on behalf of them both.

Yaḥyā b. ʿAbdullah b. ʿAbduʾl-Raḥmān b. Abū ʿAmra from Yazīd b. Ṭalḥa b. Yazīd b. Rukāna told me that when ʿAlī came from the Yaman to meet the apostle in Mecca he hurried to him and left in charge of his army one of his companions who went and covered every man in the force with clothes from the linen ʿAlī had. When the army approached he went out to meet them and found them dressed in the clothes. When he asked what on earth had happened the man said that he had dressed the men so that they might appear seemly when they mingled with the people. He told him to take off the clothes before they came to the apostle and they did so and put them back among the spoil. The army showed resentment at their treatment.

ʿAbdullah b. ʿAbduʾl-Raḥmān b. Maʿmar b. Ḥazm from Sulaymān b. Muhammad b. Kaʿb b. ʿUjra from his aunt Zaynab d. Kaʿb who was married to Abū Saʿīd al-Khudrī, on the authority of the latter told me that when the men complained of ʿAlī the apostle arose to address them and he heard him say: 'Do not blame ʿAlī, for he is too scrupulous in the things of God, or in the way of God, to be blamed.'

Then the apostle continued his pilgrimage and showed the men the rites and taught them the customs of their *ḥajj*. He made a speech in which he made things clear. He praised and glorified God, then he said: 'O men, listen to my words. I do not know whether I shall ever meet you in this place again after this year. Your blood and your property are sacrosanct until you meet your Lord, as this day and this month are holy. You will surely meet your Lord and He will ask you of your works. I have told you. He who has a pledge let him return it to him who entrusted him with it; all usury is abolished, but you have your capital. Wrong not and you shall not be wronged. God has decreed that there is to be no usury and the usury of ʿAbbās b. ʿAbduʾl-Muṭṭalib is abolished, all of it. All blood shed in the pagan period is to be left unavenged. The first claim on blood I abolish is that of b. Rabīʿa b. al-Ḥārith b. ʿAbduʾl-Muṭṭalib (who was fostered among the B. Layth and whom Hudhayl killed). It is the first blood shed in the pagan period which I deal with. Satan despairs of ever being worshipped in your land, but if he can be obeyed in anything short of worship he will be pleased in matters you may be disposed to think of little account, so beware of him in your religion. "Postponement of a sacred month is only an excess of disbelief whereby those who disbelieve are misled; they allow it one year and forbid it another year that they may make up the number of the months which God has hallowed, so that they permit what God has forbidden, and forbid what God has allowed."[24] Time has completed its cycle and is as it was on the day that God created the heavens and the earth. The number of months with God is twelve; four of them are sacred, three consecutive and the Rajab of Muḍar, which is between Jumādā and Shaʿbān.

You have rights over your wives and they have rights over you. You have the right that they should not defile your bed and that they should not behave with open unseemliness. If they do, God allows you to put them in separate rooms and to beat them but not with

---

[24] Sūra 9.37.

severity. If they refrain from these things they have the right to their food and clothing with kindness. Lay injunctions on women kindly, for they are prisoners with you having no control of their persons. You have taken them only as a trust from God, and you have the enjoyment of their persons by the words of God, so understand (Ṭ. and listen to) my words, O men, for I have told you. I have left with you something which if you will hold fast to it you will never fall into error—a plain indication, the book of God and the practice of His prophet, so give good heed to what I say.

Know that every Muslim is a Muslim's brother, and that the Muslims are brethren. It is only lawful to take from a brother what he gives you willingly, so wrong not yourselves. O God, have I not told you?'

I was told that the men said 'O God, yes,' and the apostle said 'O God, bear witness.'

Yaḥyā b. ʿAbbād b. ʿAbdullah b. al-Zubayr from his father told me that the man who used to act as crier for the apostle when he was on ʿArafa was Rabīʿa b. Umayya b. Khalaf. The apostle said to him, 'Say: O men, the apostle of God says, Do you know what month this is?' and they would say the holy month. Then he said, 'Say to them: God has hallowed your blood and your property until you meet your Lord like the sanctity of this month. Do you know what country this is?' And they said 'The holy land' and he said the same as before.'Do you know what day this is?' and they said the day of the great *ḥajj*, and he said the same again.

Layth b. Abū Sulaym from Shahr b. Ḥaushab al-Ashʿarī from ʿAsma b. Khārija told me: ʿAttāb b. Usayd sent me to the apostle on a matter while the apostle was standing on ʿArafa. I came to him and stood beneath his camel and its foam was falling on my head. I heard him say: 'God has assigned to everyone his due. Testamentary bequests to an heir are not lawful. The child belongs to the bed and the adulterer must be stoned. He who claims as father him who is not his father, or a client a master who is not his master, on him rests the curse of God, the angels and men everywhere. God will not receive from him compensatory atonement, however great.'

ʿAbdullah b. Abū Najīḥ told me that when the apostle stood on ʿArafa he said, 'This station goes with the mountain that is above it and all ʿArafa is a station.' When he stood on Quzaḥ on the morning of al-Muzdalifa he said, 'This is the station and all al-Muzdalifa is a station.' Then when he had slaughtered in the slaughtering place in Minā he said, 'This is the slaughtering place and all Minā is a slaughtering place.' The apostle completed the *ḥajj* and showed men the rites, and taught them what God has prescribed as to their *ḥajj*, the station, the throwing of stones, the circumambulation of the temple, and what He had permitted and forbidden. It was the pilgrimage of completion and the pilgrimage of farewell because the apostle did not go on pilgrimage after that.

Translated by Alfred Guillaume.

9

ʿUmar Ibn Abî Rabîʿah *

"Blame me no more, O comrades! but to-day
Quietly with me beside the howdahs stay.
Blame not my love for Zaynab, for to her
And hers my heart is pledged a prisoner.
Ah, can I ever think of how we met
Once at al-Khayf, and feel no fond regret?
My song of other women was but jest:
She reigns alone, eclipsing all the rest.
Hers is my love sincere, 'tis she the flame
Of passion kindles—so, a truce to blame!"

Translated by R. A. Nicholson

*Died 719 A.D. Muslim poet. He lived in Mecca and was famous (and infamous) for his wine and love poems.

10

AL-BALÂDHURÎ*

Correspondence Between Muʿâwiyah ibn Abî Sufyân and al-Ḥusayn ibn ʿAlî

MUʿÂWIYAH'S LETTER

According to the scholars, Muʿâwiyah wrote the following letter to Ḥusayn b. ʿAlî, may Allâh have mercy on them:

'After the customary greetings: News has reached me about activities of yours that made me quite angry at you and if it is true I shall not let you get away with it. For by my life whoever has shaken hands on a bargain and has taken a solemn oath to Allâh, must, indeed, fulfill it. But if the rumors are false, then you are the luckiest man in that respect and you will begin in the happiness of your soul and will die in bond with Allâh. So, do not anger me by cutting off the bonds of kinship or because of your evil thoughts. For when I disown you, you disown me, and when you plot against me, I plot against you. Guard against causing a breach in this community and against their resorting to discord with your connivance. I have tried the people and have tested them. In fact, your Father was far better than you and yet, the opinions of those who now flock to you were unanimously against him. I do not believe that these same people give you good advice now (lit.: what had been bad for you formerly, will be good for you from them). Look out for yourself and your faith and "Let not those who do not believe make you foolish" (Sûrah 30, v. 60).'

AL-ḤUSAYN'S ANSWER

Al-Ḥusayn answered him as follows:

'After the customary greetings: Your letter reached me in which you mention that you have heard things about me at which you were angry. If they were correct, you would not agree with me about them; but only Allâh will ever lead to good deeds and show the way to them. As for the things you were told, only flatterers and slanderers and those who try to divide the community would bring them up in their

*Died 892 A.D. (See Index s.v. al-Balâdhurî.)

reports. I do not wish to make war or transgress against you, and by Allâh I have given up that idea. For I fear Allâh too much to abandon Him, yet I do not think that Allâh would be pleased with me if I left judgment about you entirely to Him. Nor would He like my exonerating you without asking His pardon for you and for your wrongdoing, irreligious friends, who act like sinners and friends of Satans. Aren't you the one who killed Ḥujr b. ʿAdî and his god-fearing, pious companions who abhor wickedness and disapprove strongly of innovations and who "do not fear with regard to Allâh the blame of a blaming one" (Sûrah 5, 54=Flügel 59), because of alleged wrongdoing and trespasses, when they had given trust to bonds and firm compacts exacted on strict conditions. Or was it not you who killed ʿAmr b. al-Ḥamiq, the Companion of the Messenger of Allâh, Peace be with him, whose piety you sapped and whose color you made yellow and whose body you emaciated. Or was it not you who claimed Ziyâd b. Sumayya who was born 'on the bed' of ʿUbayda b. Thaqîf and whom you pretended to be the son of your own father.[1] Yet the Messenger of Allâh, Peace be on him, has said: "The child belongs to "the bed" and the adulterer deserves to be stoned".[2] Thus you have left the Path (*Sunnah*) of the Messenger of Allâh, Peace be on Him, and you have disobeyed his command, by intentionally committing a sin; you have followed your lust, lying without guidance from Allâh; then you have made him ruler over the two ʿIrâqs (i.e. ʿIrâq and Irân). He cut off the hands of the Muslims and gouged out their eyes and crucified them on the trunks of palms. You have acted as if you were not part of the *Ummah* (Community of Islam) and as if the *Ummah* did not concern you. And yet the Messenger of Allâh, Peace be on him, has said: "Whoever attaches himself to a tribe by a relationship to which he is not entitled, is accursed".[3] And are you not the man in the (affair of the) Ḥaḍramawt people, about whom Ibn Sumayya wrote to you that they adhere to the religion of ʿAlî, and you wrote to him "kill any one who professes the religion and the ideas of ʿAlî" and he killed them and mutilated them by your command. But the faith of ʿAlî is the faith of Muḥammad, Peace be on him, whom your father took as a model, and which, since you have embraced it, put you into your present high position. If it had not been for him, the highest degree of nobility for you would have been the office of the "Two

[1] He was known as Ziyâd b. Abîhi, 'Ziyād the son of his Father.'

[2] cp. Wensinck, *Handbook, s.v.* Child.

[3] See Goldziher, *Muhammedanische Studien,* I, p. 134 (English translation: p. 126).

Caravans" in search of intoxicating drinks.[4] But you have said: "Look at yourself and your religion and at the *Ummah* and beware of causing a split in the community of friends and of driving the people to civil war." But I do not know of any discord worse for the *Ummah* than your reign over it, and I do not know any view for myself and my faith to be better than my war against you. And if I do make war, then it is a good deed for the sake of my Lord, and if I desist from it, it would be a sin—Allâh may forgive me for my many shortcomings, and I ask Allâh for help, that my work will be rightly guided. However, as concerns your ruse against me: no one will ever have greater need for Allâh's mercy than you, because of the way you acted against those persons that you killed and mutilated after peace had been made. They would not have fought against you, nor broken the treaty with you except for fear of a cause in which they would have died (anyhow) had you not killed them before they had carried it out, or they would have died before they had achieved their aim. Therefore, oh Muʿâwiya, acknowledge the Punishment and believe firmly in the Reckoning, and know that Allâh has a Book of which He will not omit either a small or a large bit unless He has accounted for it. Nor is Allâh a person Whom you can take in by dubious means and Whose Friends (Saints) you can kill on a doubt and a suspicion or by deceiving the people by forcing them to do homage to your son, a foolish youth who drinks strong drinks and plays with dogs! I need only tell you that you have misled yourself and destroyed your faith and forfeited loyalty to you and betrayed your flock and have taken possession of your seat in Hellfire and "Away with Unjust People" (Sûrah 23, v. 43).'

---

[4] cp. Sûrah 106; the B. Umaiya were thought to be addicted to "wine, women and song".

11

AL-BUKHÂRÎ *

Selections of Traditions

On Mutual Help Between Believers

On the authority of Abû Mûsà al-Ashʿarî, may Allâh be pleased with him: from the Prophet, Peace be upon him and his family. He said: "Verily, the Believers are like buildings supporting each other; then he intertwined his fingers (to demonstrate the closeness among them)."

* * *

On the authority of Abû Saʿîd al-Khudrî, may Allâh be pleased with him, who heard the Messenger of Allâh, Peace be upon him and his family, say: "When a man becomes a Muslim, and his conversion to Islam is sincere (lit., beautiful) God forgives all evil that he has committed up to that time. Afterwards the reward for good deeds is ten times up to sevenhundred times as much, but the punishment for evil is also that much, except if Allâh forgives him."

* * *

On the authority of Abû Saʿîd al-Khudrî from the Prophet, Peace be on him, who said: "When the Believers are saved from Hell Fire, they are detained (from entering Paradise) by a bridge between Paradise and Hell and they will compensate each other, or demand compensation from one another, for any wrongdoing that existed between them on earth, until, after they are cleansed and purified, they are given permission to enter Paradise. And by Him in Whose hands lies Muhammad's soul, each of them will occupy a place in Paradise that indicates the position he has occupied on earth."

* * *

On the authority of Abû Hurayra, who said: "A man came to the Messenger of Allâh and asked him: Oh, Messenger of Allâh,

*Died 870 A.D. (See p. 70 ff.)

who has the greatest right to my companionship in good spirit?" The Prophet said: "Thy mother." The man asked again: "Then who?", he answered: "thy mother;" again he asked: "then who?" He answered: "thy mother"—he asked once more: "then who?" The Prophet said: "Thy father."

* * *

On the authority of Anas ibn Mâlik, may Allâh be pleased with him. He said: "The Messenger of Allâh, Peace be on Him, was neither of tall stature, nor short, neither deadly white, nor too brown; his hair was neither short and curly nor long and limp. Allâh sent him when he was just forty years old, he stayed (after that) ten years in Mecca and ten years in Medînah. Allâh took him when he was in his early sixties and there were not twenty white hairs on his head or in his beard."

* * *

On the authority of Ṣâliḥ ibn Ḥayy Abu'l-Ḥasan, who said: "I heard al-Shaʿbî say: Abû Burda told me that he heard his father, may Allâh be pleased with him, say: The Prophet, Peace be on him, said: Three kinds of people will receive their reward twice: the man who has a slave-girl whom he teaches and gives her a good education, and whom he educates and brings up well, and then sets her free and then marries her—he has two rewards [namely, God's reward for having set her free, and the pleasure of having a well-bred wife]. Further, a Believer from the People of the Book who believes in [either Mûsà or ʿIsà] and then believes in the Prophet, Peace be on Him (i.e., a Jew or a Christian who becomes a Muslim)—he will gain two rewards. Further the slave who fulfills the laws of Allâh [i.e., prayer, fast, etc.] and then acts sincerely towards his former master, he will gain two rewards (i.e., from his master and from God)."

AL-ṬABARÎ *

Tafsîr

Commentary on Sûrah II (*al-Baqarah,* The Cow), verse 127

Comments in explanation of the Koran verse: "When Ibrâhîm and Ismaʿîl raised up the foundations of the House."

Abû Jaʿfar (i.e., al-Ṭabarî) says: "When God the Exalted said: 'and when Ibrâhîm raised the foundations of the House,' he meant Remember when Ibrâhîm raised the foundations of the House. . . ."

Later the Commentators differed in their explanation of the term "foundations of the House" which Ibrâhîm and Ismaʿîl raised: were they making new foundations or were these the ones that it had had before these two came. Some people said, they were the foundations that Adam the Father of Man built at the command of Allâh. Later the site became effaced and its traces became extinct, until Allâh pointed the site out to Ibrâhîm and he rebuilt it.

A report on those who maintain that tradition

Al-Ḥasan ibn Yaḥyà said: ʿAbd al-Razzâq told us: he said: Ibn Jurayḥ told us on the authority of (ʿ*an*) ʿAṭâʾ who said: "Adam said: Oh, Lord, I do not hear the voices of the Angels!" He answered: "That is because of your sins. But descend to the earth and build me a House, then circle around it the way you have seen the Angels circle around my House that is in Heaven." The people think that he built it (with wood, earth and stones) from five mountains: from Ḥirâʾ[1], and Mount Olive, and Mount Sinai, and Mount Lubnân and al-Jûdà, but its center was taken from Ḥirâʾ. That was the building of Adam, until Ibrâhîm rebuilt it afterwards.

*Died 922 A.D. (See Index, s.v.)

---

[1] Near Mecca, the site of Muhammad's retreat.

Al-Ḥasan b. Yaḥyâ . . . ʿAbd al-Razzâq . . . Maʿmar on the authority of Aiyûb, *ʿan* Saʿîd b. Jubayr, *ʿan* Ibn ʿAbbâs who said: "When Ibrâhîm raised the foundations of the House that means, the foundations that had been those of the previous House."

Others said: "No, but they are the foundations of the House onto which Allâh made Adam descend from Heaven to earth, around which he circled the way he used to circle around His Throne in Heaven. Then He raised it to Heaven during the time of the Flood, and Ibrâhîm reërected the foundations of that House."

Report on those who said that

Muhammad ibn Bashshâr . . . ʿAbd al-Wahhâb . . . Aiyûb, *ʿan* Abû Qilâbah *ʿan* ʿAbd Allâh ibn ʿAmr who said: "When Allâh expelled Adam from Paradise He said: 'I am sending down with you a House which will be circled the way My Throne is being circled and where prayers will be said the way prayers are said at My Throne'—until Allâh sent Ibrâhîm to it and showed him its place. Ibrâhîm built it from five mountains, Ḥirâʾ, Thabîr, Lubnân, Mount al-Ṭûr, and Mount al-Khamr[2]. Yaʿqûb ibn Ibrâhîm told me, he said, Ismâʿîl ibn ʿAliyah said Aiyûb said, *ʿan* Abû Qilâbah who told the story (in this way): "When Adam fell . . ." then he continued as above.

Al-Ḥasan ibn Yaḥyâ . . . ʿAbd al-Razzâq . . . Hishâm ibn Ḥassân told us, *ʿan* Siwâr (the son-in-law of ʿAṭâʾ) *ʿan* ʿAṭâʾ b. Abî Rabâḥ, who said: "When Allâh expelled Adam from Paradise, his two feet were on earth and his head remained in Heaven; he could hear the talk of the Heavenly Hordes and their prayers, and talked to them familiarly. The Angels stood in awe of him until they complained about him to Allâh in their supplications and prayers. Then He lowered him to earth. But when he was deprived of their prayers and incantations (lit., of what he used to hear from them) he became lonely, until he complained about it to Allâh in his supplications and prayers. He was sent to Mecca and any place where he put down his feet became a city and his steps a desert, until he reached Mecca. Allâh sent down one of the gems (*yâqût*) of Paradise and it landed on the site of the present House. And he continued to circle around it until Allâh sent the Flood. It carried away that gem until Allâh sent Ibrâhîm and he built the

[2] The mount on which the *Bayt al-Maqdis* stood, (i.e., Jerusalem).

House and that is the meaning of Allâh's Word 'And when we pointed out to Ibrâhîm the place of the House'."

Al-Ḥasan ibn Yaḥyâ said, al-Razzâq told us, Maᶜmar said *ᶜan* Qatâdah who said: "Allâh threw down the House with Adam when Allâh thrust Adam down to earth; and his descent ended in the land of Hind. His head was in Heaven, his two feet on earth. The Angels regarded him with awe, for he was almost sixty ells (*dhirâᶜ*) high. But Adam was grieved that he was deprived of hearing the voices of the Angels and their praising Allâh and he complained about that to Allâh the Exalted. Allâh said: 'Oh Adam, I have thrown down for you a House around which you can circle the way My Throne is being circled around and where you can pray the way prayer is offered at My Throne.' Adam was cheered by that and set forth; his steps covered a large distance and between each two steps there arose a desert; these deserts remained afterwards. Adam came to the House and circled around it and so did the prophets after him."

* * *

Ibn Ḥamîd . . . Salma . . . *ᶜan* Ibn Isḥâq who said: "ᶜAbdallâh b. Abî Nujayḥ *ᶜan* Mujâhid and others of the scholars told us that when Allâh pointed out the site of the House to Ibrâhîm, he set out towards it from Shâm (Syria). With him went Ismâᶜîl and his mother Hagar—Ismâᶜîl was still a little nursing baby. They were borne—according to what I was told—on (the heavenly horse) al-Burâq, with whom was Gabriel directing him towards the House and instructing him about the landmarks of the Sanctuary (*Ḥaram*). Ibrâhîm set forth and with him went Gabriel." The narrator went on: He did not pass by a city without asking: 'Is this where you ordered me to go?' and Gabriel would say: 'Go on!', until he came with him to Mecca—which was at that time nothing but brown shrubs and acacia bushes. There were people called al-ᶜAmâlîq outside of Mecca and its environs; the House itself was at that time a hill of red clay. Ibrâhîm said to Gabriel: "Is it here where you order me to leave these two?" He answered: "Yes". He turned with them to a place called al-Ḥijr and made them stay there, and he ordered Hagar, Ismâᶜîl's mother to take shelter there. Then he said: "Oh my Lord, I have made some of my seed dwell in a valley where there is no sown, by Thy Sacred House" [and so on] to His Word: "Haply they may give thanks" (Sûrah 13, verse 40).

Ibn Ḥamîd . . . Salamah . . . Ibn Isḥâq who said: "Some people think—but Allâh knows best—that one of the Angels came to Hagar, the mother of Ismâᶜîl, when Ibrâhîm had settled them in Mecca, before

Ibrâhîm and Ismâ'îl raised the foundations of the House, and pointed out to her the (future) House while it was (still only) a hill of red clay: 'This is the first House that was put on earth and it is the ancient House of Allâh; and know thou that Ibrâhîm and Ismâ'îl will reërect it for mankind'."

* * *

Abû Ja'far (i.e., al-Ṭabarî) said: The reasonable gist of all this, in our opinion, is to say that Allâh, may He be exalted by mentioning His name (*dhikr*), told about His Friend Ibrâhîm that he and his son Ismâ'îl raised the foundations of the Holy House, and it is permissible (to assume) that these were the foundations of a House that He had sent down with Adam and had established on the site of the Holy House that is in Mecca. And it is further permissible to assume that that was the domed building (*qubba*) that 'Aṭâ' has mentioned which Allâh created from the mud of the water. And it is further permissible to assume that the gem or the pearl was thrown down from Heaven. It is also permissible to think that it was possible that Adam had built it and that it later lay in ruins until Ibrâhîm and Ismâ'îl raised its foundations. But we have no certain knowledge of the facts (lit., what was what) because the essence of this story comes to us only through a tale from Allâh and from His Messenger, Peace be on Him, by widespread (oral) transmission (*al-naql al-mustafîḍ*). No story about this is supported by proof and one must just accept it, and it is not—since there is no report about it, as we have described—of a character to which one could point by way of demonstration or analogy. It may be compared with other such stories, and knowledge about it may be elucidated by way of *Ijtihâd* (thinking about it and making one's own decision). But that is not to say that that would be closer to a correct understanding than what we have just said. But Allâh, may He be exalted, knows best!

IBN KATHÎR *

Tafsîr al-Qur'ân al-ʿAẓîm

Commentary on Sûrah 17, (al-Isrà) verse 1

The story, as transmitted by Anas ibn Mâlik.
The Imâm ʿAbd Allâh al-Bukhârî said: ʿAbd al-ʿAzîz ibn ʿAbd Allâh told me that Sulaymân, that is Ibn Bilâl, told us on the authority (*ʿan*) of Shurayk ibn ʿAbd Allâh who said:

"I heard Anas ibn Mâlik tell the story of the night in which Allâh made the Messenger of Allâh travel from the mosque of the Kaʿbah (in this way): "Three people came to him before he received the Revelation, while he was sleeping in the Holy Mosque. The first man said: 'Which of them is he?' the second said: 'he is the best of them'; the last one said: 'take the best of them'. That happened in that night—and he did not see them. But they came back to him another night in which his heart was seeing but his eye was asleep, and his heart was not asleep—that is the way with prophets, their eyes are asleep, but their hearts are not sleeping. The men did not talk to him, but carried him away and put him down at the Zemzem well; there Gabriel took charge of him from them. Gabriel split open his throat and the upper part of his breast until the heart and its cavity were laid bare; then he washed it by his own hand with Zemzem water until he had cleansed its cavity. Then he brought a golden basin, in which there was a smaller golden vessel filled with faith and wisdom; he filled his breast and his *laghâdîd*—that is the blood vessels of his throat. Then he wrapped him up and ascended with him to the lowest Heaven.

He knocked at one of the gates and the Heavenly Hordes called out: 'Who is that?' He answered: 'Gabriel', they asked 'Who is with you?', he replied 'Muhammad is with me.' They inquired: 'Has he received a Call?' He answered 'Yes', and then they exclaimed: 'Welcome to him, welcome!' The Heavenly Hordes rejoiced in him, but did not know yet what Allâh had in mind for him to do on earth, until He made it known

*Died 1373. Lived in Damascus and was the author of a famous Koran commentary.

to them. In the lowest Heaven dwelt Adam, and Gabriel said to Muhammad: 'This is thy father Adam' and he greeted him and greeted him again. Adam returned the greeting and said: 'Welcome and again welcome, my son; indeed thou art my son.'

In the lowest Heaven there were two rivers. Muhammad asked: 'What are these two rivers, oh Gabriel?' Gabriel replied: 'They are the sources of the Nile and the Euphrates.' Then he walked with him around in the heaven, and there was another river with a castle of pearls and topaz. He clapped his hands and there was the smell of the purest musk. Muhammad asked again: 'What is that, oh Gabriel?' 'That is the river Kawthar which the Lord has concealed to you (but is now revealing to you).' Then he ascended with him to the second Heaven, and the Angels said to him the same words as had the first (group of Angels): 'Who is that?' He said: 'It is Gabriel.' They asked: 'And who is with you?' He answered: 'Muhammad, Peace be on him.' They inquired: 'Has he received a revelation?' He replied: 'Yes.' Then they said: 'Welcome, welcome!' Then he ascended with him to the third Heaven, and they repeated the same words as the first and the second groups had said. Then they ascended to the fourth Heaven and the same words were spoken; then they ascended to the fifth, where the same thing happened, then to the sixth, where they said to him the same as before. Then he ascended with him to the seventh Heaven, and again they said the same words as before. In all the Heavens, there were prophets whom he called by name while Muhammad paid attention; among them was Idrîs in the second, Hârûn in the fourth and others in the fifth whose names I did not retain, Ibrâhîm in the sixth and Mûsà in the seventh, by special distinction by the word of Allâh, may he be exalted, for Mûsà had said: 'My Lord, I do not think that you should raise any one above me.' Thus Allâh elevated above him only some one whom only Almighty Allâh knows.

At last, he (Gabriel with Muhammad) came to the *Sidrat al-Muntahà* (the most remote Lotus Tree) where the Most Powerful (*al-Jabbâr*) the Lord of Might was suspended, until he was remote from him the distance of two bows or nearer (Sûrah 51, verse 5 ff.). And Allâh revealed to him among other revelations 'fifty prayers day and night for your *ummah*'. Then he descended with him until he reached Mûsà who kept him back and asked 'Oh Muhammad, what duty has thy Lord imposed upon you?' He answered: 'He imposed on me fifty prayers, by day and night!' Mûsà replied: 'Thy *ummah* cannot do that—go back that thy Lord may lighten that burden from you and from them.' The Prophet, Peace be on him, turned to Gabriel as if he were asking his advice about this matter, and Gabriel indicated to him 'Yes, if you wish.' Then he went up again with him to the All-Powerful, may He be exalted and praised, and he said while He was in His place (i.e. on His Throne): 'Oh Lord, lighten it from us, for my *ummah* cannot do that.' Then He remitted ten prayers. Muhammad returned to Mûsà who kept him back again and continued to send him back to his Lord, until there remained only five (daily) prayers. Mûsà again held him back at the five prayers and said: 'Oh Muhammad, I had to impose less than that on my people, the Children of Isrâ'îl, and they got weak and abandoned that. Thy *ummah* is weaker in flesh and heart and body, and in insight and obedience (lit., seeing and hearing). So go back and thy Lord may lighten if from you.' With all that the Prophet turned to Gabriel for advice. Gabriel did not disapprove of it and took him up (even) at these five prayers. The Prophet said: 'Oh my Lord, my *ummah* is weak in flesh and hearts and in insight and obedience and in their bodies; so, lighten the burden for us.' Then the All-Powerful, may He be exalted and praised, said: 'Oh Muhammad'. He exclaimed: '*Labbaika wa-saʿdaika!* (I am entirely at your service)'. He said: 'The Word cannot be altered, before me, as it was imposed upon you in the *Umm al-Kitâb* (the Heavenly Book), namely, every good deed will be rewarded by ten times its equivalent; thus, there are fifty prayers in the *Umm al-Kitâb,* and therefore, there are five obligatory prayers for you.'

The Prophet returned to Mûsà who said: 'How did you make out?' He answered: 'He lifted it by giving us for every good deed ten times its equivalent.' Mûsà replied: 'By Allâh, I had to impose on the Children of Isrâ'îl less than that and they abandoned it. Return to thy Lord and let him lighten it from you once again.' But the Prophet, Peace be on him, said: 'By Allâh, I am ashamed that I have so repeatedly disputed Him.' Then Mûsà said: 'Then descend in the name of Allâh.' (Anas b. Mâlik) said: He awoke and he was back in the Holy Mosque at Mecca."

12

AL-GHAZÂLÎ *

Deliverance from Error and Attachment to the Lord of Might and Majesty

In the name of God, the Merciful and Compassionate

I *Introduction*

Praise be to Him with Whose praise every message and every discourse commences. And blessings be upon Muhammad the Chosen, the Prophet and Messenger, and on his house and his Companions, who guide men away from error.

You have asked me, my brother in religion, to show you the aims and inmost nature of the sciences and the perplexing depths of the religious systems. You have begged me to relate to you the difficulties I encountered in my attempt to extricate the truth from the confusion of contending sects and to distinguish the different ways and methods, and the venture I made in climbing from the plain of naive and second-hand belief (*taqlīd*) to the peak of direct vision. You want me to describe, firstly what profit I derived from the science of theology (*kalām*), secondly, what I disapprove of in the methods of the party of *taʿlīm* (authoritative instruction), who restrict the apprehension of truth to the blind following (*taqlīd*) of the Imam, thirdly, what I rejected of the methods of philosophy, and lastly, what I approved in the Sufi way of life. You would know, too, what essential truths became clear to me in my manifold investigations into the doctrines held by men, why I gave up teaching in Baghdad although I had many students, and why I returned to it at Naysābūr (Nīshāpūr) after a long interval. I am proceeding to answer your request, for I recognise that your desire is genuine. In this I seek the help of God and trust in Him; I ask His succour and take refuge with Him. . . .

From my early youth, since I attained the age of puberty before I was twenty, until the present time when I am over fifty, I have ever recklessly launched out into the midst of these ocean depths, I have

*Died 1111 A.D. in Ṭûs. Famous philosopher. (See Index, s.v.)

ever bravely embarked on this open sea, throwing aside all craven caution; I have poked into every dark recess, I have made an assault on every problem, I have plunged into every abyss, I have scrutinized the creed of every sect, I have tried to lay bare the inmost doctrines of every community. All this have I done that I might distinguish between true and false, between sound tradition and heretical innovation. Whenever I meet one of the Bāṭinīyah, I like to study his creed; whenever I meet one of the Ẓāhirīyah, I want to know the essentials of his belief. If it is a philosopher, I try to become acquainted with the essence of his philosophy; if a scholastic theologian I busy myself in examining his theological reasoning; if a Sufi, I yearn to fathom the secret of his mysticism; if an ascetic (*mutaʿabbid*), I investigate the basis of his ascetic practices; if one of the Zanādiqah or Muʿaṭṭilah, I look beneath the surface to discover the reasons for his bold adoption of such a creed.

To thirst after a comprehension of things as they really are was my habit and custom from a very early age. It was instinctive with me, a part of my God-given nature, a matter of temperament and not of my choice or contriving. Consequently as I drew near the age of adolescence the bonds of mere authority (*taqlīd*) ceased to hold me and inherited beliefs lost their grip upon me, for I saw that Christian youths always grew up to be Christians, Jewish youths to be Jews and Muslim youths to be Muslims. I heard, too, the Tradition related of the Prophet of God according to which he said: 'Everyone who is born is born with a sound nature;[1] it is his parents who make him a Jew or a Christian or a Magian.' My inmost being was moved to discover what this original nature really was and what the beliefs derived from the authority of parents and teachers really were. The attempt to distinguish between these authority-based opinions and their principles developed the mind. for in distinguishing the true in them from the false differences appeared.

I therefore said within myself: 'To begin with, what I am looking for is knowledge of what things really are, so I must undoubtedly try to find what knowledge really is.' It was plain to me that sure and certain knowledge is that knowledge in which the object is disclosed in such a fashion that no doubt remains along with it, that no possibility of error or illusion accompanies it, and that the mind cannot even entertain such a supposition. Certain knowledge must also be infallible; and this infallibility or security from error is such that no attempt to show the

[1] The interpretation of this tradition has been much discussed; cp. art. Fitra by D. B. Macdonald in EI. The above meaning appears to be that adopted by al-Ghazālī.

falsity of the knowledge can occasion doubt or denial, even though the attempt is made by someone who turns stones into gold or a rod into a serpent. Thus, I know that ten is more than three. Let us suppose that someone says to me: 'No, three is more than ten, and in proof of that I shall change this rod into a serpent'; and let us suppose that he actually changes the rod into a serpent and that I witness him doing so. No doubts about what I know are raised in me because of this. The only result is that I wonder precisely how he is able to produce this change. Of doubt about my knowledge there is no trace.

After these reflections I knew that whatever I do not know in this fashion and with this mode of certainty is not reliable and infallible knowledge; and knowledge that is not infallible is not certain knowledge.

II *Preliminaries:*

Scepticism and the Denial of all Knowledge

Thereupon I investigated the various kinds of knowledge I had, and found myself destitute of all knowledge with this characteristic of infallibility except in the case of sense-perception and necessary truths. . . .

I proceeded therefore with extreme earnestness to reflect on sense-perception and on necessary truths, to see whether I could make myself doubt them. The outcome of this protracted effort to induce doubt was that I could no longer trust sense-perception either. . . .

When these thoughts had occurred to me and penetrated my being, I tried to find some way of treating my unhealthy condition; but it was not easy. Such ideas can only be repelled by demonstration; but a demonstration needs a combination of first principles; since this is not admitted, however, it is impossible to make the demonstration. The disease was baffling, and lasted almost two months, during which I was a sceptic in fact though not in theory nor in outward expression. At length God cured me of the malady; my being was restored to health and an even balance; the necessary truths of the intellect became once more accepted, as I regained confidence in their certain and trustworthy character.

This did not come about by systematic demonstration or marshalled argument, but by a light which God most high cast into my breast. That light is the key to the greater part of knowledge. Whoever thinks that the understanding of things Divine rests upon strict proofs has in his thought narrowed down the wideness of God's mercy. . . .

The majority of men, I maintain, are dominated by a high opinion of their own skill and accomplishments, especially the perfection of their intellects for distinguishing true from false and sure guidance from misleading suggestion. It is therefore necessary, I maintain, to shut the gate so as to keep the general public from reading the books of the misguided as far as possible. The public are not free from the infection of the second bad tendency we are about to discuss, even if they are uninfected by the one just mentioned.

To some of the statements made in our published works on the principles of the religious sciences an objection has been raised by a group of men whose understanding has not fully grasped the sciences and whose insight has not penetrated to the fundamentals of the systems. They think that these statements are taken from the works of the ancient philosophers, whereas the fact is that some of them are the product of reflections which occurred to me independently—it is not improbable that one shoe should fall on another shoe-mark—while others come from the revealed Scriptures, and in the case of the majority the sense though perhaps not the actual words is found in the works of the mystics.

Suppose, however, that the statements are found only in the philosophers' books. If they are reasonable in themselves and supported by proof, and if they do not contradict the Book and the Sunnah (the example of Muhammad), then it is not necessary to abstain from using them. If we open this door, if we adopt the attitude of abstaining from every truth that the mind of a heretic has apprehended before us, we should be obliged to abstain from much that is true. We should be obliged to leave aside a great number of the verses of the Qur'an and the Traditions of the Messenger and the accounts of the early Muslims, and all the sayings of the philosophers and the mystics. The reason for that is that the author of the book of the 'Brethren of Purity' has cited them in his work. He argues from them, and by means of them he has gradually enticed men of weaker understanding to accept his falsehoods; he goes on making those claims until the heretics wrest truth from our hands by thus depositing it in their writings.

The lowest degree of education is to distinguish oneself from the ignorant ordinary man. The educated man does not loathe honey even if he finds it in the surgeon's cupping-glass; he realizes that the cupping-glass does not essentially alter the honey. The natural aversion from it in such a case rests on popular ignorance, arising from the fact that the cupping-glass is made only for impure blood. Men imagine that the blood is impure because it is in the cupping-glass, and are not aware that the impurity is due to a property of the blood itself. Since this property is absent from the honey, the fact that the honey is in such a container does not produce this property in it. Impurity, therefore, should not be attributed to the honey. To do so is fanciful and false.

Yet this is the prevalent idea among the majority of men. Wherever one ascribes a statement to an author of whom they approve, they accept it, even although it is false; wherever one ascribes it to an author of whom they disapprove, they reject it even although it is true. They always make the man the criterion of truth and not truth the criterion of the man; and that is erroneous in the extreme.

This is the wrong tendency towards rejection of the ethics of the philosophers.

There is also a wrong tendency towards accepting it. When a man looks into their books, such as the 'Brethren of Purity' and others, and sees how, mingled with their teaching, are maxims of the prophets and utterances of the mystics, he often approves of these, and accepts them and forms a high opinion of them. Next, however, he readily accepts the falsehood they mix with that, because of the good opinion resulting from what he noticed and approved. That is a way of gradually slipping into falsehood.

Because of this tendency it is necessary to abstain from reading their books on account of the deception and danger in them. Just as the poor swimmer must be kept from the slippery banks, so must mankind be kept from reading these books; just as the boy must be kept from touching the snake, so must the ears be kept from receiving such utterances. Indeed, just as the snake-charmer must refrain from touching the snake in front of his small boy, because he knows that the boy imagines he is like his father and will imitate him, and must even caution the boy by himself showing caution in front of him, so the first-rate scholar too must act in similar fashion. And just as the good snake-charmer on receiving a snake distinguishes between the antidote and the poison, and extracts the antidote while destroying the poison, and would not withhold the antidote from any in need; and just as the acute and experienced money-changer, after putting his hand into the bag of the counterfeiter and extracting from it the pure gold and throwing away the spurious and counterfeit coins, would not withhold the good and acceptable money from one in need; even so does the scholar act.

Again, when a man has been bitten by a snake and needs the antidote, his being turns from it in loathing because he learns it is extracted from the snake, the source of the poison, and he requires to be shown the value of the antidote despite its source. Likewise, a poor man in need of money, who shrinks from receiving the gold taken out of the bag of the counterfeiter, ought to have it brought to his notice that his shrinking is pure ignorance and is the cause of his missing the benefit he seeks; he ought to be informed that the proximity between the counterfeit and the good coin does not make the good coin counterfeit nor the counterfeit good. In the same way the proximity between truth and falsehood does not make truth falsehood nor falsehood truth.

This much we wanted to say about the baneful and mischievous influence of philosophy.

The Danger of 'Authoritative Instruction'.

By the time I had done with the science of philosophy—acquiring an understanding of it and marking what was spurious in it—I had realized that this too did not satisfy my aim in full and that the intellect neither comprehends all it attempts to know nor solves all its problems. The heresy of the Taʿlīmīyah had already appeared, and everyone was speaking about their talk of gaining knowledge of the meaning of things from an infallible Imam who has charge of the truth. It had already occurred to me to study their views and become acquainted with what is in their books, when it happened that I received a definite command from His Majesty the Caliph to write a book showing what their religious system really is. The fact that I could not excuse myself from doing this was an external motive reinforcing the original impulse from within. I began to search for their books and collect their doctrines. There had already come to my ears some of their novel utterances, the product of the thoughts of contemporary members of the sect, which differed from the familiar formulations of their predecessors.

I made a collection, then, of these utterances, arranged them in logical order and formulated them correctly. I also gave a complete answer to them. In consequence some of the orthodox (*Ahl al-Ḥaqq*) criticized me for my painstaking restatement of their arguments. 'You are doing their work for them', they said, 'for they would have been unable to uphold their system in view of these dubious and ambiguous utterances had you not restated them and put them in order'. . . .

The Ways of Mysticism.

When I had finished with these sciences, I next turned with set purpose to the method of mysticism (or Sufism). I knew that the complete mystic 'way' includes both intellectual belief and practical activity; the latter consists in getting rid of the obstacles in the self and in stripping off its base characteristics and vicious morals, so that the heart may attain to freedom from what is not God and to constant recollection of Him.

The intellectual belief was easier to me than the practical activity. I began to acquaint myself with their belief by reading their books, such as *The Food of the Hearts* by Abū Ṭālib al-Makkī (God have mercy upon him), the works of al-Ḥārith al-Muḥāsibī, the various anecdotes about al-Junayd, ash-Shiblī and Abū Yazīd al-Bisṭāmī (may God sanctify their spirits), and other discourses of their leading men. I thus comprehended their fundamental teachings on the intellectual side, and progressed, as far as is possible by study and oral instruction, in the knowledge of mysticism. It became clear to me, however, that what is most distinctive of mysticism is something which cannot be apprehended by study, but only by immediate experience (*dhawq*—literally 'tasting'), by ecstasy and by a moral change. What a difference there is between *knowing* the definition of health and satiety, together with their causes and presuppositions, and *being* healthy and satisfied! What a difference between being acquainted with the definition of drunkenness—namely, that it designates a state arising from the domination of the seat of the intellect by vapours arising from the stomach—and being drunk! Indeed, the drunken man while in that condition does not know the definition of drunkenness nor the scientific account of it; he has not the very least scientific knowledge of it. The sober man, on the other hand, knows the definition of drunkenness and its basis, yet he is not drunk in the very least. Again the doctor, when he is himself ill, knows the definition and causes of health and the remedies which restore it, and yet is lacking in health. Similarly there is a difference between knowing the true nature and causes and conditions of the ascetic life and actually leading such a life and forsaking the world.

I apprehended clearly that the mystics were men who had real experiences, not men of words, and that I had already progressed as far as was possible by way of intellectual apprehension. What remained for me was not to be attained by oral instruction and study but only by immediate experience and by walking in the mystic way.

Now from the sciences I had laboured at and the paths I had traversed in my investigation of the revelational and rational sciences (that is, presumably, theology and philosophy), there had come to me a sure faith in God most high, in prophethood (or revelation), and in the Last Day. These three credal principles were firmly rooted in my being, not through any carefully argued proofs, but by reason of various causes, coincidences and experiences which are not capable of being stated in detail.

It had already become clear to me that I had no hope of the bliss of the world to come save through a God-fearing life and the withdrawal of myself from vain desire. It was clear to me too that the key to all this was to sever the attachment of the heart to worldly things by leaving the mansion of deception and returning to that of eternity, and to advance towards God most high with all earnestness. It was also clear that this was only to be achieved by turning away from wealth and position and fleeing from all time-consuming entanglements.

Next I considered the circumstances of my life, and realized that I was caught in a veritable thicket of attachments. I also considered my activities, of which the best was my teaching and lecturing, and realized that in them I was dealing with sciences that were unimportant and contributed nothing to the attainment of eternal life.

After that I examined my motive in my work of teaching, and realized that it was not a pure desire for the things of God, but that the impulse moving me was the desire for an influential position and public recognition. I saw for certain that I was on the brink of a crumbling bank of sand and in imminent danger of hell-fire unless I set about to mend my ways.

I reflected on this continuously for a time, while the choice still remained open to me. One day I would form the resolution to quit Baghdad and get rid of these adverse circumstances; the next day I would abandon my resolution. I put one foot forward and drew the other back. If in the morning I had a genuine longing to seek eternal life, by the evening the attack of a whole host of desires had reduced it to impotence. Worldly desires were striving to keep me by their chains just where I was, while the voice of faith was calling, 'To the road! to the road! What is left of life is but little and the journey before you is long. All that keeps you busy, both intellectually and practically, is but hypocrisy and delusion. If you do not prepare *now* for eternal life, when will you prepare? If you do not now sever these attachments, when will you sever them?' On hearing that, the impulse would be stirred and the resolution made to take to flight.

Soon, however, Satan would return. 'This is a passing mood', he would say; 'do not yield to it, for it will quickly disappear; if you comply with it and leave this influential position, these comfortable and dignified circumstances where you are free from troubles and disturbances, this state of safety and security where you are untouched by the contentions of your adversaries, then you will probably come to yourself again and will not find it easy to return to all this.'

For nearly six months beginning with Rajab 488 A.H. (=July 1095 A.D.), I was continuously tossed about between the attractions of worldly desires and the impulses towards eternal life. In that month the matter ceased to be one of choice and became one of compulsion. God caused my tongue to dry up so that I was prevented from lecturing. One particular day I would make an effort to lecture in order to gratify the hearts of my following, but my tongue would not utter a single word nor could I accomplish anything at all.

This impediment in my speech produced grief in my heart, and at the same time my power to digest and assimilate food and drink was impaired; I could hardly swallow or digest a single mouthful of food. My powers became so weakened that the doctors gave up all hope of successful treatment. 'This trouble arises from the heart', they said, 'and from there it has spread through the constitution; the only method of treatment is that the anxiety which has come over the heart should be allayed.'

Thereupon, perceiving my impotence and having altogether lost my power of choice, I sought refuge with God most high as one who is driven to Him, because he is without further resources of his own. He answered me, He who 'answers him who is driven (to Him by affliction) when he calls upon Him' (Qur'an 27, 63). He made it easy for my heart to turn away from position and wealth, from children and friends. I openly professed that I had resolved to set out for Mecca, while privately I made arrangements to travel to Syria. I took this precaution in case the Caliph and all my friends should oppose my resolve to make my residence in Syria. This stratagem for my departure from Baghdad I gracefully executed, and had it in my mind never to return there. There was much talk about me among all the religious leaders of ʿIraq, since none of them would allow that withdrawal from such a state of life as I was in could have a religious cause, for they looked upon that as the culmination of a religious career; that was the sum of their knowledge.

Much confusion now came into people's minds as they tried to account for my conduct. Those at a distance from ʿIraq supposed that it was due to some apprehension I had of action by the government. On the other hand those who were close to the governing circles and had witnessed how eagerly and assiduously they sought me and how I withdrew from them and showed no great regard for what they said, would say, 'This is a supernatural affair; it must be an evil influence which has befallen the people of Islam and especially the circle of the learned.'

I left Baghdad, then. I distributed what wealth I had, retaining only as much as would suffice myself and provide sustenance for my children. This I could easily manage, as the wealth of ʿIraq was available for good works, since it constitutes a trust fund for the benefit of the Muslims. Nowhere in the world have I seen better financial arrangements to assist a scholar to provide for his children.

In due course I entered Damascus, and there I remained for nearly two years with no other occupation than the cultivation of retirement and solitude, together with religious and ascetic exercises, as I busied myself purifying my soul, improving my character and cleansing my heart for the constant recollection of God most high, as I had learnt from my study of mysticism. I used to go into retreat for a period in the mosque of Damascus, going up the minaret of the mosque for the whole day and shutting myself in so as to be alone.

At length I made my way from Damascus to the Holy House (that is, Jerusalem). There I used to enter into the precinct of the Rock every day and shut myself in.

Next there arose in me a prompting to fulfil the duty of the Pilgrimage, gain the blessings of Mecca and Medina, and perform the visitation of the Messenger of God most high (peace be upon him), after first performing the visitation of al-Khalīl, the Friend of God (God bless him).[2] I therefore made the journey to the Hijaz. Before long, however, various concerns, together with the entreaties of my children, drew me back to my home (country); and so I came to it again, though at one time no one had seemed less likely than myself to return to it. Here, too, I sought retirement, still longing for solitude and the purification of the heart for the recollection (of God). The events of the interval, the anxieties about my family, and the necessities of my livelihood altered the aspect of my purpose and impaired the quality of my solitude, for I experienced pure ecstasy only occasionally, although I did not cease to hope for that; obstacles would hold me back, yet I always returned to it.

I continued at this stage for the space of ten years, and during these periods of solitude there were revealed to me things innumerable and unfathomable. This much I shall say about that in order that others may be helped: I learnt with certainty that it is above all the mystics who walk on the road of God; their life is the best life, their method the soundest method, their character the purest character; indeed, were the intellect of the intellectuals and the learning of the learned and the scholarship of the scholars, who are versed in the profundities of revealed truth, brought together in the attempt to improve the life and character of the mystics, they would find no way of doing so; for to the mystics all movement and all rest, whether external or internal, brings

[2] That is, Abraham, who is buried in the cave of Machpelah under the mosque at Hebron, which is called 'al-Khalīl' in Arabic; similarly the visitation of the Messenger is the formal visit to his tomb at Medina.

illumination from the light of the lamp of prophetic revelation; and behind the light of prophetic revelation there is no other light on the face of the earth from which illumination may be received. . . .

THE REASON FOR TEACHING AGAIN AFTER MY WITHDRAWAL FROM IT

I had persevered thus for nearly ten years in retirement and solitude. I had come of necessity—from reasons which I do not enumerate, partly immediate experience, partly demonstrative knowledge, partly acceptance in faith—to a realization of various truths. I saw that man was constituted of body and heart; by 'heart' I mean the real nature of his spirit which is the seat of his knowledge of God, and not the flesh and blood which he shares with the corpse and the brute beast. I saw that just as there is health and disease in the body, respectively causing it to prosper and to perish, so also there is in the heart, on the one hand, health and soundness—and 'only he who comes to God with a sound heart' (Q. 26, 89) is saved—and, on the other hand, disease, in which is eternal and other-worldly destruction—as God most high says, 'in their hearts is disease' (Q. 2, 9). I saw that to be ignorant of God is destructive poison, and to disobey Him by following desire is the thing which produces the disease, while to know God most high is the life-giving antidote and to obey Him by opposing desire is the healing medicine. I saw, too, that the only way to treat the heart, to end its disease and procure its health, is by medicines, just as that is the only way of treating the body.

Moreover, the medicines of the body are effective in producing health through some property in them which the intellectuals do not apprehend with their intellectual apparatus, but in respect of which one must accept the statement of the doctors; and these in turn are dependent on the prophets who by the property of prophethood have grasped the properties of things. Similarly I came of necessity to realize that in the case of the medicines of formal worship, which have been fixed and determined by the prophets, the manner of their effectiveness is not apprehended by the intellectual explanations of the intellectuals; one must rather accept the statements (*taqlīd*) of the prophets who apprehended those properties by the light of prophecy, not by intellectual explanation.

Again, medicines are composed of ingredients differing in kind and quantity—one, for instance, is twice another in weight and amount; and this quantitative difference involves secret lore of the same type as knowledge of the properties. Similarly, formal worship, which is the medicine for the disease of the hearts is compounded of acts differing in kind and amount; the prostration (*sujūd*) is the double of the bowing (*rukū*ʿ) in amount, and the morning worship half of the afternoon worship; and such arrangements are not without a mystery of the same type as the properties which are grasped by the light of prophecy. Indeed a man is very foolish and very ignorant if he tries to show by intellectual means that these arrangements are wise or if he fancies that they are specified accidentally and not from a Divine mystery in them which fixes them by way of the property.

Yet again, medicines have bases, which are the principal active ingredients, and 'additions' (auxiliaries or correctives), which are complementary, each of them having its specific influence on the action of the bases. Similarly, the supererogatory practices and the 'customs' are complements which perfect the efficacy of the basic elements of formal worship.

In general, the prophets are the physicians of the diseases of hearts. The only advantage of the intellect is that it informed us of that, bearing witness to prophetic revelation by believing (*sc.* the trustworthiness of the prophets) and also to its own inability to apprehend what is apprehended by the eye of prophecy; then it took us by the hand and entrusted us to prophetic revelation, as the blind are entrusted to their guides and anxious patients to sympathetic doctors. Thus far may the intellect proceed. In what lies beyond it has no part, save in the understanding of what the physician communicates to it. . . .

I believed that it was permissible for me in the sight of God to continue in retirement on the ground of my inability to demonstrate the truth by argument. But God most high determined Himself to stir up the impulse of the sovereign of the time, though not by any external means; the latter gave me strict orders to hasten to Naysābūr (Nīshāpūr) to tackle the problem of this lukewarmness in religious matters. So strict was the injunction that, had I persisted in disobeying it, I should at length have been cut off! I came to realize, too, that the grounds which had made retirement permissible had lost their force. 'It is not right that your motive for clinging to retirement should be laziness and love of ease, the quest for spiritual power and preservation from worldly contamination. It was not because of the difficulty of restoring men to health that you gave yourself this permission.'. . .

On this matter I consulted a number of men skilled in the science of the heart and with experience of contemplation. They unanimously advised me to abandon my retirement and leave the *zāwiyah* (hospice). My resolution was further strengthened by numerous visions of good men in all of which alike I was given the assurance that this impulse was a source of good, was genuine guidance, and had been determined by God most high for the beginning of this century; for God most high has promised to revive His religion at the beginning of each century.[3] My hope became strong, and all these considerations caused the favourable view of the project to prevail.

God most high facilitated my move to Naysābūr to deal with this serious problem in Dhu'l-Qaʿdah, the eleventh month of 499 (= July, 1106 A.D.). I had originally left Baghdad in Dhu'l-Qaʿdah, 488, (=November, 1095), so that my period of retirement had extended to eleven years. It was God most high who determined this move, and it is an example of the wonderful way in which He determines events, since there was not a whisper of it in my heart while I was living in retirement. In the same way my departure from Baghdad and withdrawal from my position there had not even occurred to my mind as a possibility. But God is the upsetter of hearts[4] and positions. As the Tradition has it, 'The heart of the believer is between two of the fingers of the Merciful'.

In myself I know that, even if I went back to the work of disseminating knowledge, yet I did not go back. To go back is to return to the previous state of things. Previously, however, I had been disseminating the knowledge by which worldly success is attained; by word and deed I had called men to it; and that had been my aim and intention. But now I am calling men to the knowledge whereby worldly success is given up and its low position in the scale of real worth is recognized. This is now my intention, my aim, my desire; God knows that this is so. It is my earnest longing that I may make myself and others better. I do not know whether I shall reach my goal or whether I shall be taken away while short of my object. I believe, however, both by certain faith and by intuition that there is no power and no might save with God, the high, the mighty, and that I do not move of myself but am moved by Him, I do not work of myself but am used by Him. I ask Him first of all to reform me and then to reform through me, to guide me and then to guide through me, to show me the truth of what is true and to grant of His bounty that I may follow it, and to show me the falsity of what is false and to grant of His bounty that I may turn away from it.

Translated by W. Montgomery Watt

[3] There was a well-known Tradition to the effect that at the beginning of each century God would send a man to revive religion. The events in question took place a few months before the beginning of the sixth century A.H.

[4] *Muqallib al-qulūb*—with a play on the words.

13

IMÂM RÂZÎ *

ʿIlm al-Akhlâq

On Explaining the Ranks of Human Spirits

You must know that the precise discussion of this subject cannot be made in a regular manner without advancing an introduction which is as follows: We evidently know that we like something and dislike some other thing. We, therefore, say that here there is either something which is essentially liked or something which is essentially disliked.

Or, it may be said that a thing must either be liked because it contains something, or disliked because it contains something else. The second possibility is absurd, as it leads to a continuous chain of argument or to a circular argument with infinite regress both of which are absurd.

Even if we agree with the genuineness of continuity and circularity, it is certain that on the supposition of the continuous or circular matter there is no such thing as to be liked or disliked in itself. According to this view everything that is liked is disliked in itself. According to this view everything that is liked is liked because it contains something else. It is therefore necessary to hold that there is nothing which is absolutely desirable or absolutely undesirable. But we have explained that it is evidently known that there is surely something which is liked or disliked. Hence, the case is contrary to the assumption. It is, therefore, established that there is someone who is essentially liked and something which is essentially disliked.

Now, after a thorough discussion and consideration we find nothing about which it may be possibly said that it is essentially liked, except "pleasure" and "perfection". Truly speaking, there is no difference between the two, since what is "pleasant" is the cause of achieving a perfect state of pleasure, and what is "perfect" is "pleasant". Only we call what is physically pleasant "pleasure" and what is spiritually pleasant "perfection".

Again, what is essentially disliked is "pain" and "loss" which have,

*Died 925 A.D. (See p. 103 ff.)

in fact, for the reason mentioned above, no difference in reality. For, "perfection" is essentially liked due to its essence in so far as it is perfection, and "loss" is essentially disliked due to its essence in so far as it is "loss".

After the strong argument has been cited, this introduction is well-established by several reasons:

1. Firstly, when an imperfect one is described with the attributes of praise and eulogised, he feels pleased though he is aware that the speaker is a liar. And when a perfect man is condemned with the attributes of disparagement, he feels aggrieved though he is aware that the speaker has lied. This is only because of the fact that the very idea of achieving perfection is "pleasant" in its essence and that of incurring loss is repugnant in its essence.

2. Secondly, when you listen to the story of Rustam and Isfandiyar and hear of their immense courage and their victory over their contemporaries, you feel in your heart extreme admiration for them. This is the reason why the story-teller causes the people to crowd around him by telling stories of a similar nature and induces them to take money out of their pockets and offer it to him. This indicates that "perfection" is desired for its essence.

3. Thirdly, when we undertake any kind of trade, we put the question to ourselves: "Why have we undertaken to bear the burden of this profession?" We answer, "We have only undertaken this to make money". When we ask, again, "Why do we seek money?" The answer is given by us: "We need money in order to be able to secure pleasures". When we repeat by saying: "Why should we seek pleasures?" We say and our intellect decides that we seek pleasure for its own sake. The case is similar to "perfection" which is also sought for its own sake.

When this introduction is established we say: "Perfection causes strength either in the essence or in the attributes." Perfection in the essence must be essentially necessary in so far as it does not accept, in any way, the absence of existence and annihilation. But to achieve this perfection is not possible, since a thing is either essentially necessary or not. If it is essentially necessary the necessity will be achieved for the essence. What is achieved cannot further be achieved, and if it is not essentially necessary, it becomes impossible for it to turn into what is essentially necessary. Now, that of which the existence is not possible cannot be an object of desire.

It is, therefore, established that the perfection achieved through inherent necessity cannot be the desired object. On the other hand, what is essentially possible comes into being only through something else and whenever it exists due to something else it is a necessary being as long as this "something else" exists. Hence, it is this "something else" through which the necessity of its existence is accomplished. When the necessity of existence is desired for its own sake, then anything that causes it is also desired. Now, due to this concept anything that causes the existence of an object and its continued subsistence in accordance with its best possible condition will be desired for its own sake; and anything that causes the non-existence of something in itself due to the absence of its excellent conditions will be disliked for its own sake.

Since the True, the Exalted and the Eulogized, is a Necessary Being in His Essence, He is the Lover of His Essence, and is the Beloved by virtue of His Essence, and since it is a necessary function of His Essence to cause the possible objects to emanate from Him and we have already explained that which emanates from the beloved is also lovable, therefore, the actions of Allah are lovable. It is for this reason that Allah said: "He loves them and they love Him." Some of the leading Ṣûfîs who listened to this verse said: "It is sure that though Allah loves them, He, in reality, loves His self only".

As for perfection in attributes, we have pondered but found nothing of this kind except Knowledge and Power. Since Knowledge is perfection in its essence, it is essentially lovable.

When you have known this we say: Human spirits, as you have realized, have no way of achieving the essential necessity. They, therefore, desire to achieve necessity through something else. Hence, everything that is the cause of man's life and the continuity of his existence is dear to him essentially and whatever is the cause of his death and annihilation is essentially disliked by him.

As for the discourse on Knowledge and Power, you have known that human spirits have two functions of receiving effects and acting on their own initiative. When they attend to the Divine world they receive effects and when they attend to the corporeal material world, they act on their own initiative.

When they receive effects from the Divine world, they sometimes receive existence and sometimes the sacred manifestations and spiritual forms which constitute the sciences.

As for their acting upon the material world, this is because they possess authority over this world in so far as they possess the power of dissolving and composing (things) according to their will.

Since there is no end to the stages of knowledge and power, there is also no end to the stages of human love for the two (Knowledge and Power), nor is there any end to brooding over the means of achieving the two desired objects. But it is impossible that a man should attain knowledge without limitation or have power over the objects without any limitation. The knowledge attained by human spirits is limited despite its wide scope and the power over material existents. Whatever its extent, is also limited. Evidently, the human soul does not reach a stage in knowledge and power where it may achieve unlimited things. Hence, it is impossible for the substance of soul to be free from lust and demand. Human lust for securing wealth is only because he wants power over inanimate beings, his lust for attaining a high position is only because he wants power over the spirits of the intelligents, and his lust for contending with figures and wrestling with the brave ones is only because he wants to be powerful and dislikes to be overpowered. All this goes back in origins to the root of power which is an attribute of perfection.

If a man is able to enforce his commands in a town his self aspires to be able to enforce his commands over the whole country, and when he is able to do this, he aspires to execute his commands over the countries, seas and mountains; nay, he aspires to gain command over the stars and heavenly bodies. Nevertheless, sometimes he does not want this power due to a cause that renders it impossible for him to achieve such power. Hence, he refrains from such an attempt due to some obstacle that stands in his way, and not because he is devoid of such ambition.

Here there is a delicate point, that is, a man does not very much desire to achieve this position before he enjoys the pleasure of power and authority. His longing for achieving this state increases when he tastes it and becomes familiar with it. His inclination towards this can be compared to the faculty of taste. For example, a man hears the name of a beautiful woman and falls in love with her by merely hearing her name without seeing her. When he tastes the pleasure of executive power and authority over her, he loves the woman because of the fact that he saw her, liked her and enjoyed the pleasure of mating with her. Now, mating simply strengthens his love in the substance of his spirit and adds to his lust for mating with her. Similarly, whenever he has access to lofty positions in state and authority, his lust for having more power and more authority increases. It is, therefore, established that there is no end to the lust of a man for achieving knowledge and power. It is also established that the whole of the corporeal world is limited. So, when we suppose that a man governs the whole of the world, the necessary result is that he enjoys a limited kingdom.

We have already explained that man wants unlimited power. The assertion is therefore that even if man enjoys power over the whole of the corporeal world he does not refrain from demanding more power. If a man achieves the knowledge of all that is covered by existence, his lust for achieving knowledge necessarily remains, as we have explained that what knowledge and power he has achieved is limited and what is absent from him is unlimited, though it lies within his power that the law-giver (peace be upon him!) said: "There are two greedy persons who are never satisfied—a seeker of knowledge and a seeker of the world."

Now that you know this, we say: "Though the achievement of power to exercise sway over the lower sphere, *i.e.,* the corporeal world, is a perfection, it entails a limited affair." I mean, the power of the soul to exercise sway over the corporeal world is conditioned by the continuous connection of the soul with body. But this connection may be severed. Now, when the connection is severed, the power is lost; the loss of the beloved after having a long love-affair and suffering a loss that cannot be repaired necessitates a great catastrophe and a strong desire that brings destruction. As a precaution against falling into this undesirable state, this desired object becomes the object of dislike.

As for the engagement of the soul in seeking perfect knowledge, it is pleasure in the present and happiness in the future. This is because the authority of the Soul over the corporeal world is conditioned with the connection of the soul with the body.

As for the fact that the soul receives the Pure manifestations and Divine Knowledge, this does not depend upon the connection of the Soul with the body, rather this connection is, as it were, an obstruction in achieving perfection. When this connection is broken, the Divine Manifestations become illumined. It is, therefore, established by what we have mentioned, that attention to the higher sphere for a seeker who receives the Divine Manifestations necessitates perfection in the present and in the future.

Attending to the lower sphere for the sake of achieving domination over the corporeal world, necessitates pleasure in the present time but, at the same time, it necessitates great pain after death. This is why the people of intelligence have agreed that it is their duty to keep themselves engaged in attaching their spirit to the higher world by turning it away from the lower world. Those who attend to the world of purity surely enjoy continuity without annihilation, honour without disgrace, pleasure without pain and peace without fear.

When you have known this, it becomes evident that the souls are of three kinds:—

1. The highest is the position of those who attend to the Divine World, and sink themselves in these everlasting lights, and in the branches of Divine gnosis (Knowledge) and are sometimes called in the Qur'ân, "the foremost", as the Qur'ân says: "The foremost in the race, the foremost in the race: Those are they who will be brought nigh", sometimes they are called, "those who will be brought nigh", as the Qur'ân has it. "Thus if he is of those brought nigh".[1]
2. In the middle position are those souls which attend to both the worlds. Sometimes, they advance upward to the higher world by obeisance and devotion, and, sometimes, descend to the lower world for the sake of administering the affairs of the world and exercising sway over it. They are the people of the right-hand (or righteousness) and the balanced-people.
3. The third position belongs to those who attend to the lower world and are exceedingly occupied in seeking its pleasures. They are the people of the left-hand and are transgressors.

Now, Knowledge that leads to the path of the nearly-placed souls is the science of the spiritual exercises and discipline, and the Knowledge that leads to the path of the people of the right-hand is the science of morals (Ethics).

On the Relation of the Faculties to the Substance of the Soul

You must know that the savants have mentioned many similes in this connection. The first simile is that the substance of the soul is like a king and the body as its kingdom. This king has two kinds of armies—the army that the eyes can see—it is the external bodies—and the army that is seen by inner visions which are those faculties which we have already mentioned.

You should know that for the internal faculties engaged in accomplishing the welfare of the soul and in completing the welfare of the body [there is a different faculty].

The First Kind of the internal faculties. It is that the perfection of the rational soul consists in realizing the truth in itself and the form by acting through it. But the activity of the form is also conditioned by the light of gnosis. The most important enterprise of the soul is to acquire gnosis. But it has been created *prima facie* free from the knowledge of many things and has been favoured with external and internal senses so that when the soul feels through these senses the

[1] Sûrah lvi, 11; 88.

sensible objects it awakens to the consciousness of distinction between homogeneous and heterogeneous objects, the form of which enables the substance of the soul to realize as to why the objects are homogeneous and why they are distinguished; and then the soul obtains the absolute form in itself.

This form is, again, of two kinds: those objects the mere perception of which necessitates the mental determination of ascribing negation to some and affirmation to some others, and those which are not like this. The first of this kind is the axiomatic truths the existence of which must necessarily be acknowledged. For, were they not present, the mental determination would have surely needed in every case assistance from others and would have entailed either continuation *ad infinitum* or an infinite regress.

The Second Division: It consists of those speculative sciences which are achieved and the mere conception of which does not necessitate the mental assertion of their negation or affirmation. It is therefore established that if there were no senses, the soul would not have been able to achieve either axiomatic or speculative sciences. That is why there goes the saying, "whoever has lost senses has lost knowledge." This explains the assistance of senses in perfecting the substance of the soul. As for their assistance in perfecting the substance of the body, this is clear from the fact, as we have explained, that the body having been hot and moist is constantly suffering decadence and extinction and is therefore in need of importing a substitute for what is being extinguished and it is necessary for it to distinguish between what is agreeable and what is disagreeable.

The senses, thus, assist the man in imparting him awareness of what is useful and what would do him harm. He accordingly engages himself in acquiring the useful and driving away the harmful. This is the explanation of the assistance of the senses in perfecting the substance of the body.

You must know that this is an attempt to reform the important factors of the substance of the soul. This is because the soul has only entered this corporeal world to acquire useful knowledge and righteous deeds. The sole organ that the soul has for achieving this is the body. As long as the organ does not function properly, it will not enable the agent to achieve its object. It is, therefore, established that to undertake the reform of the important functions of the body is an attempt to reform the important functions of the soul.

The Second Simile: The heart in the body is like the governor, its faculties and organs stand in place of the country, the rational imaginative faculty is like the sincere adviser, appetition is like the servant who carries food to the town, and anger like the chief of the police. Then, the appetition which is like a servant who brings food to the town may be devilish, deceitful and cunning. He appears in the form of an admonisher whose admonition brings in all kinds of dreadful evils, and deadly poisons. He habitually quarrels with the sincere minister in his administration. Now, just as it is necessary for an intelligent king to keep the sincere minister in a dominant position as against the deceitful slave who carries food, and as against the chief of the police, and that he should pay no attention to their intrigues against the minister, in order to keep the affairs of the town in good state, similarly, when the rational soul is illumined with the light of intellect and is enlightened with knowledge and wisdom, and subjugates appetition and anger, the affair of this corporeal life is well-established. Whoever deviates from this path is like one concerning whom Allah, the Exalted, says: "Hast thou seen him who chooseth for his god his own lust?" and says: "(but clung to the earth) and followed his own lust. Therefore his likeness is as the likeness of a dog;" and says, "and restrained his soul from lust, Lo! the Garden will be his home."[1]

The Third Simile: The body is like the town and the rational soul is like a king, the external and internal senses are like an army, the bodies are like the subjects, appetition and anger are like an enemy who quarrels with the king concerning his kingdom and tries to destroy his subjects. If the king intends to subjugate this enemy the kingdom remains in good state and the struggle is removed, as Allah, the Exalted, has said: "Allah hath conferred on those who strive with their wealth and live a rank above the sedentary."[2] If, however, the king does not fight with his enemy and destroy his kingdom, his own kingdom would suffer troubles and turmoils and as a consequence thereof it would meet with destruction.

The Fourth Simile: The simile of the rational soul is like that of a horseman who rides in pursuit of a game, his appetition being his horse, and anger his dog. Now, when the rider is experienced, his horse well-trained and obedient, and his dog trained, he is deserving of success. But when he is burning within himself, when his horse is disobedient and his dog is a devourer, and neither does his horse move in accordance with his intention nor his dog run as instructed by him, he is apt to perish, rather than attain his object.

The Fifth Simile: You must know that your body is like a perfect house which has been built complete with its treasures (inner portion)

---

[1] Sûrah xxv, 45; xlv, 22; vii, 176; lxxix, 40f.

[2] Sûrah iv, 95.

and whose doors are kept open, with all necessary materials well-prepared for the master of the house. The head is like the upper chamber on the top of the house and the hole and inlets in the head like small windows and ventilators in the chamber of the house. The middle of the brain is like lights in the house and the eye like the door of the chamber, the nose like the wall-shelf above the door, the two lips like two sides of the door, the teeth like gate-keepers, the tongue like the chamberlain, the back like a strong wall which is the fortress of the house, the face like the front of the house, the lungs which draw in the cold-breathing like the summer house, the running of the breath into the house like the air that passes through the summer house, the heart with its natural heat like the winter house, the stomach with the cooked nutrition therein like the kitchen, the liver with the blood in it like the tavern, the veins in which the blood flows like the owner of the house, the spleen together with the black-bile which it contains like reservoirs which contain burnt substances, the bladder with the hot yellow bile like the magazine (the house of arms), intestines along with the remnant of food like the latrine, the bladder containing urine like the well, and the two courses in the lower part of the body like the spots through which the filth is disposed of from the house, the two legs like an obedient riding beast, the bones upon which the body has been built like the plank of wood upon which is based the house, the flesh in the midst of bones like the matter, the sinews with which some bones are tied are like boxes. Glory be to Him Who has prepared in the house of your body with the nails of your Rational Soul all these wonderful measures and rare beauties! This is what concerns the rooms of this house.

Again, the rational soul in the house is like the king and the authoritative manager who sees with the eye, hears with the ear, smells with the nostrils, tastes with the tongue, speaks with the mouth and holds with the hands, acts the artful deeds with fingers, walks with the feet, and kneels down upon the knees, sits on the two buttocks, sleeps on two flanks, reclines against the back and carries burdens on two shoulders, thinks with the front of the brain, imagines through the middle of the brain, remembers with the posterior of the brain, produces sound with the throat, inhales air through nostrils, chews with teeth and swallows through the nutrition pipe. The purpose of all these organs and instruments is that he should decorate himself with the ornament of knowledge and characterize the human soul with the mood of cognition. This soul then breathes with the soul of celestial region and is equipped with the light of Divinity.

Again, Allah, the Exalted, has entrusted the management of this kingdom to three Chiefs: One of them is Appetition which holds its sway over the liver, and flows with the blood in static veins. For this reason there goes the saying of the Prophet: "The devil moves in the son of Adam like the moving of blood." This is for the fact that the Appetitive Faculty does not flow with the blood into the veins except from the liver.

The second Chief is the faculty of Anger which is located in the heart. It passes through the veins which move about on all sides of the body.

The third Chief is the administrative psychical faculty which is located in the brain and which passes through the limbs to all sides of the body.

Again, these three chiefs are not heterogeneous, independent in themselves. They are, rather, like tributaries which have originated from one root, like branches that have grown from one tree, like a source from which there flow three streams, like a father who causes the birth of many children, and like a man who performs three works designated with three names: the blacksmith, the goldsmith and the mason.

These three are like the kings of the surrounding countries who are appointed by the great king. The activities of Appetition resemble the activities of women, children, and idiots from among the people when they go against the will of their fathers and their spouses, whereas the functions of anger resemble those of the strategists and assassins when they do not act according to the commands of their rulers. The functions of the administrative psychical faculty resemble those of the philosophers, jurists and the people of virtue and righteousness.

On the Explanations that the Mental Pleasures are Nobler and more Perfect than the Sensual Pleasures

You must know that dispositions are under the influence of the souls. The strongest pleasures and the most perfect bliss are the pleasures of eating, sexual action, and possession. Now the view that in the Hereafter they should not enjoy a pleasure, nor should they find the pleasant food, nor the appetitive sexual pleasures over there, is a view that cannot be maintained according to the learned researchers and the people of mystic exercises. There is more than one reason which leads to this conclusion.

The First Proof: If the nobility of man consisted in fulfilling appetition and executing anger the animal which is strongest in this respect would have been stronger than man and would have felt more pleasure. The lion is, for example, stronger (than man) in controlling his anger, a sparrow is stronger in sexual action than man. As the case is not like this, we are certain that human happiness does not concern these matters.

The Second Proof: Everything exists as a means for obtaining bliss and perfection, and as the object is achieved in greater quantity, bliss and perfection are achieved in greater quantity. Now, if the fulfilment of the appetition of stomach and sex would have caused the perfection and bliss of man, then man would have made greater progress in the perfection of his humanity and would have attained a higher position by indulging himself in satisfying the appetition of stomach and sex. But the second premise is absurd, since a man realizes the harm of eating more than he needs, and it is considered a mark of his meanness and avarice, if he does so. Similar is the view concerning all corporeal pleasures. When the matter is like this it is established that it is not bliss and perfection to engage oneself in fulfilling appetitions, rather it is a means for satisfying his needs.

The Third Proof: A man shares with all kinds of animals even the mean ones, the pleasure of eating and drinking. If this pleasure could be equated with bliss and perfection, it would have necessarily followed that man enjoyed no superiority over animals. A leech is, for example, pleased to eat dungs just as man is pleased by taking sugar and the like.

This may be asserted by saying: were human bliss concerned with the sensuous pleasures, man would have necessarily been the meanest of animals. As the second premise is evidently absurd, the first premise meets with a similar fate. Hence, there is no necessary connection between the two.

We, therefore, say that the lower animals share the corporeal sensory pleasures with man. But man having been endowed with intellectual ability, considers these pleasures to be imperfect. For, when the intelligent man thinks of the past which was pleasant and sweet, his heart is afflicted with the pain of having missed it. In case the past was annoying and harmful, his heart feels pained by its remembrance. If he ponders over the present, he is not pleased with what he has achieved. On the contrary, he desires to have more. If he considers the future, a severe fear overtakes him not knowing what his fate will be in the future. It is, therefore, proved that the lower animals are just like man in corporeal sensual pleasures except that his pleasures appear to him to be imperfect, because of his intellect, while the animals who have no intelligence do not think of the future and enjoy their pleasures without considering them imperfect.

It is a known fact that to obtain perfection without any trouble and defect is better and nobler than achieving perfection with trouble and toil. This shows that if the corporeal sensuous pleasures necessarily led to the state of perfection, man would be lower than ants, insects and flies, which is absurd. We, therefore, know that the sensuous pleasures necessarily involve ambition and bliss.

The Fourth Proof: When considered minutely, it is discovered that the sensuous pleasures are no pleasures; their sum-total, on the contrary, amounts only to the removal of pains. The proof is this: the more hungry a man grows the more pleased he feels in eating, and the less hungry he is the less pleased he feels in eating. Similarly, when copulation is avoided for a long time the semen accumulates in its vessels which feel severe pain, extraction and heaviness. The more severe these states grow the stronger is the pleasure obtained from the discharging of the semen. It is for this reason that the pleasure of copulation in case of one whose chances of copulating have been occasional is greater than the one whose chances have been frequent. It is therefore established that these states which are considered to be bodily pleasures are in reality no other than methods of removing pains. Similar is the case with the pleasure felt by wearing clothes, as the pleasure is achieved only by removing the pain of heat and cold.

Having ascertained that the bodily pleasures result only from removing pains, we say: human bliss does not only mean the absence of pains—a fact which exists even in the absence of mankind. It is therefore established that the real bliss of man is something other than these states.

The Fifth Proof: A man is like the rest of animals in respect of eating, drinking, cohabiting and doing harm to his opponent. He is, however, undoubtedly nobler in so far as he is a man than in his capacity as animal. This surely entails equality between the point of view of nobility and that of meanness in all that necessitates nobility and perfection. This is absurd.

The Sixth Proof: It is evidently known that the glory and bliss of the angels excel in nobility those of the animals, no matter whether some of them fly, swim, float and run fast even if we leave aside the little insects and the reptiles.

Again, there is no difference with respect to the fact that the angels do not enjoy the pleasure of eating, drinking and cohabiting, nor are the animals nobler and superior in state and position than the angels who are nearest to Allah. Since this is obviously absurd, we know that the foregoing premise is also absurd.

You must know that there is a stronger and higher rank than what we have so far mentioned. I mean there is no relation between the perfection of the Necessary Being, His Grace, Nobility and Honour and the states of those other than Him, notwithstanding the fact that these mean pleasures cannot be applicable to Him. We are therefore sure that perfection and nobility sometimes exist in states other than the state in which these bodily pleasures are obtained.

If, however, they say that this perfection is only due to attaining the stage of Godhead which is impossible in respect of the created, we answer; There is no dispute that Godhead is impossible in respect of the created, but the Prophet has said, "Adorn yourself with the attributes of Allah". It is therefore necessary for us to know the meaning of *takhalluq* in order to realize that the perfect state of man is only achieved by means of adopting Divine attributes and not by obtaining bodily pleasures. It is known that this *takhalluq,* that is, adopting Divine attributes, is only achieved by meeting needs and displaying virtues and good deeds, and not by excessive eating and drinking.

The Seventh Proof: Verily when those who decide that human happiness lies in achieving bodily pleasures, see a man abstain from seeking such bodily pleasures and observing, for example, fast constantly and perfectly satisfied with such earthly pleasures as have been permitted, their faith in him grows enormously and they consider him not to belong to mankind but to the genre of angels counting their own selves in relation to him as wretched and mean. And, when they find a man absorbed in obtaining food and drink and copulation, well-known in the courage necessary for finding means which lead to the satisfaction of bodily states and keeping away from knowledge, worship, and renunciation of the world, they give their judgement about him and accuse him of being an animal, a cheat, an absurd man, mean and cursed. Were it not well established in their minds that to be preoccupied by these bodily pleasures is a defect, meanness and misery and elevation above all these states is a blessing and a perfect state, the matter would not have been as we described, or else it would have been necessary for them to have pronounced their judgement against one who turns away from these pleasures saying that he is in a miserable and accursed state and their judgement would have been in favour of the man who kept himself preoccupied with them. Such a man would have been considered to have attained bliss and perfection. Since the matter is not like this but quite the opposite, we are sure of the genuineness of what we have mentioned.

The Eighth Proof: Everything that is a perfection and blessing in itself must display itself without feeling shame and embarrassment, rather it is necessary that it should feel proud of such display and meet with success by its action.

We are obviously sure that an intelligent man does not boast of excessive eating, drinking and cohabitation, nor of his preoccupation all the time with these activities. Again, people do not proceed to mating but in privacy. No one from among the intelligent ever allows himself to agree to mating in the presence of people. This also shows that it is a low and mean action and people feel ashamed of it.

It is also habitual with the low people to abuse one another by mentioning words connected with mating. When a debased person relates in the presence of a big crowd as to how a particular man cohabits with his wife, the man concerned feels ashamed of this speech and feels as if he has been tortured by the speaker. All this indicates that the action of sexual mating is no perfection and no bliss, rather it is an indecent deed and a shameful action.

The Ninth Proof: Every animal that inclines more to eating, drinking and doing harm and less to exercise, is rated by the people at a low worth, and every animal that inclines to eating and drinking least and is quickest in undertaking exercise, is highly regarded by the people. Don't you see that a horse which accepts training and agrees to exercises, makes a charge, and runs away and moves fast, is sold at a high price? A horse which is thin in waist is most swift and excels the fat one with a big belly. Every horse which does not undergo any exercise and displays none of the actions (described above), and is loaded with a pack-saddle and bears burdens, and is regarded as the equal of an ass is sold at a low price. When these irrational animals are judged for their merits and excellences not by eating and drinking but by other criteria, what should you, then, think of the rational intelligent animals?

The Tenth Proof: The inhabitants of the remote parts of the earth who have made no progress in their intellects, habits, customs and knowledge, have necessarily grown extremely debased and low. Don't you see that since the inhabitants of the first Iqlîm (region)—the negroes—and those of the Seventh Iqlîm (region)—the Slavs possess but little share of real knowledge and sciences, excellent manners, and intellects necessarily confirm their low positions in the minds of men and prove that their stage of progress is very low? As for the inhabitants of the middle part of the earth, since they possess real knowledge and sciences and excellent manners, they have necessarily been, by common consent, confirmed as the best of human races. This indicates that the excellence and perfection of a man is only realised by means of the sciences, knowledge and excellent manners and not by his eating, drinking, and mating.

On the Explanation of the Causes of Blame and Defect that Lie in Sensuous Pleasures

You must know that an object is either condemnable *per se* or condemnable due to something else. The sensuous pleasures contain both the cases. That they are condemnable *per se* is indicated by more than one reason:

Firstly, the original and the best of all that has been discussed in this chapter is the fact that these pleasures are in fact no pleasures, rather their net result is to remove pains. The pleasure of eating, for example, means only to remove the pain of hunger, the pleasure of mating to remove the sexual appetition caused by the semen which increases and gets choked in the semen-pods and causes the extraction of the pods and painful vibration, and its discharge removes necessarily those kinds of pain. The pleasure of clothing also consists in removing the pain of heat and cold. . . .

Having understood this, it is clear to you that what is considered by some people as pleasure is in fact not so, rather it is the effort undertaken to remove pains and to engage the soul in matters like this is another pain. They are, therefore, not at all blessings and perfections.

Secondly, anything that is needed most causes the strongest feeling of pleasure when it is achieved and is most painful when the case is reverse. Whenever an object is wanted least, the pleasure caused by its presence is least. Don't you see when you throw a necklace of pearls towards a dog the dog does not pay any heed to it, as it is not wanted, and when you throw a piece of bone it would leap to it, snatch it away and fight for it with all those who would contend with him? The case is quite different with a man who feels happy and overjoyed on finding a necklace of pearls. He feels pleased either by the idea of decorating himself with it or by selling it at a profit. If a piece of bone is thrown to him he would pay no heed to it, as he does not want it. It is therefore established that pleasure and demand are in accordance with the extent of need. But the need is a calamity, a trial and a misfortune and the object which is only obtained by a trial and calamity is also of a similar nature. It is thus established that the bodily pleasures are like a poisoned sweet in the bodies which feel pleased with its sweetness although it is a whim and a deadly poison.

One may, however, point out that this objection is applicable to you concerning the spiritual pleasures as well. But we say, the reply to this will come soon.

Thirdly, these pleasures are so called in so far as they are pleasures *per se.* But to enjoy them is only possible when they come into being. If they continue they do not remain pleasant, the reason being that the pleasure which is signified on their accomplishment perceives the agreeable and is influenced by them—a state which arises only in the beginning of their occurrence. The state after the occurrence of pleasures is one of continuity and persistence and in this case there is no impression and, therefore, no awareness, and when there is no awareness there cannot be any feeling of pleasure.

Fourthly, when a man enjoys these pleasures to the extent of his want and sufficiency, he does not feel pleased in employing the means for the furtherance of those pleasures, rather he feels satiated and disgusted with them. Then, after feeling disgusted with them if he is urged to fulfil them a second time, he surely feels pain in perceiving them. For example, when one eats to his fill and is compelled to overeat, one would feel pain. Similarly, if he who has accomplished mating to his utmost desire is compelled to do it in excess, he is sure to feel pain in it. This indicates that these pleasures hold no goodness and bliss in themselves but they are useful only as long as they meet a need. When the need is fulfilled these things become a burden and a curse on the souls and spirits.

Fifthly, the objects which are considered to be pleasant and desirable in the world are sometimes described with undesirable and hateful descriptions, and they may turn up again like that. Don't you see that wheat before growing into wheat gives off a bad smell in the moisture of the earth? Then, it grows into a plant and drinks the moisture of the refuse and dung. Then, when it stands erect and is fully prepared it is eaten and is mixed with the moisture of the mouth and the saliva which if it were seen by the eating agent would be disliked by him and he would consider it filthy. Again, it turns, in the end, into a bad smelling dung and an object which is thrown away. Similar is the case with meats, sweets and fruits. When an intelligent man ponders over it, he finds it originally obnoxious in smell, filthy in substance and corrupt in origin. But Allah, the Exalted, has conferred on them a colour, smell and taste for a small period of time to the extent of what is useful for a matured man, so that he may be able to obey Allah and understand what is beneficial for him in his livelihood. Then they, shortly, return to the original filth and natural corruption.

Sixthly, surely the use of these pleasures conflicts with the essence of humanity. This is because a man is a man only in so far as he attains the light of intelligence and is aware of the unseen presence (of God) and of the Divine Lights. Now, when a man is engaged in fulfilling these bodily pleasures his intellectual faculty becomes hazy, the door of knowledge is closed to him, and he remains overpowered by animality, and devoid of humanity.

Since the nobility of man lies in fulfilling the sensuous pleasures which nullify the meaning of humanity for him, it is confirmed that to be preoccupied by these pleasures is extremely reprehensible.

Seventhly, the real human condition is to engage oneself in knowing Allah, the Exalted, in order to be able to obey Him and to lose oneself in His Love. His engagement in bodily pleasures and permissible objects of sense prevents him from worshipping and remembering Allah. Since these objects of knowledge are the noblest ideals for a human creature and the sensuous pleasures prevent one from them, these pleasures are the lowest of all objects. Whenever there is a noble object worthy of attainment its opposite object which prevents a man from achieving the good is low to that extent.

All these arguments indicate that the world *per se* is condemnable.

As for the reasons which indicate that the world is condemnable due to matters which are necessarily connected with it, they are many. We shall mention some of them as follows:

1. The world is transient and nearing extinction, and it is known that when a man likes something or meets his beloved he enjoys pleasure in its company and association. But when he faces separation, or keeps apart he feels the pain of separation. The pain of separation felt by him is the same in extent and intensity as the pleasure achieved by his meeting. The matter being so, the severer the love for the worldly life, the stronger and severer is the pain felt by separation after death. Then, though the pleasures and pains seem to be equal in this respect the preference is claimed by the side of pains, since the pleasures come to an end, while the pains are interminable. It is for this reason that to the people of intelligence the bodily pleasures are condemnable.

2. The worldly pleasures are not pure. They are mixed with pains and loss, rather, if the man ponders over this, he is sure to find that the pleasure is like a drop of water and the pain like an ocean that flows for him. We warn against the knotty problems of this preference.

We say: this preference is caused by more than one reason: (a) the harm caused by it, it is threefold and concerns the past, the present and the future.

As for the past, we say: the conditions available to a man in the past are either the means of bliss and pleasure or those of pleasure and pain, or they cause neither bliss nor pain. If we suppose that they necessitate bliss and ambition, then either it is said that they have persisted or not, both of which necessitate bliss. If they have persisted till the present time, it is a known fact that there is no stage over and above which there are not more stages, each more sublime and more perfect than the previous ones. The matter being so, whenever a man is pleased with the bliss which he enjoyed in the past, and which has continued up to the present time, his mind is fully conscious of all the stages which he has found and attained. He will therefore feel in his heart various kinds of sorrow due to the bliss which he has missed. But if the past conditions necessitated bliss but did not persist and vanished away, then whenever the man would recall the memory of those lost stages the fire of sorrow would get kindled in his heart due to losing them after they had been achieved, and their passing away after their coming into being.

If, however, these conditions were neither means for bliss nor for misery then they were something useless which carried no value. And whenever a man remembers those conditions he recognises that he has wasted that part of his life in vain without having any gain though it was possible for him to spend his time in attaining higher blessings and greater positions. At this time, he will find his heart blazing with the fire of melancholy and sorrow due to the wastage of his age. Then, he often finds that his mates and friends have attempted in their past life to achieve excellences and have succeeded in their efforts and have attained high achievements and noble positions. But when he finds himself descending low behind his companions and mates, he dies of sorrow and misery. It is therefore confirmed that his remembrance of past conditions would only bring him sorrow and misery.

As for the persisting condition which continues, it is surprising, because it is indispensable and must be the end of the past and the beginning of the future. When this is the position, it must be divisible. But it is not so. For, if this time were divisible, some parts, already in operation, must precede some others. The whole will not then be present. This is contrary to the proposition.

Having learned this, it is clear that time, which is as short as the twinkling of an eye, cannot be present, because in this time the eye-lid moves on the surface of the eye-ball which is divisible into numberless divisions according to the philosophers, and into a limited number according to others, and on this supposition the present 'now' is a part from the multitude of parts which are beyond limit and numeration belonging to one and the same glance. This little part is so insignificant that it is not perceived by mind nor is it recorded in perception and imagination. Hence, it is not possible to feel pleased, and have, in fact, real enjoyment. What is beyond the indivisible 'now' is either the past in parts or the future which both do not exist in the present. It is therefore established that the objects that are considered blessings are *per se* not so. They are, rather, absurd ideas and useless whims.

(*b*) It is the habit of man that he does not feel pleased with, nor does he incline to, anything that is available to him in actual fact. On the contrary, he feels only pleased in getting what is missing and wanting that which does not exist. We know therefore that man does not feel pleased with what exists in the present. As for the future, it may agree or disagree with him. Such being the case, he will not see things in the future due to severe fear and complete awe. It is, thus, established by what we have mentioned that there are three times, past, present and future, and his looking into any one of these necessitates severe sorrow, pain, dislike and excessive fear. It is therefore confirmed by what we have mentioned that man never escapes from sorrow and distress and other such states.

(*c*) The second thing that necessarily causes a man to be afflicted by sorrow and distress is the fact that the man either lives in the society of people or separately. The first state is a strong cause which inflicts sorrow, distress and strange feelings upon him, because keeping the company of some people necessitates dissension in the present or in the future, in all affairs or in some affairs and the dissension necessarily causes either of the two rivals to dominate the other in a way. The domination necessarily causes sorrow and distress.

The other state, that is, his living separately from the society is also a strong factor in causing him distress, since man is a creature whose interests cannot be secured except by living in large populations. Once separated from the mass of men his interests become different. It is therefore confirmed that the living of a man in the company of others necessitates trouble and turmoil, while by living in separation he is afflicted with sorrow and sadness. Thus it is confirmed that he has no escape from sorrows and pains.

(*d*) The third factor that necessitates sorrow and distress is that man is either more perfect than another or equal to him or more defective than him. If he is more perfect than another man, this other man must be defective. But defect in itself is disliked and is essentially loathed.

Now, what is defective cannot drive away its defect but by nullifying what is more perfect and by attaining all that entails the purpose essentially. It is for this reason that the imperfect man plans to try to nullify the perfection of the perfect either by nullifying perfection in itself essentially, or by concealing the perfection from the eyes of the people. Either state is essentially contrary to perfection and necessitates sorrow, pain and disturbance of heart.

In case both are equal, we say, perfection is desired essentially, so either of the two will necessarily intend with determination to make himself more perfect, noble and sublime than the other. Now, either of the two cannot be higher than the other. It is for this reason that there would occur severe fighting and struggle between them and you have learned that the struggle is a cause of fear, sorrow and loneliness. Again, if either of the two equals became subordinate, the heart of the other would be afflicted with pain, because subordination is essentially disliked, and it distresses the heart. In case one dominates the other, the heart of the dominated would be distressed.

Then, the dominated would try his utmost to remove domination. But the removal of domination would necessitate the disappearance of the domination of the dominating agent which is essentially disliked by the agent. The dominating agent therefore fears the loss of his power—a fear that entails pain. It is therefore established that if a man finds himself with his equals he is not free from sorrow and melancholy. If he happens to be dominated in relation to someone else, then whenever the dominated will look at the dominating person he will find him in a high position full of pleasure and happiness, and will find himself deprived of all these. So, without doubt, the fire of sorrow and loss shall burn his heart. Again, the dominating person will render the dominated a target of the troubling objects and the harmful things. All these distress the heart. It is therefore established that a man, no matter whether he is more perfect or less perfect than the other, or equal to him, never escapes sorrow, loss, heartache and pain of heart.

(*e*) The fourth cause which entails sorrow and distress is the fact that man possesses undoubtedly intelligence which guides him aright, and passion that destroys him. The latter has many accessories which are appetition, anger, greed and external and internal senses.

But the intellect does not find any other quality in the essence of man which could give it strength. For this reason the intellect is inevitably weaker than desire. Again, man is, from the beginning of his nature, submissive to the sensuous pleasures, is devoted to them and readily accepts them.

As for the light of intellect, it does not appear in him except after a certain period of his age. And, they say: knowledge in childhood is like an engraved image in the stone. The philosophers say: repetition causes the achievement of rational habits. The matter being so, the attraction of the soul to the sensuous pleasures must be stronger than the mental pleasures. Desire means nothing but absorption in physical pleasures and sensuous happiness. It is therefore established that the side of desire is extremely dominant over the side of the intellect.

When you have known this, we say: the sum and substance of what we have mentioned is that most of the actions coming forth from man are in accordance with the demand of desire and belong to the *genus* of blameworthy actions. Then, after man ventures upon them, accomplishes them and turns away from them, his intellect becomes free from the contention of desire. It is in this state that man becomes aware of their deformity, ugliness and their containing many undesirable and blameworthy means. But, since man becomes aware of these evils through his intellect only after their occurrence and after the act is complete, these evils cannot be removed or prevented. Therefore, man is left only with sorrow, shame, and repentance.

Since we have explained that man mostly ventures upon the demands of his desire just in accordance with the argument we have advanced, he mostly remains in sorrow, and repentance. This indicates that man is necessarily in most of the cases attached to sorrows and is afflicted by deep sighs.

(*f*) The fifth cause that necessitates distress is the fact that stages of bliss and nobility are unlimited and to achieve that which has no end is impossible; the result is that all positions cannot be achieved by man. It has been established that the repetition of intellect causes habit. So, whenever man is more constantly attached to the bodily pleasures, the greater and stronger is his inclination to seek these pleasures. When his inclination to seek pleasure is stronger, his care for achieving that which is missing is greater. Since the achievement of the stages which have no end is impossible, it entails, at the end, the excessively repeated demand of seeking endless pleasures; this will continue with the impossibility of achieving the end, and this would, then, inflict pain.

It is established that to incline to pleasure causes pains in case they are achieved. In case they are not obtained, the appearance of the pain is manifest. It is for this reason that some deeply learned philosophers have said: Whosoever intends to be free from the world through the world is like one who wants to extinguish fire with straw. It is therefore established by all these arguments that it is impossible that the worldly pleasures be free from sorrow and pains, rather they are all pains and defects.

Then, when you ponder over the conditions of the poor people you will think of their affairs and the troubles they find themselves in—annoyance, attachment to the painful, advancing straight to the enemies, association with sorrows—you will find them as if they were an ocean without a shore, whereas the pleasure obtained by man is like a drop in the ocean. It is therefore established by what we have mentioned that the bodily pleasures are mixed with pains, diseases and harmful things. Therefore, there is no doubt that they are blameworthy.

3. The third external cause that necessitates the condemnation of the world is the fact that mostly a man who is mean in himself, in his faculties, position and lineage, surpasses in physical pleasures the one who is noble in himself, in his mind, position, lineage and faith. That is why the Prophet said: Had the world to Allah weighed as much as the wing of a fly, He would not have surely allowed an infidel even a single drink out of it.

4. As for the fourth cause, it is the characteristic of the corporeal pleasures that whenever you repair a breach in it there would open up a multitude of breaches to you and this would occur without any limit. For example, when a man finds himself too weak to do anything and purchases a horse, he needs a servant to look after the horse, a village to obtain its food, a stable wherein he would tie the horse. Now, his need to have each one of these objects would open up a multitude of doors to more needs. This continues without limit. It has, for this reason, been related on the authority of Jesus Christ (peace be upon him) that he said: Surely the important affairs of the world are not accomplished by improvement and perfection but are only accomplished by abandoning them and withdrawing from them.

Translated by M.S.H. Masumi.

14

IBN ABÎ UṢAYBÎYAH,*

Abu'l-Walîd Ibn Rushd (=Averroës)

The Judge (*Qâḍî*) Abu'l-Walîd Muhammad ibn Aḥmad ibn Muhammad ibn Rushd was born and brought up in Cordova. He was eminently famous, intensely engaged in scientific studies, outstanding in the study of canon and criminal law, and a fine stylist. He studied under the Jurist al-Ḥâfiẓ Abû Muhammad ibn Rizq. He was also distinguished in the science of medicine and composed a great many excellent books, e.g., in medicine, a book called *al-Kullîyât [fi'l-Ṭibb]* ('A Compendium of Medicine'), which is a comprehensive work. He and Abû Marwân ibn Zuhr [i.e., Avenzoar, another famous Spanish-Arab scientist] were friends; therefore, when Ibn Rushd composed this book of his, he requested Ibn Zuhr to write a book on pharmaceutical matters, so that the two works together would form a complete compendium on the science and practice of medicine. In this connexion, Ibn Rushd said in a passage at the conclusion of his own work: "This is not its end. This work deals with the treatment of all kinds of diseases in the most comprehensive and concise form possible. However, we have still to compose a work on treatment of every possible symptom that affects every single organ, for that topic is, if not absolutely essential, yet part of it, on the strength of the discussions in the preceding chapters of the *Kullîyah.* In this work (of Ibn Zuhr's) there will be a complete discussion of (medical) practice, because in it we enter into a discussion of the treatment of disease, symptom after symptom, for that is the method introduced by the school of the Cynics. The result will be that we will combine in these chapters of ours the matters discussed in the *Kullîyah* and the pharmaceutical approach (to the illness). This coöperation is the most appropriate approach possible through which we can undertake a study of pharmacology, unless we delay it to some later time when we would be less occupied than at present with other, more important, works. Any one who happens to read this work (the *Kullîyah*) without this (additional)

*Died 1270 in Damascus. (See p. 59.)

part (on pharmacy), must look, after having perused it, into the works of the Cynics, for their ideas agree with his. The book, with the title *al-Taysîr [fi'l-Mudâwâh wa'l-Tadbîr]* which Abû Marwân ibn Zuhr composed in our own time, is the one that I have asked him to write and which I have copied; and that was the way in which it was produced. It contains, as we have said, treatises dealing with pharmaceutical matters concerning the same subjects which I have classified in the *Kullîyah*, except that here (in the *Taysîr*) they are mixed with the therapy of symptoms and the presentation of their causes according to the usage of the school of the Cynics. Therefore there is no need for the reader of this book of ours to go back to that school, but it is sufficient merely to study the treatment (recommended here): any one who studies the chapters of the *Kullîyah* can judge about the correct or wrong remedies (used by) the school of the Cynics in their *Tafsîr al-ʿIlâj wa'l-Tarkîb* ('Commentary on Treatment and Ingredients [of their medicines])."

The Qâḍî Abû Marwân al-Bajjà told me the following: The Qâḍî Abu'l-Walîd Ibn Rushd had sound opinions, he was intelligent, had a lean figure and a strong mind; he had studied mathematics and medicine under Abû Jaʿfar ibn Hârûn and continued with him for some time taking many courses in the natural sciences. Ibn Rushd had been a judge in Seville before he came to Cordova, and was respected by al-Manṣûr and highly regarded in his reign (*dawlah*); his son al-Nâṣir also honored him greatly. He (Abû Marwân al-Bâjjà) said: When al-Manṣûr was in Cordova during the war against Alfonso—that was in the year 591 A.H. (/1194 A.D.)—he summoned Abu'l-Walîd and when he came into his presence, he accorded him great honor and invited him to sit close by his side, until he occupied a higher rank than that accorded to Abû Muhammad ʿAbd al-Wâḥid ibn al-Shaikh Abî Ḥafṣ al-Hintâtî, the friend of ʿAbd al-Mu'min; that is, he became the third or fourth in rank in the caliph's entourage. This Abû Muhammad ʿAbd al-Wâḥid was al-Manṣûr's son-in-law, for he had given him his daughter in marriage, because he had such a high opinion of him. ʿAbd al-Wâḥid was blessed with a son by her whose name is ʿAlî and who is at present the governor of Ifriqîyah. Al-Manṣûr bade Ibn Rushd approach and made him sit by his side to talk with him; when he left his presence, all the students and many of his friends were waiting for him and congratulated him for the rank accorded him by al-Manṣûr and for the reception he had received from him. But Ibn Rushd said: "By Allâh, this is nothing that deserves congratulations, for the Prince of the Faithful had granted me my fondest wish once, or, he has (now) fulfilled all that I could (ever) hope for." However, some of his enemies had spread the slanderous rumors that the Prince of the Faithful had ordered to kill him; but when he emerged safely, he ordered one of his servants to go to his house and tell them to prepare a dish of boiled pigeon hens to be ready for him when he would come to them: he ordered them to do that only to reassure them about his well-being. But somewhat later, al-Manṣûr punished Ibn Rushd and ordered him to stay in al-Yasânah, a town near Cordova that had previously been the residence of (lit., belonged to) the Jews, and not leave it; he also punished a number of other high-ranking and famous men and ordered them to stay in various other places. It appears that he did that because they were alleged to be engaged in (the study of) science and Greek philosophy. This group consisted of Ibn Rushd and Abû Jaʿfar al-Dhahabî, and the Canon Lawyer Abû ʿAbd Allâh Muhammad ibn Ibrâhîm, the Judge of Bujâya, and Abu'l-Rabiʿ al-Kafîf (The Blind), and Abu'l-ʿAbbâs, al-Ḥâfiẓ (the Koran scholar) and poet, al-Qirâbî, and that banishment remained in force for a while. Then a number of prominent people of Seville testified that Ibn Rushd was innocent of the activities that were ascribed to him. Al-Manṣûr was satisfied that he, and the rest of the group, was innocent. This happened in the year 595 A.H. (/1198 A.D.) and he appointed Abû Jaʿfar al-Dhahabî as a consultant for the students and a consultant for physicians. Al-Manṣûr praised him and thanked him saying: "Abû Jaʿfar al-Dhahabî is like pure gold (*dhahab:* a pun on his *nisbah*) that does not increase in excellence by smelting."

Judge Abû Marwân said further: An indication of the feeling in al-Manṣûr's heart towards Ibn Rushd was the way he addressed him; when he attended his court and Ibn Rushd talked with him or discussed scientific matters in his presence, al-Manṣûr would say to him: "you hear, oh my brother". But then Ibn Rushd had composed a book on animals, in which he talked about the various species of animals describing each of them; when he came to the description of the giraffe, he added: "I have seen the giraffe at the king of the Berbers (البربر)", referring to al-Manṣûr. When al-Manṣûr heard that, he hardened against him, and that was one of the reasons that caused him to punish him with exile. Ibn Rushd is said to have apologized by saying: "I said only 'the king of the two lands' (البرّين i.e., Spain and Africa), and it was misread by a reader who pronounced instead of *Malik al-Barrayn* 'king of the two lands' *Malik al-Barbar* 'king of the Berbers (Barbarians)'[1]."

[1] In unvocalized handwriting, without "diacritical" points, the two words can easily be mistaken for each other.

The Qâḍi Abu'l-Walîd Ibn Rushd, may Allâh have mercy on him, died in Marrakesh early in the year 595 A.H. (/1198 A.D.), in the beginning of the reign of al-Nâṣir. Ibn Rushd had a long life; he was survived by a son who was a physician and an outstanding scholar[1], whose name was Abû Muhammad ibn ʿAbd Allâh, and other sons who were authorities on Canon law and served as district judges.

---

[1] For the translation of the term *ṣinâʿah* used here, cp. F. Rosenthal, *Das Fortleben der Antike im Islam,* Zürich und Stuttgart, (1965), p. 367, note 44.

15

RÂBIʿAH AL-ʿADAWÎYAH *

"Two ways I love Thee: selfishly,
And next, as worthy is of Thee.
'Tis selfish love that I do naught
Save think on Thee with every thought;
'Tis purest love when Thou dost raise
The veil to my adoring gaze.
Not mine the praise in that or this,
Thine is the praise in both, I wis."

Translated by R. A. Nicholson

*Died 801 A.D. Famous woman mystic; born in Baṣra, died in Jerusalem, where her tomb was venerated in the Middle Ages.

16

AL-MAʿARRÎ *

The Meditations

LIFE AND DEATH

1

In the casket of the Hours
Events deep-hid
Wait on their guardian Powers
To raise the lid.

And the Maker infinite,
Whose poem is Time,
He need not weave in it
A forced stale rhyme.

The Nights pass so,
Voices dumb,
Without sense quick or slow
Of what shall come.

* * * * *

By Allah's will preserving
From misflight,
The barbs of Time unswerving
On us alight.

A loan is all he gives
And takes again;
With his gift happy lives
The folly of men.

*Died 1057 A.D. (See p. 109.)

2

The greatest of all the gifts of Time is to give up all:
Whate'er he bestows on thee, his hand is outstretched to seize.
More excellence hath a life of want than a life of wealth,
And better than monarch's fine apparel the hermit's garb.
I doubt not but Time one day will raise an event of power
To scatter from Night's swart brow her clustering Pleiades.
Ere Noah and Adam, he the twins of the Lesser Bear
Unveiled: they are called not yet amongst bears grown grey and old.
Let others run deep in talk, preferring this creed or that,
But mine is a creed of use: to hold me aloof from men.
Methinks, on the Hours we ride to foray as cavaliers:
They speed us along like mares of tall make and big of bone.
What most wears Life's vesture out is grief which a soul endures,
Unable to bring once back a happiness past and gone.

3

O Death! be thou my guest; I am tired of living,
And I have tried both sorts in joy and sorrow.
My morrow shall be my yesterday, none doubts it;
My yesterday nevermore shall be my morrow.

4

I welcome Death in his onset and the return thereof,
That he may cover me with his garment's redundancy.
This world is such an abode that if those present here
Have their wits entire, they will never weep for the absent ones.
Calamities exceeding count hath it brought to light;
Beneath its arm and embosomed close how many more!
It cleaves us all with its swords asunder and smites us down
With its spears and finds us out, right home, with its sure-winged
shafts.
Its prize-winners, who won the power and the wealth of it,
Are but little distant in plight from those who lost its prize.

* * * * *

And a strange thing 'tis, how lovingly doth every man
Desire the Mother of stench[1] thewhile he rails at her.

[1] i.e., the world.

5

O purblind men, is none clear-eyed amongst you?
Alas, have ye none to guide you towards the summit?
We people the world in youthtide and in greyness
Of eld, and in woe we sleep and in woe we waken;
And all lands we inhabit at every season,
And find earth's hills the same as we found its valleys.
A bed is made smooth and soft for the rich man's slumber—
Oh, gladder for him a grave than a couch to lie on!
Whenever a soul is joined to a living body,
Between them is war of Moslem and unbeliever.

6

'Tis pain to live and pain to die,
Oh, would that far-off fate were nigh!
An empty hand, a palate dry,
A craving soul, a staring eye.

Who kindles fires in the night
For glory's sake he shows a light;
But man, to live, needs little wealth—
A shirt, a bellyful, and health.

Clasped in the tomb, he careth not
For anything he gave or got;
Silken touch and iron thrust
Are one to him that now is dust.

* * * * *

We smile on happy friends awhile,
Though nothing here is worth a smile.
Give joy to those, more blest than I,
Who gained their dearest wish—to die!

7

The stars we ought to glorify,
Which God hath honoured and set high

For all the world. And Life, how be
It ne'er so fondly loved by thee,
Is like a chain of pearls ill-strung,
That chafed the neck on which it hung.

HUMAN SOCIETY

8

(Metre: *Ṭawîl.*)
Who knows? Some that fill the mosque with terror whene'er they preach
No better may be than some that drink to a tavern-tune.
If God's public worship serve them only to engine fraud,
Then nearer to Him are those forsaking it purposely.
Let none vaunt himself who soon returns to an element
Of clay which the potter takes and cunningly moulds for use.
A vessel, if so it hap, anon will be made of him,
From whence any common churl at pleasure may eat and drink;
And he, unaware the while, transported from land to land—
O sorrow for him! his bones have crumbled, he wanders on.

9

O sons of Learning, ever were ye lured
By rhetoric empty as the buzz of flies.
Your poets are very wolves—the robber's way
They take in panegyric and love-song,
Doing their friends worse injury than foes;
And when they verses write, out-thieve the rat.
I lend you praise repaid with praise as false,
Whence 'tis as though between us taunts had passed.
Shall I let run to waste my time of eld
Amongst you, squandered like my days of youth?

* * * * *

Fine eloquence I do cast off from my tongue,
Resigning to the Arabs who have wit
Base occupations uncommendable,
Whereof the whole return is utter loss.
Leave me, that I may babble in vain no more
But, waiting Death, close on myself my door.

PHILOSOPHY AND RELIGION

10

Reason forbade me many things whereto
Instinctively my nature's bias drew;
And 'tis perpetual loss if, knowing, I
Believe a falsehood or give Truth the lie.

11

O spirit, how long wilt thou with pleasure wear
This body? Fling it off, 'tis worn threadbare.
If thou hast chosen to lodge thus all these years,
Thine is the blame—and smiles oft end in tears.
Or if the fault was Fate's, then thou art blind,
As water feels no barrier, though confined.
Wert thou not there, to sin it ne'er had stirred,
But would have lain like earth without a word.
The lamp of mind neglecting, thou dost stray,
Although in Reason's light thou hast a God-given ray.

12

Ye cast the creeds behind,
Tho' nowhere do ye find
In Wisdom they should be rejected and dismissed.

Obedience ye refuse
The Moslem judge, the Jews'
Rabbi, the Christian bishop, and the Magian priest.

Let *your* law be in turn
Offered to them ye spurn,
All will cry, "Nay; we don't desire it in the least."

13

How for her dead should Earth have care,
When in the moment of despair
Men cast away their not yet dead
Uncared for and uncomforted?
If God please, when the burst tombs quake,
He'll punish them for what they did and spake.

14

Give a drink of water as alms to the birds which go forth at
morning, and deem that they have a better right than men
(to thy charity),
For their race brings not harm upon thee in any wise, when thou
fearest it from thine own race.

Translated by R. A. Nicholson

17

IBN AL-FÂRIḌ *

The Jîmîyah

Mâ bayna muʿtaraki ʾl-aḥdâqi waʾl-muhaji,
Anâ ʾl-qatîlu bi-lâ ithmin wa-lâ ḥaraji

1. In the midst of the battle of glances and souls I am slain with neither sin nor transgression.
2. I bade farewell to my soul even before love, because of the beauty of that happy vision my eyes beheld.
3. For God's sake are lashes keeping vigil over you, out of longing for you; for His sake is a heart saddened by passion;
4. And a body become emaciated, because of its intense passion. which my emblazened heart almost straightened from its twistedness;
5. And tears shed—were it not for a gasp of the fire of love, I would not even have been near to rescue from the enundations.
6. How marvellous are the pains for your sake! I have disappeared from myself because of them; my evidence before Love rests upon them.
7. For your sake my morning was like my evening—sorrowful; but I did not say out of anxiety, O crisis, be thou dispelled.
8. I hasten to every heart whose occupation is with love, and to every tongue which constantly speaks of love,
9. And to every ear deaf to blame, and to every lash which descends not to doze.
10. Be there no ecstasy in which the eyes are rigid! Be there no love where longing are not turbulent.
11. Torment me with what you will—except separation from you. You will find the most faithful lover rejoicing in what pleases you.
12. Take the rest of the last breath of life which you have left (to me). There is no goodness in love if it has pity on the soul.

*Died 1235 A.D. (See p. 84.)

13. Who will have compassion on me to destroy my soul in the love of a young gazelle of beautiful character, mingled with souls?
14. He who dies for it out of passion lives elevated among the people of love, of the most sublime degree.
15. Were a veiled one to pass during the night through the likes of his forelock, his beautiful countenance would render him needless of lamps.
16. And if I went astray in one of the nights of his tresses, the morning of his shining countenance would guide the right path to my eye.
17. And if he took a breath, musk would say, confessing to those who know its perfume, "My aroma is from his diffusion."
18. Years of proximity to him are like a day in brevity; a day of his evasion is like years in length.
19. If he goes away journeying, O my soul, travel thou also; if he approaches as a visitor, O mine eyes, rejoice
20. Say to him who censures and rebukes me for his sake, "Leave me alone! Turn back from your hateful advice!"
21. Blame is baseness: no one has ever been lauded for it; have you ever seen a lover satirized for his infatuation?
22. O you whose heart is motionless, gaze not upon my contentment and gain steadfast your heart and beware the sedition of his eyes!
23. O my friend! I am pious, benevolent: I have expended my counsel: Don't you settle in that quarter
24. In which I have thrown off all restraint; where I have tossed off the acceptance of my worship and the acceptability of my pilgrimages.
25. The face of my passion has whitened in his love; the path of blaming me for it has blackened with proofs.
26. Blessed be God! How beautiful are his characteristics: how many souls have they killed and brought again to life!
27. My ear loves him who persists in rebuking me because of the mention of his name: yet his blame did not enter (my ear).

I have pity on the lightening in its night journey—as it is kin to his mouth—, since it is ashamed before the glistening of his teeth.

29. Every limb (of my body) sees him, even if he be absent from me, in every delicate, clear, joyous essence:

30. In the tune of the melodious lute and flute when they blend together in trilling strains,
31. And in luxurious pasturage of gazelles in the coolness of twilight and in the first rays of dawning,
32. And in misty rains falling from a cloud on a carpet woven of flowers,
33. And where the breeze sweeps her train, guiding to me most fragrant attar at sweet dawn,
34. And when I kiss the lip of the cup, sipping the clear wine in pleasure and joy.
35. I knew not estrangement from my homeland when he was with me: my mind was undisturbed where we were—
36. That place was my home while my beloved was present; when the sloping dune appeared, that was my halting-place.
37. Pleasant be riders who travel by night with you in their train, on a dawn breaking because of you.
38. Let the riders do as they please with themselves—they are the people of Badr, hence they fear not transgression.
39. (I swear) by my disobedience to him who reproaches me on your account and the tongue of flame in my heart because of obedience to ecstasy.
40. Gaze upon a heart withered from love-sickness with you, and an eye in the depths of the blood of tears.
41. Have mercy upon the poverty of my hopes and my return to humility of wishing for the promise of happiness;
42. And have sympathy for my humble desires with a "maybe" and a "perhaps", and bestow upon me happiness instead of perplexity.
43. O welcome, that which I am not worthy to expect!—the pronouncement of the bearer of glad tidings of joy after despair:
44. "Good news for you—so take off what is upon you, for 'there' has been mentioned, in spite of the deviation which is in you!"

Translated by Wheeler McIntosh Thackston, Jr.

18

Al-Ḥallâj *

A Biographical Introduction.

by Herbert Mason[1]

The stage was set; it might've been an aspect
Of your past that led to your imprisonment
And death: grandfather a Zoroastrian;
Or seen with negroes at the time of the revolt;
Or knew practitioners of the occult;
Your trips to India; or all the rest. . . .

It didn't help that persons in high places
Fought your cause, or that professors
Held debates, or that disciples marched;
It only meant the end would be more public.
You didn't live for fame. You had spoken out
About reform, but in a private way, reforming first
Yourself, though no one knew what 'private' meant.
You called attention to the uses of the tax—
The private pockets into which it went,
The immoral acts committed in the public name
As if it were consensus . . .

It wasn't this. All sermons are absorbed
And neutralized like shocks to the economy:
Once in the running, they're forgotten.
It wasn't your morality or justice
Or your sense of truth that made the sages
Jealous or the rulers shake with rage,

*Died as a martyr 922 A.D. (See p. 84.)

[1] First published in a German translation by Annemarie Schimmel as an "Einleitung" to her *Al-Halladsch, Märtyrer der Gottesliebe,* Köln, 1968.

But love—the way He came to you,
Your fellow prisoner and friend
More intimate than your children or your wife,
More personal than thought,
And never left . . . You let Him love you
As the law allows, yet it was He
Who loved and not an edict or a code.
One jealous mystic called you mad at the trial
And one aroused conservative called you a saint;
Both names were damning in official eyes.

Nine years in prison He never left you,
And the day they brought you out to hang
You had no name to call Him, only "I",
The One Who never left and never died.

THREE ODES OF AL-ḤALLÂJ

I

Qaṣîda I

The cry of the pilgrim on the threshold of Union.

Here I am! Here I am!
My secret One, my trusted One.
I have answered Your call.
You are my meaning, and my hope.

I call to You . . . or, no,
You call me to Yourself.
Do I say 'It is You'?
Or do You whisper 'It is I'?

You are the distance I must go,
My spring of springs,
My reasoning, my words,
These stammerings.

You are everything I am.
My hearing and my sight,
My universe,
My trifling things.

The sum of everything I am
You are. And everything I am
Is Mystery. I have confused You
With my little meaning.

It is You I've been in love with
And been crushed, in moments
When You let Yourself become
My prisoner in love.

I mourn in being exiled
From my home—I chose it so;
My enemies are happy
In my sorrow . . .

I come near You,
My fear excites me.
Desire steadies me
In my inmost heart . . .

What can I do with One
With Whom I am this much in love?
O Lord, the doctors say
They're tired of my sickness.

They say, Cure it through Him.
I say to them, O people
What sickness can be cured
By its disease?

My love for my Lord
Consumes and makes me weak.
How can I say to Him,
It is Your doing. . .

I look . . . my heart perceives,
But how can I explain
His ways except
By wordless gestures . . ?

My self's at fault,
O woe to me!
I am the source
Of my own agony . . .

Like a person drowning
In the sea
Who reaches out for help
With fingertips alone . .

Only He Who has come down
To depths known in the heart,
Only He, descends
Into this melancholy.

He knows what I have known
In the long illness;
And in His will I see
My death and resurrection.

O my request and hope,
My home, my very breath,
My faith . .
My worldly fate . . .

Say to me 'I have rescued you' . . .
O my hearing and my sight,
Why do You keep me still
At such a distance?

Though You are hidden
To my eyes,
My heart perceives You
In the distance. . . .

II

Qaṣîda VI

Recited by Ḥallâj on the night before his execution, the poem is about the sorrow which follows ecstasy.

I cry to You for souls whose present witness (I myself)
Now goes beyond the Where to meet the Witness of Eternity.

I cry to You for hearts so long refreshed
By clouds of revelation which once were filled with seas of wisdom.

I cry to hear the Word of God, which since it perished long ago
Has faded into nothingness in our memory.

I cry to You for the inspired speech which silences
The brilliant words of eloquent and learned orators.

I cry to You for signs that have been gathered up by intellects;
Nothing now remains of them in books except debris.

I cry to You, I swear it by Your love, for the Virtues
Of those whose only mount for reaching You was silence.

All have crossed the desert, leaving neither well nor trace behind;
Vanished like the ʿÂd tribe and their lost city of Iram.

And after them stumbles an abandoned crowd, looking for their trails,
Blinder even than she-camels, blinder than the dumbest of beasts.

III

Qaṣîda X

Murder me now, my faithful friends,
For in my murder is my Life.

My death would be to go on living
And my Life would be to die.

To me removal of my self
Would be the noblest gift to give

And my survival in my flesh
The ugliest offence, because

My life has tired out my soul
Among its fading artifacts.

So kill me, set aflame
My dried out bones

And when you pass by my remains
In their deserted grave,

You will perceive the secret of my Friend
In the inmost folds of what survives.

One moment I'm a sheikh
Who holds the highest rank,

And then I am a little child
Dependent on a nurse

Or sleeping in a box
Within the brackish earth.

My mother gave her father birth,[2]
Which was a marvel I perceived,

And my own daughters whom I made
Became my sisters in this way to me,

Not in the world of time
Nor through adulteries.

---

[2] A reference to Fâṭimâh, the Prophet's daughter, who was nicknamed by the Ismâʿîlîs *Umm Abîhâ* "her Father's Mother". See L. Massignon, *Diwan* (1955 edition), p. 26, for a discussion of the Shiʿite meaning of this line.

So gather all the parts together
Of the glowing forms

Of air and fire,
And pure water

And sow them in unwatered soil;
Then water it from cups

Of serving maids
And flowing rivulets;

And, then, when seven days have passed,
A perfect plant will grow.

Translated by Herbert Mason

19

AL-BÂQILLÂNÎ *

"Criticism of Imruʾul-Qais' *Muʿallaqa*"

You do not doubt the excellence of Imruʾulqais' poetry, nor are you sceptical regarding its perfection, and you do not hesitate (to affirm) the purity of his language (*faṣâḥa*). You also know that he has introduced new elements into the poetical style which have been followed (ever since), beginning with the (deserted) tent-places (*diyâr*) and halting at them, to the innovations introduced by him in connection therewith. (You are likewise familiar with) the comparisons (*tashbîh*) which he brought into use, the elegance (*tamlîḥ*) to be found in his poems, the great versatility (or: variety; *taṣarruf*) you encounter in his speech, and the different categories into which (the virtues of) his diction may be divided, such as artistic finesse (*ṣinâʿa*), naturalness, easiness (of elocution), elevation, strength and softness, and (other) laudable qualities and points deserving adoption and appreciation.

You often see men of literary understanding at first weighing (the work of) one or the other poet against (Imruʾulqais') poetry and holding the poetry of newly arising poets against that of Imruʾulqais (for the purpose of comparing and judging them by his standards), so much so that they at times draw the balance between the poetical work of contemporary poets and Imruʾulqais in regard to pleasantness of detail and originality of phrase. And many times the (critics) give them preference over Imruʾulqais, or consider them equal to him, or concede to them, or to him (as the case may be) a small margin of superiority. After the critics had chosen his *qaṣîda* among the Seven (*fîʾs-sabʿiyyât*)[1] they added to it similar *qaṣîdas* and joined to it others of equal structure. You hear (the critics) challenging a poet: (compose a) *lâmiyya* like (the *muʿallaqa* of Imruʾulqais)! Then you see the souls of the poets wrestling to match (*muʿâraḍa*) or equal it in its style. Frequently they stumble in many respects as compared to him, or again excel him in some points, truly astounding. But when it comes

*Died 1013 A.D. Theologian and critic of Arabic poetry, stressing the stylistic superiority of the Koran because of its divine origin.

[1] i.e., the *Muʿallaqât*.

to counting the beauties (*maḥâsin*) of Imru'ulqais' poetry you will find them limited in number and a thing within your ken. You meet with rhetorical figures (or: original traits; *badîʿ*) just like his or even more beautiful in poetry other than his, and you perceive the same excellence in the diction of other poets. Look at the modern poets (*al-muḥdathûn*): how they go deep into (the process of) gathering beautiful traits (*maḥâsin*). Some of them unite graveness of speech (*raṣâna*) with easiness of elocution (*salâsa*), strength with sweetness, and pertinence (*iṣâba*) of the idea with brilliant elegance of expression, so that there are some amongst them who though they may fall short of (Imru'ulqais) in some respects excel him in others.

For the kind (*jins*) of (aspiration) to which they dedicate themselves, and the aim which they are pursuing are within the orbit of human possibilities and are of a type mankind can match. So everybody shoots here with one arrow and obtains one dart. And then the arrows reach different marks and (the bowmen) are unequal (in their achievements). They come near (the aim) in proportion to their familiarity with the technical devices (*ṣanâ'iʿ*) and their share in the resources of the craft. The composition of the Koran, (however), is a thing apart and a special process not to be equalled, free of rivals. If you wish to realize the grandeur (of the Koran) reflect on what we are going to say in this chapter on Imru'ulqais (with respect to) his best poem, and on what we shall explain in detail to you about his defects.[2]

Now here is what (Imru'ulqais) says:

1. "Halt ye two, let us weep in remembrance of a beloved one and of a dwelling-place at Saqṭ at-Liwà, between ad-Dakhûl and Ḥaumal,
2. and Tûḍiḥ and al-Miqrât; its traces have not been effaced by what Southwind and Northwind have woven over it."

Those who are his eager partisans or claim all the beauties of poetry (for him) say: this is an innovation (*badîʿ*) for he halts and asks to halt, sheds tears and asks to shed tears, mentions the past (*ʿahd*), the mansion and the beloved, gives vent to his pain and wishes (the past) to return, and all this in one verse; and (his partisans list) more merits of like kind.

We have explained this only lest you might think we overlook the points of beauty (in his poems) whenever they occur, and neglect

[2] As this is not the place to present a critical translation of the *muʿallaqa* of Imru'ulqais the commentary has been limited to such explanations as will—so it is hoped—enable the reader to understand fully al-Bâqillânî's line of thought. The *muʿallaqa* is perhaps the most referred to poem in all Arabic literature. [For full interpretative notes cf. the translator's work from which this excerpt is taken. I. L.]

the signs of craftsmanship (*ṣinâʿa*) whenever they are to be found. Consider—may Allâh lead you the right way—and look—may Allâh give you guidance: You know that in these two lines there is nothing whereby he has outstripped any other poet on the race-track or beaten any other artist. Both in wording and meaning there are defects (in these verses).

The first of them is that he invites him who weeps for the memory of the beloved to halt. The mention (or: thought) of her does not, however, demand that the unconcerned should weep. For the latter the striving for happiness would be the only natural thing, though he might weep because of his (friend's) weeping and feel sorry for his friend because of the narrowness of his straits. As for his weeping for his friend's beloved and his companion's mistress, that is absurd. For if it is the poet's intention to let (the companion) halt and shed tears as a lover, the wording is correct but the sense is bad from another point of view: It is the height of folly (*sakhf*) to assume that the poet should not be jealous of his beloved and should ask another man to dally with her, and to display his love jointly with himself.

Further, the recording of the places and the naming of the localities: ad-Dakhûl, Ḥaumal, Tûḍiḥ al-Miqrât and Saqṭ al-Liwà, does not serve any purpose in these two verses. It would have been sufficient to mention some of them in laying out the scene (of his grief; *taʿrîf*). This prolixity (*taṭwîl*), since it avails nothing, (shows) a certain lack of (poetical) power (*ʿayy*).

Further, his words *lam yaʿfu rasmu-hâ* (its traces have not been effaced). Al-Aṣmaʿî mentions amongst the beauties of (this poem) that (the traces) are remaining. We, however, regret his testimony. Had they been wiped out we would feel (more) at ease, (and this) because (as the text stands now) this is one of (the poem's) ugly features (*masâwî*). For if he is sincere in his love the effacing of the traces could only increase the intensity of his affection and the strength of his passion. Al-Aṣmaʿî upholds the propriety of this clause only for fear lest (Imruʾulqais) be blamed for it and the (following) questions be raised: What is the purpose of his informing us that the vestiges of the abodes of his beloved have not been effaced? And: What meaning (can be ascribed) to this padding (of the verse)? So (al-Aṣmaʿî) adduces whatever he can (in Imruʾulqais' defense) but he has not succeeded by his help in absolving him from his blunder (*khalal*). Then there is in this (group of) word(s) one more defect: for he finishes the (sequence of) verses, saying (vs. 4b): *fa-hal ʿinda rasmin dârisin min muʿawwali* (but is an effaced trace a place for excessive wailing?). So (already)

Abû ʿUbaida points out that he goes back on himself and gives himself the lie, just as does Zuhair:

"Halt at the abodes which the (bygone) times have not effaced; oh yes, but winds and rains have changed them."

Another (scholar) says: with the first verse (Imruʾulqais) intends (to say) that the traces have not been entirely obliterated, and with the second (i.e., 4b) that they have partly disappeared, so that the two terms do not contradict each other. This assumption does not help, for *ʿafâ* and *darasa* have the same meaning. Hence, when he says *lam yaʿfu rasmu-hâ,* and then *ʿafâ,* this is doubtless a contradiction. The attempted justification of Abû ʿUbaida (*iʿtidhâr*) would be nearer the mark if only it were correct. But (Imruʾulqais) does not introduce his saying (i.e., 4b) in order to rectify (*istidrâk*; his statement in 2a) as does Zuhair. So (Abû ʿUbaida) is still farther off the mark.

(For) *li-mâ nasajat-hâ* (by what have woven . . .), (Imruʾulqais) should have said *li-mâ nasaja-hâ.* He expressed himself incorrectly and chose by way of comment the feminine form, for they (i.e., the words *janûb* and *shamʾal*) are applied here in the meaning of winds (and winds are feminine). Only the metre forced him to take this improper license.

lam yaʿfu rasmu-hâ (its traces have not been effaced):—the best wording would have been *lam yaʿfu rasmu-hu*; for he mentions *al-manzil* (the abode; masc.). If (the feminine) refers to the plains (*biqâʿ*) and regions in which the abode is situated, it is still a mistake. For he wants to qualify as obliterated only the abode where his beloved had alighted, or (to describe it as) not having been effaced, as distinguished from the neighboring places. If, however, by *al-manzil* (the abode) he means *ad-dâr* (the homestead) and therefore uses the feminine (*ad-dâr* being feminine), it is again a mistake. And even if (these lines) should be free from all (the defects referred to) and from all other shortcomings which we do not care to mention because of our aversion to profusion, we still would not doubt that the poetry of our own contemporaries is by no means inferior to these verses, nay, that it even surpasses and excels them.

Imruʾulqais continues:

3. "There my companions halted their mounts beside me and said: Do not perish from grief, compose yourself.
4. And verily, my cure is a shed tear. But is an effaced trace a place for excessive wailing?"

In these two verses again there is no new motif and no beautiful expression, any more than there was in the first two verses. The first verse (of this group) is tied to his words *qifâ nabki* (halt ye two, let us weep), as though he had said *qifâ wuqûfa ṣaḥbî ʿalayya maṭiyya-hum,* or *qifâ ḥâla wuqûfi ṣaḥbî* (halt the way my companions halt). According to the sense *bihâ* (there) should follow later, but in the text (actually) occurs too early. This constitutes restraint (*takalluf*) and a departure from the harmony of speech (*iʿtidâl al-kalâm*). The second verse is faulty as he seems to consider tears a sufficient remedy (for love-pains). So why should he have to ask for another expedient, and for endurance and a wailing place at the traces? If he had wanted to render his speech really beautified he ought to have stated that in view of the intensity of his grief tears could not heal him, and then he ought to have asked whether there be another device (*ḥîla*) at the spring-encampment (to effect a change in his situation).

5. "As it was your wont with Umm al-Ḥuwairith before her, and with her neighbor, Umm ar-Rabâb, at Maʾsal.
6. When the two rose (the scent of) musk spread from them like the breeze (*nasîm*) of the Eastwind bringing the sweet flavor of the cloves (*qaranful*)."

You cannot fail to realize that the first verse contributes little and, besides, (that its wording) has no splendor. For it often happens that a saying is well worded, but not sustained by any worthwhile meaning. As for the second verse, the words *idhâ qâmatâ taḍawwaʿ aʾl-misku* (when the two rose, musk spread from them) show constraint. If he had wished to express great praise, it would have been best to ascribe to them sweet odor under any circumstances, but when (they are said to be fragrant only while) getting up, this is a restriction (of praise; *taqṣîr*). Then there is another mistake in it: for after comparing her (natural) perfume to musk (Imruʾulqais) likens it to the scent (lit.: breeze, *nasîm*) of cloves, and mentioning this after the musk constitutes an anti-climax (*naqṣ*). His words *nasîm aṣ-ṣabâ* (breeze of the Eastwind), (added) for (further) determination (*taqdîr*), cut off from the first hemistich, have not been connected with (that first half-verse) in the way they should have been.

7. "For tender passion the tears of my eye streamed down copiously on my breast until they moistened my sword-belt.
8. Oh many a perfect (*ṣâliḥ*) day was granted to you by them, and especially a day at Dâra Juljul."

He says: *fa-fâḍat dumûʿu ʾl-ʿaini* (so the tears of the eye streamed down copiously), then he supplements the phrase by adding *minnî* (of me), a poor supplement (even) if employed by poets of lesser skill. This word (i.e., *minnî*) is a padding, neither pleasant nor original. *ʿalà ʾn-naḥri* (on my breast) is another padding, for *balla damʿiya miḥmalî* (my tears moistened my sword-belt) is quite clear and sufficient, nor is *ʿalà ʾn-naḥri* a beautiful padding. Then *ḥattà balla damʿiya miḥmalî* (until my tears moistened my sword belt), another reference to the tears, is a third padding. It would have been enough to say *ḥattà ballat miḥmalî* (until they moistened my sword-belt); the rest of the verse he added only for the establishment of the metre. Further his implication that he exceeded all bounds (of despair) by "shedding tears until his sword-belt was moistened," is an exaggeration and at the same time an (unwarranted) diminution. Had he introduced an innovation (*abdaʿa*), he would have said: until my tears had moistened their abodes and courts. It looks as though his aim had just been to establish metre and rhyme, since the tears are far from moistening the sword-belt and only trickle to the ground or to the seam of his dress when a man is standing or sitting. And if they moistened (the sword-belt), (they did) so because (the tears) were so few and because they did not stream (to the ground). You will find in al-Khubzuruzzî's poems (some ideas) more beautiful than this verse, stronger (*amtan*), and more startling (*aʿjab*).

The second verse is lacking in beautiful and original features and is devoid of any idea. There is no pleasing (*yarûqu*) word in it nor any idea beyond the natural abilities of the common crowd. And his attempt to overawe you by mentioning an out-of-the-way place (certainly) will not impress (lit.: scare) you.

9. "And the day when I hamstrung (and killed) my riding-camel for the maidens; and what a pack-saddle had to be carried (after the mount had been killed)!
10. And the maidens threw each other its flesh and fat like the fringes of twisted raw-silk."

(The poet) either means to say: remember the day when I hamstrung my mount, or he supplements his saying: on the day of Dâra Juljul. The first half of this verse (vs. 9) contains nothing but silliness. Some of the literary experts (*udabâʾ*) say: his words *yâ ʿajaban* (oh wonder!) are meant to divert (the critics) by an exclamation from his silly juvenile attitude when he slaughters his camel for (the girls). He does not want to have the second hemistich cut off from the first, but wishes to have it harmoniously connected with it (*mulâʾim*). What he says, however, is far-fetched and it (still remains) cut off from the first (hemistich). According to the literal meaning (*ẓâhir*) of his saying he professes amazement at the maidens carrying his saddle, but there is no essential reason for amazement in this any more than in his slaughtering his camel for them. And (even) if he should have meant to say that they carried his saddle and that some of the (girls) carried him, so that he would have referred to his person by (referring to his) saddle, there would still have been little cause for surprise in it. The text, however, evinces no evidence for this assumption. It rather leads away from it. Even if the verse should be free of defects, there would be nothing unusual (*gharîb*) in it and no new idea (*badî*ʿ), outweighing its silliness, its poverty of meaning, the platitude (*taqârub*) of the (whole) scene and its similarity to the character of the epigones amongst our own contemporaries. So up to there (Imruʾulqais) has not composed one impressive verse, nor one superior phrase.

The second verse (vs. 10) is generally considered beautiful and the comparison held pretty (*malîḥ*) and pertinent (*wâqi*ʿ). There is, however, a flaw in it, viz. that though (in his comparison) Imruʾulqais takes into account the meat, he disregards the fat, so that one does not recognize that he wishes to describe the fatness (of the slaughtered camel). He compares one of the elements to an appropriate object, but is unable to provide (such an object) for the comparison of the first part which, therefore, remains unintegrated (in the comparison; *mursal*). This is lack of craftsmanship and inability to satisfy the requirements of proper diction (*kalâm*).

This verse is open to another objection from the point of view of the contents: (Imruʾulqais) describes the food with which he feeds his guests as excellent, and this at times meets objection. Some people say: the Arabs boast of the food they serve and do not find any fault in this; only the Persians consider it an ugly and blameworthy way of behaving. The comparison of the fat to the raw-silk (*dimaqs*) is a motif which might arise in the mind and on the tongue of the vulgar. Thus he was not the first to use this comparison. He adds *al-mufattal* (the twisted) for the rhyme's sake only,but this expression really adds to the meaning. Nonetheless, I am not aware that the vulgar use *ad-dimaqs al-mufattal* in their speech, and the literary experts (*ahl aṣ-ṣanʿa*) do not count this phrase as rhetorically commendable (or: original; *badî*ʿ), but rather consider it a platitude (*qarîb*). And there is one more objection to (the line): his joy at entertaining his girl-friends is in bad taste and so is his exultation over what he serves to his guests, unless it be that he has composed the passage in the style of the libertins (*mujûn*), like Abû Nuwâs, in gaiety and facetiousness.

11. "And the day when I entered the litter (or perhaps: And on that day I entered . . .), the litter of ʿUnaiza. Then she said: Woe to you: you are forcing me to walk!
12. She said, while the saddle inclined to the side with us: you are ruining my mount! oh Imruʾulqais. So alight!"

dakhaltu ʾl-khidra khidra ʿUnaizata (I entered the litter, the litter of

ʿUnaiza). The repetition is employed for the sake of the metre only, there is no other reason for it, nor is any elegance (*malâḥa*) or splendor (*raunaq*) (accruing to the passage on account of it). *fa-qâlat laka'l-waylâtu inna-ka murjilî* (woe to you, you are forcing me to walk) is a feminine manner of speech which he adopts into his poetry for the very reason (of its being feminine). Outside of this there is no (merit) in it. The repetition of *taqûlu wa-qad mâla 'l-ghabîṭu* (she says while the *ghabîṭ*—the saddle on which the litter rests—inclined to the side with us) after *fa-qâlat . . . murjilî* has no point except for the completion of the metre (*taqdîr al-wazn*), otherwise the first indication that she is speaking would be sufficient. (Moreover), it makes for bad composition, since once he says *fa-qâlat* (in the perfect tense) and then *taqûlu* (in the aorist), both in (practically) the same sense and with an exceedingly slight difference of meaning (*faṣl khafîf*). In the second hemistich again there is a touch of feminine speech. Abû ʿUbaida records that (Imru'ulqais) says: *ʿaqarta baʿîri* (you are ruining my male camel) instead of *nâqatî* (my female camel), because women (used to be) carried on male camels which are stronger. This admits of some doubt. For evidently *baʿîr* is a common name for male and female (camels), and (Imru'ulqais) had to use (the word) *baʿîr* in order to establish the metre.

13. "And I said to her: just go on and loosen his bridle, and do not push me away from your thirst-quenching fruit.
14. And to many a pregnant one like you I came at night-time, and to many a one who suckled, whom I distracted from her amulet-bedecked one-year-old (baby)."

The first verse (vs. 13) is cheap, containing no original idea, nor any elevated (*sharîf*) expression, as though it were a composition produced by one of low craftsmanship. His words *fa-mithli-ki ḥublà qad ṭaraqtu* (and to many a pregnant one like you I came at night-time) meet with reproach on the part of all authorities on the Arabic language. According to them the text will have to be set right as follows: *fa-rubba mithli-ki ḥublà qad ṭaraqtu,* the implication being that he is a frequent visitor of women whom he depraves and diverts from their pregnancy and from nourishing (their children), for pregnant women and such as nurse their children are least addicted to love and the desire for men.

The second verse (vs. 14) deals with *iʿtidhâr* (apology), with yielding to passion and with love-madness, and is entirely unrelated to the idea contained in the first vs. (vs. 13). For it says as much as: do not push me away from you, for I am conquering women, driving them with deceit out of their wits and depraving them by love-making. (And this he argues) while, as a matter of fact, his habit of depraving women does not necessarily entail their attachment to him nor the abandonment of their aloofness from him, but should, on the very contrary, entail their separation from, and their disregard for him, because of his levity, his foul habits and his wicked doings. He shows so much obscenity and foulness that the decent (*karîm*) would loathe (men) like him and abstain from (as much as) mentioning his (name).

The same applies to:

15. "Whenever (the child) cried behind her she turned a part (of her body) to him, but the part underneath me was not turned away.
16. But one day, on the grade of the sand-hill, she withdrew from me with an oath not open to subterfuge."

The first verse (vs. 15) represents extreme obscenity and levity. What is the point in telling his mistress how he perpetrated these foul deeds and behaved in this (outrageous) way and acted in this (abominable) manner? Truly, this must render him an object of hate in the eyes of whoever hears his words and must needs provoke aversion. If he has spoken the truth, he would be wicked, and how may we assume that he is a liar? Further, the verse contains neither an original expression nor a beautiful idea. The verse is connected with the preceding one that speaks about the nursing woman who has a one-year-old baby.

The second verse (beginning with) *wa-yauman* (and one day) is odd. She only pretends aversion and harshness to him and binds herself by oath against him. This is a badly composed passage. There is no point in telling us that his beloved feigned to balk against him on a (particular) day and at a (particular) place which he names and describes. You can find in the works of the modern poets (specimens) of this sort of love-song which melt the mind and move the heart. But the soul abhors this (kind of poetry that Imruʾulqais represents) and the heart is disgusted by it. There is nothing in it to evoke approval or to be considered beautiful.

17. "Oh Fâṭima, gently! restrain your coquetry! If you really have decided on separation from me, act fairly (at least; *fa-ajmilî*)!
18. It has deceived you about me that my love of you was murdering me, and that whatever you would command my heart it would do."

The first verse (vs. 17) exhibits a great amount of poor judgment (*rakâka*), and a feminine touch and delicacy, yea, (even) effeminacy. One might perhaps insist that the language of women on (a subject) so congenial to them is appropriate and constitutes superior love poetry. But this is not so. For you find that poets in verses dealing with the affairs of women do not renounce their sedateness (*raṣâna*) in their diction. The second half-verse is unrelated to the first and does not accord with it. This will become clear to you when you confront it with the next preceding verse. How can he disapprove of her coquetry when (according to poetical convention) the wooing lover (or: the composer of love-poems: *mutaghazzil*) rejoices at the coquetry of his beloved and her playfulness?

(Imru'ulqais) was criticized for the second verse (vs. 18) on the (following ground): he informs us that the proper thing for her would be not to let herself be deceived by his display of love which is murdering him, nor by his protestations that she rules his heart and that he would do whatever she might demand. (For) if the lover makes such a statement (in a poem, he is supposed to) speak the truth. If, on the other hand, his intention differs from the one for which he has been criticized and he has something else in mind, namely a display of hardiness, this would contradict his exhibition of love and of tears for the beloved friends (as expressed) in the preceding verses, and would in another way lead him into contradiction and inconsistency. (Further criticism attaches to) the phrase *ta'murî ʿl-qualba yafʿali* (whatever you command the heart it will do), (where) the meaning is: you command me; whereas (in reality) the heart cannot be commanded. This metaphor is therefore neither appropriate (*wâqiʿ*) nor beautiful.

19. "If you are displeased with my character, disentangle your clothes from mine and be gone.
20. And your eyes never weep without wounding (lit.: but to wound) the prize parts of my murdered heart with your two darts (your eyes)."

In the interpretation of the first verse (vs. 19) it has been argued: he mentions the garment, but means the body, just as Allâh has said: "Thy raiment—purify it!"[3] Abû ʿUbaida says: This (verse) is an example of foul language (*hujr*). *tansulî* means "clear out." The whole verse has little meaning, its inanity being the cause of its lowness. Everything he says about himself makes him contemptible, silly, and indecent, and had better be omitted. If (Imru'ulqais) had not thus passed judgment against himself, but had shown in some way that his character was not such as to demand separation from him and severance of all ties with him, and that (on the contrary) he had the qualities of good breeding and a noble disposition, everybody would have felt obliged to maintain friendly relations with him. The metaphor in the second hemistich (is tainted) with lowness and (represents) a platitude (*tawâḍaʿa wataqâraba*), though it may be unprecedented (*gharîb*).

The second verse (vs. 20) is considered one of the beautiful and

[3] Korân 74; 4.

original features of the *qaṣîda*. The meaning is: you are shedding tears only to wound a heart which is already broken into little pieces (*muʿashshar*), i.e., *mukassar*, as one says *burma* (stone-pot) *aʿshâr*, when it is broken into pieces. This is the interpretation recorded by al-Aṣmaʿi and most (scholars) accept it as the most likely. Others, however, say: The phrase alludes to the parts (*aʿshâr*) into which the slaughtered camel is divided. By *bi-sahmai-ki* (with your two arrows) he refers to *al-muʿallà* (the best arrow in the game), which commands seven lots, and the *raqîb*, commanding three lots.[4] So he wants to convey (the following idea): you have taken my heart in its entirety. By *muqattal* (murdered) he means *mudhallal* (humiliated).

You will realize that whatever he may mean to say does not accord with the preceding verses because of the contradiction which we have indicated. It seems that whoever adopts the second interpretation does so for fear (that the poet might be criticized), for he considers the words of Imruʾulqais objectionable in their first interpretation. For if somebody should say: "he beats (*ḍaraba*) the mark with his arrow," meaning: "he hits (*aṣâba*) the mark," he would use faulty and corrupt language. He interprets the above expression as "her eyes when hitting his wounded heart are like two piercing arrows, and when they weep and shed tears they strike his heart." He who adopts the second interpretation is avoiding a wrong construction suggested by the wording, but renders the meaning itself corrupt and faulty. For if (the poet) yearns (for her) in accord with the passion he ascribes to himself, his whole heart already is hers: so why must it be her tears that have to conquer his heart for her?

Understand after all this (discussion) that this verse has no connection with the first verse (vs. 19) and that its contents are not related to it, but that it is cut off from it, because nothing that precedes necessitates her weeping, nor shows any reason for it. So when he introduces this sentence (*kalâm*) after what preceded it, he leaves a gap in his presentation. Now, even if one verse in twenty should have proved free of blame and beyond reproach and original (*badîʿ*), it would not have been an astounding achievement. For nobody claims vis-à-vis his ilk that all they say is contradictory and all they compose disharmonious (*mutabâyin*). It is quite sufficient to have demonstrated that all preceding verses up to this line cannot be declared superior to any composed by the later poets, leave alone by the earlier poets. As a

[4] The reference is to the *maisir* game: on this game see Carra de Vaux, *E.I.*, III, 155–56, and the literature there noted.

matter of fact, he did create some verses in which he excels and exhibits his skill. We only deny that his poetry is homogeneously excellent and on the same level throughout in regard to soundness of meaning and phrasing. We maintain that he moves between (*yataṣarrafu baina*) the uncouth (*waḥshî*) and the unusual (*gharîb*), an objectionable Arabic style, altogether loathsome like pus, and again a sound and well-balanced (*mutawassiṭ*; style), between the popular and the vulgar in wording and meaning, beautiful wisdom and repellent inanity. On this subject Allâh said: "If it were from any other than Allâh, they would find in it (the Koran) many a contradiction."[3]

21. "And with many a noble and secluded virgin (*baiḍat khidr*) (access to) whose chamber (*khibâʾ*) nobody (dares to) covet, I have enjoyed pleasure leisurely.
22. On my way to her I passed guards and kin, bent on divulging the time of my death."

It is (generally) maintained that he wishes to compare her to the "egg of a tent" in her purity and delicacy. This is a nice expression, though he is not the first to use it; it is rather frequent amongst the Arabs and a common comparison. By *ghair muʿjal* (not hurried) he intimates this does not happen on rare occasions and only from time to time but that he enjoys such favors again and again. Others hold that he perseveres in his determination so that fear of her inaccessibility and inapproachability does not induce him to hurry when he comes close to her. This verse is of no great value, for it only repeats what has been stated in the other verses and does not develop his love-theme and his absorption by her. Thus a repetition such as that contained in this verse is of small import, except that it adds the statement of her inaccessibility. Nonetheless, the first half of the verse is sound in its wording, but not so the second.

The second verse (vs. 22) is weak. His words *lau yusirrûna maqtalî* (if they could divulge the time of my death) stand for *lau asarrû*. And the change (from the past tense to the aorist) is weak and resembles a fall from the steed in the hippodrome of metrical necessity, and the fault of this construction is so evident that a careful (poet) would have been on his guard against (a mistake like this).

23. "When the Pleiades appeared (*taʿarraḍat*) in the sky like the (sparkling) parts of the sash, studded with gems."

Some find fault with his phrase "when the Pleiades passed along in the sky obliquely," asserting that the Pleiades do not pass along in

---

[3] Koran 4.84.

the sky obliquely (*taʿarraḍa*). Some even go so far as to say: he names the Pleiades but means the Gemini (*al-Jauzâʾ*), since these do pass along in the sky obliquely (or: indirectly). The Arabs sometimes (use substitute designations). So (e.g.) Zuhair says: *ka-Aḥmar ʿÂd* (like Aḥmar of ʿÂd) when he means: *Aḥmar Thamûd* (Aḥmar of Thamûd). Some, however, in order to justify (the term) *taʿarruḍ*, say: It designates something (the broadside of which) appears first, just like a girdle when encircling (your waist) touches you with its broadside (*ʿurḍ*), that is, with its lateral part (*nâḥiya*). (This usage compares to what) the poet says:

> "They showed to me their sides with worn-out shields just as the filly on the tether shows its flank."

(The poet) says: (The filly) shows you its flank while it is tied by the rope. Says Abû ʿAmr (b. al-ʿAlâʾ): (Imruʾulqais) means to say: When the Pleiades take their place in the center of the sky as the belt takes its place in the middle part of a woman. We, however, feel that the verse is irreproachable from the points of view from which they criticize it and that it constitutes one of the beauties of this *qaṣîda*. And were it not for a number of (such irreproachable) verses, anybody's poetry could match his. Yet he does not offer anything (in the verse) passing the limit and reaching the height (of mastery).

You know that neither the earlier nor the later poets have accorded such adequate treatment to any star as they have to the Pleiades. Every one of them has produced something new and beautiful, or matched or added to (the traditional treatment of the motive). Thus, e.g., the verse of Dhû ʾr-Rumma:

> "I descended to the water-place riding at random while the Pleiades over my head looked like a high-circling crane."

Likewise the verse of Ibn al-Muʿtazz:

> "And you see the Pleiades in the sky (bright) as though they were eggs of an ostrich's hatching-place shining in the desert-ground."

And his verse:

> "The Pleiades in the latter part of the night resemble the opening of a blossom or a silverstudded bridle."

Further his verse:

> "He handed me (the wine) while the Pleiades shone as though they were freshly plucked narcissi with which the cupbearer greets the boon-companions."

Likewise the verse of al-Ashhab b. Rumaila (an-Nahshalî):

> "To him who nightly travelled through (the desert) the Pleiades

shone as though they were ear-rings chained (*musalsal*) near the Western brim of the horizon."

Ibn al-Muʿtazz (further) said:

"The Pleiades (*an-najm*) drop and the gemini follow them like a woman who reaches out for her ear-rings which have fallen to the ground."

He has taken over this (idea) from Ibn ar-Rûmî who says:

"His saliva is sweet when you taste his mouth while the Pleiades in the Western sky are ear-rings."

Ibn al-Muʿtazz says:

"He gave me wine to drink when the morning was still wrapped in the night
and when the Pleiades like the blossoms of a twig scattered (their sparkling) over the earth."

And he also says:

"The Pleiades are eager to set
Just as a fiery horse bends down its head when on the point of getting into harness (bridle: *lijâm*)."

Ibn aṭ-Ṭathriyya says:

"When the Pleiades were in the sky as though they were pearls scattered from their (broken) string."

If I had compiled for you all the original phrases (*badîʿ*) the (poets) have employed in the description of the Pleiades this book would have become too long and have exceeded its purpose. We only wish to make you realize that originality (*ibdâʿ*) in this field is easy (*qarîb*) and by no means unusual (*gharîb*). With reference to our quotations (Imruʾulqais) adds nothing to the beauty of the comparisons (in use for the Pleiades). He either approaches or matches them. So you understand that what has been ascribed and attributed to him by his adherents, to wit, that he alone has attained mastery (in the application of an apt comparison to the Pleiades), is (in reality) an achievement in which he has many associates, a trodden road, a travelled path, and a wide-open door. And if this is the most perfect verse of the *qaṣîda,* the (main) pearl of the necklace, the central gem of the jewel-string, and it ranks no higher (than stated above), then what about (the verses) you disapprove of? Besides there is a sort of constraint (in the verse). For (Imruʾulqais) says: "when the Pleiades presented their broadside in the center of) the sky as the parts of the belt present themselves." The words *taʿarraḍat fîʾs-samâʾ* (presented their broadside in [the center of] the sky) could be dispensed with, since he compares (the Pleiades) to the parts of the girdle regardless of whether they stand in the center of the sky or at the points where they rise or set. So the pompous array of using *at-taʿarruḍ*, etc., and the amplification of the phrase are pointless. He wishes to say that the Pleiades are like one piece of the gem-studded girdle. So his phrase *taʿarruḍa athnâʾiʾl-wishâḥi* (as the parts of the girdle present themselves) is meaningless. He meant to say: *taʿarruḍa qiṭʿatin min athnâʾiʾl-wishâḥi* (as one of the parts of the girdle presents itself) but the proper words did not occur to him to that he compares to a plural what can only be compared to a singular form.

24. "When I arrived she had already put aside her clothes near the curtain to sleep, except for the undergarment.
25. And she said: By the oath of Allâh! There is no escape from you. Methinks your wickedness (or: folly) will never cease."

Look at the first (of these two) verses and those preceding it—how confused and ill cared for is his composition! He has already mentioned his enjoyment of her favors, the time the circumstances and the guardians, and only now does he begin to describe her appearance when he entered and joined her, how she had put aside her clothes with the exception of her undergarment. *al-mutafaḍḍil* is one who is dressed in a single garment, and *al-mutafaḍḍil* is the same as *al-fuḍul*. What he ought to have said at the beginning he only mentions at the end. His words *ladà ʾs-sitr* (near the curtain) are a padding; they are neither beautiful nor original (*badîʿ*). The whole verse does not contain any beauty nor excellence.

The second verse is both related and unrelated (to what precedes it; *fîhi taʿlîq waʾkhtilâl*). Al-Aṣmaʿî notes that *mâ laka ḥîlatun* means: you cannot come to me while people are around. The idea in the second hemistich is totally unrelated to the first, and joining the two half-verses causes a certain incongruity (*ḍarb min at-tafâwut*).

26. "And I arose with her and walked forth while she dragged the trains of a cloak adorned with figures (to efface) our traces behind us.
27. And when we had passed the quarters of the tribe and the depression of Khabt (or: of a grove) with its sandy hillocks took us sideways."

The first verse describes her assistance to him, until she arises with him in order to be alone with him. She drags over their traces the trains of her embroidered cloak.—*al-murjal* is a sort of garment the embroidery (*washy*) of which is called *tarjîl*—There is constraint (*takalluf*) in this phrase, for he says: behind us over our trace. It would have been sufficient to say: over our trace. After all, the train drags only behind the walker, so there is no point in adding: behind us. (Besides,) he really means to say (*taqdîr*): *fa-qumtu amshî bihâ* (so I arose to walk forth with her; instead of: *fa-qumtu bihâ amshî*, so I arose with her and walked forth). This again is a sort of constraint (or: forced construction). Then he should have said: *dhail mirṭ* (train of a cloak) instead of *adhyâl mirṭ* (trains of a cloak). But even if the verse would have been free from all these (defects) it would have been commonplace (*qarîb*). With a verse like this you cannot surpass nor outdo any other verse. The saying of Ibn al-Muʿtazz is much more beautiful:

"All night long I spread my cheek (as a carpet) under his feet in humility and I dragged my trains (*adhyâlî*) over (his trace."

In the second verse (vs. 27) *ajaznâ* (is used) in the sense of *qaṭaʿnâ* (we crossed, passed); *khabt* is a depressed tract of land; *ḥiqf* is a sloping sand ridge; *ʿaqanqal* is compact sand the strata of which are interlocked.

This verse contrasts with the preceding verses. For what is easy in it to pronounce (*salis*) is very common (*qarîb*), resembling the manner of speech of people born of a foreign mother or employed in lowly, ordinary life (*bidhla*). And right in the midst of this diction he uses unusual words and introduces uncouth and complicated expressions. There is nothing gained by mentioning them nor by choosing to insert them in his speech. We praise an unusual and forceful phrase contrasting with the general style (*nasj*) if it occurs where it is needed to describe what is commensurate with it, like (e.g.) His word used in the description of the Day of Resurrection: *yauman ʿabûsan qamṭarîran* (a day grim and calamitous).[6] But if it occurs in another place it is objectionable and blameworthy in inverse proportion to the praise it deserves when used in its proper place. It is said that Jarîr recited before one of the Umayyad caliphs his *qaṣîda* (beginning):

"The companion tribe (*khalîṭ*) parted at Râmatân and bade farewell. Will you always feel afflicted when they make ready to part?

How can I find consolation as, since your departure, I have not found a soothing heart nor a drink to quench my thirst."

(The caliph) was carried away by the beauty of this poem until (Jarîr) reached the verse:

"And Bauzaʿ says: you are crawling along (leaning) on your staff (because of old age). Why didst thou not scoff at people other than me, Oh Bauzaʿ?"

[6] Koran 76.10.

Then (the caliph) said: You have marred your poem using this name.[7]

28. "I drew to me the two branches of the *dauḥa*-tree and she swayed to me, of slender waist, plump above the ankles (lit.: in the place of the leg-rings),
29. of slim figure, white, not too plump, her breasts smooth (or: radiant; lit.: polished) like a mirror."

The meaning of *haṣartu* is: I drew near and bent down. *bi-ghuṣnay dauḥa* (the two branches of the *dauḥa*-tree) is an uncommendable expression. It is not proper to speak of two (branches). The second hemistich (of vs. 28) is sounder. It contains, however, nothing by way of description which is not on everybody's tongue. You can find it in the descriptive passages of every poet. But despite its triteness it is correct (*ṣâliḥ*). The meaning of *muhafhafa* is: light, not heavy; *al-mufâḍa* is a woman who has become flabby in frame. If you consider the contrast of this verse to the preceding verses, (Imru'ulqais') weakness for objectionable words, and the mistake of singling out her breasts as radiant after having already stated that she is white all over her body, the verse is (to be judged as) of no value, but rather commonplace (*qarîb*) and mediocre (*mutawassiṭ*).

30. "She turns and shows an oval (cheek), and she protects herself with the eye of a deer of Wajra, mother of a young;
31. (and she shows) a neck like that of an antelope (*ri'm*), not too long when she stretches it, nor unadorned."

The meaning of *'an asîl* is *bi-asîl*. He means a cheek that is not ugly (*kazz*). *tattaqî* (she protects herself): one says; *ittaqâ-hu bi-tursi-hi*, i.e., he puts his shield between himself and (his opponent). His expression *taṣuddu wa-tubdî 'an asîlin* (she turns away and shows an oval cheek) is misplaced since you disclose your face when turning towards (a person) not when turning away (from a person). *tattaqî bi-nâẓiratin* (she protects herself with an eye) is an elegant (*malîḥ*) expression, but (unfortunately) he has joined it to the rest of the composition which is faulty, namely the words *min waḥshi Wajrata* (of the deer of Wajra). The passage ought to be quite different. He should have proceeded to mention "the eyes of gazelles or of (wild) kine" without using the general term *waḥsh* (deer), because amongst (the *waḥsh*) are animals whose eyes are not pleasing. *mutfil* (having a young one) is explained

---

[7] *Aghâni*, V, 169–70, Ḥammâd ar-Râwiya relates how he is beaten at the order of Ja'far b. Manṣûr when he recites this poem. The prince tells him Bauza' is the name of a *ghûla* rather than a human woman and the ugly name will cause him a sleepless night.

as designating (an animal) that is not quite young but rather fully developed. This, (however), is a forced excuse (for the poet's use of the word). On the basis of this explanation, which is mentioned by al-Aṣmaʿî, *muṭfil* is a useless addition. But in my opinion it may serve another purpose, viz. to intimate that when (the deer) has a kid she looks on her young with the eyes of tenderness, and this look (for the poet) represents the tenderness of the loving eye. The entire passage constitutes an appendage of mediocre value.

In the second verse (vs. 31) *laisa bi-fâḥishin* means: it (the neck) is not of excessive length. And *naṣṣat-hu* means: she lifted (the neck). To say *laisa bi-fâḥishin* in praise of the neck is abominable (*fâḥish*), and his own invention. If you examine Arab poetry you meet with descriptions of the neck (as charming) as sorcery. How did this particular word (viz. *fâḥish*) occur to him and how did he come to use it? Why did he not say as Abû Nuwâs did:

> "Like gazelles ascending (fresh) meadows, climbing up from a pond"?

I do not mean to prolong (this discussion) lest you might find it annoying nor do I plan to employ many more words of blame lest you might feel bewildered. So I hasten to sum up what I have said. If you are an expert you have by now penetrated (into the subject) and are satisfied (with my argument) and understand why we reproach (Imru'ulqais) and you require no further (explanations). In case, however, you do not belong to this class and are lacking in thorough knowledge of this field, no explanation would be sufficient for you even if we had all his poems read (to you), should pursue all his phrases, and point out in every single letter (what is wrong).

Understand that this *qaṣîda* represents a mixture of styles: (comprising) vulgar and common, mediocre, weak and worthless, uncouth, obscure and objectionable verses, and a restricted number of original ones. We have pointed out the common style in them and you will not be in doubt regarding the uncouth and detestable elements which frighten the ear, terrify the heart, and are a strain on the tongue. Their meaning brings a frown to every noble man's face, their appearance looks gloomy to every enquirer or onlooker. Such poetry cannot be commended nor considered elegant, since it is far removed from what it intends to convey (*ifhâm*) and contrary to the mutual understanding (*tafâhum*) which forms the purpose of speech. Thus, naturally, (this kind of poetry) cannot attain its aim and reaches into (the sphere of) vague and enigmatic allusions.

Translated by G. E. von Grunebaum

20

AL-ḤARÎRÎ *

Maqâmah

I ride and I ride through the waste far and wide, and I fling away pride
to be gay as the swallow;
Stem the torrent's fierce speed, tame the mettlesome steed, that wherever I lead Youth and Pleasure may follow.
I bid gravity pack, and I strip bare my back lest liquor I lack when the
goblet is lifted:
Did I never incline to the quaffing of wine, I had ne'er been with fine
wit and eloquence gifted.
Is it wonderful, pray, that an old man should stay in a well stored seray
by a cask overflowing?
Wine strengthens the knees, physics every disease, and from sorrow it
frees, the oblivion-bestowing!
Oh, the purest of joys is to live sans disguise unconstrained by the ties of
a grave reputation,
And the sweetest of love that the lover can prove is when fear and hope
move him to utter his passion.
Thy love then proclaim, quench the smouldering flame, for 'twill spark
out thy shame and betray thee to laughter:
Heal the wounds of thine heart and assuage thou the smart by the cups
that impart a delight men seek after;
While to hand thee the bowl damsels wait who cajole and enravish the
soul with eyes tenderly glancing,
And singers whose throats pour such high-mounting notes, when the
melody floats, iron rocks would be dancing!
Obey not the fool who forbids thee to pull beauty's rose when in
full bloom thou'rt free to posses it;
Pursue thine end still, tho' it seem past thy skill: let them say what they
will, take thy pleasure and bless it!
Get thee gone from thy sire, if he thwart thy desire; spread thy nets nor
enquire what the nets are receiving;

*Died 1122 A.D. (See p. 112.)

But be true to a friend, shun the miser and spend, ways of charity wend,
be unwearied in giving.
He that knocks enters straight at the Merciful's gate, so repent or e'er
Fate call thee forth from the living!'

Translated by R. A. Nicholson

21

IBN AL-JAWZÎ *

"The Devil's Delusion"

Most of the philosophers take the view that God Almighty knows Himself, but nothing else; it is admitted that the creature knows both himself and his Creator; hence the rank of the creature must be superior to the Creator's.

This in my opinion is too clearly horrible to be worthy of discussion; only look at the traps set by the Devil for these fools for all their profession of consummate intelligence. Avicenna differs from them on this point, holding that God knows Himself, and knows Universals, but not particulars. This doctrine was learned from them by the Muʿtazilîs, who seem to have thought knowledge of both too much. Praise be to God who has made us of those who reject from Him ignorance and deficiency, and believe in His word *Knoweth He not whom He hath created* (Sûrah lxvii. 14) and *He knoweth what is on land and sea, and there falleth not a leaf but He knoweth it* (Sûrah vi. 59). And they took the view that God's knowledge and power are His substance, in order to avoid making two eternals. The reply to them is to say that He is one eternal possessing attributes.

Further the philosophers reject the resurrection of the bodies and the return of the spirits into the bodies, and the existence of material Heaven and Hell. They assert that these are figures used for the sake of the common people who reject spiritual reward and punishment. They hold that the soul endures after death eternally either in indescribable pleasure—such being perfect souls—or indescribable pain—such being polluted souls. The degrees of suffering vary with different people and the pain will be removed from some and cease. To them it may be said: We do not deny the existence of the soul after death, and its return is in consequence called restoration: nor that it is to have felicity or damnation; only what prevents the resurrection of the bodies? And why should we reject bodily pleasures and pains in Paradise and Hell, when the Code affirms them? We believe in a combination of

*Died 1200 A.D. Famous and prolific author in all branches of Arabic literature.

the two felicities and damnations, the spiritual and the bodily. Your treating realities as figures is arbitrary, having no evidence. If they say: Bodies are dissolved, devoured, and changed: we answer: Nothing can stand before Might. Further, man is man and, supposing a body were to be made for him from mould other than that whereof he was made, he would not cease to be himself, as indeed his parts change from youth to age and to emaciation and obesity. If they say: The body is not a body until it ascends from one state to another till it becomes flesh and veins: we reply that the might of God is not restricted to what we understand and witness. Further we have been told by our Prophet that the bodies will grow in the graves before resurrection. There is a tradition, traced to Abû Hurairah, that the Prophet said: Between the two blasts there are but forty. They said: O Abû Hurairah, forty days?—He said: I decline to answer.—Forty months?—He said; I decline.—Forty years?—He said: I decline. Then God will send down water from the heaven and they will grow like vegetables. He added: There is no part of a man but will decay except one bone, the *os sacrum;* from that he was created, and thence will mankind be recomposed on the Day of Resurrection.—The Tradition is to be found in the two *Ṣaḥîḥ*.

Now the Devil has deluded some of our coreligionists and got at them through the door of their sagacity and intelligence, showing them that it is right to follow the philosophers, owing to their being sages, from whom there have proceeded deeds and words which indicate their extreme sagacity and perfection of intellect, as is recorded of the wisdom of Socrates, Hippocrates, Plato, Aristotle, and Galen. These persons certainly possessed attainments in mechanics, logic, and natural science, and by their sagacity they discovered hidden things. Only when they talked of theology they mixed things up, and so differed on this subject, whereas they did not differ about things of the senses and mechanics. We have recorded the confusion of their tenets, and the cause of this confusion is that human abilities do not apprehend the sciences save generally, and recourse must be had therein to the Codes.

Now these people of latter days in our community were told that those sages denied the Creator and rejected the codes, believing them to be cunningly devised expedients; the former accepted what was told them of the latter, repudiated the badge of religion, neglected prayer, handled forbidden things, despised the precepts of the code, and threw off the bonds of Islam. The Jews and Christians are more excusable than they, because the former do hold to codes proved by miracles. The religious innovators are also more excusable, because they profess to study the evidences. Whereas these have no support for their unbelief except their knowledge that the philosophers were sages. Do you suppose they do not know that the Prophets were sages and something more?

What has been told these philosophers about the denial of the Creator is absurd; for most people affirm the existence of the Creator, and do not reject prophecies, only have neglected to study them; a few of them are exceptional and follow the materialists, whose minds are simply corrupt. We have seen among the philosophers of our own community a number whose philosophizing has gained for them nothing but bewilderment. They act neither according to its precepts nor those of Islam. Nay, there are some of them who fast during Ramaḍân, and say their prayers, and then start objecting to the Creator and the prophecies, and in their talk reject the resurrection of the bodies. Scarcely any of them are to be seen who are not afflicted with poverty and injured thereby. Such a person spends most of his time in railing at fate and objecting to the Disposer; indeed one of them said to me: I quarrel only with Him who is above the sphere. He composed many verses on this theme. One of them was about this world:

> Without a craftsman is it work of craft?
> Without an archer possibly a shaft?

Others:

> Strange this existence, with no option brought
> To us beforehand and no knowledge taught!
> 'Tis like some labyrinth from which no skill
> Can rescue, no, nor wisdom nor strong will.
> We grope in darkness which no sun makes bright.
> Nor moon, nor firestick gives a ray of light.
> Bewildered, dazed, held fast in her embrace
> By Ignorance, with frown upon her face.
> And what is wrought therein is doubtless work;
> But what is said thereon is idle talk.

Since both philosophy and monasticism were near in time to that of our law, some of our coreligionists stretched out their hands to take hold of the one and others to take hold of the other. So you will find many foolish people who when they study doctrine philosophize, and when they study asceticism become eremites. We pray God to keep us steadfast in our religion and safe from our enemy. Truly He is one who answers.

Translated by D. S. Margoliouth

AL-TANÛKHÎ,*

The Table Talk of a Mesopotamian Judge

I was told by Abû ʿAlî b. Abî Ḥâmid the following. I heard, he said, several people in Ḥalab narrate how Abu'l-Ṭayyib Aḥmad b. al-Ḥusain who at the time was claiming to be a prophet there[1] had been in the desert of Samâwah and the neighbouring regions till Lu'lu' was despatched against him from Ḥims by the Ikhshîdî rulers, fought against him, and captured him, while his followers from Kalb, Kilâb, and other Arab tribes dispersed. Lu'lu' kept him in prison a long time till he fell ill and came near dying. Being petitioned on his behalf, Lu'lu' demanded that he should retract, and drew up a deed wherein he attested that his former claims were false, that he reverted to Islam, that he repented of his profession and would not resume it. Lu'lu' then discharged him. He had recited to the Beduin a discourse which he declared to be Qur'ân revealed to him; and they repeated numerous Sûrahs by him, of which I took down one. I lost it, but retained the commencement in my memory. It is as follows:

> By the travelling star, and the revolving sphere, and night and day, verily the unbeliever is in a risky way. Proceed on thy road, and follow the track which the Muslims before thee trod. For by thee will Allah suppress the error of those who have perverted His faith, and erred from His path.

The Sûrah (he added) is lengthy, and this is all of it that I can remember. When Mutanabbî monopolized attention in the audience-chamber of Saif al-daulah—we were at the time in Ḥalab—we used to remind him of this Qur'ân of his and other similar things which were told of him, and he used to repudiate them.—The grammarian Ibn Khâlûyah said to him one day in the chamber of Saif al-daulah: Were not someone a fool, he would not consent to be called Mutanabbî, "Prophetaster", which means "liar"; a man who consents to be known as the Liar must be a fool.—

*Died 994 A.D. Studied with Abu'l-Faraj al-Isfahânî, the author of the *Kitâb al-Aghânî* (see p. 110); was a judge in Baghdâd.

---

[1] He was in consequence called Mutanabbî (Prophetaster).

Mutanabbî replied: I do not consent to be called by that name: only people who wish to lower me in general estimation call me by it, and I do not know how to get out of it. I myself[2], when I was passing through Aḥwâz on my way to Fars in the year 354 in the course of a long conversation which I had with Mutanabbî asked him the import of his name, as I wished to hear from himself whether he had really claimed to be a prophet. He gave an elusive answer, saying: This was something which happened in my youth, and which the circumstances justified.—I was ashamed to demand details, and so left the matter alone.

Abû ʿAlî b. Abî Ḥâmid proceeded to say: My father said to me, when we were in Ḥalab and he heard some people reciting the Sûrah of Abû'l-Ṭayyib al-Mutanabbî which has been mentioned: Were it not for his stupidity, how could his words *Proceed on thy road,* etc., be compared with the verses of God Almighty (Sûrah xv. 94) *So utter what thou art bidden and turn aside from the polytheists, verily we have defended thee from the mockers* etc. Is there any comparison between the eloquence of the two or any resemblance between the two utterances?

Translated by D. S. Margoliouth

---

[2] The author of the *Table Talk* is speaking here.

22

IBN QUTAYBAH *

ʿ*Uyûn al-Akhbâr*

When I had become aware of the wide-spread decrease, and disappearance of learning, of Government being too busy to set up a market for Adab, so that it became effaced and erased, I took it upon myself to compose a book on knowledge and on the rectification of tongue and hand for the benefit of those of the scribes whose education was scanty: a book through which I reached my soul's desire for them, and my heart's ease, and in which I registered for their sake all that God had presented me with for the day of victory. But I impose upon them the condition not only to study it, but also to learn by heart the original sources of the sayings, so as to introduce them as similes into the spaces between their lines when they write, and to make use of their beautiful conceits and their elegant expressions when they speak. After having undertaken to look after part of their equipment, zeal called me to satisfy their wants, for I was afraid lest, if I left them to themselves for the remaining needs and trusted them to select it, their perseverance might not last against neglect and out of weakness they might not find their riding beasts easy so that they might turn away from the end, as they had turned away from the beginning; or lest they might attempt this with weakness of purpose and languidness of application so that weakness of natural disposition and disgust at inconvenience might overpower them. Therefore I finished for them what I had begun, and coated with plaster the building of which I had laid the foundations; and I behaved towards them like one who acts kindly towards him he loves, rather like a tender father towards a son who shows filial piety. But I shall be satisfied with their casual thanks, relying upon God for reward and remuneration.

This book, although not dealing with Qur'ân or Sunna, the religious law or the knowledge of what is lawful and what is forbidden, yet leads on to the heights of things and shows the way to noble character; it restrains from baseness, turns away from ugly things, incites to

*Died 889 A.D. Famous authority on pre-Islamic poetry and author of *Adab* works. (See p. 111 and Index, s.v.)

right conduct and fair management, to mild administration and to rendering the land prosperous. For the way to Allâh is not one nor is all that is good confined to nightprayers and continued fasting and the knowledge of the lawful and the forbidden. On the contrary, the ways to Him are many and the doors of the good are wide; and the soundness of religion depends on the soundness of time and the soundness of time on the soundness of government, whilst the soundness of government depends—beside the help of Allâh—on leading aright and providing proper understanding.

I have arranged these *'Uyûn al-Akhbâr* as an eye-opening for those whose upbringing is scanty, as a reminder for the learned, as an education for the leaders of men and those whom they lead, as a place for the kings to rest from the toil of endeavour and weariness. I have classified it into chapters and connected one chapter with one that is like it, one narrative with one that resembles it, one word with its sister; so that he who studies may find it easy to learn, and he who reads remember it, and he who is in search for something may turn to it. Through it the minds of the learned are impregnated, the thoughts of the wise are assisted in being brought forth; it contains the fresh butter of pure milk, the ornament of culture, the fruits of prolonged thought, the choicest words for the eloquent, the intelligence of poets, the lifestory of kings, the traditions of preceding generations. I have collected for you a great deal in this book of all this, that you may train your soul with the best of it, that you may straighten it with its *thiqâf*[1], free it from its bad qualities, as you would free the white silver from its dross; and drill it to accept good behaviour, upright mode of life, noble culture and grand character, as taught in it. Let it enter your speech when you hold a conference, and your eloquent style when you write; with its help you will succeed in what you ask for, you will use beautiful words in intercession, and escape blame by means of the best excuses, when you apologize. For words are the pitfalls of hearts, and lawful sorcery. Make use of its culture in the company of your ruler, and in setting aright administration, in making his policy mild, and in managing his wars. Enliven your company through it, whether in earnest or joke, render your proofs obvious with the help of its similes, humiliate your adversary by taking them into account so that truth may manifest itself in the most beautiful shape and that you reach your aim with the lightest of provision and gain your goal calmly; and that you may overtake the tracked beast, bending part of your rein and walking gently and

[1] An instrument used for the straightening of lances.

come in first. All this, provided your natural disposition be compliant, your temper ready and your feeling tractable; should this not be the case, those whose intelligence points out to them the defects of their soul, and who consequently manage it well and cover its defects with patience and reflection; who put the remedies of this book on the illness of their natural disposition, drench their soul with its (the book's) water and strike fire from it through its lights, will find this book able to restore the sick and sharpen the blunt and arouse the drowsy and awake the slumbering; until with the help of Allâh even they come near the ranks of those that are gifted by nature.

I did not think it right for this book of mine to be a bequest for those who pursue this world, as opposed to those who pursue the next world; nor to the chiefs, as opposed to the masses, nor to the kings as opposed to the subjects. On the contrary, I have given every one of these parties their share and made their part copious. And I have included in the book new examples from the beautiful sayings of the ascetics about the world and its misfortunes, and decay and death; sayings that they quote to each other, whenever they assemble, and which they introduce into their correspondence, when they are separated one from another; sermons and sayings about asceticism, self-restraint, fear of God, certainty of belief and the like of these. Perhaps Allâh will lead back through them those who turn aside, bend towards repentance those who deviate, restrain those who act wrongly, and soften through their delicacies the hardness of hearts. But with all this I did not deprive the book of strange curiosities, witty and sagacious sayings, words that please and others that make laugh; lest there should be omitted from the book any of the roads that travellers have travelled or any way of speech to which speakers have had recourse; and in order to give rest to the reader from the toil of seriousness and the tiring effect of truth for "the ear is wont to reject, while the mind has eager desire" (for what it deems elegant). For if a joke is suitable or almost so, and fitting in with its time and the conditions that bring it forth, it is not bad nor to be disapproved of, belonging neither to the big nor even the small sins, if God will. Therefore this our book will take you in the end to the chapter on jests and merriment and to such of them as have been handed down from Sharîfs and Imâms. If then you, who show a grave mien, come across a saying you hold in light esteem or you find good or you admire or you laugh at, know our method and our intention. Remember also that if you, in your asceticism, can dispense with it, there are others, easygoing in those things in which you exert yourself, who may want it. The book has not been composed for you to the exclusion of others and could not therefore have been arranged according to your outward predilections. Had it been influenced by the fear of those that don grave miens, half of its beauty would have gone and half of its juice, and those would have turned away from it whom we should love to turn towards it along with you.

Abû Muhammad[2] said: I wrote a letter to one of the rulers and in one part of it I said: The resolute men have always found sweet the bitter words of the sincere, they have always wished to be guided aright in their faults and to inquire after the right judgment from everybody down to the foolish maidservant. Whilst there are those who are in need of proving the love they claim for him and the purity of their intention, Allâh has made this unnecessary for me through that which compulsion has rendered obligatory; since I have always been hoping for an increase of my present state from the lasting of your privilege and the rising of your scale and the unfolding of your high rank and power.

And in another passage I wrote: In this letter I have taken upon myself a certain amount of blame, and have acted contrary to my own knowledge by offering my judgment without having been asked for advice, and have put myself in the place of the special officers without having been placed there. But my soul burning with anger and feeling uneasy at what it heard, dragged me away from a path right for it, to one right for you, when I saw the tongue of your enemy unfolding itself with its charges against you and its arrows piercing you: whilst I was your friend incapable of arguing since he did not find an excuse, and whilst I saw the common people engage in all kinds of talk regarding you. For there is nothing more harmful for the ruler in some cases nor more useful for him in others, than they: for horsemen carry along what Allâh makes run down their tongues and stories remain and remembrance holds out against time and the ends prevail and news which has become manifest has more weight in their eyes, than the testimony of trustworthy witnesses.

And again in another passage: He who leads people and manages their affairs is in need of a wide chest and he must gird himself with patience and bear up with the want of culture of the common people; he must make the ignorant understand and satisfy the man against whom the decision has gone and who has been denied his request by pointing out whence he has been denied it; for since people are not universally satisfied, even if all the causes of satisfaction have been put

---

[2] *i.e.* The author of the *ʿUyûn,* Abû Muhammad ʿAbdullah ibn Muslim ibn Qutaybah.

together for their benefit, much less will they be satisfied if some have been withheld from them. And they do not accept obvious excuses, even less dubious ones. And your brother is he who tells you the truth and is grieved for you, not he who follows you in your passion and afterwards disappears from you without bringing you near.

Ziyâd said to a man who consulted him: All those who ask for advice have confidence and every secret has its depository. But there are two things in men that cripple them in their efforts: the squandering of secrets and the venting of advice. There is no room for a secret except in one of two men: the man of Future Life who hopes for God's reward or the man of this world who has nobility in his soul and an intelligence with which to preserve his rank; and I have tested both of them for you.

One of the scribes wrote: Know that he gives you good advice and is anxious for you, who examines for you with his sight the things behind the ends and who shows you the likeness of the things of which you are afraid; who mixes for you the rough and the smooth in his speech and his advice, in order that your fear may equal your hope and your gratitude correspond with the benefit bestowed on you. And know further that he cheats you and instigates others against you, who helps your being seduced, who levels for you the smooth ground of oppression, who runs with you in your bridle obedient to your passion.

And in a passage: If I am suspect in your eyes at present, you will find on reflecting on the various sides of this advice things that will show you that it issued from truth and sincerity.

Ibrâhîm ibn al-Mundhir said: Ziyâd ibn ʿUbeydallâh al-Ḥârithî[3] asked ʿUbeydallâh ibn ʿUmar about his brother Abû Bakr as to whether to appoint him judge, and he advised him to do it. But when he sent to Abû Bakr he refused, whereupon Ziyâd sent for ʿUbeydallâh asking him to help him against Abû Bakr. Abû Bakr said to ʿUbeydallâh: "I beseech you by God, do you think it right for me to take charge of the judgeship?" He said, "By God, no." Whereupon Ziyâd said: "God is far from such imperfection! I asked your advice and you advised me to appoint him and now I hear you forbidding him!" He said: "O Amîr, you asked my advice, so I exerted my judgment for your benefit and gave you my sincere advice, now he asked my advice, so I exerted my judgment for his benefit and gave him my sincere advice."

Naṣr ibn Mâlik was at the head of Abû Muslim's police. When Abû Muslim received Abû Jaʿfar's leave to come to see him he asked Naṣr's

[3] Governor of Medina from 133 to 136 A.H.

advice and he told him not to go and said: I do not trust him with regard to you. Abû Jaʿfar said to him, when he came to him: "did Abû Muslim ask your advice with regard to coming to see me and did you forbid him?" "Yes." "How is this?" "I heard your brother Ibrâhîm the Imâm quote in the name of his father Muhammad ibn ʿAlî: 'Men will go on receiving an increase in their judgment, as long as they give sincere advice to those who ask for their advice.' So I behaved to him accordingly, and now I behave toward you as I did toward him."

Muʿâwiya said: "I used to meet an Arab of whom I knew that there was in his heart hatred against me and I used to ask his advice, whereupon he would stir up his hatred against me in the measure he felt it in his soul. While he went on to overwhelm me with insult, I overwhelmed him with forbearance until he turned into a friend whom I asked for help and who gave it, and whom I asked for assistance and who answered my call."

Translated by Josef Horovitz.

23

ABÛ ḤAYYÂN AL-TAWḤÎDÎ *

The Book of Enjoyment and Good Company[1]

I went to the vizier's house another evening, and the first thing which he addressed to the gathered circle was, "Do you prefer the Arabs over the non-Arabs or the non-Arabs over the Arabs?"

I said, "In the opinion of the learned men, there are four nations: the Greeks, the Arabs, the Persians and the Indians. Three of these are non-Arab, and it is difficult to say that the Arabs by themselves are preferable to the other three, in spite of both their common collections and their differentiations." He said, "However, I like from this group the Persians." And I said, "Before I decide anything, speaking for myself, I will relate a conversation by Ibn al-Muqaffaʿ,[2] who is of pure Persian origin and is deep-rooted among non-Arabs, a man superior among the people of merit. . . . " The vizier said, "Bring me unto the blessing of God and His assistance."

I then related the conversation of Shabîb ibn Shabba, who said: We were standing in the courtyard of the camel station (in Basra)—the standing place of the nobles and the meeting place of the people, with the notables of Egypt present—when Ibn al-Muqaffaʿ came into view. There was not among us anyone who did not take delight in him or who did not derive satisfaction in questioning him, and we rejoiced at his appearance. He said, "What keeps you upon the backs of your animals in this place? By God, if the Caliph were to send out to the people of the earth, seeking the likes of you, he should not locate anyone like you. Now go to the house of Ibn Barthan, in extended shade and shielded from the sun, facing the northerly breeze. Give rest to your animals and servants. We will sit on the ground, for it is a fine carpet,

*Died 1023 A.D.

[1] Al-Tawḥîdî (died 414 A.H./1023 A.D.) lived in Baghdâd, then under Buwayhid rule. The Book is a record of conversations held at the house of a Buwayhid vizier.

[2] Early Persian convert to Islam and the source of many stories in Arabic *Adab* works. He was burnt to death as a suspected heretic in 159 A.H./757 A.D.

most tread upon." Some of us were listening, for he is the most accomplished of the circle and the most prolific at conversation. So we hastened to do what he had said and alighted from our animals at the house of Ibn Barthan, inhaling the northerly breeze, when Ibn al-Muqaffaʿ drew near to us and said, "Which nation is most intelligent?" We thought that he had in mind the Persians, so we said, "The Persians are the most intelligent," seeking to ingratiate ourselves and having in mind to flatter him. But he said, "Not at all. That ability is not theirs, nor is it among them. They are a people who were taught and who then learned, who were given an example and who then imitated and followed after, who were started on a matter and who then went on to pursue it. They have neither invention nor discovery." So we said to him, "The Greeks." But he said, "It is not them either. Though they have strong bodies and are masters at building and architecture, they do not know anything other than those two, nor have they perfected anything else."

We said, "The Chinese." He replied, "Masters of furniture and crafts, but they have neither thought nor deliberation." We said, "The Turks." He answered, "Lions for quarrel." We said, "The Indians." He responded, "Masters of imagination, trickery, sleight-of-hand, and deception." We said, "The Negroes." He said, "Roving cattle." So we handed over the matter to him, and he said, "The Arabs." We exchanged glances and whispered to one another; that enraged him, his color turning pale. Then he said, "It seems that you suspect me of ingratiating myself with you. By God, I wish that this thing were otherwise, but I would be disgusted if the matter escaped me and its correct solution eluded me. I will not leave you until I explain why I said what I did, in order to clear myself of the suspicion of deception and the imputation of flattery.

"The Arabs did not have a proper condition to follow as a pattern nor a Book to guide them. They are people of a poor land, deserted from mankind; everyone among them, in his loneliness, has need of his thought, his contemplation, and his mind. They knew that their livelihood came from the plants of the earth, so they marked each of them and attributed to each its type, and they knew the benefit that was in the fresh plant and the dry plant, and their growth cycles, and which were suitable for sheep and camels. Then they contemplated time and its succession and rendered it as spring, summer, mid-summer and winter. They knew that their drink was from the heavens, so they invented for them the constellations. And they were aware of the changing of time, so they made for it divisions of the year. They needed to spread out on the earth, so they made of the heavenly stars guides for the sections of the earth and its regions, and followed the land by means of them. And they made among themselves something which would prevent them from doing evil and which would make them desirous of the beautiful, by which they would avoid baseness and which would spur them on to excellent qualities, even to the extent that a member of their nation, though he be in any remote spot of the earth, describes these excellent qualities, not omitting a thing from his description, and he is immoderate in the censure of evil acts and condemns them at length. They do not discourse except in discussion which encourages good deeds, the preservation of the neighbor, the giving away of goods, and the setting up of commendable acts. Everyone of them achieves that by his mind and deduces it by his native intelligence and his thought, without learning or becoming well-mannered; instead, his natural disposition is well-bred and his mind is perceptive. This is why I said they are the most intelligent nation, because of the soundness of natural endowment, correctness of thought, and acuteness of understanding." This was the end of the conversation.

The vizier said, "How good is what Ibn al-Muqaffaʿ said! How good is what you narrated and what you brought! Bring me now what you have heard and have deduced."

I replied, "If what this man, skillful in his manners and excellent of mind, has said is sufficient, then anything added to it would be a superfluity, unnecessary to it, and following it with something similar would be of no use."

The vizier said, "The range of description varies in beautifying and making ugly; the different characteristics depend upon what is thought correct and incorrect. This question—I mean the preference of one nation over another—is, among nations, a thing over which people have contended and have pushed each other around. Nor, since we have exchanged words in this room, have they come to a firm settlement and an apparent agreement."

I responded, "This happens of necessity, for it is not in the Persian's nature nor his custom nor his origin to acknowledge the merit of the Arab, and neither is it in the nature of the Arab nor in his habit that he be delighted at the merit of the Persian. And the same applies to the Indian, the Greek, the Turk, the Dailamite, and others, for the consideration of merit and nobility rests upon two things. The first is that by which one people became distinguished from another, at the time of the creation, by the choice of good and bad, by correct and erroneous opinion, and by the contemplation of the beginning and the end. The matter depends upon this, but secondly, every nation has virtues and vices and every people has good and bad qualities, and every group of people is both complete and deficient in its industry and its wielding of influence. And it is decreed that bounties and merits and faults be poured forth over all mankind, scattered among them all.

"Thus the Persians have politics, manners of government, restraints, and ceremonies; the Greeks have science and wisdom; the Indians have thought, deliberation, agility, beguilement, and perseverence; the Turks have courage and boldness; the Negroes have patience, the ability for hard labor, and joy; and the Arabs have bravery, hospitable reception, fidelity, gallantry, generosity, responsibility to obligation, oratory, and a gift for explanation.

"Moreover, the merits mentioned above, in these famous nations, are not possessed by everyone of their individuals but rather are widespread among them. But there are some in their group who are devoid of all of them and are characterized by their opposite; that is, the Persians do not lack a man ignorant of politics and lacking in manners, found among the riffraff and the rabble. Similarly, the Arabs do not lack a cowardly or an ignorant or a foolish or a miserly or an inarticulate man. And the same holds true for the Indians, the Greeks, and others. Accordingly, when the people of merit and perfection from the Greeks are compared with the people of merit and perfection from the Persians, they come together on an even path. There is no difference between them except in the degrees of merit and the extents of perfection, and those are general rather than specific. In a like manner, when the people of shortcoming and vileness of one nation are compared with those of shortcoming and vileness of another nation, they come together on a single path. There is no difference between them except in degrees and extents. And no attention is paid to that nor any blame put upon it. Thus it has become clear from this list that all the nations have divided among themselves merits and shortcomings by the necessity of natural endowment and the choice of thought. Beyond that, people only compete among themselves regarding inheritance, native custom, overwhelming passion of irascible souls, and the angry impulse of emotional force.

"Here is another thing, an important principle which it is not possible to avoid pointing out in our discussion. Every nation has a period of domination over its opponents. This is clearly evident when you imagine for a moment the Greeks at the time of Alexander the Great, when they conquered, governed, ruled, sowed and unsowed, prescribed, managed and commanded, incited and restrained, erased and recorded, acted and reported. Similarly, when you turn your attention to discussing Chosroës Anûshîrvân [Sasanid Emperor, 531–578 A.D.], you find these same conditions. . . . And for this reason, Abû Muslim,[3] when asked which people he found most courageous, said, 'All people are courageous when their fortune is rising.' He had spoken truly. And accordingly, every nation at the beginning of its prosperity is virtuous, courageous, brave, worthy of glory, generous, outstanding, eloquent, perceptive, and reliable. This point of view is extrapolated from a phenomenon common to all nations, to one universal to each nation at a time, to a thing embracing each group, to one prevalent to each tribe, to something customary in each family, to one special to each person and each man. And this change from nation to nation illustrates the abundance of the generosity of God to all His creation and creatures in proportion to their fulfillment of His demand and their readiness to exert themselves at length in attaining it."

Translated by John Damis

Muslim Culture in Baghdâd[1]

When I wandered about in the city after a long absence, I found it in an expansion of prosperity that I had not observed before this time. The resplendent buildings that rose in the city of al-Manṣûr were not sufficient for its wealthy people until they extended to the houses of the eastern quarter known as Rusâfa. They built high castles and ornamented homes in this quarter, and set up markets, mosques and public baths.[2] The attention of al-Rashîd and the Barmakids was directed toward adorning it with public buildings, until the old Baghdâd became

---

[3] A Persian *Mawlà* of 'Iraq, sent to Khurâsân by the Hashimites in 126 A.H./743 A.D. as confidential agent and propagandist to the Persian *Mawâlî*. Despite his considerable success among the Persian population and his decisive role in the military victories of the 'Abbâsids over the Umayyads, Abû Muslim was executed by the 'Abbâsids soon after their victory was secured in 133 A.H./750 A.D.

[1] Letter written by the son of Khurâsânî nobleman to his father from Baghdâd, in the last years of the eighth century A.D. The anonymous well-connected author records conversations with high state officials, and, as told in a later letter, was received in audience by the caliph Hârûn al-Rashîd.

[2] A later writer numbered the public baths in Baghdâd at this time at 65,000.

like an ancient town whose beauties were assembled in a section of the city which was created near by it.

I admired the arrival of buildings in Baghdâd because of the over-crowdedness of the people I had seen in its sections. Their billowing is like the sea in its expanses; their number is said to exceed 1,500,000, and no other city in the world has such a sum or even half its amount. Moreover, the social life of the people points to this great sum, although there are no cities to the right or the left of the place in which the people band together like sand. Then I marvelled at the arrival of comfort among the people, for I saw many of them aiming toward arts whose need is not confined to the necessities of civilization. Moreover, the usefulness of their crafts and what they produce expands to the demands of affluence which occurs among nations at the end of their rule and at the time when commanding becomes difficult.

It is difficult for me, with this pen which is of limited substance, to describe the glorious qualities of the city which are but a small part of the honor it achieves, such that it prides itself in the splendor of power. The city brings together a great many notable persons, even to the extent that if the traveler meets a group of them on the road, he does not understand where the multitude is from, although even the least of them has wealth and rank. It is difficult for the largest of cities to support its inhabitants and to extend its soldiery and its retinue and those expectant to it from every direction. The people of wealth walk with slave boys and retinue whose number the listener will fancy to be far from the truth. I witnessed at Attâbiyya station a prince who was riding with a hundred horsemen and was surrounded by slave boys, even filling the road and blocking the path of the people until they passed. I witnessed at the water hole of a sugar cane field along the Tigris a youth from the people of wealth who was going in a grand procession of horses and men, and it was as if I was with a Byzantine emperor upon his mount or a Persian king in the splendor of his procession. The number of those counted in the ʿAbbâsid house is probably more than the thousand men riding in such a group as this, and all of them are of great wealth and affluence of civilization. Moreover, prosperity prevailed among the Baghdâdîs, even resembling the affluence of al-Rashîd which they saw in his concern in the world for seeking comfort, even verifying the saying which says, "The people are in debt of the king." For it was he who clothed the world, throughout its expanses, with this beauty. Nor was any Caliph ever known to be more generous than he in the handing out of wealth. It is said that he spent ten thousand dirhams every day for his food, and perhaps the cooks would prepare for him thirty kinds of food. Abû Yûsuf[3] informed me that when the Caliph consummated his marriage to Zubaida, the daughter of Jaʿfar the Barmakid, he gave a banquet unprecedented in Islam. He gave away unlimited presents at this banquet, even giving containers of gold filled with silver, containers of silver filled with gold, bags of musk and pieces of ambergris. The total expenditure on this banquet reached 55,000,000 dirhams. The Caliph commanded that Zubaida be presented in a gown of pearls whose price no one was able to appraise. He adorned her with pieces of jewelry, so much so that she was not able to walk because of the great number of jewels which were upon her. This example of extravagance had no precedent among the kings of Persia, the emperors of Byzantium or the princes of the Umayyads, despite the great amounts of money which they had at their disposal.

Part of the beauty of the world in these days is that al-Rashîd is not unique in the greatness of his spending and squandering. His wife, Zubaida, designs works which surpass the spending of the kings, as in an example of her making, a carpet of silk brocade. This carpet contained the picture of all animals of all the species, and of every bird in gold and their eyes in sapphires and jewels. It is said that she spent about 1,000,000 dînârs on it. Or for example, her making vessels of gold inlaid with jewels, and dresses of exquisite embroidery whose price exceeds 50,000 dînârs, and domes of silver, ebony, and sandalwood, upon which are daggers of gold adorned with embroidery, silk brocade, sable and types of silk. Or for example, her making candles of ambergris, and slippers adorned with jewels, and her taking from among the servants hirelings who followed on donkeys and tended after her needs and ran her errands. And other examples of the affairs which are recorded in the annals of the kings to enhance their position of power and the tales of the amenities which they had at their disposal.

I did not see the likes of this affluence in other houses of the Caliphate except among the glorious Barmakids, where the beauty of the kings and their radiance reached their limit. When they decided to ride out, more people gathered to see them than gathered to see the Caliph. I saw one of their young men at the Muhawwal Gate in the western quarter in a grand procession. His clothes were embroidered and he was thronged by soldiers and slave boys, offspring and notables. He placed his glance upon the mane of his horse, and the people were looking at him, but he did not turn toward them because of his eminence and loftiness.

---

[3] The author of the *Kitâb al-Kharâj*, see page 74.

When al-Rashîd himself was in the presence of the Barmakids, he found himself amidst inlaid containers, marbled vaults, and seats of embroidery and silk brocade. Slave girls trailed garments of silk and jewels, and received him with perfumes whose scent was unknown, and it seemed to him that he was in Paradise, surrounded by beauty, jewels and perfume.

The affluence of the Barmakids reached, in the end, the highest level of enjoyment with an ampleness of comfort. Their sessions of entertainment in their houses were more splendid than those in the houses of al-Rashîd and more complete with devices of entertainment. This was because they possessed female singers who were unrivaled in the country, especially the famous Fauz, Farîda and Manna, who were the finest female singers and the best at plucking the lute.

The singing for the Barmakids was not known in the houses of princes, except for the yellow-skinned and the black-skinned. When the Barmakid children grew up, they wanted the beautiful slave girls to know how to sing in order that their beauty would increase from the influence which singing would have on souls. Nâfidh, from the account of one of their doormen, told me that when al-Rashîd visited them on one of the days of his vacation, they had the slave girls brought out to the garden. There they fell into double-column formation like soldiers, and sang and played lutes and struck tambourines until they reached the steps of the castle.

We do not know any preceding king who possessed the good things which are abundant among our kings in this age. It is as if Baghdâd had dropped its quarters onto the bed of life's richness, and, from the abundance of wealth, the causes of ease and eminence had been found for the people.

The Affluence of the Baghdâdîs and Their Immersion in the Good Things of Life

Affluence is abundant among the upper rank of those who are masters of the state. It then diminishes little by little among those of lesser rank, until only a small amount remains for the general public. As for those who do not enjoy the exalted power and breadth of bounty of the kings, they begin to equip themselves with all the good things after they have gone on journeys which gain them experience, show them wonderous things, and give them profits. The people in the provinces come to them with the grandest of all the types of their wares, until markets have become plentiful in Baghdâd. They have advanced from requesting necessities to the acquisition of things for beautification and decoration. This may be seen in the case of their purchase of arms inlaid with gold, their competing in costly jewels, ornamented vessels, and splendid furniture, and their acquisition of a large number of slave boys, female singers, and those things which they send out their retainers to seek in the provinces. When every expensive and rare thing in the country was brought to them, I realized that the beauties of the world had been assembled in Baghdâd.

I witnessed the market of the female slaves after my return from Khorâsân, when I was living in the place known as the market of the slave traders. They are the men who have the girls brought to Baghdâd from the ends of the earth. I saw among these girls Ethiopians, Greeks, Georgians, Circassians, and Arabs born in Medina, Ṭâʾif, Yamâma and Egypt, possessing sweet tongues and ready answers. The singers among them were known by their very fine dresses, and their headbands which they arranged with pearls and jewels and wrote upon with gold leaf.

The observer imagines on his first trip to this market that, while he is circulating among the girls, they are being sold in injustice and slavery. But he does not retain this sudden fancy after he sees how they embrace the people of ease. I had heard that some of the beautiful girls luxuriously adorned were rescued secretly from places they disliked. Then they would come to the market disguised from the eyes of the guards until a prospective buyer stopped before one of the people. Their masters are unaware of them, and the slave traders oversee their sale like merchants overseeing their goods. When their buyer stops before a man, he grabs with his hand at the hand of the slave trader, just as the custom is known in buying and selling. I had stopped that day, with the guide calling to those about him who were interested, describing for them one slave girl after another, using the best descriptions of beauty. The noise was resounding and the market was brisk.

I return now to what I had started to speak of concerning the excessive affluence of the Baghdâdîs. I saw them beautifying their chambers with magnificent furnishings and costly furniture. They cover their walls with embroidery and silk brocade, and take an interest in planting flowers in their gardens, even to the extent that they have rare flowers brought to them from India. It reaches the point that the price of one of these gardens is valued at 10,000 dînârs. They select their slave boys from the most graceful of people and the most lively in energy; they desire entertainment and amusement from their concern, which I had mentioned, for their acquisition of female singers. They indulge in luscious food to the point of buying game and fruit out of season, paying for them their weight in silver. They enjoy the taste in some of their foods from perfume which they chew, and Indian betel leaves which they mix with wet lime to improve the taste and the food, and produce delight and cheerfulness in the soul. When it is hot they place their chairs among water gushing from statues of lions and among forms of birds and apples and other forms which they chisel in marble. When their bodies have obtained sufficient water to refresh the soul, they place fans on the ceiling. They work the fans by ropes which pull them, and pulling them, they draw the cool breeze over themselves. They indulge in clothes and ornamentation and in riding horses with silk brocade and heavy finery of silvery, to a degree which no affluent nations before them have reached.

Translated by John Damis

24

IBN BAṬṬÛṬAH.*

The Travels in Asia and Africa

[INDIA AND CHINA]

The king of China had sent valuable gifts to the sultan, including a hundred slaves of both sexes, five hundred pieces of velvet and silk cloth, musk, jewelled garments and weapons, with a request that the sultan would permit him to rebuild the idol-temple which is near the mountains called Qarájíl [Himalaya]. It is in a place known as Samhal, to which the Chinese go on pilgrimage; the Muslim army in India had captured it, laid it in ruins and sacked it. The sultan, on receiving this gift, wrote to the king saying that the request could not be granted by Islamic law, as permission to build a temple in the territories of the Muslims was granted only to those who paid a poll-tax; to which he added "If thou wilt pay the *jizya* we shall empower thee to build it. And peace be on those who follow the True Guidance." He requited his present with an even richer one—a hundred thoroughbred horses, a hundred white slaves, a hundred Hindu dancing- and singing-girls, twelve hundred pieces of various kinds of cloth, gold and silver candelabra and basins, brocade robes, caps, quivers, swords, gloves embroidered with pearls, and fifteen eunuchs. As my fellow-ambassadors the sultan appointed the amír Zahír ad-Dín of Zanján, one of the most eminent men of learning, and the eunuch Káfúr, the cup-bearer, into whose keeping the present was entrusted. He sent the amír Muhammad of Herát with a thousand horsemen to escort us to the port of embarkation, and we were accompanied by the Chinese ambassadors, fifteen in number, along with their servants, about a hundred men in all.

We set out therefore in imposing force and formed a large camp. The sultan gave instructions that we were to be supplied with provisions while we were travelling through his dominions. Our journey began on the 17th of Safar 743 [22nd July 1342]. That was the day selected because

*Died 1377 A.D. Famous traveller who visited Africa, the Near and Middle East, Central and South Asia, and even parts of China. (See p. 100.)

they choose either the 2nd, 7th, 12th, 17th, 22nd, or 27th of the month as the day for setting out. On the first day's journey we halted at the post-station of Tilbat, seven miles from Delhi, and travelled thence through Bayána, a large and well-built town with a magnificent mosque, to Kúl [Koel, Aligarh], where we encamped in a wide plain outside the town.

On reaching Koel we heard that certain Hindu infidels had invested and surrounded the town of al-Jalálí. Now this town lies at a distance of seven miles from Koel, so we made in that direction. Meanwhile the infidels were engaged in battle with its inhabitants and the latter were on the verge of destruction. The infidels knew nothing of our approach until we charged down upon them, though they numbered about a thousand cavalry and three thousand foot, and we killed them to the last man and took possession of their horses and their weapons. Of our party twenty-three horsemen and fifty-five foot-soldiers suffered martyrdom, amongst them the eunuch Káfúr, the cup-bearer, into whose hands the present had been entrusted. We informed the sultan by letter of his death and halted to await his reply. During that time the infidels used to swoop down from an inaccessible hill which is in those parts and raid the environs of al-Jalálí and our party used to ride out every day with the commander of that district to assist him in driving them off.

On one of these occasions I rode out with several of my friends and we went into a garden to take our siesta, for this was in the hot season. Then we heard some shouting, so we mounted our horses and overtook some infidels who had attacked one of the villages of al-Jalálí. When we pursued them they broke up into small parties; our troop in following them did the same, and I was isolated with five others. At this point we were attacked by a body of cavalry and foot-soldiers from a thicket thereabouts, and we fled from them because of their numbers. About ten of them pursued me, but afterwards all but three of them gave up the chase. There was no road at all before me and the ground there was very stony. My horse's forefeet got caught between the stones, so I dismounted, freed its foot and mounted again. It is customary for a man in India to carry two swords, one, called the stirrup-sword, attached to the saddle, and the other in his quiver. My stirrup-sword fell out of its scabbard, and as its ornaments were of gold I dismounted, picked it up, slung it on me and mounted, my pursuers chasing me all the while. After this I came to a deep nullah, so I dismounted and climbed down to the bottom of it, and that was the last I saw of them.

I came out of this into a valley amidst a patch of tangled wood, traversed by a road, so I walked along it, not knowing where it led to. At this juncture about forty of the infidels, carrying bows in their hands, came out upon me and surrounded me. I was afraid that they would all shoot at me at once if I fled from them, and I was wearing no armour, so I threw myself to the ground and surrendered, as they do not kill those who do that. They seized me and stripped me of everything that I was carrying except a tunic, shirt and trousers, then they took me into that patch of jungle, and finally brought me to the part of it where they stayed, near a tank of water situated amongst those trees. They gave me bread made of peas, and I ate some of it and drank some water. In their company there were two Muslims who spoke to me in Persian, and asked me all about myself. I told them part of my story, but concealed the fact that I had come from the Sultan. Then they said to me: "You are sure to be put to death either by these men or by others, but this man here (pointing to one of them) is their leader." So I spoke to him, using the two Muslims as interpreters, and tried to conciliate him. He gave me in charge of three of the band, one of them an old man, with whom was his son, and the third an evil black fellow. These three spoke to me and I understood from them that they had received orders to kill me. In the evening of the same day they carried me off to a cave, but God sent an ague upon the black, so he put his feet upon me, and the old man and his son went to sleep. In the morning they talked among themselves and made signs to me to accompany them down to the tank. I realized that they were going to kill me, so I spoke to the old man and tried to gain his favour, and he took pity on me. I cut off the sleeves of my shirt and gave them to him so that the other members of the band should not blame him on my account if I escaped.

About noon we heard voices near the tank and they thought that it was their comrades, so they made signs to me to go down with them, but when we went down we found some other people. The newcomers advised my guards to accompany them but they refused, and the three of them sat down in front of me, keeping me facing them, and laid on the ground a hempen rope which they had with them. I was watching them all the time and saying to myself: "It is with this rope that they will bind me when they kill me." I remained thus for a time, then three of their party, the party that had captured me, came up and spoke to them and I understood that they said to them "Why have you not killed him?" The old man pointed to the black, as though he were excusing himself on the ground of his illness. One of these three was a pleasant-looking youth, and he said to me: "Do you wish me to set you at liberty?" I said

"Yes" and he answered "Go." So I took the tunic which I was wearing and gave it to him and he gave me a worn double-woven cloak which he had, and showed me the way. I went off but I was afraid lest they should change their minds and overtake me, so I went into a reed thicket and hid there till sunset.

Then I made my way out and followed the road which the youth had shewn me. This led to a stream from which I drank. I went on till near midnight and came to a hill under which I slept. In the morning I continued along the road, and sometime before noon reached a high rocky hill on which there were sweet lote-trees and zizyphus bushes. I started to pull and eat the lotus berries so eagerly that the thorn left scars on my arms that remain there to this day. Coming down from that hill I entered a plain sown with cotton and containing castor-oil trees. Here there was a *bâʾin*, which in their language means a very broad well with a stone casing and steps by which you go down to reach the water. Some of them have stone pavilions, arcades, and seats in the centre and on the sides, and the kings and nobles of the country vie with one another in constructing them along the highroads where there is no water. When I reached the *bâʾin* I drank some water from it and I found on it some mustard shoots which had been dropped by their owner when he washed them. Some of these I ate and saved up the rest, then I lay down under a castor-oil tree. While I was there about forty mailed horsemen came to the *bâʾin* to get water and some of them entered the sown fields, then they went away, and God sealed their eyes that they did not see me. After them came about fifty others carrying arms and they too went down into the *bâʾin*. One of them came up to a tree opposite the one I was under, yet he did not discover me. At this point I made my way into the field of cotton and stayed there the rest of the day, while they stayed at the *bâʾin* washing their clothes and whiling away the time. At night time their voices died away, so I knew that they had either passed on or fallen asleep. Thereupon I emerged and followed the track of the horses, for it was a moonlit night, continuing till I came to another *bâʾin* with a dome over it. I went down to it, drank some water, ate some of the mustard shoots which I had, and went into the dome. I found it full of grasses collected by birds, so I went to sleep in it. Now and again I felt the movement of an animal amongst the grass; I suppose it was a snake, but I was too worn out to pay any attention to it.

The next morning I went along a broad road, which led to a ruined village. Then I took another road, but with the same result as before. Several days passed in this manner. One day I came to some tangled trees with a tank of water between them. The space under these trees was like a room, and at the sides of the tạnk were plants like dittany and others. I intended to stop there until God should send someone to bring me to inhabited country, but I recovered a little strength, so I arose and walked along a road on which I found the tracks of cattle. I found a bull carrying a packsaddle and a sickle, but after all this road led to the villages of the infidels. Then I followed up another road, and this brought me to a ruined village. There I saw two naked blacks, and in fear of them I remained under some tree there. At nightfall I entered the village and found a house in one of whose rooms there was something like a large jar of the sort they make to store grain in. At the bottom of it there was a hole large enough to admit a man, so I crept into it and found inside it a layer of chopped straw, and amongst this a stone on which I laid my head and went to sleep. On the top of the jar there was a bird which kept fluttering its wings most of the night—I suppose it was frightened, so we made a pair of frightened creatures. This went on for seven days from the day on which I was taken prisoner, which was a Saturday. On the seventh day I came to a village of the unbelievers which was inhabited and possessed a tank of water and plots of vegetables. I asked them for some food but they refused to give me any. However, in the neighbourhood of a well I found some radish leaves and ate them. I went into the village, and found a troop of infidels with sentries posted. The sentries challenged me but I did not answer them and sat down on the ground. One of them came over with a drawn sword and raised it to strike me, but I paid no attention to him, so utterly weary did I feel. Then he searched me but found nothing on me, so he took the shirt whose sleeves I had given to the old man who had had charge of me.

On the eighth day I was consumed with thirst and I had no water at all. I came to a ruined village but found no tank in it. They have a custom in those villages of making tanks in which the rain-water collects, and this supplies them with drinking water all the year round. Then I went along a road and this brought me to an uncased well over which was a rope of vegetable fibre, but there was no vessel on it to draw water with. I took a piece of cloth which I had on my head and tied it to the rope and sucked the water that soaked into it, but that did not slake my thirst. I tied on my shoe next and drew up water in it, but that did not satisfy me either, so I drew water with it a second time, but the rope broke and the shoe fell back into the well. I then tied on the other shoe and drank until my thirst was assuaged. After that I cut the shoe and tied its uppers on my foot with the rope off the well and bits of cloth which I found there. While I was tying this on and wondering what to do, a person appeared before me. I looked at him, and lo! it was a black-skinned man, carrying a jug and a staff in his hand, and a wallet on his shoulder. He gave me the Muslim greeting "Peace be upon you" and I replied "Upon you be peace and the mercy and blessings of God." Then he asked me in Persian who I was, and I answered "A man astray," and he said: "So am I." Thereupon he tied his jug to a rope which he had with him and drew up some water. I wished to drink but he saying "Have patience," opened his wallet and brought out a handful of black chick-peas fried with a little rice. After I had eaten some of this and drunk, he made his ablutions and prayed two prostrations and I did the same. Thereupon he asked me my name. I answered "Muhammad" and asked him his, to which he replied "Joyous Heart." I took this as a good omen and rejoiced at it. After this he said to me "In the name of God accompany me." I said "Yes," and walked on with him for a little, then I found my limbs giving way, and as I was unable to stand up I sat down. He said "What is the matter with you?" I answered "I was able to walk before meeting you, but now that I have met you I cannot." Whereupon he said "Glory be to God! Mount on my shoulders." I said to him "You are weak, and have not strength for that," but he replied "God will give me strength. You must do so." So I got up on his shoulders and he said to me "Say *God is sufficient for us and an excellent guardian.*" I repeated this over and over again, but I could not keep my eyes open, and regained consciousness only on feeling myself falling to the ground. Then I woke up, but found no trace of the man, and lo! I was in an inhabited village. I entered it and found it was a village of Hindu peasants with a Muslim governor. They informed him about me and he came to meet me. I asked him the name of this village and he replied "Táj Búra." The distance from there to Koel, where our party was, is two farsakhs. The governor provided a horse to take me to his house and gave me hot food, and I washed. Then he said to me: "I have here a garment and a turban which were left in my charge by a certain Arab from Egypt, one of the soldiers belonging to the corps at Koel." I said to him "Bring them: I shall wear them until I reach camp." When he brought them I found that they were two of my own garments which I had given to that very Arab when we came to Koel. I was extremely astonished at this, then I thought of the man who had carried me on his shoulders and I remembered what the saint Abú ʿAbdalláh al-Murshidí had told me, as I have related in the first journey, when he said to me: "You will enter the land of India and meet there my brother Dilshád, who will deliver you from a misfortune which will befall you there." I remembered too how he had said, when I asked him his name, "Joyous Heart" which, translated into Persian, is *Dilshád.* So I knew that it was he whom the saint had foretold that I should meet, and that he too was one of the saints, but I enjoyed no more of his company than the short space which I have related.

The same night I wrote to my friends at Koel to inform them of my safety, and they came, bringing me a horse and clothes and rejoiced at my escape. I found that the sultan's reply had reached them and that he had sent a eunuch named Sunbul, the keeper of the wardrobe, in place of the martyred Káfúr, with orders to pursue our journey. I found, too, that they had written to the sultan about me, and that they regarded the journey as ill-omened on account of what had happened to me and to Káfúr, and were wanting to go back. But when I saw that the sultan insisted upon the journey, I urged them on with great determination. They answered: "Do you not see what has befallen us at the very outset of this mission? The sultan will excuse you, so let us return to him, or stay here until his reply reaches us." But I said: "We cannot stay, and wherever we are his reply will overtake us."

We left Koel, therefore, and encamped at Burj Búra [Burjpur], where there is a fine hermitage in which lives a beautiful and virtuous shaykh called Muhammad the Naked, because he wears nothing but a cloth from his navel to the ground. Thence we travelled to the river known as *Āb-i-Siyah* ["Black Water," Kalindi] and from there reached the city of Qinawj [Kanauj]. It is a large, well-built and strongly fortified city; prices there are cheap and sugar plentiful, and it is surrounded by a great wall. We spent three days here and during this time received the sultan's reply to the letter about me. It ran thus "If no trace is found of so-and-so [*i.e.* Ibn Baṭṭúṭah], let Wajíh al-Mulk, the qádí of Dawlat Ābád, go in his place." We came next to the small town of Mawri, and thence reached Marh, a large town, inhabited chiefly by infidels under Muslim control. It takes its name from the Málawa, a tribe of Hindus, of very powerful build and good-looking; their women especially are exceedingly beautiful and famous for the charms of their company. From Marh we travelled to ʿAlábúr [Alapur], a small town inhabited like the former by infidels under Muslim control. A day's journey from there lived an infidel sultan, named Qatam, who was sultan of Janbíl and was killed after besieging Guyályur [Gwalior]. The governor of ʿAlábúr was the Abyssinian Badr, a slave of the sultan's, a man whose bravery passed into a proverb. He was continually making raids on the infidels alone and single handed, killing and taking captive, so that his fame spread far and wide and the infidels went in fear of him.

He was tall and corpulent, and used to eat a whole sheep at a meal, and I was told that after eating he would drink about a pound and a half of ghee, following the custom of the Abyssinians in their own country. He had a son nearly as brave as himself. During a raid on a village belonging to some Hindus Badr's horse fell with him into a matamore and the villagers surrounded him and killed him.

We journeyed thereafter to Gályúr or Guyályur [Gwalior], a large town with an impregnable fortress isolated on the summit of a lofty hill. Over its gate is an elephant with its mahout carved in stone. The governor of this town was a man of upright character, and he treated me very honourably when I stayed with him on a previous occasion. One day I came before him as he was about to have an infidel cut in two. I said to him "By God I beseech you, do not do this, for I have never seen anyone put to death in my presence." He ordered the man to be put in prison so my intervention was the means of his escape. From Gályúr we went to Parwán, a small town belonging to the Muslims, but situated in the land of the infidels. There are many tigers there, and one of the inhabitants told me that a certain tiger used to enter the town by night, although the gates were shut, and used to seize people. It killed quite a number of the townsfolk in this way. They used to wonder how it made its way in. Here is an amazing thing: a man told me that it was not a tiger who did this but a human being, one of the magicians known as *Júgis* [Yogis], appearing in the shape of a tiger. When I heard this I refused to believe it, but a number of people said the same, so let us give at this point some account of these magicians.

The men of this class do some marvellous things. One of them will spend months without eating or drinking, and many of them have holes dug for them in the earth which are then built in on top of them, leaving only a space for air to enter. They stay in these for months, and I heard tell of one of them who remained thus for a year. The people say that they make up pills, one of which they take for a given number of days or months, and during that time they require no food or drink. They can tell what is happening at a distance. The sultan holds them in esteem and admits them to his company. Some eat nothing but vegetables, and others, the majority, eat no meat; it is obvious that they have so disciplined themselves in ascetic practices that they have no need of any of the goods or vanities of this world. There are amongst them some who merely look at a man and he falls dead on the spot. The common people say that if the breast of a man killed in this way is cut open, it is found to contain no heart, and they assert that his heart has been eaten. This is commonest in the case of women, and a woman who acts thus is called a *kaftár*. During the famine in Delhi they brought one of these women to me, saying that she had eaten the heart of a boy. I ordered them to take her to the sultan's lieutenant, who commanded that she should be put to the test. They filled four jars with water, tied them to her hands and feet and threw her into the river Jumna. As she did not sink she was known to be a *kaftár*; had she not floated she would not have been one. He ordered her then to be burned in the fire. Her ashes were collected by the men and women of the town, for they believe that anyone who fumigates himself with them is safe against a *kaftár*'s enchantments during that year.

The sultan sent for me once when I was in Delhi, and on entering I found him in a private apartment with some of his intimates and two of these *júgís*. One of them squatted on the ground, then rose into the air above our heads, still sitting. I was so astonished and frightened that I fell to the floor in a faint. A potion was administered to me, and I revived and sat up. Meantime this man remained in his sitting posture. His companion then took a sandal from a bag he had with him, and beat it on the ground like one infuriated. The sandal rose in the air until it came above the neck of the sitting man and then began hitting him on the neck while he descended little by little until he sat down alongside us. Then the sultan said "If I did not fear for your reason I would have ordered them to do still stranger things than this you have seen." I took my leave, but was affected with palpitation and fell ill, until he ordered me to be given a draught which removed it all.

. . . The sultan of Cálicút is an infidel, known as "the Sámari." He is an aged man and shaves his beard as some of the Greeks do. In this town too lives the famous shipowner Mithqál, who possesses vast wealth and many ships for his trade with India, China, Yemen, and Fars. When we reached the city, the principal inhabitants and merchants and the sultan's representative came out to welcome us, with drums, trumpets, bugles and standards on their ships. We entered the harbour in great pomp, the like of which I have never seen in those lands, but it was a joy to be followed by distress. We stopped in the port of Cálicút, in which there were at the time thirteen Chinese vessels, and disembarked. Every one of us was lodged in a house and we stayed there three months as the guests of the infidel, awaiting the season of the voyage to China. On the Sea of China travelling is done in Chinese ships only, so we shall describe their arrangements.

The Chinese vessels are of three kinds: large ships called *chunks*, middle-sized ones called *zaws* [dhows], and small ones called *kakams*. The large ships have anything from twelve down to three sails, which are made of bamboo rods plaited like mats. They are never lowered, but turned according to the direction of the wind; at anchor they are left floating in the wind. A ship carries a complement of a thousand men, six hundred of whom are sailors and four hundred men-at-arms, including archers, men with shields and arbalists, who throw naphtha. Each large vessel is accompanied by three smaller ones, the "half," the "third," and the "quarter." These vessels are built only in the towns of Zaytún and Sin-Kalán [Canton]. The vessel has four decks and contains rooms, cabins, and saloons for merchants; the cabin has chambers and a lavatory, and can be locked by its occupant, who takes along with him slave girls and wives. Often a man will live in his cabin unknown to any of the others on board until they meet on reaching some town. The sailors have their children living on board ship, and they cultivate green stuffs, vegetables and ginger in wooden tanks. The owner's factor on board ship is like a great amír. When he goes on shore he is preceded by archers and Abyssinians with javelins, swords, drums, trumpets and bugles. On reaching the house where he stays they stand their lances on both sides of the door, and continue thus during his stay. Some of the Chinese own large numbers of ships on which their factors are sent to foreign countries. There is no people in the world wealthier than the Chinese.

When the time came for the voyage to China, the sultan Sámarí equipped for us one of the thirteen junks in the port of Cálicút. The factor on the junk was called Sulaymán of Safad, in Syria [Palestine]. I had previously made his acquaintance, and I said to him "I want a cabin to myself because of the slave-girls, for it is my habit never to travel without them." He replied "The merchants from China have taken the cabins for the forward and return journey. My son-in-law has a cabin which I can give you, but it has no lavatory; perhaps you may be a)le to exchange it for another." So I told my companions to take on board all my effects, and the male and female slaves embarked on the junk. This was on a Thursday, and I stayed on shore in order to attend the Friday prayers and join them afterwards. The *king* Sunbul and Zahír ad-Dín also went on board with the present. On the Friday morning a slave boy of mine named Hilál came to me and said that the cabin we had taken on the junk was small and unsuitable. When I spoke of this to the captain he said "It cannot be helped, but if you like to transfer to the kakam there are cabins on it at your choice." I agreed to this and gave orders accordingly to my companions, who transferred the slave girls and effects to the kakam and were established in it before the hour of the Friday prayer. Now it is usual for this sea to become stormy every day in the late afternoon, and no one can embark then. The junks had already set sail, and none of them were left but the one which contained the present, another junk whose owner had decided to pass the winter at Fandaraynā, and the kakam referred to. We spent the Friday night on shore, we unable to embark on it, and those on board unable to disembark and join us. I had nothing left with me but a carpet to sleep on. On the Saturday morning the junk and kakam were both at a distance from the port, and the junk which was to have made for Fandaraynā was driven ashore and broken in pieces. Some of those who were on board were drowned and some escaped. That night the same fate met the junk which carried the sultan's present, and all on board were drowned. Next morning we found the bodies of Sunbul and Zahír ad-Dín, and having prayed over them buried them. I saw the infidel, the sultan of Cálicút, wearing a large white cloth round his waist and a small turban, bare-footed, with the parasol carried by a slave over his head and a fire lit in front of him on the beach; his police officers were beating the people to prevent them from plundering what the sea cast up. In all the lands of Mulaybár, except in this one land alone, it is the custom that whenever a ship is wrecked all that is taken from it belongs to the treasury. At Cálicút however it is retained by its owners and for that reason Cálicút has become a flourishing city and attracts large numbers of merchants. When those on the kakam saw what had happened to the junk they spread their sails and went off with all my goods and slave-boys and slave-girls on board, leaving me alone on the beach with but one slave whom I had enfranchised. When he saw what had befallen me he deserted me, and I had nothing left with me at all except ten dinars and the carpet I had slept on.

As I was told that the kakam would have to put in at Kawlam, I decided to travel thither, it being a ten days' journey either by land or by the river, if anyone prefers that route. I set out therefore by the river, and hired one of the Muslims to carry the carpet for me. Their custom is to disembark in the evening and pass the night in the village on its banks, returning to the boat in the morning. We did this too. There was no Muslim on the boat except the man I had hired, and he used to drink wine with the infidels when we went ashore and annoy me with his brawling, which made things all the worse for me. On the fifth day of our journey we came to Kunjá-Karí which is on the top of a hill there; it is inhabited by Jews, who have one of their own number as their governor, and pay a polltax to the sultan of Kawlam. All the trees along this river are cinnamon and brazil trees. They used them for firewood in those parts and we used to light fires with them to cook our food on this journey. On the tenth day we reached the city of Kawlam [Quilon], one of the finest towns in the Mulaybár lands. It has fine bazaars, and its merchants are called Súlís. They are immensely wealthy; a single merchant will buy a vessel with all that is in it and load it with goods from his own house. There is a colony of Muslim merchants; the cathedral mosque is a magnificent building, constructed by the merchant Khwája Muhazzab. This city is the nearest of the Mulaybár towns to China and it is to it that most of the merchants [from China] come. Muslims are honoured and respected in it. The sultan of Kawlam is an infidel called the Tírawarí; he respects the Muslims and has severe laws against thieves and profligates. I stayed some time at Kawlam in a hospice, but heard no news of the kakam. During my stay the ambassadors from the king of China who had been with us arrived there also. They had embarked on one of the junks which was wrecked like the others. The Chinese merchants provided them with clothes and they returned to China, where I met them again later.

I intended at first to return from Kawlam to the sultan to tell him what had happened to the present, but afterwards I was afraid that he would find fault with what I had done and ask me why I had not stayed with the present. I determined therefore to return to Sultan Jamál ad-Dín of Hinawr and stay with him until I should obtain news of the kakam. So I went back to Cálicút and found there a vessel belonging to the sultan [of India], on which I embarked. It was then the end of the season for voyaging, and we used to sail only during the first half of the day, then anchor until the next day. We met four fighting vessels on our way and were afraid of them, but after all they did us no harm. On reaching Hinawr, I went to the sultan and saluted him; he assigned me a lodging, but without a servant, and asked me to recite the prayers with him. I spent most of my time in the mosque and used to read the Koran through every day, and later twice a day.

Sultan Jamál ad-Dín had fitted out fifty-two vessels for an expedition to Sandabúr [Goa]. A quarrel had broken out there between the sultan and his son, and the latter had written to Jamál ad-Dín inviting him to seize the town and promising to accept Islám and marry his daughter. When the ships were made ready I thought of setting out with them to the Holy War, so I opened the Koran to take an augury, and found at the top of the page *In them is the name of God frequently mentioned, and verily God will aid those who aid Him.* I took this as a good omen, and when the sultan came for the afternoon prayer, I said to him "I wish to join the expedition." "In that case" he replied "you will be their commander." I related to him the incident of my augury from the Koran, which so delighted him that he resolved to join the expedition himself, though previously he had not intended to do so. He embarked on one of the vessels, I being with him, on a Saturday, and we reached Sandabúr on the Monday evening. The inhabitants were prepared for the battle and had set up mangonels, which they discharged against the vessels when they advanced in the morning. Those on the ships jumped into the water, shields and swords in hand, and I jumped with them, and God granted the victory to the Muslims. We entered the city at the point of the sword and the greater part of the infidels fled into their sultan's palace, but when we threw fire into it they came out and we seized them. The sultan thereafter set them free and returned their wives and children to them. They numbered about ten thousand, and he assigned to them one of the suburbs of the city and himself occupied the palace, giving the neighbouring houses to his courtiers.

When I had stayed with him at Sandabúr for three months after the conquest of the town, I asked him for permission to travel and he made me promise to return to him. So I sailed to Hinawr and thence by Manjarúr and the other towns as before to Cálicút. I went on from there to ash-Sháliyát, a most beautiful town, in which the fabrics called by its name are manufactured. After a long stay in this town I returned to Cálicút. Two slaves of mine who had been on the kakam arrived at Cálicút and told me that the ruler of Sumatra had taken my slave-girls, that my goods had been seized by various hands, and that my companions were scattered to China, Sumatra and Bengal. On hearing this I returned to Hinawr and Sandabúr, reaching it after an absence of five months, and stayed there two months.

Translated by H.A.R. Gibb.

25

IBN JUBAYR*

A Description of the Sacred Mosque and the Ancient House

May God bless and exalt it

The venerable House has four corners and is almost square. The chief of the Banû Shayba who are the custodians of the House, one Muhammad ibn Ismâʿîl ibn ʿAbd al-Raḥmân of the stock of ʿUthmân ibn Ṭalḥah ibn Shaybah ibn Ṭalḥah ibn ʿAbd al-Dâr, the Companion of the Prophet—may God bless and preserve him—and the incumbent of the chamberlainship of the House, informed me that its height, on the side which faces the Bâb [Gate] al-Ṣafā' and which extends from the Black Stone to the Rukn al-Yamanî [Yemen Corner], is twenty-nine cubits. The remaining sides are twenty-eight cubits because of the slope of the roof towards the waterspout.

The principal corner is the one containing the Black Stone. There the circumambulation begins, the circumambulator drawing back (a little) from it so that all of his body might pass by it, the blessed House being on his left. The first thing that is met after that is the ʿIraq corner, which faces the north, then the Syrian corner which faces west, then the Yemen corner which faces south, and then back to the Black corner which faces east. That completes one *shauṭ* [single course]. The door of the blessed House is on the side between the ʿIraq corner and the Black Stone corner, and is close to the Stone at a distance of barely ten spans. That part of the side of the House which is between them is called the Multazam: a place where prayers are answered.

The venerable door is raised above the ground eleven and a half spans. It is of silver gilt and of exquisite workmanship and beautiful design, holding the eyes for its excellence and in emotion for the awe God has clothed His House in. After the same fashion are two posts, and the upper lintel over which is a slab of pure gold about two spans long. The door has two large silver staples on which is hung the lock.

*Died 1217 A.D. Spanish traveller to the Near East.

It faces to the east, and is eight spans wide and thirteen high. The thickness of the wall in which it turns is five spans. The inside of the blessed House is overlaid with variegated marbles, and the walls are all variegated marbles. (The ceiling) is sustained by three teak pillars of great height, four paces apart, and punctuating the length of the House, and down its middle. One of these columns, the first, faces the centre of the side enclosed by the two Yemen corners, and is three paces distant from it. The third column, the last, faces the side enclosed by the ʿIraq and Syrian corners.

The whole circuit of the upper half of the House is plated with silver, thickly gilt, which the beholder would imagine, from its thickness, to be a sheet of gold. It encompasses the four sides and covers the upper half of the walls. The ceiling of the House is covered by a veil of coloured silk.

The outside of the Kaʿbah, on all its four sides, is clothed in coverings of green silk with cotton warps; and on their upper parts is a band of red silk on which is written the verse, 'Verily the first House founded for mankind was that at Bakkah [Mecca]' [Koran III, 96]. The name of the Imâm al Nâṣir li-Dîn Ilâh, in depth three cubits, encircles it all. On these coverings there has been shaped remarkable designs resembling handsome pulpits, and inscriptions entertaining the name of God Most High and calling blessings on Nâṣir, the aforementioned ʿAbbâside (Caḷiph) who had ordered its instalment. With all this, there was no clash of colour. The number of covers on all four sides is thirty-four, there being eighteen on the two long sides, and sixteen on the two short sides.

The Kaʿbah has five windows of ʿIraq glass, richly stained. One of them is in the middle of the ceiling, and at each corner is a window, one of which is not seen because it is beneath the vaulted passage described later. Between the pillars (hang) thirteen vessels, of silver save one that is gold.

The first thing which he who enters at the door will find to his left is the corner outside which is the Black Stone. Here are two chests containing Korans. Above them in the corner are two small silver doors like windows set in the angle of the corner, and more than a man's stature from the ground. In the angle which follows, the Yemen, it is the same, but the doors have been torn out and only the wood to which they were attached remains. In the Syrian corner it is the same and the small doors remain. It is the same in the ʿIraq corner, which is to the right of him who enters. In the ʿIraq corner is a door called the Bâb al-Raḥmah [Door of Mercy, usually called the Door of Repentance, Bâb al-Taubah] from which ascent is made to the roof of the blessed House. It leads to a vaulted passage connecting with the roof of the House and having in it a stairway and, at its beginning, the vault containing the venerable *maqâm* [the standing-stone of Abraham]. Because of this passage the Ancient House has five corners. The height of both its sides is two statures and it encloses the ʿIraq corner with the halves of each of those two sides. Two-thirds of the circuit of this passage is dressed with pieces of coloured silk, as if it had been previously wrapped in them and then set in place.

This venerable *maqâm* that is inside the passage is the *maqâm* of Abraham—God's blessings on our Prophet and on him—and is a stone covered with silver. Its height is three spans, its width two and its upper part is larger than the lower. If it is not frivolous to draw the comparison it is like a large potter's oven, its middle being narrower than its top or bottom. We gazed upon it and were blessed by touching and kissing it. The water of Zamzam was poured for us into the imprints of the two blessed feet [of Abraham who stood on this stone when he built the Kaʿbah], and we drank it—may God profit us by it. The traces of both feet are visible, as are the traces of the honoured and blessed big toes. Glory to God who softened the stone beneath the tread so that it left its trace as no trace of foot is left in the soft sand. Glory to God who made it a manifest sign. The contemplation of this *maqâm* and the venerable House is an awful sight which distracts the senses in amazement, and ravishes the heart and mind. You will see only reverent gazes, flowing tears, eyes dissolved in weeping, and tongues in humble entreaty to Great and Glorious God.

Between the venerable door and the ʿIraq corner is a basin twelve spans long, five and a half spans wide, and about one in depth. It runs from opposite the door post, on the side of the ʿIraq corner, towards that corner, and is the mark of the place of the *maqâm* at the time of Abraham—on whom be (eternal) happiness—until the Prophet—may God bless and preserve him—moved it to the place where now it is a *muṣallà* [place of worship]. The basin remained as a conduit for the water of the House when it is washed. It is a blessed spot [called al-Maʿjan] and is said to be one of the pools of Paradise, with men crowding to pray at it. Its bottom is spread with soft white sand.

The place of the venerated Maqâm, behind which prayers are said, faces the space between the blessed door and the ʿIraq corner, well towards the side of the door. Over it is a wooden dome, a man's stature or more high, angulated and sharp-edged [i.e. pyramidal], of excellent modelling, and having four spans from one angle to another. It was erected on the place where once was the *maqâm* [standing-stone], and around it is a stone projection built on the edge like an oblong basin about a span deep, five paces long, and three paces wide. The *maqâm* was put into the place we have described in the blessed House as a measure of safety. Between the *maqâm* and the side of the House opposite it lie seventeen paces, a pace being three spans. The place of the Maqâm also has a dome made of steel and placed beside the dome of Zamzam. During the months of the pilgrimage, when many men have assembled and those from ʿIraq and Khurasan have arrived, the wooden dome is removed and the steel dome put in its place that it might better support the press of men.

From the corner containing the Black Stone to the ʿIraq corner is scarcely fifty-four spans. From the Black Stone to the ground is six spans, so that the tall man must bend to it and the short man raise himself (to kiss it). From the ʿIraq corner to the Syrian corner is scarcely forty-eight spans, and that is through the inside of the Ḥijr [an adjacent enclosure]; but around it from the one corner to the other is forty paces or almost one hundred and twenty spans. The *ṭawwâf* [circumambulator] moves outside. (The distance from) the Syrian corner to the Yemen corner is the same as that from the Black corner to the ʿIraq corner for they are opposite sides. From the Yemen to the Black is the same, inside the Ḥijr, as from the ʿIraq to the Syrian for they are opposite sides.

The place of circumambulation is paved with wide stones like marble [they are in fact of fine polished granite] and very beautiful, some black, some brown and some white. They are joined to each other, and reach nine paces from the House save in the part facing the Maqâm where they reach out to embrace it. The remainder of the Ḥaram, including the colonnades, is wholly spread with white sand. The place of circumambulation for the women is at the edge of the paved stones.

Between the ʿIraq corner and the beginning of the wall of the Ḥijr is the entrance to the Ḥijr; it is four paces wide, that is six cubits exactly, for we measured it by hand. This place is not enclosed in the Ḥijr, and is that part of the House which the Quraysh left, and is, as true tradition has it, six cubits. Opposite this entrance, at the Syrian corner, is another of the same size. Between that part of the wall of the House which is under the Mîzâb [waterspout] and the wall of the Ḥijr opposite, following the straight line which cuts through the middle of the aforementioned Ḥijr, lie forty spans. The distance from entrance to entrance is sixteen paces, which is forty-eight spans. This place, I mean the surroundings of the wall (of the Kaʿbah, under the Mîzâb), is all tessellated marble, wonderfully joined with bands of gilded copper worked into its surface like a chess-board, being interlaced with each other and with shapes of *miḥrâbs.* When the sun strikes them, such light and brightness shine from them that the beholder conceives them to be gold, dazzling the eyes with their rays. The height of the marble wall of this Ḥijr is five and a half spans and its width four and a half. Inside the Ḥijr is a wide paving, round which the Ḥijr bends as it were in two-thirds of a circle. It is laid with tessellated marble, cut in discs the size of the palm of the hand, of a dinar and more minute than that, and joined with remarkable precision. It is composed with wonderful art, is of singular perfection, beautifully inlaid and checkered, and is superbly set and laid. The beholder will see bendings, inlays, mosaics of tiles, chess-board forms and the like, of various forms and attributes, such as will fix his gaze for their beauty. Or let his looks roam from the carpet of flowers of many colours to the *miḥrâbs* over which bend arches of marble, and in which are these forms we have described and the arts we have mentioned.

Beside it are two slabs of marble adjacent to the wall of the Ḥijr opposite the Mîzâb, on which art has worked such delicate leaves, branches, and trees as could not be done by skilled hands cutting with scissors from paper. It is a remarkable sight. The one who decreed that they should be worked in this fashion is the Imâm of the East, Abû ʾl-ʿAbbâs Aḥmad al-Nâṣir b. al-Mustaḍiʾ billâh al-ʿAbbâsî—may God hold him in His favour. Facing the waterspout, in the middle of the Ḥijr and the centre of the marble wall, is a marble slab of most excellent chiselling with a cornice round it bearing an inscription in striking black in which is written, '(This is) among the things ordered to be done by the servant and Caliph of God Abû ʾl-ʿAbbâs Aḥmad al-Nâṣir li-dîni Ilâh, Prince of the Faithful, in the year 576 [1180]'.

The Mîzâb is on the top of the wall which overlooks the Ḥijr. It is of gilded copper and projects four cubits over the Ḥijr, its breadth being a span. This place under the waterspout is also considered as being a place where, by the favour of God Most High, prayers are answered. The Yemen corner is the same. The wall connecting this place with the Syrian corner is called al-Mustajâr [The Place of Refuge]. Underneath the waterspout, and in the court of the Ḥijr near to the wall of the blessed House, is the tomb of Ismaʿîl [Ishmael]—may God bless and preserve him. Its mark is a slab of green marble, almost oblong and in the form of a *miḥrâb.* Beside it is a round green slab of marble, and both [they are *verde antico*] are remarkable to look upon. There are spots on them both which turn them from their colour to something of yellow so that they are like a mosaic of colours, and I compare them to the spots that are left in the crucible after the gold has been melted in it. Beside this tomb, and on the side towards the ʿIraq corner, is the tomb of his mother Hâjar [Hagar]—may God hold her in His favour—its mark being a green stone a span and a half wide. Men are blessed by praying in these two places in the Ḥijr, and men are right to do so, for they are part of the Ancient House and shelter the two holy and venerated bodies. May God cast His light upon them and advantage with their blessings all who pray over them. Seven spans lie between the two holy tombs.

The dome of the Well of Zamzam is opposite the Black Corner, and lies twenty-four paces from it. The Maqâm, which we have already mentioned and behind which prayers are said, is to the right of this dome, from the corner of which to the other is ten paces. The inside of the dome is paved with pure white marble. The orifice of the blessed well is in the centre of the dome deviating towards the wall which faces the venerated House. Its depth is eleven statures of a man as we measured it, and the depth of the water is seven statures, as it is said. The door of this dome faces east, and the door of the dome of ʿAbbâs and that of the Jewish dome face north. The angle of that side of the dome named after the Jews, which faces the Ancient House, reaches the left corner of the back wall of the ʿAbbâside corner which faces east. Between them lies that amount of deviation. Beside the dome of the Well of Zamzam and behind it stands the *Qubbat al-Sharab* [the dome of drinking], which was erected by ʿAbbâs—may God hold him in His favour. Beside this ʿAbbâside dome, obliquely to it, is the dome named after the Jews. These two domes are used as storerooms for pious endowments made to the blessed House, such as Korans, books, candlesticks, and the like. The ʿAbbâside dome is called *al-Sharabiyyah* because it was a place of drinking for the pilgrims; and there, until to-day, the water of Zamzam is put therein to cool in earthenware jars and brought forth at eventide for the pilgrims to drink. These jars are called *dawraq* and have one handle only. The orifice of the Well of Zamzam is of marble stones so well joined, with lead poured into the interstices, that time will not ravage them. The inside of the orifice is similar, and round it are lead props attached to it to reinforce the strength of the binding and the lead overlay. These props number thirty-two, and their tops protrude to hold the brim of the well round the whole of the orifice. The circumference of the orifice is forty spans, its depth four spans and a half, and its thickness a span and a half. Round the inside of the dome runs a trough of width one span, and depth about two spans and raised five spans from the ground, and it is filled with water for the ritual ablutions. Around it runs a stone block on which men mount to perform the ablutions.

The blessed Black Stone is enchased in the corner facing east. The depth to which it penetrates it is not known, but it is said to extend two cubits into the wall. Its breadth is two-thirds of a span, its length one span and a finger joint. It has four pieces, joined together, and it is said that it was the Qarmata [Carmathians]—may God curse them—who broke it. Its edges have been braced with a sheet of silver whose white shines brightly against the black sheen and polished brilliance of the Stone, presenting the observer a striking spectacle which will hold his looks. The Stone, when kissed, has a softness and moistness which so enchants the mouth that he who puts his lips to it would wish them never to be removed. This is one of the special favours of Divine Providence, and it is enough that the Prophet—may God bless and preserve him—declare to be a covenant of God on earth. May God profit us by the kissing and touching of it. By His favour may all who yearn fervently for it be brought to it. In the sound piece of the stone, to the right of him who presents himself to kiss it, is a small white spot that shines and appears like a mole on the blessed surface. Concerning this white mole, there is a tradition that he who looks upon it clears his vision, and when kissing it one should direct one's lips as closely as one can to the place of the mole.

The sacred Mosque is encompassed by colonnades in three (horizontal) ranges on three rows of marble columns so arranged as to make it like a single colonnade. Its measurement in length is four hundred cubits, its width three hundred, and its area is exactly forty-eight *marâja*ʿ [sing. *maraj*ʿ, a measure of area amongst the western Arabs equalling fifty square cubits]. The area between the colonnades is great, but at the time of the Prophet—may God bless and preserve him—it was small and the dome of Zamzam was outside it. Facing the Syrian corner, wedged in the ground, is the capital of a column which at first was the limit of the Ḥaram. Between this capital and the Syrian corner are twenty-two paces. The Kaʿbah is in the centre (of the Ḥaram) and its four sides run directly to the east, south, north and west. The number of the marble columns, which myself I counted, is four hundred and seventy-one, excluding the stuccoed column that is in the *Dâr al-Nadwah* (House of Counsel), which was added to the Ḥaram. This is within the colonnade which runs from the west to the north and is faced by the Maqâm and the ʿIraq corner. It has a large court and is entered from the colonnade. Against the whole length of this colonnade are benches under vaulted arches where sit the copyists, the readers of the Koran, and some who ply the tailor's trade.

The Ḥaram enfolds rings of students sitting around their teachers, and learned men. Along the wall of the colonnade facing it are also benches under arches in the same fashion. This is the colonnade which runs from the south to the east. In the other colonnades, the benches against the walls have no arches over them. The buildings now in the Ḥaram are at the height of perfection. At the *Bâb Ibrâhîm* [Abraham's Gate] is another entrance from the colonnade which runs from the west to the south and has also stuccoed columns. I found in the writing of Abû Jaʿfar ibn [ʿAlî] al-Fanakî al-Qurṭubî, the jurisprudent and traditionalist, that the number of columns was four hundred and eighty; for I had not counted those outside the Ṣafa Gate.

Of the enlarging of the Sacred Ḥaram and the adornment of its buildings by the Mahdî Muḥammad ibn Abî Jaʿfar al-Manṣûr al-ʿAbbâsî there is noble evidence. On the side running from west to north high on the wall of the cloister I found written, 'The servant of God Muḥammad al-Mahdî, Prince of the Faithful—may God have him in His care—ordered the enlargement of the Sacred Mosque for the pilgrims to God's House and for those upon the *ʿumrah.* In the year 167 [A.D. 783].'

The Ḥaram has seven minarets. Four are at each corner, another is at the Dâr al-Nadwah, and another at the Ṣafa Gate indicates the Gate and is the smallest of them, no one being able to climb up to it for its narrowness. The seventh stands at the Abraham Gate which we shall mention later.

The Ṣafa Gate faces the Black corner in the colonnade which runs from the south to the east. In the middle of the colonnade which is opposite the door are two columns facing the aforementioned corner and bearing this engraved inscription: 'The Servant of God Muḥammad al-Mahdî, Prince of the Faithful—may God have him in His favour—ordered the erection of these two columns to indicate the path of the Messenger of God [Muhammad]—may God bless and preserve him—to al-Ṣafa, that the pilgrims to the House of God and those that dwell therein might follow him. (Done) by the hand of Yaqtin ibn Mûsà and Ibrâhim ibn Ṣâliḥ in the year 167 [A.D. 783].'

On the door of the holy Kaʿbah is engraved in gold, with graceful characters long and thick, that hold the eyes for their form and beauty, this writing: 'This is amongst those things erected by order of the servant and Caliph of God, the Imâm Abû ʿAbdullâh Muḥammad al-Muqtafi li-Amri Ilâh, Prince of the Faithful. May God bless him and the Imâms his righteous ancestors, perpetuating for him the prophetic inheritance and making it an enduring word for his prosperity until the Day of Resurrection. In the year 550 [A.D. 1155].' In this wise (was it written) on the faces of the two door-leaves. These two noble door-leaves are enclosed by a thick band of silver gilt, excellently carved, which rises to the blessed lintel, passes over it and then goes round the sides of the two door-leaves. Between them, when they are closed together, is a sort of broad strip of silver gilt which runs the length of the doors and is attached to the door-leaf which is to the left of him who enters the House.

The *Kiswah* [lit. 'robe', covering] of the sacred Kaʿbah is of green silk as we have said. There are thirty-four pieces: nine on the side between the Yemen and Syrian corners, nine also on the opposite side between the Black corner and the ʿIraq corner, and eight on both the side between the ʿIraq and Syrian corners and on that between the Yemen and the Black. Together they come to appear as one single cover comprehending the four sides. The lower part of the Kaʿbah is surrounded by a projecting border built of stucco, more than a span in depth and two spans or a little more in width, inside which is wood, not discernible. Into this are driven iron pegs which have at their ends iron rings that are visible. Through these is inserted a rope of hemp, thick and strongly made, which encircles the four sides, and which is sewn with strong, twisted, cotton thread to a girdle, like that of the *sirwâl* [the Arab cotton bloomers], fixed to the hems of the covers. At the juncture of the covers at the four corners, they are sewn together for more than a man's stature, and above that they are brought together by iron hooks engaged in each other. At the top, round the sides of the terrace, runs another projecting border to which the upper parts of the covers are attached with iron rings, after the fashion described. Thus the blessed *Kiswah* is sewn top and bottom, and firmly buttoned, being never removed save at its renewal year by year. Glory to God who perpetuates its honour until the Day of Resurrection. There is no God but He.

The door of the sacred Kaʿbah is opened every Monday and Friday, except in the month of Rajab, when it is opened every day. It is opened at the first rising to the sun. The custodians of the House, the *Shayba*, advance, seeking to forestall each other in moving a big stairway that resembles a large pulpit. It has nine long steps, and wooden supports that reach the ground and have attached to them four large wheels, plated with iron as against their contact with the ground, on which the ladder moves until it reaches the Sacred House. The highest step reaches the blessed threshold of the door. The chief of the *Shayba,* a mature man of handsome mien and aspect, then ascends it, carrying the key of the blessed lock. With him is a custodian holding up a black veil that is (hung) before the door and under which his arms sag while the aforesaid chief of the *Shayba* opens the door. When he has opened the lock, he kisses the threshold, enters the House alone, closes the door behind him and stays there the time of two *rakʿah.* The other *Shayba* then enter and also close the door and perform the *rakʿah.* The door is then opened and men compete to enter. While the venerated door is being opened, the people stand before it with lowered looks and hands outstretched in humble supplication to God. When it is opened they cry, '*Allâhu Akbar*' [God is Great], raising a clamour and calling in a loud voice, 'Ah, my God, open to us the gates of Your mercy and pardon, Most Merciful of the Merciful.' They then 'enter in peace, secure' [Koran XV, 46].

In the wall facing the entrant, which is that running from the Yemen corner to the Syrian, are five marble panels set lengthways as if they were doors. They come down to a distance of five spans from the ground, and each one of them is about a man's stature in height. Three of them are red, and two green, and all have white tessellations so that I have never seen a more beautiful sight. They are as if speckled. A red one adjoins the Yemen corner, and next to it a distance of five spans is a green. At the place opposite this, falling back from it three cubits, is the *muṣallà* [praying place] of the Prophet—may God bless and preserve him—and men crowd to pray at it and be blessed. They are all sited in this manner, there being between each panel and the other the distance we have stated. Between each pair is a marble slab of pure and unstained whiteness on which Great and Glorious God had fashioned, at its first creation, remarkable designs, inclining to blue, of trees and branches, and another beside it with the same designs exactly, as if they were parts (of the same stone); and if one were placed over the other each design would correspond with its opposite. Beyond a peradventure each slab is the half of the other, and when the cut was made they divided to make these designs and each was placed beside its sister. The space between a green and a red panel is that of two slabs, their combined width being five spans, according to the number mentioned above. The designs on these slabs vary in shape, and each slab lies beside its sister. The sides of these marble slabs are braced by cornices, two fingers wide, of marble tessellated with spotted greens and reds, and speckled whites, that are like wands worked on a lathe, such as to stagger the imagination. In this wall there are six spaces with white marble. In the wall, which is to the left of him who enters, which is from the Black corner to the Yemen, there are four marble panels, two green and two red. Between them are five [two spaces must therefore be on the flanks] spaces with white marble, and all in the fashion described. In the wall to the right of the entrant, which is that from the Black corner to the ʿIraq, there are three panels, two red and one green, interspersed with three spaces of white marble. This is the wall that runs to the corner containing the *Bâb al-Raḥmah* [the Door of Mercy or to-day the *Bâb al-Taubah*] which is three spans wide and seven spans high. That side-piece of this door which is to your right as you face it is of green marble and two-thirds of a span wide. In the wall from the Syrian to the ʿIraq corner are three panels of marble, two red and one green, connected by three spaces of white marble in the manner described. These slabs of marble are crowned with two fasciae, one over the other, each being two spans wide, and of gold with an inscription in lapis-lazuli of fine hand. These fasciae reach the gold engraving on the upper half of the wall. The side on the right of the entrant has one fascia. In these double fasciae some parts (of the inscription) have been effaced.

In each of the four corners, towards the ground, are two small tablets of green marble which enclose the corner (on both sides). Similarly, both of the two (small) silver doors which, in the form of windows, are found in each corner, are enclosed by small side-pieces of green marble the size of the openings. At the beginning of all the walls described comes a red marble panel and at the end also comes a red, while the green are distributed between them after the manner related, save on the wall to the left of the entrant, for there the first marble you find, beside the Black corner, is green; then comes a red, and so on until the end of the arrangement we have explained.

Beside the noble Maqâm is the preacher's pulpit [*minbar*] which also is on four wheels in the mode we have explained. When, on Fridays, the time of prayer approaches, it is brought to the side of the Kaʿbah that faces the Maqâm, which is that which runs between the Black and the ʿIraq corners, and is propped against it. The *khâṭib* [preacher] comes through the Gate of the Prophet—may God bless and preserve him—which is opposite the Maqâm and in the colonnade which runs from east to north. He wears a black dress, worked with gold, a black turban similarly worked, and a *ṭaylasân* of fine linen. All this is the livery of the Caliph, which he sends to the preachers of his land. With lofty gait, calm and stately, he slowly paces between two black banners held by two muezzins of his tribe. Before him goes another of his people bearing a red staff, turned on a lathe, and having tied to its top a cord of twisted skin, long and thin, with a small thong at its tip. He cracks it in the air with so loud a report that it is heard both within the Ḥaram and without, like a warning of the arrival of the preacher. He does not cease to crack it until they are near the pulpit. They call (this whip) the *farqaʿah*.

Coming to the pulpit, the *khâṭib* turns aside to the Black Stone, kisses it, and prays before it. Then he goes to the pulpit, led by the Zamzam muezzin, who is the chief of the muezzins of the noble Ḥaram and also dressed in black clothes. He bears on his shoulder a sword which he holds in his hand without girding it. The muezzin girds the *khâṭib* with the sword as he ascends the first step, which then, with the ferrule of his scabbard, he strikes a blow which all present can hear. He strikes it again on the second step and on the third. When he reaches the top step, he strikes the fourth blow, and stands facing the Kaʿbah praying in low tones. Then he turns to right and left and says, 'Peace upon you, and the mercy and blessings of God.' The congregation returns the salutation ['Upon you be peace'] and he then sits. The muezzins place themselves in front of him and call the *adhân* in one voice. When they have finished, the *khâṭib* delivers the address, reminding, exhorting, inspiring, and waxing eloquent. He then sits down in the conventional sitting of the preacher and strikes with the sword a fifth time. He then delivers the second (part of) the *Khuṭbah* multiplying prayers for Muhammad—may God bless and preserve him—and for his family, begging God's favour for his Companions and naming in particular the four Caliphs—may God have them all in His favour—praying for the two uncles of the Prophet—may God bless and preserve them—Ḥamzah and ʿAbbâs, and for al-Ḥasan and al-Ḥusayn, uniting to all (the words): 'May God hold them in His favour.' He then prayed for the Mothers of the Faithful, wives of the Prophet—may God bless and preserve them—and begged God's favour for Fâṭimah the Fair and for Khadîjah the Great in this language.

. . . The messenger gave notice that the new moon had been seen on the night of Thursday. The news passed from one to the other and was confirmed before the Qâḍi, thus obliging him to deliver the *khuṭbah* that day, in accordance with the established custom, the 7th of Dhu ʾl-Ḥijjah after the midday prayers. In this sermon he advised the people of the rites they should observe, and told them that the morrow, being Yaum al-Tarwiyah, would be the day of their ascent to Minà, and that the 'standing' (on Mount ʿArafât) would be observed on

Friday. He reminded them that the venerated tradition that comes directly from the Prophet—may God bless and preserve him—has it that a 'standing' on this day is equivalent to seventy on any other, and that the superiority of a year in which this standing (falls on a Friday) is as the superiority of Friday over all the other days (of the week).

Early on the morning of Thursday the people began their ascent to Minà, and thence passed on to ʿArafât. It is the rule that the night should be passed there, but perforce they omitted this in fear of the Banu Shuʿbah, who make raids on the pilgrims on their way to ʿArafât.

The ascent of the people continued all that day, all night, and all Friday so that there was assembled on ʿArafât a multitude whose numbers could not be counted save by Great and Glorious God. Muzdalifah lies between Minà and ʿArafât; from Minà to Muzdalifah lies the same distance as from Mecca to Minà, which is about five miles; and from Muzdalifah to ʿArafât is the same or a little more. Muzdalifah is also called al-Maʿshar al-Ḥaram [the place of ritual ceremonies] as well as Jamʿ [reunion], and therefore has three names. Before coming to it, about a mile away, is the Wadi [valley of] Muḥaṣṣir, which it is the custom to pass through with a brisk step. It is the boundary between Muzdalifah and Minà, for it lies between them. Muzdalifah is a wide stretch of land between two mountains, and around it are the reservoirs and cisterns that were used for water in the time of Zubaydah—may God's mercy rest upon her soul. In the middle of this plain is an enclosure at whose centre is a rounded knoll on the top of which is a mosque that is approached by steps on both sides. Men crowd as they climb up to it and at the prayers inside it, the night they pass at Muzdalifah.

ʿArafât also is a wide plain, and if it were men's place of congregation on the Day of Resurrection it could contain them all. This broad plain is enfolded by many mountains, and at its extremity is the Jabal al-Raḥmah [Mount of Mercy] on and around which is the standing ground of the pilgrims. The 'Two Signs' [Al-ʿAlamân] come about two miles before this place, and the area stretching from the 'Two Signs' to ʿArafât is neutral [lit. 'lawful' *ḥill*], while that on the hither side is sacred. Near to them on the ʿArafât side, is the valley of ʿUranah, from which place the Prophet—may God bless and preserve him—has enjoined that avoidance be made by saying, ʿArafât is all a standing ground. But turn aside from the valley of ʿUranah.' He who 'stands' there invalidates his pilgrimage, and this should be kept in mind, for on the evening of the 'standing' the camel-masters often hurry many pilgrims, making them apprehensive of the crowding in the return from ʿArafât and taking them down by the 'Two Signs' that face them, until they come to the valley of ʿUranah or overreach it and so annul their pilgrimage. The prudent will not therefore leave his standing ground on ʿArafât until the disc of the sun has completely subsided.

The Mount of Mercy rises in the middle of the plain, apart from the other mountains. It consists wholly of separate blocks of (granite) stone and it is difficult of ascent. Jamâl al-Dîn, whose memorable works we have already mentioned in this journal, provided on its four sides low steps that can be climbed by laden beasts, and spent great sums upon it. At its summit is a cupola that is attributed to Umm Salîmah —may God hold her in His favour—but it is not certain whether this is true. In the centre of the cupola is a mosque into which men crowd to pray, and around this venerated mosque runs a terrace, broad and handsome to look upon, that overlooks the plain of ʿArafât. To the south is a wall against which are erected the *miḥrâbs* that the people pray in. At the foot of this sacred mountain, to the left of him who looks towards the *qiblah* [direction of Mecca], is a house of ancient construction in whose upper part is a vaulted upper chamber, attributed to Adam—may God bless and preserve him. On the left of this house, facing the *qiblah,* is the rock beside which was the standing ground of the Prophet—may God bless and preserve him—and it is on a small hill. Around the Mount of Mercy and this venerated house are water cisterns and wells. Also to the left of the house and near to it is a small mosque. Fast by the 'Two Signs', and to the left on him who faces the *qiblah,* is an ancient mosque of large proportions, of which the south wall that is named after Abraham—may God bless and preserve him—remains. The preacher delivers a sermon in it on the day of the 'standing', and then leads the combined midday and afternoon prayers. Also to the left of the 'Two Signs', when facing the *qiblah,* is the Wadi ʾl-Arâk [the valley of the Thorn Tree, *Salvadora persica*] which is the green thorn that stretches before the eye a long way over the plain.

The assembling of the people on ʿArafât is completed during Thursday and all the night of Friday. Near the third part of this night of Friday, the Emir of ʿIraq pilgrimage arrived and pitched his tent in the wide plain that, for him who faces *qiblah*, is contiguous with the right side of the Mount of Mercy. The *qiblah,* relative to ʿArafât, is to the west, for the sacred Kaʿbah is in that direction.

Upon that Friday morning there was on ʿArafât a multitude that could have no like save that which there will be on the Day of Resurrection; but, within the will of God Most High, it was a gathering that will win reward, giving promise as it does of God's mercy and forgiveness when men assemble for the Day of Reckoning. Some truth-demanding sheiks of the *mujâwir* [settled pilgrims] asserted that never had they seen on ʿArafât a more numerous concourse, and I do not believe that since the time of al-Rashîd, who was the last Caliph to make the pilgrimage, there had ever been such a concourse in Islam. May God by His favour grant that it bring mercy and immunity from sin.

When, on Friday, the midday and afternoon prayers were said together, the people stood contrite and in tears, humbly beseeching the mercy of Great and Glorious God. The cries of 'God is Great' rose high, and loud were the voices of men in prayer. Never has there been seen a day of such weeping, such penitence of heart, and such bending of the neck in reverential submission and humility before God. In this fashion the pilgrims continued, with the sun burning their faces, until its orb had sunk and the time of the sunset prayers was at hand.

For their return from ʿArafât, they had appointed the Mâlikite imâm as their guide and model, for the practice of Mâlik—may God hold him in His favour—demands that there should be no departure from ʿArafât until the sun's disc has fallen below the horizon and the time for sunset prayers has come. Yet some of the Yemenite Saru had taken their leave before this. So when the time had come, the Mâlikite imâm gave the sign with his hands and descended from his post. The people then pressed forward on their return with such a surge that the earth trembled and the mountains quaked. What a standing it had been, how awesome to regard and what hopes of happy reward it had brought to the soul. God grant that we may be among those on whom He there conferred His approbation and covered with His bounty. For He is bounteous, generous, compassionate, and beneficent.

The people departed after the sun had set as we have said, and in the late evening came to Muzdalifah, where they recited the combined sunset and early night prayers according to the rule laid down by the Prophet—may God bless and preserve him. Throughout the night the Maʿshar al-Ḥaram [Muzdalifah] was illuminated by candle-wick lamps. As for the mosque which we mentioned before, it was all light, seeming to the beholder as if all the stars of the sky shone upon it. After the same fashion was the Mount of Mercy and its mosque on the night of Friday . . . That night which was the night of Saturday, men spent in al-Maʿshar al-Ḥaram, and when they had said the morning prayer, they early left it for Minà. They stood and prayed (upon the way), for all Muzdalifah is standing ground save the valley of Muḥaṣṣir, where one must move speedily [*harwala*] in the direction of Minà until emerging from it. At Muzdalifah most of the pilgrims provide themselves with stones (to cast at) the cairns. This is the more favoured custom, but there are others who collect them from around the mosque of al-Khayf in Minà, and it is as they wish.

When the pilgrims arrived at Minà they made speed to throw seven stones on the Cairn of ʿAqabah and then slaughtered in sacrifice, after which it became lawful for them to do everything save (to have contact with) women and (to use) scent, (from which they must still abstain) until they have performed the *ṭawâf* of the *ifâdah* [return to Mecca]. This cairn was stoned at the rising of the sun on the Day of Sacrifice, and most of the pilgrims then left to do the *ṭawâf* of the *ifâdah*. Some of them stayed until the second day, and some until the third, which is the day of the descent to Mecca. The second day, following the Day of Sacrifice, at the declension of the sun, the pilgrims cast seven stones at the First Cairn, and then did the same at the Centre Cairn, stopping at both for prayers. They did the same at the Cairn of al-ʿAqabah, but did not stop here, imitating in all this the actions of the Prophet—may God bless and preserve him. The Cairn of the ʿAqabah is stoned last on these two days; but on the Day of the Sacrifice it is the first and only cairn to be stoned, the others not being associated with it on that day.

The day following the Day of Sacrifice, after the casting of the stones, the *khâṭib* preached a sermon in the mosque of al-Khayf, and then conducted the combined midday and afternoon prayers. This *khâṭib* came with the ʿIraqi Emir, being delegated by the Caliph to deliver the khuṭbah and to discharge the duties of Qâḍî in Mecca as it is said. His name is Tâj al-Dîn. It became clear that he was dull and stupid; his discourse revealed this, and his speech did not observe the rules of grammatical analysis. On the third day, the pilgrims hastened to descend to Mecca. They had completed the throwing of forty-nine stones, seven on the Day of Sacrifice at al-ʿAqabah which are those that release from abstentions, twenty-one on the second day, after the declension of the sun with seven at each cairn, and the same number on the third day, returning then to Mecca. Some there were who said the afternoon prayers in the bed of the torrent, others in the sacred Mosque, and some had made haste and said the midday prayers in the torrent bed. It had anciently been the practice to stay at Minà three days after the Day of Sacrifice in order to complete the throwing of seventy stones. But in these times it is despatched in two days in accordance with the saying of God—may He be blessed and exalted—'Whoso hasteneth (his departure) two days, it is no sin for him; and whoso delayeth, it is also no sin for him' [Koran II, 203). This is done in fear of the Banû Shuʿbah and what might be sprung on them by the Meccan robbers.

Translated by R. J. C. Broadhurst